Blind Ambition:
The End of the Story

OTHER BOOKS BY THE AUTHOR

Lost Honor (1982)

The Rehnquist Choice: The Untold Story of the Nixon Appointment that Redefined the Supreme Court (2001)

Unmasking Deep Throat: History's Most Elusive News Source (2002)

Warren G. Harding (2004)

Worse Than Watergate: The Secret Presidency of George W. Bush (2004)

Conservatives Without Conscience (2006)

Broken Government: How Republican Rule Destroyed the Legislative, Executive, and Judicial Branches (2008)

Pure Goldwater (2008)

Blind Ambition:

The End of the Story

John W. Dean

**Polimedia
Publishers**

All Polimedia titles, imprints, and distributed lines are available at special quantity discounts for bulk purchases for sales promotion, premiums, fund-raising, educational, or institutional use.

Special book excerpts or customized printings can also be created to fit specific needs. For details, write or contact the office of Polimedia Publishing at:

Polimedia Publishers
100 S. Sunrise Way #A670
Palm Springs, CA 92262
info@polimediaent.com
www.polimediaent.com

2 3 4 5 6 7 8 9 10

Published by Polimedia Publishers
© 2009 John W. Dean

ISBN-10: 097868617-5-5
ISBN-13: 978-0-97686017-5-1

Printed in the United States of America

PRAISE FOR THE UPDATED EDITION OF *BLIND AMBITION: THE END OF THE STORY*

"Faust writes his own story. In the vast literature of those who came to Washington and lived to tell the tale there is nothing else like this. Blind Ambition *is not only the best and most enduring book written from inside the Nixon White House, it is a classic of lost illusions. Now, in this new edition, John W. Dean, who has gained his understanding of the past through unsparing honesty, defends history itself from the charlatans and quacks who would distort it."*

Sidney Blumenthal
Journalist, political editor of *The Daily Beast*, and author of *The Clinton Wars* and *The Permanent Campaign: Inside the World of Elite Political Operatives*

"John Dean's Blind Ambition *happily is available again - and with a brilliant Afterword that provides an up-to-date account of the Watergate affair, using new documentation. Dean's memoir reminds us again of his crucial role in laying bare the sordid facts of Richard Nixon and all the President's men. He offers a unique accounting of the events and his own role in them. Rare indeed is a memoir so utterly lacking in self-righteousness, false piety, and special pleading. It is a sobering reminder of the perils of ambition.*

Stanley Kutler
Historian and author of *The Wars of Watergate* and *Abuse of Power: The New Nixon Tapes*

"Blind Ambition *uniquely takes the reader inside the Nixon White House, of particular interest as the Nixon administration crumbled under the impact of Watergate.* Blind Ambition *was a classic of its kind. Now* Blind Ambition *has been re-issued with an indispensable Afterword providing further valuable information."*

Jeffery Hart
Professor Emeritus of English at Dartmouth College, a longtime senior editor at the *National Review*, and occasional speechwriter for Ronald Reagan and Richard Nixon.

"Over the past three and a half decades many historians, journalists and outright fraudulent hacks have attempted to write and even rewrite the history of Watergate. So too have many of the Watergate partici-pants. However, as more and more of the Nixon White House materials continue to be released by the National Archives, no work on this incredible episode has been buttressed more by the evidence than Blind Ambition. *John Dean's memoir is by far the most fascinating, compel-ling and revealing book that has ever been published on life inside the Nixon White House and Watergate, bar none."*

Thomas Maxwell-Long
Professor of History at California State University San Bernardino and co-author of *Watergate and the Resignation of Richard Nixon: Impact of a Constitutional Crisis*

"Amid the vast wasteland that is political autobiography, John Dean's was always a thing apart: a literary accomplishment. Now updated with a detailed and illuminating new afterward, it's one of the best books for one-stop shopping to understand what Watergate was all about and why it still matters."

Rick Perstein
Author of *Before the Storm: Barry Goldwater and the Unmaking of the American Consensus* and *Nixonland: The Rise of a Presi-dent and the Fracturing of America*

CONTENTS

UPDATED EDITION PREFACE

WHAT WAS WATERGATE? The answer is not simple and could take any of a number of varying legal, ethical, moral, social, historical, and political perspectives. Clearly, Watergate became much more than a hotel, office, and apartment complex alongside the Potomac River in Washington, DC, when, on June 17, 1972, Gordon Liddy's team of five men dressed in business suits and wearing surgical gloves were arrested in the offices of the Democratic National Committee. In a study of how Americans collectively remember Watergate, the complexity of this question was noted by Michael Schudson's *Watergate In American Memory: How we Remember, Forget, and Reconstruct the Past* (1992). Schudson found, "There is no agreement on what Watergate is. The interesting question becomes how, not whether, we remember Watergate, which face or facet of Watergate we recall and why. Not surprisingly, this varies across different groups." I came upon the best definition I have yet found when browsing in a bookstore in the mid-1970s. I opened a newly-released dictionary that defined Watergate as "a scandal involving the abuse of high office occurring during the presidency of Richard Nixon." I no longer recall the dictionary, but I have never forgotten the definition, for it is the way I have used the term "Watergate" in all the years since discovering it. Still, as Schudson pointed out, it is how we remember these events. In the pages that follow, written shortly after the events occurred, I recorded my memory of them.

Blind Ambition: The White House Years was first published over three decades ago in 1976. It has been out of print for two decades. Since reading it in galleys and then page proofs, I had (until now) never re-read it from cover to cover, although I should add I have never re-read any of my other nine published books either. The reason is that I am intimately familiar with

i

their contents. Books are like children, and you know your own well. Frankly, in re-reading this material after all these years, I was surprised at my own candor. I pulled no punches, and made no effort to spare myself. My thinking at the time was why bother to tell a story like this except with complete candor? Otherwise, I knew my story would not be much use to anyone else in avoiding mistakes similar to those I made then. Given the feedback I have received over the years, I believe my being honest and open did help, and I have not changed a word of my original account. I am republishing that account because I have something to add, information and insights I did not possess when it was first written. Since then, I have learned the answers to many questions about the events that ended the Nixon presidency, and for a time changed the American presidency for the better.

For reasons that are more fully apparent in the new Afterword, the time has come for me not only to fill in a few blanks, but also to call attention to the sham efforts by a few to falsely rewrite this history with which I am so familiar. In addition, it is clear that the lessons of Watergate, which were real and which influenced the operations of government for the better during several decades afterwards, have been lost. As I have written in other books, those lessons and the positive influence of Watergate ended when George W. Bush became president and, during his tenure in office, subscribed to the efforts of Vice President Dick Cheney to remove all the restraints and responsibilities that Watergate had imposed on the presidents who had followed Nixon.[*]

Since this book went out of print, I have been approached several times about republishing it, but there seemed to me no point in doing so until I had something I thought needed to be

---

[*] See *Worse Than Watergate: The Secret Presidency of George W. Bush* (2004); *Conservatives Without Conscience* (2006); and *Broken Government: How Republican Rule Destroyed the Legislative, Executive and Judicial Branches* (2008).

said. In 1980, I published *Lost Honor*, where I discussed the aftermath of Watergate as it played out during the presidencies of Gerald Ford and Jimmy Carter. However, after the Carter Administration, I stopped talking about Watergate publicly, because I was involved in private business and wanted to lower my public profile.

During the mid-1980s, I began hearing about efforts to rewrite the Watergate story, but I ignored this revisionism at that time because it struck me as absurd. Accordingly, when I was asked to review the first book revising the Watergate story, Jim Hougan's *Secret Agenda: Watergate, Deep Throat and the CIA* (1984), I passed. At the time, I was unaware that Hougan's work was merely the first effort of many, for a number of Nixon's apologists, including many of my former White House colleagues, were busy inventing another totally new – and patently false – account of Watergate, turning history upside down by claiming that virtually everything I had written in the following pages was false, as was my testimony.

According to these revisionists, I had fooled the FBI, the Senate Watergate Committee, the House Impeachment Inquiry, and the Watergate Special Prosecutors, not to mention countless journalists and historians – everyone except a retired liquor salesman in Tampa, Florida: a man with limited formal education, but an endless supply of conspiracy theories. When St. Martin's Press published his remarkable and fabricated story, *Silent Coup: The Removal of a President*, it became impossible to ignore, for it sensationalized Watergate by making my wife, Maureen, who had nothing whatsoever to do with these events, the central part of a sordid and grossly false new account. We filed a defamation lawsuit and aggressively pursued it. After nine years in which the defendants spent $15 million of insurance company money fighting us and trying to make us go away, and during which time we used the power of subpoenas to uncover and discover a great deal of new information about Watergate along with overwhelming evidence to prove the

iii

revisionists' account was bogus, we agreed to settle our lawsuit. But I am getting ahead of myself. Suffice it to say that because of this nine-year effort, I actually know more about Watergate today, and understand it better, than when I lived through it.

Had I not uncovered all this new information and had I not discovered how the public memory of these events has almost totally faded, I would not be reissuing *Blind Ambition*. I am republishing this account now in order to add information that is not widely known, to share the rest of the story, and to provide solid information to those who missed these remarkable events and are curious about this sorry chapter of American history. Finally, I believed that those in government who believe historical truth is important, need to understand that there are individuals trying to distort that truth for their personal reasons. Our government works best when it understands true history, not when our history is distorted, particularly for a chapter as significant as Watergate.

ORIGINAL
AUTHOR'S NOTE

THIS BOOK IS A PORTRAIT—not a black-and-white photograph—of five years of my life. It represents my best effort to paint what I saw and reproduce what I heard. I have included detail, texture and tone to make this history more vivid—though, I trust, no prettier. I prepared for the writing of *Blind Ambition* the same way I prepared to testify before the Ervin Committee, before the special prosecutors, and in the cover-up trial. But in the book I have included dialogue and enclosed it in quotation marks, whereas in my testimony I deliberately refrained from dramatizing the events I was relating.

While many White House conversations were taped, many were not. To reconstruct what occurred, I reviewed an enormous number of documents as well as my own testimony. Wherever possible, I spoke to others who were present with me during discussions, or I talked to people to whom I'd related conversations shortly after they took place, and I referred to notes I had kept. I have also, of course, relied on my memory in this account of my experiences in the White House, and while I do not claim to report the dialogues verbatim, I vouch for their essential accuracy. To borrow my lawyer's phrase: "I'm ready to get on the box" take a lie-detector test.

A final matter of importance. I have often read authors' acknowledgments, but I never before quite realized what they were saying. Now I do, and it is not merely a gesture when I offer thanks to all those who helped with this book. I sincerely thank Marcia Nassiter and David Obst for their early encouragement; Estelle Oppenheim and Marie Ralphs for typing and retyping many drafts; Patty Firestone and Hays Gorey for critical readings and helpful suggestions; Richard Snyder,

v

Sophie Sorkin, Vera Schneider, Harriet Ripinsky, David Nettles, Frank Metz, Joanna Ekman, and the staff of Simon and Schuster for their enthusiastic and professional support; Taylor Branch for his talented assistance and patient tutoring; and Alice Mayhew, my editor, for guiding—more truly, forcefully but thoughtfully driving—the book to completion.

JOHN DEAN
Los Angeles
August 1976

CHAPTER ONE:

REACHING FOR THE TOP,

TOUCHING BOTTOM

"WOULD YOU BE INTERESTED in working at the White House?" Bud Krogh asked me casually.

It was a warm afternoon in May 1970, and we were walking toward a park bench that was well shaded by the aged trees surrounding the Ellipse. Bud had invited me to his White House office and, when I arrived, had suggested that we take a stroll so that we could talk, but I had had no idea what he wanted to talk about. I was pleasantly surprised by the question.

"Why do you ask?" I countered, trying to check my impulse to give way to the flattery.

As I listened to Bud telling me he had recommended me for President Nixon's White House staff, I was also paying attention to the little voice in the back of my head that was telling me to act reserved, to remember the negative impressions I had collected about the White House: friends haggard and drained from long hours of pressure, able men reduced to "gophers" and errand boys, breaking their necks whenever one of the President's top aides had a whim. That was not for me even if it was the White House. My job at the Justice Department was relaxed and enjoyable, with importance and promise for advancement. "Bud, thank you," I said, "but I really like it at Justice."

I did not want to act coy, just properly cautious, so that he would carry back the message that I would not be lured by just any job. He was scouting, and I wanted to find out exactly how interested the White House was. As always, I was mask-

1

ing my inner calculations and feelings, this time behind an appearance of friendly sincerity. So was Krogh. We had both come a long way in the government at thirty.

Speaking as if he were musing on whether I could move my desk down the hall, Bud inquired whether I thought the Attorney General, John N. Mitchell, would let me move to the White House.

"I really don't know," I replied.

Bud said that his boss, John Ehrlichman, the President's former counsel and present domestic affairs adviser, or Bob Haldeman, the White House chief of staff, might raise the possibility with Mitchell. I liked the notion of these powerful men negotiating for my talents.

Nothing happened, but several weeks later John Mitchell called me into his office to tell me that my going to work at the White House had been discussed, and that he had raised no objections. But Mitchell did not encourage me to go. On the contrary, he told me that I could expect to be promoted at Justice in time and that I would be better off staying where I was. In an almost fatherly way he suggested that the White House was not a healthy place; his distaste for the President's staff was vague but real. I knew there was some jealousy between Mitchell and the White House, but I had no idea the animosity cut deep. I would learn.

In early July, I was eating lunch at the Congressional Hotel on Capitol Hill, discussing the Administration's drug legislation with a key House Commerce Committee member, when I was paged to the phone. It was, Lawrence Higby, Haldeman's chief gopher, and he was in a hurry. The legendary White House operators had tracked me down at my obscure corner table for Higby, who was across the country at the Western White House. He asked me to catch the next plane to California because "Mr. Haldeman wants to meet with you." Immediately. Drop everything. With the efficiency that was the stamp of Haldeman's staff, Higby reeled off the available flight times. I thought I could catch the three-o'clock flight from Baltimore's Friendship Airport with a mad dash. I would be met in Los Angeles, he told me, but he failed to say why I was being summoned to San Clemente. I assumed it was about the White House job. "Don't miss the plane," Higby said and hung up.

I went back to the lunch table and whispered to my Justice Department colleague, Mike Sonnenreich, that he would have to carry on without me. As nonchalantly as possible, I mentioned that I had to leave at once for San Clemente on urgent business.

His jaw dropped, his composure momentarily lost. "You what?"

Having secured the name dropper's most savored prize, I smiled and rushed off.

Richard G. Kleindienst, the Deputy Attorney General, was in a meeting. I interrupted to tell him the news. We had talked about my moving to the White House, and he was more opposed than Mitchell. Half seriously and half to flatter, he said again that he didn't want to lose me, and that the last place in the world he wanted to see me was in "that zoo up the street." No title and no amount of money could induce him to work there, he said. Despite the overstatement, he was serious. When I said Haldeman had summoned me, he observed, "Haldeman's the only son-of-a-bitch in the whole place who can think straight. You'll like Bob."

I dashed home to pack, carefully selecting suits, shirts, ties, and shoes consonant with my image of the Nixon White House. As I drove my Porsche through the early-afternoon traffic on the Baltimore-Washington Parkway, I wondered whether I could beat a speeding ticket by telling a policeman I was on my way to the Western White House. Luck spared me, and I caught the flight with five minutes to spare.

3

Five hours, a few Scotch-and-sodas, a meal, some thoughts about the White House, some promising conversations with the stewardesses, and we were landing. The passengers in the first-class cabin were pulling their coats from the overhead racks when an officious airline executive stepped briskly on board.

"Excuse me," he said to the startled passengers, "would you all wait just a moment, please?" He whispered to the stewardess and then followed her to my seat. "Mr. Dean?"

"Yes."

"Are you going to San Clemente?"

"Yes."

"Do you have any luggage?"

"Only what I'm carrying."

He took my bag and marched off the plane ahead of me. The other passengers were held up until I made my exit, pleasantly embarrassed. Just outside the plane's door the executive stopped in the folding passageway to unlock a door that led down to the ground. By this time, the flight crew had gathered to watch. I noted the curiosity on their faces and tried to look as though I were accustomed to this royal treatment. I planned to step smartly into the limousine I expected below, but instead of a limousine I saw, not a hundred yards away, a shiny brown-and-white Marine helicopter with a corporal in full-dress uniform standing at attention at the foot of its boarding ramp.

The airline executive handed my suitcase to a young Marine lieutenant who stepped out of the helicopter as we approached. The corporal, still at attention and expressionless, snapped a salute at me without even glancing at my face. I stopped at the top of the boarding ramp to look back at the crew while the chopper pilot gunned the engine. I decided I had handled my escalating headiness fairly well. I had been

4

cool, had controlled my excitement, yet had managed a little hustling. Well, I thought, if nothing else came of this trip I could at least call the stewardess whose name and phone number I had managed to acquire. I figured I wouldn't have any trouble getting a date—she must be wondering just who I was. I was wondering the same thing.

The pilot asked me if I'd ever been in a helicopter before. I told him yes, in military helicopters much like his, except not as plush. Shortly after I went to work at the Justice Department, the senior officials had gone through a nuclear evacuation drill, and a helicopter had whisked us to a secret subterranean retreat where we would operate the government in the event of a real attack. Also, I had once surveyed an antiwar demonstration from a helicopter. I preferred not to think about those previous trips, because now I was relishing the glamour without the unsettling idea of living like a mole under scorched earth or of watching police bang heads.

As we headed south toward San Clemente, the pilot pointed out landmarks and towns along the coast: the drydocked Queen Mary, being converted into a hotel but looking from the air like an old and rusting toy; the indistinguishable beach towns of Newport and Laguna; and hundreds of white dots on the water, the luxury boats marking the leisure and wealth that abound in Southern California. We landed at a helicopter pad a few miles from the Western White House, and I was driven to "the compound" by another Marine corporal. The grounds and the buildings looked like the campus of a well-endowed small college. I heard my driver receive instructions on his two-way radio to take me to the "admin building," where Higby was waiting.

Higby asked if I would like to freshen up before I met Mr. Haldeman. My God, I thought, I'm meeting with Haldeman tonight. As I splashed cold water on my face, I realized I was tired from the trip and from the meal and the drinks on the flight. I began thinking, maybe I am really too interested in

5

this job, maybe that's the wrong frame of mind. I suspect it is the fear of failure or rejection that sets off this defense mechanism in me before any interview. I wanted to make a mental adjustment. I would have to collect my thoughts fast, and I would have to start telling myself I did not even want to work at the White House.

I was still working on convincing myself later in Haldeman's outer office, when Haldeman emerged. We had never met before, but when he saw me he bounded across the small reception area, his right hand extended, a broad smile on his face. Athletically built, with crew-cut hair, and deeply tanned skin, he looked like a college football coach recruiting a new player—not like the awesome ramrod of the President's guard I had heard so much about. And he seemed genuinely pleased to meet me, which caught me off guard.

"I'm Bob Haldeman," he said. I was faced with a split-second decision on how to respond. I didn't want to become trapped as I had with Mitchell, whom I still called "Mr. Mitchell" or "General." Even though our relationship was now informal, I could not pull myself over the mental hurdle to call him John. I doubt that he would have been offended, but he had never invited me to change, either. The pattern, I thought, had been fixed at our first meeting. I wanted to do better with Haldeman. His unexpected pleasantness pushed my resolve over the edge.

"Bob," I replied, "it's nice to meet you." That took care of that.

Since he did not seem put off by my informality, I was heartened enough to comment on his suntan.

"Well, don't get the idea that all we do out here is lie around in the sun," he said with a smile. Haldeman usually managed a tan. Later I wondered if Bob's tan level was an indicator for the President as to when they should travel to the warm climates he also loved. Whenever Haldeman's tan began

6

to fade, off they would go.

He asked me into his office. Comfortable and well equipped, it was out of a catalogue for contemporary office furniture. The entire office complex adjacent to the President's house was new and expensive, and it looked it. Money had been no concern; the expenses had been safely buried in inconspicuous budgets.

The pleasantries quickly disposed of, Haldeman asked me to be seated and opened up a file which contained my resume, the FBI field investigation that had been run on me before I went to Justice, and some notes.

"I thought it would be useful for us to talk about your coming to the White House. Ehrlichman has recommended you to be his successor as counsel to the President, but you would not work directly for Ehrlichman. You would be reporting to me. So I thought we should talk. Of course," he said after a brief pause, "the President will make the final decision, but I believe he will follow my recommendation. I guess I know about your background, education, and all that crap," he said, scanning my resume, "unless there is something you'd like to add to what you've got on your resume?"

"Nothing."

"Well, tell me what you do for Mitchell over at the Justice Department."

I described my responsibilities, but it was clear that he was not listening to what I was saying but to how I was saying it. Haldeman, it seemed, lived by Polonius' advice to his son: "apparel oft proclaims the man." I watched as he checked me out and saw a reflection of his own taste in clothes. I was wearing black wing-tip shoes; he was wearing brown wing-tips. He had on a white button-down collar shirt; mine was blue. My suit was as conservative as his. Later I discovered that he and I shopped at the same men's store in Washington.

7

"Do you think you can handle the job of counsel to the President?" Haldeman asked.

"Well, Bob, I am not really sure I know what the counsel does."

He described the job. The counsel would not be involved in program or policy development. Those functions belonged to John D. Ehrlichman's newly created Domestic Council or Henry A. Kissinger's National Security Council (for foreign affairs). The counsel's office would be responsible for keeping the White House informed about domestic disorders and antiwar demonstrations, investigating possible conflicts of interest for the White House staff and Presidential appointees, handling all matters relating to Presidential clemency, and generally assisting the staff with legal problems. Or, as Haldeman said with a smirk, "Doing whatever you goddam lawyers do for those who need you."

"I think I can handle the job," I answered, though I was not at all sure. I didn't understand his description. The job sounded vague and scary. If you made a mistake at the White House, you'd be finished.

Mistakes at that level would be whoppers.

While I was worrying about my future survival, Haldeman asked a most curious question: "Do you believe that you can be loyal to Richard Nixon and work for the White House rather than for John Mitchell?"

"I'm sure I can, yes," I answered. But I was thinking, how strange, Mitchell has a close relationship with the President. Haldeman's question reflected the same mutual suspicion I had heard in Mitchell's advice. I thought I was savvy about political skirmishing, but I did not understand how one could be disloyal to Nixon if one were loyal to John Mitchell, whose fidelity to the President was, I thought, unquestioned.

At last Haldeman asked me if I really wanted the job. Following my inner game plan, I said I was not yet absolutely sure, I would like to think it over, at least overnight. He seemed surprised, but said we could talk in the morning. I thought my hesitation was having the proper effect on him—he would not take me for granted.

Haldeman offered me a ride to my hotel with him, Higby and another aide, Presidential Appointment Secretary Dwight Chapin. Just recently, I learned, Haldeman had changed his mode of transportation to and from the office. A native Southern Californian, he stayed at a family house on Lido Isle, about thirty-five miles north of San Clemente. Each morning he had been picked up at the island by a Coast Guard launch, taken across a small bay to Newport Beach, driven a few miles to a helicopter pad at the Newporter Inn Hotel, helicoptered to a pad a few miles from the President's estate, and then driven to his office at the Western White House. The operation had employed six men and four vehicles and had taken about an hour. Then Haldeman, bent on efficiency, had discovered that he could travel faster on the freeway.

So we rode back on the freeway that night, and I got my first glimpse of Haldeman's relationship with his staff. It was not a relaxed ride to Newport Beach, where Haldeman was dropped off. He fired questions at Higby and Chapin and asked me a question about the protocol of addressing federal judges. His manner with Higby and Chapin was condescending, and he bitched at them when they didn't have ready answers. I winced at what I was seeing, but as I watched Higby and Chapin I thought their obsequiousness invited the treatment. They had both worked for Haldeman at the J. Walter Thompson advertising firm in Los Angeles and had joined the 1968 Nixon election campaign with him. From there they had gone directly to the White House staff as his aides. This explained their relationship in part: Haldeman had made them. If I went to work for Haldeman, I told myself, I would never accept their trampled position.

9

Haldeman safely delivered, Higby and Chapin drove me to the exclusive Balboa Bay Club at Newport Beach, and after a round of drinks Higby told me a driver would pick me up at nine o'clock the next morning. The desk clerk directed me to my quarters, which turned out to be an elegantly furnished two-bedroom apartment. The kitchen and the bar were stocked, and fresh flowers and fruit, "compliments of the manager," had been placed in the large living room overlooking the Yacht Club and bay. The White House goes first class, I thought. If they were trying to impress me, they were succeeding.

It was only nine o'clock California time—less than twelve hours since Higby had yanked me from my lunch in Washington—and I was tired but not sleepy. The excitement had my mind spinning. I fixed myself a Scotch, took off my coat, tie and shoes, and plopped down in an easy chair to think about what I should tell Haldeman in the morning. I decided, as I had always known I would, that it was too great a chance to be turned down. What I lacked in legal skill I could compensate for by extra effort; that was what I had done all my life. If I did turn it down, I might become a marked man and never get another opportunity to move up the ladder. Settled back with my drink, I entertained a reverie about what a big shot I would be as counsel to the President. Would I drive my Porsche to the office or ride in a White House limousine? Suddenly there was a knock at the apartment door. I found a Marine Corps p.f.c. standing outside.

"Can I help you?" I asked him.

"Yes, sir, I have Mr. Ehrlichman's luggage. I was told to deliver it here, sir."

"Fine, come on ahead," I told him. He disappeared and quickly returned with a half-dozen large suitcases, thanked me, and disappeared again.

Why had Ehrlichman sent his luggage here? I glanced at it. There was a suitcase for everyone in the Ehrlichman family.

Were they coming here tonight? Was I in the wrong room? I remembered that the "compliments of the manager" envelope had a note inside which I had not bothered to read. I went to the fruit basket and found it: "Welcome, The Hon. John Ehrlichman and family." I was flushed with embarrassment. Ehrlichman and family would not be far behind their luggage. I scrambled. Shoes, tie, and coat. Repacking. I cleaned the ashtrays, washed my glass, returned the bottle of Scotch to the bar, and dashed down to the front desk. Quickly, I explained the situation to the desk clerk.

"Mr. Dean, you're using the apartment Mr. Ehrlichman was going to use, but he won't be in for several days."

"Oh, I see."

I returned, relieved, but the magic was gone. The splendor was for Ehrlichman, not me. I was only a transient. But someday, I thought, such arrangements would be made for me.

The meeting the next day in Haldeman's office had barely begun when his phone buzzed.

"Whoops," he said, bringing his feet down from his desk, "that's the President. Excuse me, this shouldn't take long." I caught a glimpse of the President's office as Haldeman rushed through the connecting doorway.

Alone, I pondered my new intimacy with power. I had already been overwhelmed by the tension and the grandeur, and I knew everything I was feeling was a minute refraction of what touched the President himself. All of San Clemente, from the helicopters and the global communications to the breathless expressions of otherwise cynical men, reached to and from the President. Presidential presence was everywhere, and the President was in the next room talking with Haldeman. I was delighting over the feel of my new title, Counsel to the President, when Haldeman came back and invited me in to meet him.

11

The President was standing behind his desk, his back to us, gazing through the huge picture windows at the Pacific Ocean. By now, the sun had burned away most of the morning haze. As Haldeman and I waited the President continued to stare out the window. I felt awkward about interrupting a man, particularly this man, so deep in thought.

Haldeman broke his trance: "Mr. President, I'd like you to meet John Dean."

The President turned from the window, forced a smile, and extended his hand to greet me. I was so nervous at that moment I have no memory of what he said, but I recall he had a rather weak handshake, not in the tradition my father had instilled in me as a youngster. Immediately I realized a President has to shake so many hands that he saves his good grip for important occasions.

Richard Nixon, I found, was taller than he appeared in his pictures and on television, and he looked older. He was dressed casually in a maroon sport coat, but his manner was formal as he directed me to be seated in a chair in front of his desk. I was glad to sit down, because my knees were shaking.

The President sat at his desk with his chair pushed to one side to enable him to cross his legs comfortably, and Haldeman made a few remarks to bring the meeting to its point. Fidgeting with a fountain pen, the President turned his chair to direct his attention at me.

"John," he said, "Bob has told me about your career as a lawyer and I want you to be my counsel." Then, almost as if he felt that had been too blunt, he quickly smiled and asked, "Would you like to be the counsel to the President?"

"Yes, sir. It would be an honor." A tremble in my voice surely revealed my nervousness.

"Good. That's good," he said with a smile.

I was annoyed with myself. Why was I frightened? The

President was trying to put me at ease. I would discover he was very concerned that his visitors be comfortable because he couldn't relax when they were uneasy. I felt the awesomeness of talking with the most important and powerful man in the world. Even more, I wanted very much to be what I thought he wanted to find, but my self-confidence had deserted me. I hoped he would not ask me a lot of questions before I caught my breath.

Fortunately, the President continued talking. He praised, with some hints of reverence, my boss and his Attorney General, John Mitchell. "Mitchell is one of the best lawyers I know," he began, and his soliloquy was woven with fond memories of the time they had practiced law together in New York. He scarcely looked at me, and I had the feeling that he was not necessarily talking to me, just thinking aloud for my benefit. But just in case, I punctuated his remarks with appropriate smiles, knowing nods and a few "yes, sirs."

"He is more than the bond lawyer the newspapers like to call him," the President said, glancing at me.

I nodded. "Yes, sir."

And then he stopped. He sat in his chair, playing with his pen, thinking about John Mitchell. No one said anything. Haldeman stared out the window. I sat watching and waiting. Finally the President looked at Haldeman and then at me, and said with a tone of emphasis, "The Attorney General carries a heavy load for the President." And again there was silence as we pondered the President's words.

The President broke the silence, talking about his "young, efficient" White House staff. "They get the job done, and done well." And he let me know that Bob was very much his man in charge. This brought a slightly embarrassed but confident smile to Haldeman's face.

Unexpectedly, the President's tone changed, as if he were

suddenly off camera. He became more personal, less Presidential, as he turned his chair to face me. He placed his pen on the desk. "John, as a young lawyer in the White House, with the title Counsel to the President, you could have an important role with the other young lawyers in the government. You know, the guys who come to Washington to work for a few years' experience. These guys are ignored. You could organize them, get together with them, tell'm what we're doing at the White House, make the poor fellows feel involved. Then when they go back home they'd have something to say. They'd carry a message back home."

I understood from my own first experiences in Washington what he was saying, and I thought his idea made good sense politically. But the way he said it, the reflective, intimate tone of his voice, gave me the impression that he was referring to more than politics, to something he had experienced himself.

Several weeks after I joined the White House staff, I read *Nixon*, the biography by Earl Mazo and Stephen Hess. I discovered that Richard Nixon first came to Washington in 1942, an obviously ambitious young lawyer five years out of law school, to participate in the government's war efforts, but that because of his Quaker background he initially entered nonmilitary government service. His biographers did not report why, after six months working for the tire-rationing bureaucracy of the Office of Price Administration, he had suddenly quit, waived his religious exemption, and joined the Navy.

I recalled the President's comments, his ruminations about young government lawyers. The President had been telling me that his first experience in Washington had been disappointing. He had been ignored when he wanted to be involved. Probably he had found the daily tedium, the routine, and the anonymous work of a bureaucrat unbearable and had quit to join a service where his energy would be rewarded.

14

One evening soon after, I was dining alone in the White House mess at a large circular table reserved for staff, when a man who looked familiar came into the room.

"May I join you?" he asked.

"Certainly," I responded. I wasn't fond of eating alone. After he had been seated and given a menu by the Filipino steward, he introduced himself: "I'm Murray Chotiner."

He was an intriguing man, an intimate part of the Nixon legend. Chotiner had been managing or advising the President on political matters since his first Congressional campaign in 1946. He was now channeling White House funds and advice to favored Congressional candidates running in the 1970 elections, a few months away. I knew that he did not swing much weight at the White House. Haldeman had frozen him out because of Murray's reputation as a slush-fund politician. Chotiner was part of the "old Nixon" image, but he seemed congenial and I decided to test my insight on him. Proudly, feeling like one of the intimate few, I told him what the President had said about young lawyers, what I had read about Richard Nixon's coming to Washington as a young lawyer, and my theory. Was I right?

Chotiner said nothing for several long and awkward moments. I felt the chagrin he intended me to feel, and I regretted my question. When he spoke, it was to offer friendly but firm advice. "John, you're new around here. If you want to get along with the President, keep what he tells you to yourself. Unless he tells you otherwise. And even more important, don't ask questions unless you have a good reason. Believe me, I know from experience what I'm saying."

He was trying to be helpful, but I was stung. I learned an important lesson: to keep my mouth shut. All loose talk about the boss is dangerous to him and forbidden to his aides. The loyal soldier is silent, and he does not pry.

15

Now the President concluded his reflections on young lawyers in government, leaned back in his chair, clasped his hands as his arms rested on the chair, and was once again most Presidential. Haldeman, seated immediately beside his desk, looked at me and said, without speaking a word, Now that you are the President's counsel, what do you have to say? It was my turn.

Mustering my courage, I told the President as briefly as possible that I would follow up his suggestion about involving young lawyers, and that I was most grateful for the opportunity to serve him on the White House staff. I failed to hide my nervousness or my excitement. The President responded with a smile and rose. The meeting was over.

We shook hands and Haldeman led me back to his office. I had been at the summit for twenty minutes.

Haldeman went to his desk and began scanning the neatly typed messages that had piled up in the twenty minutes. He tore some notes from a pad he was carrying. I presumed he had taken them during his own session with the President. After sliding them into a desk drawer, he pushed a button on his telephone which brought Larry Higby flying into his office.* Higby stood patiently, like a well-trained retriever, waiting for his master to speak. Finally Haldeman addressed him: "Call Chapin and see if he'll have lunch with us. Are those memos ready yet?" Before Higby could respond,

---

* When writing *Blind Ambition* I made this comment about Haldeman making notes because it was a regular practice but also a well-kept secret. Later, when Haldeman was given a subpoena for all his notes, he claimed to have none, for he had placed them all in the President's files, as Presidential papers. But after he left government, and Watergate was well behind him, he obtained his notes from the President and published them in *The Haldeman Diaries: Inside the Nixon White House* (New York: G.P. Putnam's Sons, 1994). My visit to San Clemente, and hiring, was not of sufficient importance to make Haldeman's diary, other than an editorial note that I began working at the White House on July 28, 1970 (my records indicate July 27, 1970).

16

Haldeman fired off more questions and instructions. Higby faded as quickly as he had appeared.

I sat on Haldeman's sofa and lit a cigarette, which tasted especially good after the ordeal. Haldeman busied himself with memos on his desk. I welcomed the brief pause and began staring out the large panel windows. This place is like a stop-and-go movie, I thought. Everyone races through moments of intense activity and then becomes motionless and distant. The pauses are therapeutic reprieves, but they are intense too. I thought about my new job with a slow, languid pleasure, as if licking an ice-cream cone. I felt I had reached a true height of success, assuring even greater future successes, and all this had happened far ahead even of my own optimistic schedule. I had arrived so fast I was apprehensive, a bit frightened. I thought about what I would tell my friends when they asked how I had pulled off this job at the age of thirty-one, after practicing law for a total of six months. Well, I would say, I just happened to be in the right place at the right time. I laughed to myself at the thought of how unsatisfying this answer would be.

Returning home, I wondered how John Mitchell would react. I was anxious for the blessings of my mentor, and a bit concerned.

Mitchell called me to his office almost as soon as I returned from San Clemente. "Well, I can understand why you took the job, it's a nice opportunity for a young lawyer," he said. "Congratulations."

I was relieved, and curious to hear any advice he had to offer before I moved on.

"It's a tough place to work," he began. "The hours are long, and sometimes the demands incredible. Everything has to be done yesterday. And it can be rough-and-tumble at times."

"I gather it's pretty competitive up there."

"That's right. Everyone wants the President's ear and he's only got two of them," he said, leaning back in his chair as the smoke from his pipe rose to form the thin haze that always hung over his desk. He thought for a moment about what he wanted to tell me.

"I'm not sure what this latest reorganization of the White House staff means," he continued. "I've been watching it." He summarized the recent division of responsibilities: Henry Kissinger running the National Security Council (foreign policy), John Ehrlichman heading the new Domestic Council (domestic affairs), George P. Shultz directing the reorganized Office of Management and Budget (money matters), with Bob Haldeman "coordinating the whole ball of wax."

"I see a head-on collision coming between Shultz and Ehrlichman. Ehrlichman is in over his head. He likes to dabble in everything," Mitchell observed with annoyance. He stopped to repack his pipe banging its charred contents into an ashtray. "I'll be curious to see if Ehrlichman ever takes his foot off your shoulder. You're going to be a threat to him."

I was flattered by the remark, which Mitchell had not intended as flattery.

"Shultz is a good man," he went on. "He's a real stand-up-type guy. Tough too. I'm glad to see the President relying on him more, and I've told the President that. Shultz can keep the President out of trouble with Ehrlichman's half-baked schemes to cure the ills of the country."

John Mitchell, usually a man of few words except after several martinis, was talking more candidly about the White House than I had ever heard him. I listened hard. It was a place I knew nothing about, and Mitchell knew a lot.

"Don't be intimidated by Haldeman," he advised. "He's really a fine, personable guy once you get to know him. The

18

President needs Haldeman. I had to talk Bob into taking that job at the White House after the campaign. Now he's the President's right and left hands. He does for the President what the President isn't any good at doing himself. Once you've proved yourself to him, well, the President will know it."

Now Mitchell grew even more personal. "The President will like you. Just sit back and do the job you're quite capable of doing and the President will discover you. Once you've gained his confidence, he'll listen to you. You can help him and tell him the way things are, which he needs to hear more often."

Mitchell wished me well at the White House and told me I was always welcome if I wished to return to Justice. We talked briefly about the future. He felt Richard Nixon would have no trouble getting reelected in 1972.

"Mr. Mitchell, what are you going to do in the next administration?" I asked. "Would you like to go to the Supreme Court?"

"Hell, no," he replied with a laugh as he got up to give me a farewell handshake. "I just want to get back to New York as soon as I can and make some money. I'm going broke in this damn job."

I arrived early for my first day on the new job, July 27, 1970, and drove to the southwest gate of the White House grounds. A guard found my name on his clipboard and instructed me to park in one of the visitors' spaces, since my permanent spot had not yet been assigned. Bud Krogh pulled in a few spaces away. He waved a greeting at me and hurried off, mumbling like the Mad Hatter that he was late. He would see me later, he called. It was not yet eight in the morning. Late, I thought. I had been worried about getting there too early. No one had told me when the work day started.

I'd barely got acquainted with my new office in the Executive Office Building when Bud called in, "Hey, John, have you had a chance to take a real look around yet?"

"No, I haven't."

He seemed pleased. "Let me take you on a tour and show you some of the places no one sees." There was a look of mischief on his face.

Bud Krogh—Egil Krogh, Jr.—was a long-time friend of John Ehrlichman and his family in Seattle. After spending much of his childhood in the Ehrlichman home, he had joined Ehrlichman's law firm and then followed Ehrlichman to the White House as his assistant. Such intimate sponsorship from Ehrlichman gave Bud a head start in the White House, and he made the most of it. Despite his youth, he was already known in the Administration for his quick grasp of complex issues and his forceful presence. Even when he was largely ignorant of the subject matter, he was sharp enough to dominate meetings and win the participants' respect. Already he was the White House man in charge of relations with the District of Columbia government, with responsibilities ranging from reviewing its budget to overseeing its response to the massive antiwar demonstrations of the early Nixon years. He was also in charge of the White House effort to combat heroin and other dangerous drugs, a subject of great concern to the President. Later he would be selected to run the highly secret Plumbers' Unit that was to stop up leaks, and still later he would go to jail for his activities there.

Bud Krogh was someone I considered a friend. We took off toward the basement of the Executive Office Building like the Hardy Boys. Hidden in the depths we found the telephone switchboard headquarters, and behind it a massive equipment room filled with transformers, generators, and electrical circuitry. Bud introduced me to the chief operator, who seemed pleased by our visit. "This equipment we have, Mr. Dean, could handle a whole city the size of Hagerstown,

Maryland," she said proudly. I wondered why she picked Hagerstown, of all places, but her domain was certainly impressive, as were the skills of the women who worked as operators. They could locate anyone, just as they had found me for Larry Higby when Haldeman wanted me to fly to San Clemente. (Only once did I abuse this skill, when I asked one of the operators to track down a woman I had met who would not give me her unlisted telephone number.) Bud and I lingered briefly and then pressed on to the basement of the White House's West Wing and the Situation Room.

The Situation Room, I had heard, was where Henry Kissinger took his dates to impress them. It operated twenty-four hours a day to keep the President aware of what was happening throughout the world, Bud explained. I pictured this nerve center as a gleaming room packed with uniformed admirals and generals seated at long computer consoles, surrounded by lesser-ranking aides and walls of incomprehensible charts and maps. Wrong. The room was dreary and overcrowded, jammed with cluttered desks, and staffed by a few young military men wearing out-of-date civilian clothes and a secretary checking the antique-looking teletypes. Even the windowless wood-paneled conference room, designed to prevent eavesdropping, was boring. This vital communications post was far less imposing than the switchboard rooms, and I decided that Kissinger must have something more than the Situation Room to impress the ladies.

Outside the "Sit Room" we peeked into a large storage area beside the mess, where workmen were building an executive dining room for senior staff and Cabinet officers, which would resemble a private men's grill at a posh country club. We walked on, peering into the White House barbershop, the limousine drivers' waiting room, the photographer's office, the vault safe for sensitive Presidential papers, and a Secret Service command post.

We went upstairs to the first floor of the West Wing, where

21

the President's Oval Office is located. Bud was amazed that I had never seen it. As we approached, he pointed out a small monitoring device that kept constant track of the President's whereabouts. It indicated that the President was in his hideaway office at the Executive Office Building next door. An Executive Protective Service officer was posted near the monitor. A thick velvet rope guarded the door to the Oval Office, which was standing open. Bud, never shy, asked the officer to remove the rope so that we could take a closer look. He obeyed reluctantly, with the request that we step just inside.

"This is The Man's office," said Bud. "What do you think?"

"Not bad, not bad at all. In fact, it's damn impressive." I could feel the importance of the office as I took it all in. My attention was caught by the conspicuous rug and the huge desk. The oval rug was deep blue, with a ring of gold stars and a huge gold eagle in the middle, a replica of the President's seal of office. It struck me as surprisingly flashy for Richard Nixon, who had such strong feelings about appearing dignified and Presidential. He would not, despite the advice of his television experts, wear a blue shirt. Blue shirts weren't Presidential, he said, and he didn't care if his white shirts made his dark features appear harsher on television; white shirts were Presidential. His blue-and-gold rug, like the short-lived Bavarian-guard uniforms he commissioned for the White House, was in odd contrast to all that.

His desk was enormous and had allegedly been used by Woodrow Wilson. Two Presidents, maybe four, could have worked at it without disturbing each other. There was a story about the desk around the White House. The President liked to sit with his feet on it, and his heels had scarred the top. Once, when he was out of the country, someone noticed the damaged mahogany surface and sent the desk out to be refinished. When he returned, Nixon noticed that his heel marks had been removed. "Dammit, I didn't order that," he snapped. "I want to leave my mark on this place just like other Presidents."

We moved on to the East Wing, with Bud pointing out places of interest along the way—the doctor's office, the chief butler's office, the Map Room, the Lincoln Library, the kitchen, the secret tunnel. We stopped briefly at the door of the secret tunnel, which ran from the basement of the White House to the Treasury Department a block away. Bud said the Secret Service had contingency plans for bringing troops through the tunnel if a hostile demonstration ever got out of hand. But the only trooper to use the tunnel was Chief Justice Warren Burger. On the day his Supreme Court nomination was announced, the tunnel enabled him to enter the White House unnoticed by the press.

Down we went to the East Wing basement, until halted by a large steel door posted "Restricted Area." Bud ignored the sign, and I followed him through a room of furnaces, low-hanging pipes, and huge valves to a second steel door with a small window. He rang the doorbell, and a face appeared that recognized him. The door opened and Bud stated his purpose: "I want to show Mr. Dean, the new counsel to the President, the area we use as a command post during demonstrations."

We walked through a corridor maze until we came to a small suite of rooms. "This," Bud announced, "is the President's bomb shelter."

I looked around. Ventilated air. Stored supplies. Beds. An appropriately Presidential desk flanked by flags. And a conference room with three built-in television sets, plus radio equipment and telephones everywhere. It looked like a President's bomb shelter.

Bud said Ehrlichman found this an ideal command post for monitoring demonstrations, which puzzled me. It was remote, to say the least, and totally out of touch with what would be occurring on the streets. I conjured an image of "Field Marshal Ehrlichman," whose interest in demonstrations Haldeman once

23

likened to that of a firehouse Dalmatian at a blaze. I knew I wouldn't use the shelter for monitoring demonstrations, although Haldeman had told me that that would be one of my responsibilities. The only time I ever returned there was for a secret screening of *Tricia's Wedding*, a pornographic movie portraying Tricia Nixon's wedding to Edward Cox, in drag. Haldeman wanted the movie killed, so a very small group of White House officials watched the cavorting transvestites in order to weigh the case for suppression. Official action proved unnecessary; the film died a natural death.

As Bud and I went past the offices of the White House staff members, I noticed furniture and files being moved. The White House, far more than any other government office, was in a state of perpetual internal flux. Offices were constantly exchanged and altered. One day I visited the President's Congressional-liaison man, Bryce N. Harlow, in his first-floor West Wing office (which later belonged to Clark MacGregor and then to William E. Timmons) and found a team of workmen busy constructing a new wall where a door had once been. Bryce explained he had been forced to give up his private bathroom because the stairwell from the basement to the second floor was being made smaller so that Henry Kissinger's office could be expanded. "In a way, I'm glad to know the place I used to shit will be Henry's office," he said with a wry smile. "That tells me who's who around here." Harlow was perhaps the only man in the White House who did not care about losing space; he was planning to leave anyway.

Everyone jockeyed for a position close to the President's ear, and even an unseasoned observer could sense minute changes in status. Success and failure could be seen in the size, décor, and location of offices. Anyone who moved to a smaller office was on the way down. If a carpenter, cabinetmaker, or wallpaper hanger was busy in someone's office, this was a sure sign he was on the rise. Every day, work men crawled over the White House complex like ants. Movers busied themselves with the continuous shuffling of furniture from one office to another as people moved in, up, down, or out. We learned to read office changes as an index of the internal bureaucratic power struggles. The expense was irrelevant to Haldeman. "For Christ's sake," he once retorted when we discussed whether we should reveal such expenses, "this place is a national monument, and I can't help it if the last three Presidents let it go to hell." Actually, the costs had less to do with the fitness of the White House than with the need of its occupants to see tangible evidence of their prestige.

Our tour ended and it was time to go back to my "temporary" EOB office and work. By all White House standards my office was shabby. The walls needed painting and the furniture looked like military discards. I was across and down the hall from Special Counsel Charles W. Colson, whose growing staff had lovely views of the White House and its tree-filled south lawn from their freshly decorated offices. From my window I could gaze on an interior asphalt courtyard filled with delivery trucks and parked cars plus the rear ends of air conditioners in other office windows.

I spoke with Larry Higby about this situation, which I felt did not befit a man with my title. "Larry, I don't want to sound like a complainer, but I'm embarrassed to invite anyone to my office for a meeting, it's such a dump. Also it's sometimes hard to concentrate, listening to the urinals flush all day, since you've got me right beside the men's room."

"It's only temporary," he said. He agreed to have the walls painted and some decent furnishings delivered, but added a teaser: "Bob hasn't decided where he wants to put you yet." Then he dangled "possibilities" before me—nice big offices of people Haldeman might move out in order to move me in. I did not have to be told what was happening. I was being tested and my performance would determine what I would get. I was at the bottom of the ladder, and instinctively I began to climb.

For a thousand days I would serve as counsel to the President. I soon learned that to make my way upward, into a position of confidence and influence, I had to travel downward through factional power plays, corruption, and finally outright crimes. Although I would be rewarded for diligence, true advancement would come from doing those things which built a common bond of trust—or guilt—between me and my superiors. In the Nixon White House, these upward and downward paths diverged, yet joined, like prongs of a tuning fork pitched to a note of expediency. Slowly, steadily, I would climb toward the moral abyss of the President's inner circle until I finally fell into it, thinking I had made it to the top just as I began to realize I had actually touched bottom.

CHAPTER TWO:

FIREFIGHTING

THE TESTS STARTED that first day at the White House. After a brief examination of my meager quarters, I had sat down at my desk. I didn't have anything to do, but then my secretary brought me a sealed envelope with a small red tag. I asked her what it was. She had not opened it; it was stamped "CONFIDENTIAL," and the red tag meant "priority." Someone had been planning work for the new counsel. The cover memorandum was a printed form, with striking blue and red instructions filled in:

ACTION MEMORANDUM

FROM THE STAFF SECRETARY

LOG NO.: P523

Date: Friday, July 24, 1970

Time: 6:30 P.M.

Due Date: Wednesday, August 5, 1970

Time: 2:00 P.M.

SUBJECT: Request that you rebut the recent attack on the Vice-President.

An attached "confidential memorandum" said that a new muckraking magazine called *Scanlan's Monthly* had published a bogus memo linking Vice-President Agnew with a top-secret plan to cancel the 1972 election and to repeal the entire Bill of Rights. Agnew had publicly denounced the memo as "completely false" and "ridiculous," and the editors of *Scanlan's* had replied: "The Vice-President's denial is as clumsy as it is fraudulent. The document came directly from Mr. Agnew's office and he knows it." My instructions were clear: "It was noted that this is a vicious attack and possibly a suit should be filed or a federal investigation ordered to follow up on it."

"Noted" by whom? Since the memorandum was signed by John Brown, a member of Haldeman's staff, I called him to find out. The "noter" was the President, I was told; he had scrawled my orders in the margin of his daily news summary. No one had to explain why the President's name was not used. He was always to be kept one step removed, insulated, to preserve his "deniability."

So this is my baptism, I thought. I was astounded that the President would be so angrily concerned about a funny article in a fledgling magazine. It did not square with my picture of his being absorbed in diplomacy, wars, and high matters of state. Was it possible that we *had* a secret plan to cancel the election and the Bill of Rights. I was embarrassed by the thought. Now I cannot look back on this episode without laughing, but then I was not at all loose about it. It was the President of the United States talking. Maybe he was right.

On the due date, I wrote my first memorandum to the President, explaining the hazards of a lawsuit and the wisdom of waiting to see what an FBI investigation produced. I thought the affair had been put to rest. Not so. Back came another action memorandum from the staff secretary. The President agreed with my conclusions, but he wasn't yet content. "It was requested," said the memorandum, "that as part of this inquiry you should have the Internal Revenue Service conduct a field investigation on the tax front."

This was the "old Nixon" at work, heavy-handed, after somebody. I began to fret. How could anything be at once so troubling and so absurd? The President was asking me to do something I thought was dangerous, unnecessary, and wrong. I did nothing for several days, but the deadline was hard upon me. I couldn't simply respond, "Dean opposes this request because it is wrong and possibly illegal." I had to find some practical reason for doing the right thing or I would be gone. I called Bud Krogh several times, but he was out. Then I thought of my recent acquaintance, Murray Chotiner, and arranged to meet him.

"I need some counsel, Murray."

"You're the lawyer. You're the one who is supposed to give counsel around here," he said with a chuckle.

"I'm still trying to find the water fountains in this place," I said. "Murray, seriously, I need some advice. The President wants me to turn the IRS loose on a shit-ass magazine called *Scanlan's Monthly* because it printed a bogus memo from the Vice-President's office about canceling the 'seventy-two election and repealing the Bill of Rights."

Murray laughed. "Hell, Agnew's got a great idea. I hope he has a good plan worked out. It would save us a lot of trouble if we dispensed with the 'seventy-two campaign." Murray wasn't taking my visit as seriously as I was. We joked about Agnew for a few minutes before I could get him to focus on my problem, and he had the answer. "If the President wants you to turn the IRS loose, then you turn the IRS loose. It's that simple, John."

"I really don't think it's necessary, Murray. The President's already got Mitchell investigating it. The FBI, I guess."[*]

"I'll tell you this, if Richard Nixon thinks it's necessary you'd better think it's necessary. If you don't, he'll find someone who does."

---

[*] Years later I would learn that Mitchell did nothing, and there was no FBI investigation.

I was not convinced and said so, but nicely. "Okay, but let me ask you this, Murray. You're a lawyer. Isn't it illegal and therefore crazy to use the IRS to attack someone the President doesn't like?"

"Not so," he snorted. He stopped and retrieved the calm he rarely lost. "John, the President is the head of the executive branch of this damn government. If he wants his tax collectors to check into the affairs of anyone, it's his prerogative. I don't see anything illegal about it. It's the way the game is played. Do you think for a second that Lyndon Johnson was above using the IRS to harass those guys who were giving him a hard time on the war? No sir. Nor was Lyndon above using the IRS against some good Republicans like Richard Nixon. I'll tell you he damn near ruined a few."

Murray was testy, or maybe defensive—I couldn't decide. It was clear that he didn't want to discuss the matter further. I thanked him and left. If I was going to play ball in Richard Nixon's league, I would have to get over my squeamishness. I am not sure what I would have done if John J. Caulfield had not walked into my office.

Jack Caulfield could easily have been born in the mind of Damon Runyon instead of in New York City. He had moved up the ranks of the New York police force, from a street beat to detective, arriving at the White House after an assignment as candidate Nixon's personal bodyguard in 1968. Bob Haldeman had assigned him to me without telling me why. Caulfield explained that he was White House liaison with the Secret Service and the local police, but his principal assignment was to investigate Senator Edward M. Kennedy's conduct in the Chappaquiddick accident for John Ehrlichman.

Jack was a bountiful source of information. He knew what everybody was doing. He could tell you how to get a refrigerator or parking privileges and who was sleeping with whose secretary. And he wanted to help me find my bearings. He seemed a natural person to turn to with my IRS orders, and I decided to show him the memos. "How would you handle this assignment?" I asked.

"This isn't any problem. I'll take care of it for you with a phone call," he answered confidently. He returned the next day to report that a tax inquiry would be fruitless because the magazine was only six months old and its owners had yet to file their first return. Being resourceful, however, he had asked the IRS to look into the owners themselves. "You can tell the President everything is taken care of," he assured me.

"I've got a good one for you to pass along to the President," Jack added proudly. His Treasury Department sources had noticed an authoritative article on U.S.-Mexico drug traffic published by *Scanlan's Monthly*. It would make excellent background reading for the President's upcoming meeting with Mexican President Diaz Ordaz. I attached a copy of the article to my memo to the President, and was amused to hear that the article was removed before the memo landed on the President's desk. No one in Haldeman's office wanted to be responsible for passing along anything from a magazine the President hated so much.

I summarized the tax situation in my report. "The fact that *Scanlan's* is a new entity does not make the tax inquiry very promising," I concluded. "Accordingly, I have also requested that the inquiry be extended to the principal organizers and promoters of the publication." Thus, within a month of coming to the White House, I had crossed an ethical line. I had no choice, as I saw it. The fact that I had not carried out the assignment myself eased my conscience slightly. I had no idea how Jack had done it so easily, nor did I ask, and I never found out what became of the IRS inquiry.

Scanlan's came back to plague me again the following month. This time it was charging the White House with inviting some "labor racketeers" to the President's famous

31

"hardhat luncheon." I was asked to have the FBI check into the magazine's charges and reported back that the labor leaders were indeed shady characters. Shortly after this report, *Scanlan's* went out of business, its editors unaware of how much trouble they stirred up at the White House.

Soon Haldeman was testing me again, with a sensitive task regarding what was to be known as the "Huston Plan." Thomas Charles Huston, its patron, was the second person Haldeman assigned to my staff, again with no explanation. He was as mysterious and complex as the label on his plan: "Top Secret/Handle Via COMINT Channels Only." Haldeman called me to his office to explain that Tom Huston had been charged with responsibility to revise domestic intelligence gathering. Every official involved agreed with the plan except FBI Director J. Edgar Hoover, who had irritated the President by blocking its implementation. Huston could do nothing further, for he had offended the powerful Hoover. My assignment was to get the plan implemented.

Before I read the plan, I thought there was nothing more than a personality clash in my way, and the fact that Huston had offended Hoover was no surprise. I had discovered his abrasiveness the hard way when I once asked Tom to draft a routine memorandum to the Attorney General asking for some information. The memo was sent, over my signature, to the Justice Department, where it exploded. Kleindienst had called me. "Listen, Junior," he yelled, "I don't like having to make this call, but John Mitchell is damn upset. I'm surprised at you acting like the rest of those assholes up there!" He then read me the memorandum Huston had drafted. It was curt and quick; I seemed to be ordering John Mitchell around like a deckhand. Horrified, I told Kleindienst I had signed the memo without reading it and assured him I would start reading my mail.

Obviously I now had to read the plan, but Huston wouldn't give me a copy until I had been given security clearance. The clearance procedure was hardly the ritual swearing to secrecy I anticipated, and it would have been funny if everyone had not been so solemn. Two CIA officials came to my office and told Jane Thomas, my secretary, and me that we had to keep the plan locked in a combination safe; we could not move these classified materials without a guard to accompany us; and, finally, we should not talk into lamps, flowerpots, or pictures if we were in a foreign hotel. Bugs, you know.

With my "Top Secret/COMINT Channel" status, I received the plan. The President, I discovered, had ordered removal of most of the legal restraints on gathering intelligence about left-wing groups. He had authorized wiretaps, mail intercepts, and burglaries. These were the hottest papers I had ever touched. The plan had the full support of the Central Intelligence Agency, the Defense Intelligence Agency, and the National Security Council of everyone except Hoover's FBI. Hoover had foot-noted the document with an objection that the risk of each illegal method was greater than the potential return.

Tom Huston came to brief me. With rabid conviction, he told me the nation would surely crumble from within if the government failed to deal with the revolutionaries and anarchists who were bent on destroying it. He was incensed that the President's orders could be blocked by Hoover merely because Hoover "wanted to ride out of the FBI on a white horse." There was nothing really new about the plan, he assured me, for the FBI used to do those things regularly when Hoover was younger.

After Huston left, I sat back to study my predicament. I was suspicious of his arguments because he was trying so hard to sell them. He had a vested interest in finding anarchy at the doors. (In fact none of the dire predictions in his report ever came true.) But I was no expert in internal security, and I knew that my arguments on the merits of the plan would convince no one. The methods would never hold up legally, and I was sensitive to my personal risk if I were involved in the decision

33

to use them. I would have preferred to let someone else handle this one, but Haldeman had selected me. Still, I wondered, how did Haldeman expect *me* to get J. Edgar Hoover to reverse himself?

After casting about for a few days, I decided that John Mitchell offered the only way out, and I arranged to see him on September 17. When I arrived at his office, he had just talked to the CIA representatives. To my relief, Mitchell said he had already made his decision. He was going to kill the plan somehow.

"John, the President loves all this stuff," he said slowly, "but it just isn't necessary." As he searched out loud for some sort of compromise, I was grateful to him for assuming my burden. He would take the heat at the White House, not I. We decided to endorse the idea of an interagency Intelligence Evaluation Committee, a toothless version of the Huston Plan. It was, in effect, a study group. Mitchell assumed the task of persuading Hoover to join the IEC as a SOP to the White House. This took some doing, for Hoover had, in a fit of pique, cut off all communications with the other intelligence agencies. While Mitchell presented the IEC to Hoover as meaningless, I was to present it to the White House as a promising first step. True, I would say, it was not the Huston Plan, but it would at least get Hoover back in harness. My report was received without joy, but no wrath fell on me. The Huston Plan was laid to rest, and Huston himself soon left the White House in disgust.[*]

---

[*]   In 1975, in the aftermath of Nixon's resignation, the U.S. Senate investigated the intelligence activities of the executive branch, including the Huston Plan. Huston's proposal and related documents would be printed in the *Hearings Before the Select Committee to Study Government Operations with Respect to Intelligence Activities* (better known as the Church Committee, named after its chairman Senator Frank Church). Today that material is online at: (continued on next page)

From *Scanlan's Monthly* to the Huston Plan, I had survived two quick tests as different as the Marx Brothers and the Gestapo, and I had learned to expect anything in special assignments. But I also focused on my regular duties and was adjusting my instincts to what I saw daily in the White House. Before I hired my first assistant, I had formulated a plan of advancement. From three dozen resumes and a dozen interviews, I selected Fred F. Fielding, a successful young Philadelphia lawyer who resembles the actor George Hamilton. Fred is personable, poised, conservative in manner, and quite witty. I liked him from our first meeting. I knew Fred wanted to succeed at the White House as badly as I did, and I explained my ideas for doing it.

"Fred, I think we have to look at our office as a small law firm at the White House," I began. "We have to build our practice like any other law firm. Our principal client, of course, is the President. But to convince the President we're not just the only law office in town but the best, we've got to convince a lot of other people first. Haldeman, Ehrlichman, and the others who surround the President. Here's how we can do it."

Our conflict-of-interest duties were the key, I explained. The work was complicated and boring, but I had already sensed that it would produce new business. "It seems that when you really get to know a man's personal financial situation," I said, "and then candidly discuss his job here to determine if he has any conflicts, you can end up in his confidence if you play it right. And once you're in his confidence, he sends you business. What we've got to do is service that business. First we go out and get it, and then we service it. When we get a question, we've got to fire back the right answer, fast."

We proceeded on that course, and it worked. We put in long grueling hours, and word soon got around that the counsel's office was eager to tackle anyone and everyone's problems and do it discreetly. We gave advice on the divorce laws to staff members whose marriages had been ruined, and we answered questions about immigration law for the Filipino stewards who worked in the mess. Although our work was technical and legal, we discovered that we could use it to get a foothold in substantive areas. If we were alert in conflict-of-interest reviews and investigations, we would have a small say in Presidential appointments. As with any law firm, our influence depended largely on our reputation, and our reputation was good. We cultivated it with care.

Haldeman's assignments always received priority, of course, and he fired questions at us regularly. A Presidential fact-finding committee had returned from Vietnam with two captured Chinese rifles for the President, and the Treasury Department wanted to disallow the gifts because they had been illegally imported. What could we do? After a crash study of the relevant law, we had no trouble persuading Treasury to classify the rifles as legal "war trophies" for the Commander in Chief. A corporation, said Haldeman, had upset the President by marketing a replica of the Presidential seal. Could anything be done? A few statutes cited on White House stationery made the company desist. Congress wanted the General Accounting Office to audit the White House budgets in which the redecorating expenses had been buried. Haldeman wanted to know if the audit could be blocked legally. We let the auditors in but assured Haldeman we could stall them for four years. Jeb Stuart Magruder, the deputy director of White House communications, wanted to make a mass mailing to Nixon supporters at government expense. Not legal, we said, but Magruder went ahead anyway. Henry Kissinger wanted to meet with members of the Senate Foreign Relations Committee; would it violate the President's principle of executive privilege for him to visit Capitol Hill? It was a close call, we said; we advised Kissinger to meet the senators on neutral ground at Blair House, the official guest mansion, to avoid precedent.

The staffers we helped recommended us to their bosses, and the bosses seemed satisfied with our work. It did not take long for Haldeman, who knew everything, to learn that business was booming at the counsel's office. He gave his blessing, which meant that I was soon enjoying some of the coveted White House status symbols: a daily copy of the President's news summary, a new twelve-line telephone in place of my two-line model, subscriptions to more magazines and newspapers than I wanted, an Army Signal Corps telephone in my home (on which I could call London faster than I could dial next door), and carte blanche to redecorate an impressive new office. The small law firm grew; within six months my professional staff was up to three lawyers, plus Caulfield. We enjoyed neither the power nor the spectacular growth of Chuck Colson's office, but we became known as a steady ground-gainer.

By the beginning of 1971, the members of my staff were hopelessly overworked; but they were well organized, and business flowed in and out routinely. I left most of the standard casework to Fred and began scouting around for more important cases. It did not take long to notice that the counsel's office could perform in intelligence work for the White House. We had already assumed the role in our conflict-of-interest investigations. And we had Jack Caulfield, who knew such waters. We advertised our office as the place where questions would be answered. I encouraged this new specialty, figuring that intelligence would be more valued by the policy-makers than would dry legal advice. All through 1971, my "warm-up" year, we were bombarded with intelligence requests. I learned a lot about some of the things my superiors were interested in.

Chuck Colson asked us to search the military records of some anti-war Vietnam veterans for unrespectable conduct. The counsel's office checked the files but found no bombshells.

Haldeman sent us frequent questions about *Millhouse: A White Comedy,* a satirical film based on the President's "Checkers Speech" and other embarrassing events. Would it hurt us with the youth vote? Could we stop it? Caulfield acquired a dossier of FBI material on Emile de Antonio, the film's creator. We planned to leak it if the movie became a hit or if the Democratic Party sponsored showings. Neither occurred.

Haldeman requested an investigation of "Richard M. Dixon," the comedian who was seeking to capitalize on his striking resemblance to the President. Caulfield did a quick undercover investigation, but Haldeman lost interest when President Dixon faded.

Colson sent me a transcript of a telephone call he had had from William Lambert, a senior investigative reporter for *Life* Magazine, whose message was as complicated as it was wild and seamy. He said Teddy Ratenoff, an old informant of his, had gone to work as a freelance consultant for the Knapp Commission, which was then investigating police corruption in New York. Ratenoff, said Lambert, had just called to say he had penetrated a high-class prostitution operation and discovered "a lot of politicians mixed up in it, even at the White House." Lambert told Colson that Ratenoff sounded menacing, as if he might peddle his information. My assignment: find out what Ratenoff knew and whether it was true.

I sent Caulfield to New York on that one. After huddling with some of his old colleagues there, he returned with a cloak-and-dagger report entitled "Interview with Special Agent XXX regarding Xaviera de Vres a.k.a. Hollander." Special Agent XXX confirmed that Ratenoff worked for the Knapp Commission, providing bugging equipment and expertise. He had wired the lush business quarters of a madam named Xaviera Hollander (later a.k.a. the Happy Hooker) and had made tapes of famous clients "having intercourse and engaging in abnormal sexual practices." Most of the clients appeared to be judges. Ratenoff had also managed to copy Ms. Hollander's address book. But there was *another* address book, for sensitive political people, and it was not known whether Ratenoff had it. Special Agent XXX said Ratenoff had already entered

38

into a financial arrangement with author Robin Moore to write a book about Hollander. Ratenoff was clearly on to something, but it was impossible to determine what he knew about White House people.

Caulfield and I decided the information cut such a wide swath there was little chance of its being put to political use. The only real danger might be political embarrassment to the White House, but even that seemed remote. Still, I decided to check around quietly to find out what kind of response I would get. It would be entertaining to drop hints of the information from Special Agent XXX, and it would also let people know that the counsel's office had ears in hidden corners. I began asking the more adventurous men at the White House if they might have anything to fear from Xaviera Hollander's address book. When I whispered my story to Press Secretary Ronald Ziegler, his face went white as a sheet. "I'll deny it," he said quickly. "I'll deny it." He turned and walked away. But over the next few weeks Ziegler kept up a steady stream of calls to me, asking for further developments. His tone was so urgent I could scarcely keep from laughing. There were no further developments, except that Ms. Hollander did quite well as a public figure.

The counsel's office built up a reputation for such intelligence investigations—some juicy, many simply laborious—and we handled them while the ordinary legal work hummed along. I became the White House collecting point for antiwar intelligence reports, and I funneled information directly to the President during emergencies. In May of 1971, for instance, we expected as many as forty thousand antiwar demonstrators to come to Washington for what became known as "Mayday." Shortly after the President announced his surprise military "incursion" into Laos, antiwar leaders had announced their intention to "close down the government" by blocking bridges, traffic intersections, and entrances to government buildings. Loosely organized radical groups were to divide up the key targets, armed mostly with their own bodies, some with rocks and trashcans to throw.

With the demonstration set for the morning of Monday, May 3, officials of the Administration mapped their opposing strategy in summit meetings the preceding weekend. Ehrlichman, Kleindienst, Police Chief Jerry Wilson, and several Pentagon generals led the sessions. I attended to hear the intelligence reports, as I had when I had monitored demonstrations for the Justice Department. There were detailed briefings on the precise transmission frequencies of the demonstrators' walkie-talkies, which would be monitored, and general estimates of the percentage of drug users in the ranks. And there were constant updates on the intentions of the demonstrators, which was no great feat since the plans were printed in antiwar newspapers, complete with maps and arrows. Shortly before the battle, Assistant Attorney General Robert C. Mardian reported that the government knew the exact target areas of every antiwar group except one faction of Gay Liberation.

On Mayday, Ziegler issued a placid statement that the President anticipated a normal business day, but the President, in fact, wanted reports every half hour, and my office was responsible for gathering the intelligence. Direct lines had been installed between my phone and the command posts at the FBI, the Metropolitan Police, the Secret Service, and the Justice Department. When I picked up any of those lines, a special White House light flashed in the command post. My staff would call each command post for its latest word—what bridges were open, how much violence there was, how many people had been arrested, the general outlook. We would write a hurried report, fire it off to the President, and begin immediately on the next one. We were an information conduit only, making no decisions, but we got a great deal of attention.

Ehrlichman kept calling for information, and Colson popped in and out of the office with questions. Colson's intrusions became so annoying that Fred Fielding finally suggested in jest that he send a crate of oranges to the demonstrators locked up in jail. Senator Edmund Muskie, his Presidential campaign already under way, had a custom of sending oranges to his volunteers. The idea was that Muskie would be identified with violent antiwar radicals.

"Yeah, Chuck, that's a great idea," I chimed in, laughing.

To our surprise, Colson stopped, looked around, and then smiled. "You're right," he said, "I'll do it," and he dashed out the door. A few hours later he strolled back in. "I sent the oranges," he said proudly, "and I tipped off the press."

There were high political stakes involved in the handling of the demonstration, but we were quite distant from the passions and fears as we monitored numbers and information. Distant enough to play war games. On Mayday, I did something I could never have hoped to do when I first became counsel. I asked for, and got, a military helicopter to fly me over the city for a firsthand view. At the last minute I asked Ehrlichman to go with me, and I considered it a coup when this powerful man accepted. Taking various assistants with us, we took off from the Ellipse, and the pilot banked and rolled in the air as we passed over knots of people on the ground. We saw burning cars in Georgetown, a confused maze of little figures running through the streets, and conclaves of demonstrators on university campuses. Flashing police lights and pitched rock battles blended into a general scene of chaos. Ehrlichman, busy with his home movie camera, said little on the flight. When we finally circled back to land at the Ellipse, the ground there was crisscrossed with demonstrators and with blue uniformed police giving chase. We could not land there, said the pilot, so Ehrlichman ordered him to set down on the south lawn of the White House. That pad was strictly reserved for the President, and Ehrlichman later smilingly said he had been chewed out by the First Lady.

By the next day the violence had subsided, and the recriminations began. Critics of the Administration denounced the mass arrest of some ten thousand demonstrators, who later won a court ruling that the arrest methods were illegal. The President announced that he was proud of the government response, and I ushered Chief Wilson and the generals of the Mayday command into his office to receive congratulations.

The Mayday demonstration was at once gruesome and sporting for the officials involved on the inside. It was one of a series of crises that year, many of which served to slowly advance the importance of the counsel's office. When Lieutenant William Calley was convicted of murder for his part in the mass killing of civilians in the Vietnam village of My Lai, we called all over Washington to order delivery of documents on military law, inundated ourselves, talked with other experts, and became instant experts on the procedures of military courts. (For both legal and political reasons, spelled out at great length, I recommended that the President stay away from the case while Calley's lawyers appealed, but I was overruled by Ehrlichman and the President.) When the commander of an American vessel caused a scandal by handing a desperate Lithuanian detector back to the Russian ship from which he had escaped, we found ourselves informing the President of what was happening and why. When the Pentagon Papers sent the whole Administration into an uproar, we dove into constitutional law and offered discouraging opinions on the chances of enjoining newspapers from publishing them. Through it all our law firm performed well, and our intelligence specialty inched us upward. But there was one crisis in the intelligence field that did not help my stature in the White House.

One day in July 1971, Jack Caulfield bolted into my office, his face flushed. I was alarmed; Jack was not easily moved to fear. Usually, Caulfield strolled casually into my office and waited patiently, rocking on the balls of his feet like a schoolboy about to tattle. As he waited, I would sense him trying to read my mail upside down. When I acknowledged him, he would hand over a deadpan report on some salacious item he had picked up from his sources. Jack labored over the prose of his memos and his feelings were easily hurt, so I would praise his report and give him another assignment. Fielding and I would often crack up over an entertaining gem such as Special Agent XXX, but we liked Caulfield. He was Jack Anderson on our side.

"Jesus Christ, John!" he shouted, without waiting for my greeting. "You've got to help me. This guy Colson is crazy! He wants me to firebomb a goddam building, and I can't do it."

"Now, wait a minute, Jack," I said. I shut the door and told my secretary to hold my calls. "Calm down and tell me from the beginning."

"Colson's been pestering me for weeks to get this guy Halperin's Vietnam papers out of the Brookings Institution." (There had been reports that Morton H. Halperin and Daniel Ellsberg had secret documents that would extend the Pentagon Papers into the Nixon years, and we were all climbing the walls about it, especially Henry Kissinger.) "Well, I told Colson I might be able to get them." He paused. "Listen, John, I didn't take this assignment until Colson assured me it was okay with Ehrlichman. Tony, my man, went over to case the place. It's a big gray building on Mass Avenue. You know where it is?"

"Yeah." I knew that "Tony" was one of Jack's operatives, but I didn't find out his last name, Ulasewicz, until years later. Jack always said his last name was something I didn't "need-to-know," in spy jargon.

"Well, Tony cased the place, and he finally figured he could buy one of the security guards to get us in the building. And he found out Halperin's papers are in this big vault safe upstairs. The security on that vault is tough. It didn't take long to figure out this wouldn't be any easy job. We'd have to get past the alarm system and crack the safe somehow." I sensed that Jack was getting a buzz off the story in spite of himself.

"I told this to Colson," he continued. "I told him this thing is impossible! I figured Chuck would forget it. But he didn't. Chuck says, 'I don't want to hear excuses! Start a fire if you need to! That'll take care of the alarms. You can go in behind the firemen. I'm not going to think of everything for you. That's your business!'"

His eyes were wide. "Now, John, I'm no chicken, but this is insane. Tony can't go in there with a bunch of firemen. There are so many holes in this thing we'd never get away with it. You've got to get me out of this."

He was pleading and stammering by the end, and there was a short silence as my head reeled. "Goddammit, Jack," I said finally, "this is what you get for messing around with Colson." I couldn't resist the dig. "You just sit tight and don't do anything until you hear from me." I was trying to sound calmly in command. "And whatever you do, don't talk to Colson."

"I won't go near him, John," he said. His face portrayed fear, relief, embarrassment, gratitude, and uncertainty that I would be able to save him.

I stared out the window and wondered if the President's mind was as cluttered as mine when he stared out his window. Garbage and tension, I thought. I knew I had to get out of this thing. It was out-and-out street crime. I saw fat burglars wearing stocking masks slipping behind firemen and felt a rush of revulsion. And now I was trapped. Caulfield was on *my* staff, and I knew the plan before the fact. In order to escape, I would have to stop it. I suppressed a dart of anger at Caulfield, and then at Colson, before focusing on strategy. I thought about going straight to Colson, but rejected the idea. He was too fired up about Halperin's papers and too forceful. He might pull out all the stops to break me down. He was powerful, and he might squeeze me to choose between this break-in and my job as counsel. Then I thought of Ehrlichman.

Ehrlichman was in San Clemente with the President. By now I could get him directly on the phone, although I did so sparingly. "John," I said, "something's come up here that requires your firm hand." I was trying to make light of it. "I can't talk to you about it on the phone, so I'd really like to come out there and see you for a few minutes, if you can work me in tomorrow. It'll only take a few minutes." He could tell I was rattled, and I worried about it; being rattled was not an admired state in the White House.

"Okay," he said evenly. Ehrlichman did not waste words.

That afternoon I flew to San Clemente on the C-135, a courier flight, and Bob Mardian sat beside me. I asked him why he was going out to San Clemente, and he replied that he had to speak directly with the President about a matter so sensitive he couldn't tell me a thing. (He was worried, I learned later, that J. Edgar Hoover might blackmail the Administration with his knowledge of the President's special wiretaps against newsmen and employees suspected of leaking.) I was impressed and bested, since I could say only that I had to speak directly with Ehrlichman on a matter so sensitive I couldn't tell Mardian a thing. We chatted and played gin rummy. Mardian, an old Arizona colleague of Dick Kleindienst and Senator Barry Goldwater, was considered tough as nails in the Administration. His shiny dome and huge hands were his most striking features. He had little sense of humor, but he tried hard to be sociable.

On the following morning I had the first of what would be many encounters that revealed John Ehrlichman to be unflappable. I was quite exercised in his office, giving him a speech about an outright break-in, which was hardly a run-of-the-mill affair. I kept waiting for him to interrupt me with some sort of question or exclamation, but he never did. He just sat there,

45

staring out over the top of his half-rimmed glasses like a professor. The only sign of interest he gave was an occasional slight twitch of an eyebrow. Meanwhile, I offered every practical argument I could think of against the scheme: criminal statutes that would be violated, the likelihood that Halperin had other copies, the security around the safe, the exposure of Caulfield, on and on.

"Yep, okay," he said finally, nodding. "I'll take care of it."

He picked up the phone and called Colson. "Chuck, that Brookings thing. We don't want it anymore. I'm telling Dean to turn Caulfield off. Right. Goodbye."

I felt a great weight lift off me, and I admired the ease with which Ehrlichman had removed it. I also admired the skill with which he had handled me. He showed no hint of a reaction— no surprise, no argument, no demonstration of his knowledge. Impulsive reactions could be telling, and Ehrlichman had protective instincts. I wondered then if this thing had been ordered by the President. Years later, I learned that the President had angrily demanded Halperin's papers, had ordered "everybody to rifle" the files, if necessary.

Back in Washington, I was visited by Bud Krogh, who had by now taken command of the Plumbers' Unit. As part of his mandate to stop leaks, he wanted to harass the Brookings Institution in any way he could, and he was checking in with me. He told me the counsel's office should play some role in the "declassification" program of the Plumbers. He seemed almost apologetic, and I sensed he was slightly embarrassed at being chosen to head an intelligence operation that should logically have been mine. It was an uneasy conversation, with much nonverbal communication, and Bud was finally moved to offer an explanation: "John, I guess there are some people around here who think you have some little old lady in you."

Bud knows about the Brookings break-in, I thought. I was upset that they thought of me as a little old lady, but I tried not to let on. Later, as if to prove myself again, I had Caulfield obtain the tax records of Brookings from the IRS as Bud had requested and sent them to him with a covering memo, noting that Brookings received many government contracts we might cut off. I also told him there were Nixon loyalists on the Brookings board whom we might use clandestinely. A week later I sent Bud another terse and self-serving memo, offering to help "turn off the spigot" of funds to Brookings, but he never called on me. Although I was never sorry about my action to stop the break-in, I was pained it might have harmed my reputation for toughness in the White House. Within my limits, I was tough, too, and it had served me well.

In the fall of 1971, my small law office reached a plateau. I had acquired additional office space next door, and the carpenters erected partitions there to accommodate another lawyer, two secretaries, and Jack Caulfield. Upstairs, on the second floor of the EOB, I commandeered another large office. With partitions, it had room for two lawyers and a secretary. Soon I would take over the remaining office in my own suite, occupied by a man whose wife was a friend of Mrs. Nixon. His job was to greet those friends of the President whom the President did not want to see, but he spent most of his time reading newspapers. It took months of delicate sessions with Haldeman's staff and the personnel people to accomplish my goal. We had to find the man a nice job in another department, handling him gently. When the lateral arabesques were accomplished, I partitioned his office, redecorated, and brought two attorneys into the suite.

I was drained after nearly a year and a half's constant work. Haldeman granted permission for a vacation, and I flew to London, Paris, the Riviera, Rome, Athens, and the Greek Isles. While basking in the high life and relaxation, I reviewed my career prospects. I was getting closer to the center of things, I thought, having arrived at the edge of the President's inner circle. Yet I knew I had risen about as high as I could go.

Ehrlichman would always have a foot on my shoulder, for he was in fact the President's counsel; I was merely a successful staff lawyer.

When I returned, I decided to look for a job living abroad, with plenty of travel and a salary between $50,000 and $100,000. I took French lessons at Berlitz and entertained some offers. My experience in government would be useful later anyhow; another President would be looking for an Attorney General one day, and I could be a candidate. I went in to tell Haldeman I was leaving.

He was not pleased. "John, you wouldn't have all those damn job offers if we hadn't brought you to the White House in the first place. The same offers will be there after the election, probably more. You owe it to the President to stay through the election. Then you can leave if you want."

Haldeman never invited argument, and I did not offer any. Pleased that he wanted me to stay, I accepted the notion of leaving government in the glory of the President's reelection— for business, or perhaps even as ambassador to a small country. In the interim, my next step upward would be to play bit parts in the power struggles among those above me.

Soon after Hugo L. Black and John M. Harlan retired from the Supreme Court in the fall of 1971, Ehrlichman called me into his office. "I want you to help me out on a little project, John," he said, almost idly. "The President has asked me to give him some recommendations on the Court vacancies. He's not too happy with the Attorney General's track record."

I nodded routinely, but my mind was clicking with the implications of Ehrlichman's attack on Mitchell. I had lived through the disastrous nominations of Clement F. Haynsworth and G. Harrold Carswell under Mitchell at Justice and knew he had been politically wounded by them, but I was stunned by the notion that he had fallen this far.

Ehrlichman noticed my double take. "You look surprised," he remarked with a smile.

"Yeah, I am. I thought Mitchell had a lock on making Supreme Court nominations."

"He used to." After this had registered, Ehrlichman laid out his assignment for me. I was to review Mitchell's favored candidates for the Court, accompanied by David Young, a young lawyer who had joined Ehrlichman's staff after burning himself out working briefly for Henry Kissinger. The top man on Mitchell's list, said Ehrlichman, was Representative Richard Poff of Virginia.

Young and I went to Poff's office and spent four hours one afternoon questioning him on his judicial philosophy, background, and potential enemies, probing for skeletons. Poff was willing to cooperate even though he had just gone through a similar ordeal with a team of Mitchell's men from the Justice Department. Young wrote a glowing report to Ehrlichman, which satisfied me immensely because I had liked Poff ever since serving under him at the House Judiciary Committee. Poff passed muster all the way up to the President, but then caught everyone off guard by suddenly withdrawing himself from consideration.

An open race commenced between Mitchell and Ehrlichman as both scanned the South for acceptable names. Ehrlichman sent Young off to study Representative Wilbur Mills, and District Judge Lewis F. Powell, Jr., rose to the top of his reserve list. Mitchell quickly sent his next two names to the White House: Herschell Friday of Arkansas and Judge Mildred Lilly of Southern California. Ehrlichman lost no time in sending Young and me to screen them. He instructed us to report back to him by phone as soon as possible.

David Young and I flew to Little Rock. Neither of us mentioned what we were both aware of: that he was along to make sure my old loyalties to Mitchell did not get in the way of

Ehrlichman's intentions, and I was there to keep Ehrlichman from looking too openly partisan.

After nine hours with Herschell Friday, I phoned Ehrlichman. "John, he's a fine man, a good smart lawyer with a very lucrative practice, but he would probably make Harrold Carswell look good as a witness in the Senate. He knows little constitutional law, and he hasn't thought much about the major social issues that would confront him on the Court. I think we would take a beating trying to get him confirmed."

Ehrlichman asked a few questions and then said, "Give me a written report when you return, but take the next flight now and meet with the lady judge." I was soon back on the phone, speaking from a private room in Judge Lilly's apartment. "She sure as hell looks like what our woman candidate for the Court should look like," I said. "She's damn bright and knows her mind. I don't think she'd have any trouble getting confirmed, but the big question is whether the ABA committee will approve her. They may not think she's experienced enough."

Back in my office, I was not surprised to learn that Ehrlichman had used my assessment of Friday to block Mitchell's recommendation. And when the American Bar Association blocked Judge Lilly, Mitchell had failed with three straight. The bases were empty and Ehrlichman stepped up to bat. He offered Lewis Powell as his candidate. Mitchell acceded, and Powell went on to the Court. I had been circulating the name of Assistant Attorney General William H. Rehnquist in the White House. It caught on, although the President could not pronounce Rehnquist's name and called him a "clown" because of his pink shirts and his sideburns. Mitchell liked Rehnquist, but he smarted because the recommendation had come from the White House. And he smarted even more when someone leaked a story to columnists Rowland Evans and Robert Novak about how the President had to rely on the White House staff for Supreme Court nominations because the Attorney General could not deliver.

50

I was astonished at the boldness of Ehrlichman's move against Mitchell and the shrewdness with which he had enlisted me. He had challenged and beaten the President's most intimate adviser in an area where Mitchell cherished his prerogatives. It was a blow to Mitchell, not the first or the last. Long before his coup on the Supreme Court nominations, Ehrlichman had mounted a patient but relentless poaching war on Mitchell's territory. He was campaigning to gather control over all the far-flung domestic agencies into the White House, where he could pull the levers, and by early 1971 he had tamed nearly all of them except Mitchell's Department of Justice. It remained a sizable gap in his empire. As Ehrlichman moved in on his last and strongest opponent, many of us in the White House spent hours discussing the fine points of his deft skills.

Typically, he would begin by instructing his Domestic Council staff to study some matter in the Attorney General's domain, such as drug abuse or antitrust policy. He would solicit and get Mitchell's cooperation in the President's name. Then a critical study would emerge, and Ehrlichman would explain privately to the President the failures in existing practices. He would recommend new solutions which always contained a transfer of authority to himself, and he would win the President's approval.

Ehrlichman gained leverage over antitrust policy by attacking the suits brought by Mitchell's Assistant Attorney General Richard McLaren against International Telephone and Telegraph (ITT). He argued that the suits not only were contrary to the President's desired antitrust policy but also were evidence of Mitchell's failure to keep McLaren in bounds. For months he needled Mitchell, who, at least partly because he did not want to lose another battle to Ehrlichman, straddled the issue. Then, on April 28, 1971, Ehrlichman delivered his *coup de grace.* "Your strong views on how the Administration should conduct antitrust enforcement are not being translated into action," he wrote the President, and he concluded with a request for power:

"You should authorize us to require all government-wide antitrust policy work to be coordinated through one White House office, preferably the working group under Krogh that has been working on this for the past 90 days." The President approved, and Ehrlichman had his foot on Mitchell's neck. As the moving force behind the effort to settle the antitrust suits against ITT, he worked to consolidate his hold.

A year later, on February 29, 1972, the ITT settlement exploded in the Administration's face when Jack Anderson published a memo purportedly written by ITT lobbyist Dita Beard, in which she baldly told her boss that the antitrust suit against ITT would be dropped in return for a $400,000 contribution of ITT cash and services to the GOP convention in San Diego.* The next day Anderson lobbed another bombshell: he charged that Kleindienst, who had just been appointed Attorney General (Mitchell having left to head the Committee to Reelect the President), had lied "outright" about the settlement of the ITT case. Impulsively, Kleindienst demanded that his confirmation hearings be reopened so that he could clear his name.

As usual, John Ehrlichman took charge at the White House. On March 8, 1972, I was invited to his office for my first of many meetings on the Kleindienst-ITT matter, along with Chuck Colson, public relations pros and Congressional-liaison men. Always the congenial host, Ehrlichman motioned us all to be seated and took his usual easy chair. We could tell that John was not scheduled for other important meetings that day by his working uniform: blue blazer, white button-down shirt, club tie, and creaseless gray slacks. His formidable stomach, which had been expanding in proportion to his power, served as a comfortable rest for the pad of white paper he always carried

---

*   [Original Footnote:] On May 5 the GOP voted to switch the convention to Miami, citing, among their reasons, labor problems, insufficient hotel space, and concern with demonstrations.

to meetings. I thought he was a copious note taker until one day I stole a glance at his doodles. He was the finest and most prolific doodler in the Nixon White House, which helped him to stay awake at many meetings. Ehrlichman's quick mind could not tolerate what others had to say once he had collected the facts and made up his mind.

At this meeting, he was collecting. "Well, fellas, what do you have to report from the boiling kettle?"

"Kleindienst is a damn fool," Colson said instantly. "Jim Eastland tried to talk him out of going back to the Hill, but Kleindienst charged off after his honor like Sir Galahad. We wouldn't be in this mess if he wasn't so stupid." James 0. Eastland, the venerable Democratic chairman of the Senate Judiciary Committee, had become even friendlier to the Administration since Mitchell had assured him he would face no Republican opposition in his reelection campaign. He chaired the Kleindienst hearings to our advantage.

When Colson finished chewing on Kleindienst, we began assessing in earnest. We faced the nearly impossible task of proving a negative—of showing there was no collusion involved in the ITT settlement. After reviewing the documented history of the ITT case, I knew that Dita Beard's memo conveyed a hopelessly inaccurate, almost naive view of the Administration's workings. She appeared to be puffing up her own influence by ignoring the other forces at play, most notably Ehrlichman's effort to wrest control of antitrust policy from Mitchell's Justice Department. I also knew, however, that the campaign's fund raisers would never hesitate to milk any decision for all it was worth.* In short, we considered the

---

*   [Original Footnote:] While at the Special Prosecutor's office in 1974, I was not at all surprised to see the following handwritten note by Haldeman on his May 13, 1971 meeting with the President: "Kalmbach a little later hit Geneen hard. Work through Kleindienst." Translated, this meant that fund raiser Herbert Kalmbach, who was Nixon's personal attorney, was to pressure ITT president Harold Geneen for a campaign

Beard memo crass, almost an insult to our professionalism, but we knew we could not stand an open investigation. An honest defense based on the intricacies of tough opportunism would only make matters worse. As we kicked "scenarios" around the room, a public-relations strategy emerged around two central themes: hide the facts and discredit the opposition.

Ehrlichman approved the strategy and left the implementation to Chuck Colson, who threw himself into the campaign night and day, oblivious to unfavorable developments and undaunted by failure. He kept coming back again like a battering ram. From the beginning, Colson's extraordinary efforts centered upon his conviction that the Dita Beard memo was a forgery. If he could prove it, he would expose the Democrats as hucksters. Bob Mardian did not share Colson's belief and was convinced Colson's effort was wasted time that would not help his friend Kleindienst get confirmed. I witnessed many table pounding debates between the two on this point, but Colson pressed on. The FBI's famous laboratory would prove him right, he said. Since J. Edgar Hoover did not like Colson, I was sent to enlist the director's cooperation, a delicate mission.

I was somewhat apprehensive about dealing with Hoover, not knowing what to expect from this legendary man I had met only once during my tenure at the Department of Justice. When I arrived five minutes early for our scheduled meeting, I was greeted by a lanky black agent neatly dressed in a dark-blue suit.

---

contribution after the antitrust settlement went through. He was to check with Kleindienst first, because Kleindienst would be well acquainted with how much benefit Geneen had reaped from the settlement. Both Kleindienst and Kalmbach say this never occurred.

"Mr. Dean, Presidential counsel, I presume?" he said, standing at the door. He bowed his head slightly as he shook my hand, and said the director would see me in a minute.

I looked around the reception office filled with Hoover memorabilia: gangsters' guns, clues from celebrated crimes, pictures, and other battle treasures placed in large glass cases.

"You've never been to the director's office before, have you, Mr. Dean?"

"No, I haven't," I answered, thinking Hoover was probably reading my FBI file before he met me.

"Well, please feel free to look around." I continued looking until he told me, without receiving any signal that I was aware of, that the director was ready to see me. "Please follow me, Mr. Dean."

He led me along a dim corridor of inner offices where aging gray faces, Hoover's personal staff, looked up from their desks as I passed their doors. Hoover was poised at the end of a long, polished conference table, waiting for me as if I were there to photograph him.

"Mr. Dean, please come in," said the immaculately dressed, perfumed director. He excused my escort as we shook hands and ended the ceremonial arrival. I risked no small talk with the formidable chief and waited for his cue, which he wasted no time in giving. "Please hold my calls," he said, flipping a switch on a large console beside his desk. "Mr. Dean, what can I do for you?"

"Mr. Hoover, we, the White House that is, Mr. Ehrlichman and others"—I wanted to get my authority established—"have good reason to believe the so-called Dita Beard memorandum is a phony, and we'd like to have your lab test it because we are sure that your test will confirm that it is a forgery."

Hoover sat back and thought for a moment. "Do you have the document with you?"

"No, sir, but I'll have it sent over if you are willing to examine it."

"Of course I'll examine it. I'd be happy to." He leaned over to his console, flipped a switch and said, "Felt." He paused, then hit the switch again, said, "Never mind," and told me to get the document to Assistant Director Mark Felt, along with samples from the typewriter it was written on and some other comparative documents which Felt would describe for me.

"Yes, sir," I answered. "This will be most helpful, because Dick Kleindienst is taking a terrible beating over that document. His confirmation hearing has nothing to do with him anymore. It's a political attack on the Administration now. Jack Anderson started it all with the memo, and if we can show it's a forgery..."

"I understand exactly, Mr. Dean, what you need," the director said with emphasis, "and I'm delighted to be of service. Jack Anderson is the lowest form of human being to walk the earth. He's a muckraker who lies, steals, and let me tell you this, Mr. Dean, he'll go lower than dog shit for a story." The director turned his red leather chair to face me as I sat in a matching-color chair beside his desk. This was not the J. Edgar Hoover I had expected.

"Lower than dog shit," he went on. "Mr. Dean, let me tell you a story. My housekeeper puts papers down in the hall, every night, for my dogs, and every morning she picks up the paper and puts it in the trashcans in the back of the house. Well, one day Anderson and his boys came out to my house to fish in my trashcans for a story. To look at my *trash,* can you believe that? Anyway, they fished all through that trash and all the way to the bottom, underneath the dog shit, to see what they could find. So when you're talking about Anderson I know you're talking about a man that'll go lower than dog shit to find his stories. Isn't that something, Mr. Dean?" he asked, shaking the fleshy jowls of his face.

I strained to hold back a chuckle, not sure if I was supposed to laugh or not. The story was funny, but he was not joking. I finally nodded and said, "It certainly is some story, Mr. Hoover, some story indeed."

I reported back to Ehrlichman and Colson that I was confident Hoover would supply the report Chuck needed to blow the Kleindienst-ITT hearings out of the headlines, and I relayed his parting offer: "Mr. Dean, if you'd like some material from our files on Jack Anderson, I'd be pleased to send it over." Colson literally applauded, warming his hands at the thought of J. Edgar Hoover reaching into his famous files for derogatory material on his publicity enemy number one.

Waiting for the FBI reports, Chuck got a tip from the President's barber, who was also Jack Anderson's barber, that Dita Beard was a drinking buddy of Anderson's long-time secretary, Opal Ginn. Chuck charged off after that one, asking me to interview the barber to see if we could discredit Anderson's testimony (that no one in his office was a friend of Dita Beard). The barber had nothing, but Chuck found a photograph of Beard and Ginn together at a party and fed a press release and the photograph to Marlow W. Cook, a Republican senator on the Judiciary Committee.

Cook's release all but said Jack Anderson was a liar, and the Senator found himself on the end of a fragile limb when Anderson rebutted with a sworn affidavit from Ginn that she had met Beard only once. Chuck soothed Cook with promises. He expected to learn more from his special consultant, E. Howard Hunt.

Clad in the ill-fitting red CIA wig that has since become famous, and equipped with a voice modifier, Hunt interviewed Beard at her bedside in a Denver hospital. He called after his first visit. She had met Opal Ginn only once.

"She's lying," Chuck insisted. "Bear down on her and get her to tell the truth."

Hunt failed to extract anything different. Senator Cook was furious. He had been made a fool of by Colson, who would soon do the same to others.

"What does the stuff Hoover sent over on Anderson look like?" Chuck asked me.

"Chuck, you're going to be amazed what's in Hoover's famous files."

"Well?"

"Newspaper and magazine clippings."

"Shit. You're kidding me."

"Nope, that's it!" That was it. In this case, at least, the poisonous files proved to be a myth.

Caulfield conducted an investigation on Anderson's brother that produced nothing. Jeb Magruder, who was now deputy director of the Reelection Committee, sent former Plumber G. Gordon Liddy to run down a tip that Jack Anderson was involved in a questionable land deal in Maryland. Nothing.

Colson was reporting to the President on his efforts. It reminded the President of the Alger Hiss case of how, as a young congressman, he had fought to prove that the State Department official was a Communist and a perjurer. "The typewriters are always the key," the President told Chuck. "We built one in the Hiss case." As were all the top Nixon aides, Chuck was frequently instructed to reread the pertinent chapter in *Six Crises* for lessons on how to run over bureaucrats and smoke out political enemies.[*]

---

[*] When *Blind Ambition* was first published, one of the items that attracted attention was Colson's statement that Nixon had claimed they built a typewriter during the Hiss investigation. I recalled vividly Colson's statement to me because like all of Nixon's aides, I had read of his work in the Hiss Case. I had been stunned by the statement, for if Nixon's team (working with the FBI or whomever) had built the typewriter used to

The original Dita Beard memo went to the FBI on March 10 at my request. The lab work did not begin for several days, and ITT had Pearl Tytell, a New York document analyst, compare a photocopy of the memo with other materials from Dita Beard's typewriter. When she had concluded that the document was phony, ITT flooded the FBI with documents.

On March 13, Colson asked me to retrieve the original memo from the FBI. Pearl Tytell, he said, would not issue a notarized report of her findings until she had inspected the original. I had been nervous about ITT's expert from the beginning; the FBI never touched evidence analyzed by anyone else. Hoover had an iron rule against competition, the possibility of contradiction. I was afraid of what Hoover might do if he found out we had sent the original to an outside expert. Colson said it was vital for Tytell to have it, and assured me no one would know. I called the FBI lab and had it picked up. ITT officials took it to New York. The next day, Tytell called Colson to say she would stake her professional reputation on her conclusion. It was clearly a fraud, but she recommended a chemical analysis.

Chuck was enchanted with Tytell's potential as a Senate witness. "Who'd dispute that nice, grandmotherly little lady?" he asked. "Even Teddy Kennedy wouldn't doubt her in public." He authorized an ITT official to fly the memo to chemical expert Walter McCrone for "paper chromatography" and "microprobe analysis" work. McCrone snipped two small corners off the original, performed his tests, and reported his support for Tytell. Chuck was ecstatic. The document was phony.

---

convict Hiss, he had been framed. Colson later denied he had made such a statement, and the matter remains unresolved. But Colson's denial makes little sense, given the context in which he said it. One day, as the continued transcription of Nixon's tapes proceeds, we may learn the truth.

Now Chuck felt confident enough to make use of Howard Hunt's report that Dita Beard denied writing the memo and was prepared to so testify before a special panel of senators who were to question her in Denver as soon as she got out of the oxygen tent she was in. A Dita Beard statement was phoned to Washington as Chuck scrambled to rehabilitate her image in the media, an image he himself had sought to discredit by leaking stories that she was a sad old drunkard. Suddenly, stories appeared concerning her distinguished career at ITT.

On March 17, Chuck incorporated her statement into a press release and had it delivered to the home of Senate Minority Leader Hugh Scott. Fielding and I watched the news that evening. Scott appeared on all three networks, proclaiming Dita Beard's denial of authorship.

"At last we've turned the corner," said Chuck. "We've started to reverse the bad news. Next we hit them with the FBI lab report, and it's all over."

J. Edgar Hoover called me. "Mr. Dean, I've arranged for you to meet with Mr. Felt to discuss the lab findings." He hung up abruptly and I called Felt.

"What have you got, Mark?"

"Well, I'm not sure it's what you need. I'm sending over a draft letter, which the director is ready to sign, but he's authorized me to let you see it first. It says we can't make a definite finding."

I read the letter with dismay. It was worse than I had expected from Felt's remark. In FBI jargon, Hoover was saying the Dita Beard memo was legitimate. Colson, outraged, called Felt to complain and then accused Bob Mardian of sabotaging the lab study by leaking word about ITT's experts to Hoover. He insisted that I persuade Felt to change the letter, at least to make it innocuous.

Felt would not budge, because the director would not budge. Colson carried the FBI's draft letter to the President's office, and when be returned he said he had never before seen the President so furious. The President penned a note to his friend Edgar, asking him to "cooperate," then gave it to Ehrlichman with instructions to turn Hoover around. Ehrlichman could not budge the director an inch. When the President was told, he mused, "I don't understand Edgar sometimes. He hates Anderson."

Colson did not tell ITT officials about the FBI report, but instead he encouraged them to release their experts' reports. They did so on March 20. The next day, Dita Beard's lawyers released her sworn affidavit that the memo was not hers, just as Senator Scott had told the world she would. On March 23 Senator Scott and the ITT officials found out that they had been left on a limb, as Hoover sawed it off by releasing the FBI letter. Public debate on the memo's authenticity ended with the FBI's pronouncement.

A fresh wave of anti-Hoover sentiment lapped through the Administration. Had he deliberately doctored the lab reports after discovering the work of ITT's experts? Speculation intensified when he threatened to have McCrone indicted for tampering with FBI evidence. We tried to trace all the people who knew about the ITT work, but the original memo had traveled thousands of miles, and through countless hands. An old proposal to make Hoover "director emeritus" was briefly recalled. Colson wanted to fire Hoover. The idea was, as always, discarded. There was a question on Hoover in each secret poll of public opinion conducted by the White House, and he always ranked extremely high. This piece of political realism, more than fear of blackmail, probably guaranteed Hoover his job until he died, unexpectedly, a few months later.

The most intense debate took place over what to do about the Kleindienst hearings in the wake of Colson's defunct memo strategy. It was election year, and the Administration was

61

getting hit every day with revelations about the ITT deal and evidence of favoritism toward big business. Once again Colson came up with the game plan: the President should end the political drain of the Kleindienst hearings by canning him. The President agreed and instructed Haldeman to inform Mitchell. But the firing was never carried out. I don't know why. Perhaps the President simply could not face anyone down in person, or perhaps Kleindienst saved himself with a message that his friend Senator Eastland would block any other nominee. The hearings dragged on through April as the President's popularity slipped.

The ITT scandal was serious enough business, but I found some hilarity in the high jinks even then. That ceased abruptly in mid-April when Haldeman and Ehrlichman sent me up to the Kleindienst hearings to order a witness to refuse to give testimony. The witness was Jack Gleason, a former Administration official who was now an ITT consultant and who was scheduled to testify about his work for the corporation.

I already knew that Gleason was scared about something. He had come to my office and said, "John, I could be in some trouble. I can't tell you the details, but I need a lawyer." I had sent him to a friend who had been my lawyer, and it didn't take me long to figure out what was bothering him. He was worried about potential *criminal* liability. I knew from Chotiner that Gleason had been involved in a secret effort in 1970 to raise and distribute political funds. Gleason had operated out of the basement of a Georgetown town house, and the records of the Town House Operation were considered radioactive in the Administration. Colson had them for a while, but he decided to turn them over to my office because I was doubly protected against having to disclose them: not only did I fall under executive privilege but, as the President's official lawyer, I could also cite attorney-client privilege.* When Colson called to say he was sending the files, he ordered me to keep them secret and said that anyone who had knowledge of the information would be endangered.

I knew all this before Haldeman summoned me to his office. To my surprise, I found Ehrlichman there, too. Obviously this was important.

"John, I've got a job for you," Ehrlichman began. "You know Jack Gleason is testifying down at the inquest today. We've decided we don't want to run any chance that he'll talk about his prior service here. I want you to see if he'll take the Fifth. You know his lawyer, don't you?"

"Yeah, I've known him for a long time. But I don't think he'll let Jack take the Fifth out of the blue. That's throwing up a red flag. They don't know anything about Gleason yet."

"And they still won't if he doesn't say anything," said Haldeman.

"When he takes the Fifth, it'll be all over the press." They knew this as well as I did, but I wanted to hear their answer. Ehrlichman and Haldeman in the Town House Operation, I was thinking. They must have sold the Washington Monument for

---

* [Original Footnote:] Executive privilege is a Presidential claim to constitutional authority for withholding information from his coequals: the Congress and the courts. With time those privileges would become useless. Years after Watergate, Independent Counsel Kenneth Starr (a former Solicitor General and Federal Judge) succeed in eliminating the attorney-client privilege between government attorneys and government employees. Today, there is no attorney-client privilege for government lawyers. In addition, Congress has never recognized this common law privilege, and they will not hesitate to such purportedly privileged matters. The answer has been for government employees (including Presidents, and Vice-Presidents) to hire private, non-governmental attorneys when the need arises.

63

one of those contributions. Or Gleason must know something else even worse. "And they'll start investigating the shit out of him within twenty-four hours."

"There are all kinds of investigations," Ehrlichman replied. "Jack works for ITT, and they'll be combing the files over there at the money factory."

"Jack has his own consulting firm," I corrected, "but it works mostly for ITT."

"Well, then, they'll look over *there,*" he said impatiently. "I just don't want them sniffing over here."

"Look, John," said Haldeman, "suppose some bright guy on the committee knows Gleason did some fund raising in 1970. And suppose they ask for the records just to check on whether ITT corrupted the Attorney General way back then. Jack can't even say who he raised the money for. What's he going to tell them?"

I searched for legal positions that Gleason might hold them off with, but I could see the box Haldeman was building: Town House hadn't been registered as a political committee, but it should have been; even if Gleason admitted that, he would have to explain where the records were. "Well, if it gets that far," I said, "he can argue that he doesn't know where the records are, which is true."

"If it gets that far," Ehrlichman said quickly, "it's already on our doorstep. If he tries to take the Fifth then, they probably won't let him. Even if they do, it won't matter. He'll have led them to the thicket. If he's going to take the Fifth, he should do it before he opens his mouth."

"The ITT people won't like that, John," I said. "They might fire him."

"ITT's used to it," said Ehrlichman, "and they don't have to run for election. Besides, Jack can take care of himself." If ITT fired Gleason, he was telling me, it would draw the investigation toward itself closer. The White House was prepared to let Jack lose his job, on this one anyway.

I tried a different tack. "Look, Gleason's lawyer is a good friend, but he's not likely to do something like this on my say-so. I don't have a lot of ammunition."

Ehrlichman answered, though I was looking at Haldeman. "John, that's the sort of dilemma a counsel to the President gets his inspirations for." He shifted in his chair, he had finished what he had to say.

I drove up to Capitol Hill, went to Vice-President Agnew's sparsely furnished office in the New Senate Office Building, and sent word to the committee's hearing room for Edward P. Taptich, Gleason's lawyer. Without using Haldeman's or Ehrlichman's name, I told him what I wanted. It was an unpleasant conversation. He went to the committee room to confer with Gleason. When he returned with Gleason's answer I called Haldeman, and Ehrlichman came on the phone also. Sitting in Agnew's chair talking, I knew they might have fired me if they had known Taptich was in the room with me. He nodded as I repeated his arguments.

"Bob," I said, "it's a pretty firm no. My lawyer friend does not feel he would be properly advising his client to tell him to take the Fifth, and Gleason doesn't want to take the heat unless he has to."

"Goddammit, he has to," Haldeman said. "He doesn't know..."

"And, besides, Bob," I was anxious to get to some good news, "my friend Ed thinks there's no problem. He's going to object to *any* question they ask about anything except Gleason's work for ITT in San Diego, the convention stuff. He'll say that anything else is not germane to the Kleindienst confirmation hearings. That will probably happen on some warm-up question before anything troublesome gets introduced."

65

"What happens," Ehrlichman pressed, "if he loses the objection?"

"Well, I don't think that will happen, because of Brother Eastland's sense of fairness. But if it does, Ed will make a speech about how he refuses to let his client be subjected to a hearing that has no boundaries and goes fishing into the man's political background. And if that doesn't work, he'll ask for a recess on account of his laryngitis, and we'll call you."

"This is too important to go in praying," said Ehrlichman. "I think maybe you should have a word with Gleason yourself."

"I can't call him out of the hearing room, John," I said. "He's sitting down there now, about to go on. Look, I think we've got a ninety-five percent chance of getting by, which will leave us a hell of a lot better off than taking the Fifth. We won't lose too much anyway by trying it the way Ed's got it planned. Besides, I'm sure they're not going to budge. They think it's their hot seat."

"Okay, John," Haldeman said. "I hope you're smiling when I see you next."

Taptich went to the hearings and I waited. He objected when Senator Kennedy asked Gleason what job he had received when the Nixon Administration took office. Eastland sustained the objection. When Senator John V. Tunney, another committee member, got wind of my presence in the building and asked about my conversations with Gleason, Taptich objected, and was again sustained after a long argument. He was home free. Two years later, when Town House came to light, Gleason and another White House aide pleaded guilty to Campaign Act violations and received suspended sentences while Herbert Kalmbach went to jail for selling ambassadorships. The prosecutors sat on a possible indictment against Bob Haldeman.

I had survived my first minor role on the front lines of a cover-up and had risen in the confidence of Haldeman and

Ehrlichman. Looking back, I wonder that I failed to see the signs of worse to come. At the time, I was relieved to have passed. The ITT scandal at last melted to the back pages of the papers, and Kleindienst was confirmed. When the White House returned to normal, I started planning another of the foreign junkets I took frequently now that I had decided to leave the Administration. Fielding and I abandoned our crisis regimen of sandwiches at our desks and resumed leisurely lunches at the mess.

"Well, Johnny," Fred said as we walked slowly back from lunch one day in mid-May, "I read back in January where Jeane Dixon predicted Nixon would have a serious scandal this year but would survive it. It's amazing, she was right. We've had it, and the President was untouched." I agreed.

We were all wrong, of course. The machinery had long been cranking through the White House toward a scandal that would grind down the President himself. And I was part of the machinery.

CHAPTER THREE:

THE TICKLER

THE WHITE HOUSE APPARATUS went into motion each morning at about seven. Bud Krogh had indeed been late when I encountered him on my first day. The daily staff meeting, chaired jointly by John Ehrlichman and George Shultz, began at 7:30. Usually by seven a sleepy-eyed handful of those who attended this meeting would be in the mess munching cereal and silently reading their news summaries to prepare for the day. Ehrlichman was a regular breakfast-clubber. He sat at a small table near the wall with the newspaper in his face, sometimes lifting one eye to see who else was there, and departing at about 7:25 for the Roosevelt Room to preside.

At 8:15 Ehrlichman and Shultz adjourned their meeting and walked down the hall to the more important session in Haldeman's office, where they were joined by Henry Kissinger, Chuck Colson, Bryce Harlow (later it was MacGregor, then Timmons), Peter M. Flanigan, an assistant to the President, and Ron Ziegler. "The 8:15" flushed up matters the President's top-level aides thought he should be thinking about that day, for Haldeman would go from the 8:15 to the President's office.

After a few months at my job, I suggested to Higby that it seemed appropriate for the counsel to attend the 8:15. Haldeman did not agree but said I could, if I wished, attend the 7:30. For several weeks I dragged my body out of bed at 5:45 to make it to the mess by seven, and then on to the Roosevelt Room. I listened to the discussion of proposed supplemental foreign-assistance appropriations; Shultz's professorial analysis of the need for a forty-five-day extension of the no-strike period in a railway labor-management dispute; a speechwriter's report on what the President might say upon signing legislation giving the Blue Lake lands back to the Taos Pueblo Indians.

All routine business not involving the counsel's office. Quietly I stopped attending, and no one missed me. The meetings were simply a mechanical technique to make sure that what the President wanted was being done. However, they were not as strict or severe a method as the tickler.

The discipline of Haldeman's tickler was unrelenting. I had felt it with my first assignment, the action memorandum on *Scanlan's Monthly,* with its due date "Wednesday, August 5, 1970, at 2:00 P.M." That one I had answered on time, but subsequently I spent too much time preparing my answers to a few action memoranda, let the due dates slide by, and discovered the consequences. First a secretary in the staff secretary's office called my secretary, asking where the answer was, and when the explanation was found unsatisfactory a very bitchy Larry Higby called to say, "What's the matter, Dean, can't you meet a deadline? Do you think you're someone special?" When I explained I was working on the response, Higby snapped, "Work a little harder." Higby was chewed out by Haldeman when the paper did not flow as the chief of staff wanted, so he leaned on others.

The tickler was an extension of Haldeman, and was probably more responsible for the chief of staff's awesome reputation than was his own aluminum personality. It was a self-perpetuating paper monster, with a computer's memory and a Portuguese man-of-war's touch. Often those who were ticklers made calls for the sake of making calls, to impress Haldeman with their efficiency. Their machine never forgot or tired. Once a staff man was nailed with responsibility for the slightest project, the tickler would keep pestering until it was fed something: a status report, a piece of paper, a bit of information to chew on. No one could ignore the tickler, because no one could afford to ignore Haldeman. It reached everywhere. Even Mitchell and Kissinger were subject to it. Each call was recorded meticulously on the tickler scorecard, on which reputations were made and broken in Haldeman's eyes. The tickler did not easily show mercy. Thus, when I received a confidential action memorandum from Haldeman on January 18, 1971, and told Higby that the January 26, 1971 due date was too soon for the complex and extremely delicate assignment, I was refused an extension. At the time, I did not know I was handling a matter of intense interest to the President, but years later this assignment would help me understand the chain of events that destroyed the Nixon Presidency.

It began on January 14, 1971, when the President went all the way to the University of Nebraska to be assured a friendly reception, free of antiwar radicals and heckling students. As television commentators did not fail to point out, the President was neither welcome nor respected at institutions of higher learning. New campus protests had just broken out against stepped-up air operations in Cambodia and Laos, and Senator Muskie, who led the Democrats in the public opinion polls, was getting extensive press coverage on his trip through the Middle East and Moscow. The President, his prospects for reelection slipping, wanted to be seen as a courageous and admired leader. But as Air Force One flew toward the Nebraska heartland he was thinking about more than his speech and his reception. He reached for his IBM dictating machine.

"This is for Haldeman," he said. "It would seem that the time is approaching when Larry O'Brien is held accountable for his retainer with Hughes. Bebe [Rebozo] has some information on this, although it is, of course, not solid. But there is no question that one of Hughes's people did have O'Brien on a very heavy retainer for 'services rendered' in the past. Perhaps Colson should check on this."

Rose Mary Woods, the President's secretary, typed the message and passed it directly to Haldeman. Back in Washington the next day, Haldeman discussed the assignment with the President. Haldeman suggested that I, rather than Colson, pursue it, and the President agreed. "Let's try Dean," Haldeman noted on the bottom of the President's memo, and three

70

days later I received a Haldeman authored directive to investigate the relationship between billionaire industrialist Howard Hughes and Democratic National Committee Chairman Lawrence F. O'Brien.

Following my pattern, I talked it over with Jack Caulfield, who knew a lot of gossip about the Hughes empire. He told me it was embroiled in an internal war, with two billion dollars at stake, private eyes swarming, nerve-jangling power plays going on, and Mafia figures lurking in the wings. I found myself as cowed as any newspaper reader by the Hughes legend. The American dream in neon lights. He had built the last financial empire that was solely in the control of one owner, made movies in Hollywood, seduced a string of starlets beginning with Jean Harlow, and set world flying records. He had not been seen in public since 1957, pulling the strings of his one-man empire as a total recluse. He was more secret than the CIA and perhaps more powerful than the President. And he was feared in the Nixon White House, where some believed that the "Hughes loan" scandal had cost Richard Nixon the 1960 election to John F. Kennedy.[*] The implications of the assignment were clear. If Larry O'Brien was in fact on the Hughes payroll while serving as chairman of the Democratic National Committee, it would be a matter of scandal.

Caulfield delighted in sharing his tales of Hughes intrigue, but after talking with his friends "who might know more," he could still confirm only that there was a rumor about O'Brien's retainer, and I needed more. At Haldeman's request I checked with Lyn Nofziger, who specialized in making certain that the press was abreast of bad news about political foes. Lyn had

---

[*]   [Original Footnote:] In 1956 (when Richard Nixon was Vice-President), Howard Hughes made a secret loan of $200,000 to the Vice-President's brother Donald. Its existence became known during the 1960 election campaign.

only heard rumors, too. Bebe Rebozo, the President's pal, repeated what he had already told the President. I was living on a diet of rumors when Chuck Colson called. He had learned of my assignment and said he knew the man with the answer: Robert Bennett.

Bob Bennett, son of Republican Senator Wallace Bennett of Utah, did have the answer. He had recently bought the Mullen public-relations firm in Washington and acquired a prize client, Howard Hughes. Bennett was unequivocal. Larry O'Brien had been retained by Howard Hughes, and the contract was still in existence. Bennett would document the facts as long as they were not used to embarrass Hughes. He promised to report back to me after visiting the Hughes people in Los Angeles.

I told this to Haldeman on my due date, January 26, in a lengthy memorandum in which I stressed how vigorously I had attacked the assignment—hoping thereby to camouflage how little hard evidence I possessed. Two days later Haldeman instructed:

> You should continue to keep in contact with Bob Bennett as well as looking for other sources of information on the subject. Once Bennett gets back to you with his final report, you and Chuck Colson should get together and come up with a way to leak the appropriate information. Frankly, I can't see any way to handle this without involving Hughes so the problem of "embarrassing" him seems to be a matter of degree. However, we should keep Bob Bennett and Bebe out of this at all costs.

Haldeman's memo led me to respect the fast rise of Bob Bennett. I had never heard of him until a few weeks earlier, and now he not only was the key to information that might influence the future of the Democratic Party chairman, but was also getting White House protection on a par with Bebe Rebo-zo's. When Bennett came to see me after his trip to Los Angeles, I took handwritten notes of the conversation, something I seldom did.

Like Howard Hughes's famous protective team of male "nurses" and the upper echelon of Hughes's corporation, Bennett is a Mormon. He neither drinks nor smokes, and has a polished, businesslike manner. He would have fit well in the Administration. When he walked into my office, he eased his lanky frame into a chair and crossed his legs in a way that made him seem conscious of their length. He made me think of Ichabod Crane, gangly and mysterious, but extremely loquacious. He spoke endlessly around the subject at hand. Unlike Ehrlichman's pithy metaphors or Haldeman's sparse commands, Bennett's speech was contoured in long, rounded sentences that imparted a softness to his words. He was discussing all manner of skullduggery, but he managed to give it the innocent air of a parson's monologue.

The real problem, he seemed to be saying, was Robert Maheu, a former FBI man who had, until recently, run the Hughes hotel and casino properties in Las Vegas. Bennett's superiors at the Hughes Tool Company had just ousted Maheu and spirited Hughes away to the Bahamas. Now, said Bennett, his superiors and the Maheu forces were "trying to destroy each other" in a battle for control of Hughes's assets, with Bennett's side having an inside advantage. It was Maheu who had hired O'Brien for Hughes. The contract had been drawn with one of O'Brien's firms to keep him one step removed. Since O'Brien was part of the ousted Maheu faction, said Bennett elliptically, "his services are no longer needed." But O'Brien, he said, was arguing that his contract was with the Hughes Tool Company and that he should continue to receive his retainer regardless of Maheu's departure. I gathered from Bennett that O'Brien was bargaining hard to keep his job, or at least to depart with a large severance settlement. Bennett performed well in concealing any distaste for O'Brien. His desire to take O'Brien's place was obvious.

It was a thorny matter, said Bennett. Maheu had handled all Hughes's political activity for the last fifteen years and had the facts on everything from the old Hughes loan to the involvement of the President's brother, Donald Nixon, with the Hughes empire. Since O'Brien was close to Maheu, there was a presumption that he knew a great deal. He had to be handled delicately.

As I tried to distill Bennett's meaning from his long, orbital speech, I recoiled at the rat's nest he was revealing. I admired how carefully he phrased his sentences, and I wondered about the things he was *not* telling me. He did not say specifically what O'Brien had done for the Hughes companies or, for that matter, what he himself was doing. And, more important from the standpoint of my assignment, he did not offer the promised documentation of O'Brien's contract. Instead he focused on Maheu. The Hughes people had been forced to fire Maheu after discovering his involvement with notorious gangsters, Bennett said in a tone of piety, and suggested that the Administration pursue a criminal investigation. The conversation ended; as far as I know, the Administration never took any action.

I puzzled over Bennett's message for several days. His superiors, I decided, must have tempered his desire to expose O'Brien. They were probably confident they could handle O'Brien in the "settlement negotiations." Maheu was their real foe, and Bennett seemed to be steering the Administration against him, not O'Brien. What a mess, I thought.

Jack Caulfield's supplementary reports tangled the situation further. Now Jack was cautioning against any hasty assault on the O'Brien-Hughes matter. "The revelation that an O'Brien-Maheu relationship exists poses significant hazards in any attempt to make O'Brien accountable to the Hughes retainer," he wrote. Any forced embarrassment of O'Brien "might well shake loose Republican skeletons from the closet." The available information about the common knowledge between Maheu and O'Brien was weak, Caulfield told me, but his sources fed him all sorts of rumors about dirt in both political houses. Jack thought we should settle for a truce.

I told Haldeman that the Hughes people had apparently backed off from their offer to document O'Brien's retainer, and that in any case we were treading in dangerous waters. I said "dangerous," and I felt it so. Even my hardening experiences inside the White House were not equal to this kind of twisted intrigue. My brief investigation had already convinced me that O'Brien, Bennett, and Maheu were mysterious characters, but I had only a glimmer of what was to come. Maheu would later surface as the point of contact for the CIA's effort to have the Mafia assassinate Fidel Castro in the early 1960s. Bennett, for his part, would later amaze me by turning up as a crucial behind-the-scenes player in most matters that came to plague the Nixon White House. He would become as mysterious in his inconspicuous presence as Howard Hughes was in his conspicuous absence.[*]

For the time being, Haldeman let the matter drop and I received no further instructions. The O'Brien inquiry lay dormant, but it was not lost from his memory, or from mine. The President began planning for his reelection campaign and reached out in a new direction, one that would later merge with a new O'Brien investigation.

Late in April 1971, the President reviewed a series of task-force proposals for the 1972 campaign, covering everything from advertising budgets to political strategies, and discovered

---

[*] Even later, Bennett would further surprise me when he proceeded to make a small fortune rather quickly in business, after leaving government. And then in 1992, he was elected to a seat in the U.S. Senate, where he represents Utah to this day.

there was no task force on campaign intelligence. He reached for his dictating machine and ordered Haldeman to rectify the mistake: Make sure we have a political intelligence capability better than we had in previous campaigns. Haldeman ordered ticklers Higby and Strachan to solicit thoughts on a campaign intelligence system.

It did not take me long to realize that Haldeman's interest in intelligence had been intensified. He called me to his office and offered a stilted explanation: "Nothing has higher priority than the President's reelection. We've got to take maximum advantage of the President's incumbency, and I want every office in the White House to be thinking about how to help in the reelection effort." He knew what he wanted from me. "One thing that can be improved, for example, is demonstration intelligence. That stuff you send over here is worthless. There's more information in the newspapers. We're not going to have a convention like the one the Democrats had in Chicago. Antiwar demonstrators would love to destroy our convention, but we're not going to let it happen."

I reflected on how I might take advantage of Haldeman's preoccupation. I was still building my law firm, seeking new business, and I knew the campaign would be a steppingstone for those who distinguished themselves. But as I looked ahead I saw the counsel's office performing rather menial campaign tasks—legal chores hardly important enough to get me admitted to the inner councils of the Nixon campaign.

If the counsel's office could play the same role at the Republican convention we had played on Mayday—special White House tie-lines, half-hourly reports—I knew we would be in the thick of things. We had a jump on other White House offices in demonstration intelligence. Why not expand our role to all intelligence that would be of interest to the President in a campaign? I wrote a memo to Haldeman, seeking a grant of authority:

My office receives a great amount of intelligence information regarding the activities of domestic insurgents of the new militant left, civil disorders, etc. Other offices receive domestic intelligence regarding such matters as crime and drug statistics, civil rights problems of note, political intelligence, and other matters of domestic intelligence that I suspect never reach the President.

I would like to recommend and urge that a digest of this information be prepared on at least a bi-weekly basis for the President, with circulation limited to you, John Ehrlichman, and the President. I suggest the limited circulation because much of the information would be extremely sensitive, and not many members of the staff would "need-to-know." I would think that if a matter reported in the digest deserved follow up by another staffer, one of you would so direct.

In late July 1971, I carried the memo into Haldeman's office and made my pitch. I reviewed my proposal with him briefly and suggested, of course, that the counsel's office would be a good place to have the intelligence digest prepared.

"We've done this before," I said, hinting at previous demonstrations, "and I think we could beef it up. I've already talked to Bernie Wells at the IEC [Intelligence Evaluation Committee], and I think those guys over there will improve themselves in the election year."

"That stuff isn't worth a damn," Haldeman said quickly.

"I know," I said, already on the defensive, "but they see everything the Bureau and the police turn up from their informants. Which isn't much. What they don't see are all the tips I pick up from the advance men and friends who come out of the woodwork. I know there's a lot more out there, political stuff, but nobody can collect it unless they have backing from you. Otherwise no one is going to send their stuff in to one place. They'll want to give it directly to you so they can get the kudos for it."

"You've got a good idea, John, but it's already coming in. Strachan collects it. Besides, I'm not so worried about collecting information as getting it in the first place."

"Jack Caulfield might be able to help," I offered. "I know he's been working on a plan for campaign security and intelligence. I don't know how good it will be, but Jack tells me he's preparing a proposal to cover everything. He wants to present it to you and Mitchell and Ehrlichman."

"Well, I don't have a lot of faith in Jack Caulfield," said Haldeman, "but let's see what he comes up with." He looked away. I could almost hear his stopwatch ticking in his head. The meeting was over. I had been shot down.

At Haldeman's instruction, his assistant, Gordon Strachan, had begun to educate himself on the kind of tactics savvy insiders used in the big time.[*] He had never been in a Presidential campaign before, and sought the advice of those who had worked in the 1968 campaign: Dwight Chapin, speechwriter Patrick J. Buchanan, and chief advance man Ronald Walker. Strachan was surprised when the veterans regaled him with tales of what Richard Nixon's opponents had done to him in 1968—infiltrated his campaign staff, disrupted and sabotaged his rallies, leaked false stories, planted rumors. Buchanan, who popularized the term "political hardball," argued for such tactics. We should expect the opponents to do what they had done in the past, and we should do it first, and better. There was general agreement. The Nixon campaign would not be soft.

---

[*] I was able to write about these matters in *Blind Ambition* largely because the information became public during the Watergate hearing. While I had no personal knowledge of many of these activities, I did know the players, and had picked up tidbits during idle chatter at the White House. As noted in the Afterword, because even more information has surfaced, it is possible to fill in additional gaps.

On August 14, 1971, Strachan wrote to Haldeman that he now had "oral recommendations for political intelligence and covert activities." Haldeman expressed interest only in independent operations, so that any slipups could not be traced back to the White House. Things began to move. Chapin called an old college friend, Donald H. Segretti, and hired him to disrupt, ridicule, and harass the Democratic candidates, and stir up as much intramural bickering as possible. Strachan called Jeb Magruder at the Reelection Committee, and Magruder agreed to infiltrate the office of Senator Muskie, the Democratic frontrunner.

Political intelligence was now lodged in the tickler, and it would remain there until Haldeman was satisfied. Every week or so, Strachan tickled me with the same questions: "Anything new on demonstrations?" "Does Caulfield have anything on Kennedy?" After making his rounds, Strachan would write a report for Haldeman. His September 18 memo was typical:

> Monitoring of Democrats – Colson submitted a memorandum expressing surprise and dismay that we did not have a list of attendees of the Muskie "Fat Cat" week-end. [We did have such a list and had sent him a copy.] His other concern is that no arrangements have been made to tape record all of Muskie's statements, including the "offhand" comments. Colson suggests that Nofziger arrange for this, but Lyn said he had no money for this type of project.

> The most recent EMK [Edward M. Kennedy] report has been submitted. It contains nothing.

> The question is whether or not the subject of intelligence shouldn't receive a greater allocation of time and resources than it is receiving now.

Strachan recommended more resources for intelligence, and Haldeman wrote his "H" in the space marked "Approve," but added a cryptic note: "Resources as to what?" Accordingly, Strachan sprayed calls around, asking for specific ideas about how to organize the intelligence operation. When he called me, I told him that Caulfield was working on a plan and Jack's project went into the tickler.

Caulfield's campaign intelligence plans had grown out of his personal disappointment. Ehrlichman had tried to have him appointed director of the Alcohol, Tax, and Firearms Division at IRS, but Internal Revenue Commissioner Randolph Thrower had blocked the move (using up his last credit at the White House in the process). Caulfield, knowing that he had no future in the counsel's office, began looking for a niche outside government. He had hit upon the idea of establishing a private security firm, using his White House connections. If he could land the President's reelection campaign as his first client, he might find entree to lucrative corporate accounts after the election. He had worked on his plans for months, and in late September he produced a twelve-page memorandum outlining "Operation Sandwedge." I assumed that the code name had something to do with Jack's love of golf. A sandwedge digs the ball out of the sand, deep weeds, or mud. Rather a sporting metaphor for political intelligence, I thought.

The plan read like a grade-B detective story, but Jack was thinking big. Sandwedge called for a budget of half a million dollars, which would pay for everything from convention security to undercover investigations and, Jack added privately, electronic surveillance on request. As support, Caulfield had enlisted some hefty names as Sandwedge partners: Joseph Woods, Rose Woods's brother, a former Cook County sheriff; Roger Barth, assistant to the commissioner of Internal Revenue; and Mike Acree, a career IRS official who would later become commissioner of customs. Tony, Jack's New York operative, would be in charge of covert activities.

I had mixed emotions when Jack asked my help in selling Sandwedge to the triumvirate of Haldeman, Ehrlichman, and

80

Mitchell. Caulfield did not really belong in the counsel's office; there was not enough demand for his specialty. He was looking for an opportunity to move, and I wanted to fill the slot with another lawyer. This weighed in favor of sponsoring Sandwedge, but I hesitated. I sensed that an Irish cop without a college education would not be entrusted with such a sensitive assignment in an Administration of WASP professional men. There was risk involved in supporting a losing proposition. I told Caulfield I would speak with "the Big Three," as he called them, after they had read Sandwedge.

I heard first from Mitchell as I was leaving his Justice Department office one day. "Say, incidentally, John, I read that damn memo Caulfield sent me on Operation Sandwich," he said.

"Oh, yes, *Sandwedge*."

"Whatever the hell he calls it. I don't know, but I don't think Caulfield should handle an operation like that, nor do I want Rose Woods's brother involved in it. I'll talk with Haldeman, but I want a hold on it for now. I want a lawyer to handle it. If Caulfield wants to work for the lawyer, fine."

"I think Jack sees himself as chief bottle washer of the operation," I said.

"Well, put a hold on it for now. Jeb was over here asking me about it, and I told him to sit tight until the thing is properly structured."

A few days later, Caulfield came to my office looking unhappy.

"What's up?" I asked.

"Jeb called me a few days ago and said that since there was a hold on Sandwedge, he had to go ahead. He's under pressure to get information on Muskie and asked me to check some guy named Buckley out as a possible informant. I checked him out with Rumsfeld, since he used to work for Don at OEO."

Caulfield was distressed about young, inexperienced people at the Reelection Committee setting up an intelligence operation. This was the kind of thing Sandwedge was designed to deal with, and he was offended. I had not told him of my discussion with Mitchell, hoping to spare his feelings until Mitchell met with Haldeman. Also, I did not want Caulfield to mount a personal lobbying effort that might displease them.

Curious to know what Jeb Magruder was doing, I called him with Jack's report on John R. Buckley.[*]

Jeb was coy. "We're setting up a little operation over here of our own," he said. "I can't wait for Caulfield."

"Jeb, if I can be of assistance let me know," I volunteered.

"I'll tell you one thing you can do. You can get Colson off my back." He said it half jokingly, but I knew he meant it. Jeb and Chuck had never gotten on well. "He's driving me crazy," Jeb claimed. "He has one request after another. There's no end to it. Currently he's all worked up that we're not providing good intelligence on Muskie's campaign, and he's got Haldeman worked up, too, Strachan tells me."

Obviously, the tickler was at work on him.

Operation Sandwedge was blocked with Mitchell's hold, but Gordon Strachan's tickler had not released it. On October 7, 1971, Strachan again raised the fate of "Sandwedge and covert activities" with Haldeman, suggesting that Haldeman and Mitchell meet to make some decisions about it and about other pending campaign matters. After the meeting, Mitchell said Sandwedge had been scratched because neither he nor

---

[*]   [Original Footnote:] Buckley later enlisted a semi-retired Washington taxi driver to infiltrate the Muskie campaign, as chauffeur and messenger, to bring him political documents. Buckley photocopied those documents he thought important and passed them to CRP.

Haldeman had confidence in Caulfield's ability. Campaign intelligence would be assigned to a lawyer, Mitchell told me. I suggested that the Reelection Committee's eventual general counsel might handle it. Mitchell agreed.

This decision was picked up by the tickler, and soon Strachan was inquiring regularly if I had found a general counsel for the Reelection Committee. Magruder wanted Fred Fielding, who had a background in Army intelligence work, but I refused Magruder without raising it with Fielding. Later, my conscience prodded me to offer Fred the opportunity, but Fred declined. He knew I planned to move on after the election, leaving him in line to succeed me. The job remained vacant.

After another call from Strachan, I talked with Bud Krogh about the possibility of having David Young go to the Committee. Not possible, Bud told me, protecting his own deputy.

"How about Gordon Liddy?" Bud suggested. "He's just finishing a project analyzing the organization of the FBI and could be available. He's a helluva lawyer. The President read one of his memos and complimented it."

"I don't really know Liddy."

"Well, he ran for Congress once, and I don't really know what he knows about the election laws. But I know he's a fast study and could learn them."

"One of the things Mitchell wants the general counsel to handle is intelligence," I added. "Demonstrations and the political stuff, too."

"Gordon is a former FBI man, and I'm sure he could handle any intelligence needs they might have. He's handled some very sensitive things here for us." Bud was selling Liddy. There were no negatives, and I respected Bud's judgment. After all, he had once recommended me.

Within a few days, I met Gordon Liddy in Bud's office. Wearing a three-piece charcoal-gray suit and groomed like a

Vitalis commercial, he bristled with energy, and talked law. He was very interested in the job and, while he did not profess expert knowledge of campaign law, he was familiar with the new election bill then winding its way through Congress. He had a quick mind and was articulate. I told Liddy he could use my election-law files if he got the job. The Liddy recommendation was passed on to Ehrlichman. He approved; so did Haldeman, Mitchell, and Magruder. On December 8, 1971, Gordon Liddy became general counsel of the Committee to Re-elect the President.[*]

Within a week, I heard from other Committee aides that Magruder was introducing Liddy as "our man in charge of dirty tricks." Liddy, who was in my office to review my election-law files, was annoyed.

"Magruder's an asshole, John," he said curtly, "and he's going to blow my cover."

"I'll take care of it," I told him, and I called Jeb to say it was less than prudent to announce that Gordon Liddy was handling dirty tricks.

Some weeks passed, and word filtered back that Liddy had jumped with both feet into the accumulated legal work of the campaign. The backlog was far too much for one man to handle, and Liddy complained that Magruder would not let him hire staff lawyers. I suggested volunteer lawyers to help him with massive projects, such as an analysis of the voluminous state election laws, and on several occasions Gordon thanked me profusely for helping him get started. Then he vanished, I assumed, into the lawbooks and I did not envy him.

---

[*]   As noted in the Afterword, this was a calamitous decision. Years later, Krogh would apologize to me for not telling me that he and Ehrlichman were pawning Liddy off on the Reelection Committee to get him out of the White House, thinking he could cause no problems as general counsel. Liddy, however, was a debacle in progress.

During that period, Bob Bennett visited me for the first time in nearly a year and made another long and delicate speech. A writer named Clifford Irving was claiming authorship of Howard Hughes's autobiography, he said, and it was a fraud. Hughes had never met Irving, much less told him the story of his life. Bennett suspected a dark plot to ruin Hughes's most valued possession, absolute privacy, and he hinted that Hughes's former confidant and current archenemy, Maheu, might be behind it. He asked me to have the Justice Department begin a criminal investigation. I responded vaguely and let the matter drop.[*]

Early in January, Liddy stopped by to tell me he was going to New York for a meeting with Caulfield and his man Tony to audit, at Jack's request, their financial accounts. Ehrlichman had promised Tony support through 1972, even though Liddy was now the man in charge of intelligence. Caulfield and Tony dropped from the picture gracefully, but the Sandwedge proposal remained as the only intelligence blueprint in the tickler. Caulfield, not the plan itself, had killed Sandwedge, and Liddy's lawyerly caution and professional demeanor were designed to make up for Caulfield's deficiencies. I thought it a good decision to have hired someone like Liddy, a man of caution, instead of Jack.

I smiled at the thought of what lay in store for Liddy at the old Sandwedge New York "headquarters," for I had spent the night there when interviewing for jobs outside government a few months before. I had to pay for the trip myself, and Jack

---

[*]   Clifford Irving's work forced the reclusive Howard Hughes to hold a telephone news conference with reporters who had covered him for many years. Hughes denounced the book as a fraud. By January 28, 1972, Irving and his cohorts confessed to the hoax. McGraw-Hill and *Life* magazine, which had paid Irving some three-quarter of a million dollars for the story, pressed charges and Irving, his wife, and an accomplice were indicted and convicted. Irving returned the money advanced from his publishers and spent seventeen months in Federal prison. In 1981, he recounted it all in *The Hoax*.

had offered to help defray my expenses by letting me stay at the planned undercover apartment. It was then being used for a special Ehrlichman-approved assignment which required a luxurious ambiance, and Jack had described it as "quite a pad." The apartment was meant to serve as a boudoir; Tony had enlisted acquaintances of amorous reputation in a mission to seduce there some of the women who had attended Kennedy's Chappaquiddick party. (The women would, according to the plan, volunteer some details of Kennedy's conduct in a moment of tenderness, or under fear of extortion.) After an elegant dinner in the company of a New York businessman and his wife, I walked to the apartment with my blind date. I was aghast. The woman, who had high expectations of the counsel to the President, had one quick drink and left. The apartment looked like a Chicago whorehouse—red velvet wallpaper, black lace curtains, white Salvation Army furniture, and a fake-fur rug. Upon my return to Washington, Jack asked me how I liked the pad, and I could not bring myself to tell him. "Well, Jack, it saved me some money," I stammered. "Thanks."

Liddy offered no comment on the apartment after his trip. He seemed tight-lipped about all his operational work, but he did seem genuinely to admire Caulfield's street smarts. "Caulfield's a good man," he said. "He's been around." It became apparent from a brief conversation that Jack and Liddy had traded war stories.

"By the way, John," Liddy added, "I've been analyzing all these intelligence requirements for the campaign, and it's a big operation. What kind of budget do you think I should have? It's expensive to do it right."

"I don't have a clue what it costs, Gordon. But I know Haldeman wants the best. He's always bitching about intelligence." Thinking of Caulfield's Sandwedge budget, I tossed out a figure idly. "Maybe half a million bucks, Gordon. Maybe more if you can justify it." Liddy, I soon realized, didn't take anything idly, and he returned to his calculations.

86

Soon afterward, he was back in my office complaining about the White House bureaucracy, which was threatening to take away his White House identification pass, and did. As he spoke, I noticed a bulky white bandage wrapped around his fist.

"What happened to your hand, Gordon?"

He shrugged. "Oh, nothing really."

"It looks serious."

"Well, some might feel that way, but I don't. It was necessary, you see, that I prove my strength to the men I'm thinking of recruiting to assist me at the convention."

"What do you mean?"

"Well, in my business, John, it's important that those I work with understand I'm a man of strength. *Macho,* as they say. So to prove myself to them I held my hand over a candle until the flesh burned, which I did without flinching. I wanted them to know that I could stand any amount of physical pain." [*]

"My God, Gordon!" I didn't really know what to say, so I told him I hoped his hand healed quickly, which he also shrugged off. After he left my office I called Bud Krogh and told him the story Liddy had just told me. "What's with this guy, Bud?"

---

[*] Years later, I would learn from Howard Hunt, who was with Liddy at the time he pulled this stunt, that Liddy and Hunt were having dinner with two women in Los Angeles and were hoping to get lucky. To impress his date that he was a man of great will, Liddy held his hand over a candle on the table until his palm started burning and all could smell his flesh cooking. Hunt said that Liddy thought this was a surefire way to hustle the young lady. In fact, it made her ill. Had Liddy told me the truth, I would have known that he had serious mental problems, and I would have had him removed from the Reelection Committee.

87

Bud did not seem surprised. "Liddy's a romantic," he said. Then he offered some advice: "Gordon needs guidance. Somebody should keep an eye on him."

I was annoyed. "Bud," I said, "this guy is a strange bird. Why didn't you tell me this before? I can't watch him." It began to dawn on me that Bud might have touted Liddy to me to unload him from his own staff. It's an old trick, sell the bad apple elsewhere; I had done it myself. But this could be serious. "Listen, Bud," I said, "I think you should call Magruder and tell him to keep an eye on Liddy. He'd listen to you because you've worked with the guy." Bud agreed, and I called Magruder too.

Jeb had heard the candle story. "Weird guy," he said.

On January 26, Jeb called with an invitation to sit in on a meeting the next morning at the Attorney General's office. Liddy was going to present his plans for campaign intelligence. I knew Magruder wanted me there for more than courtesy. I was still the collecting point at the White House for demonstration intelligence. I had recommended Liddy for the job, and Magruder wanted an intelligence man from the White House at the meeting for protection. I was both curious and apprehensive. I knew this meeting was the culmination of a long series of demands coming down through the tickler. Campaign intelligence was important, and Liddy was our professional. But I had seen enough hardball at the White House to be worried, and Liddy's hand-burning incident stuck in my mind. The counsel's job, I thought, is to recommend caution before the fact and to work miracles afterward.

When I arrived at Mitchell's office, Liddy was arranging commercially prepared charts—multicolor, three feet by four feet—on an easel. He finished soon after I walked in, and everyone took a seat after greetings were exchanged. Mitchell sat behind his Bureau of Prisons desk and began his normal slow and unconscious rocking motion. The rest of us faced

88

him in a semicircle, sitting in faded red leather chairs whose straight backs and narrow wooden armrests seemed designed to keep visitors in a state near attention, and we were. I sat on Mitchell's right. Magruder faced him directly, sitting in the center. And Liddy was on Mitchell's left, by his easel.

Jeb started the meeting, obviously nervous. "Mr. Mitchell," he said, "Gordon has prepared a presentation for you on what he believes is necessary for campaign intelligence, and handling demonstrations at the convention and in the campaign." Then he turned to Liddy, who was looking for a place to put his pipe. "Why don't you go ahead, Gordon?" Then a quick glance back at Mitchell. "If you're ready, Mr. Mitchell." Mitchell nodded his assent.

This was the first time I had ever seen Mitchell and Magruder together, and it was obvious Jeb did not have the easy rapport I had with him. Part of his discomfort grew out of political reality. Haldeman, not Mitchell, had hired Magruder to be Mitchell's deputy and run the day-to-day operations of the campaign. Mitchell, his influence waning, could do nothing about it. Jeb was Haldeman's man, or, more accurately, Larry Higby's man, since Haldeman never proclaimed a very high estimation of Magruder. Higby had put Jeb where he was, and Jeb had to walk on eggs. About the only thing Mitchell and Magruder had in common was an antipathy for Chuck Colson. Initially Jeb had been so frightened of Mitchell that he had dealt with him through me for weeks after joining the Reelection Committee. Finally I had told him he must develop his own relationship with Mitchell, but I could see that Jeb was still uncomfortable.

Gordon Liddy, on the other hand, went to his easel and began his speech with authority. He seemed to enjoy the stage, and his speech was remarkably free of the normal conversational "uhs" and nervous pauses. He began with a brisk description of his own qualifications for handling the job and followed with a recitation of the names of specialists he had consulted, with appropriate security precautions, in the course of constructing his plan. I wondered how he could possibly have done all this at a time he was swamped in legal work.

Liddy explained that he had divided his program into components, which he would discuss individually before showing how it all fit together. This ended the preview. "If you have any questions, General, please interrupt and I'll address them," he told Mitchell with gallant deference, and then turned to his first chart.

The first component dealt with Mitchell's biggest worry, convention demonstrations. It had its own code name, Operation Diamond. Liddy told how he would set up intelligence liaison with the FBI, the Secret Service, and the CIA. Also, he would gather his own information by infiltrating antiwar groups with paid informants. All the incoming information would be professionally analyzed to determine which groups and which leaders posed the greatest potential for disruption.

"Now, General," he went on, "this operation will be equipped with its own operational arm. It is my judgment that the local police and federal security forces will be of limited value. They all have their own fish to fry and their own political allegiances. They are not trustworthy, and in most cases they will not act until the situation is already out of hand. We need greater loyalty than they possess, and we need preventive action to break up demonstrations *before* they reach the television cameras. I can arrange for the services of highly trained demonstration squads, men who have worked successfully as street-fighting teams at the CIA. These men are extremely well disciplined, and they have a history of engaging in such activities that will serve us well. They will appear spontaneous and ideologically motivated. These men carry their own cover and will not be traceable to us.

"We will have a second operational arm," he continued, "that could be of even greater preventive use. These teams are experienced in surgical relocation activities. In a word, General, they can kidnap a hostile leader with maximum secrecy and a minimal use of force. If, for example, a prominent radical comes to our San Diego convention to marshal his army of demonstrators, these teams can drug him and take him across the border into Mexico until the convention is over. He would never see the face of a single one of our operatives."

Mitchell stopped rocking. "What the hell good is that going to do?" he asked with some irritation. It was his first interruption.

"Well, sir, by removing their leadership we'd throw them into confusion at a critical moment and lessen their effectiveness against us."

"Maybe," Mitchell mumbled. For a moment no one spoke. There was electricity in the room. Magruder looked at Mitchell's desk, refusing to glance at Liddy. So these were the people Liddy had burned his hand for, I thought. I waited for Mitchell to say something more, but I doubted he would.

Liddy broke the silence. "Would you like me to proceed, General, with another facet of the plan?" His voice betrayed his first sign of nervousness.

"Please," said Mitchell.

Gordon removed the top chart. Now we were into the political intelligence component. Its code name, as I recall, was Operation Ruby. Gordon said he would incorporate his existing program of "live penetrations"—currently only a chauffeur-messenger inside Muskie headquarters, code name, Sedan Chair—into a larger network. Such infiltrations would depend, of course, on the target selected, whether it was Larry O'Brien, Senator Henry M. Jackson, Senator Hubert H. Humphrey, Senator Muskie, or anyone else with an office and a staff. He had anticipated that the Democratic convention in Miami might be a target and had made preliminary studies of the hotels and the convention hall. "As you probably know," said Liddy, "most of the sensitive positions in these hotels are held by Cubans. They are the telephone operators, desk clerks, janitors, maids, and union officials there. I have already made extensive contacts in the Cuban community, and I can assure you we can provide a steady flow of information from the hotels.

"Most of that information will be routine, however, and of limited value," he continued. "But this operation contains a completely separate unit that will upgrade our intelligence. I have secured an option to lease a pleasure craft that is docked on the canal directly in front of the Fontainebleau Hotel. It is more than sixty feet long, with several staterooms, and expensively decorated in a Chinese motif. It can also be wired for both sight and sound in complete secrecy. Now, my preliminary soundings convince me that many of the prominent Democratic officials, including senators and representatives, are vulnerable to weakness of the flesh, which seems to overcome them at conventions. We can, without much trouble, compromise these officials through the charms of some ladies I have arranged to have living on the boat. This will enable us to extract the kind of information we want. The operation will blend into the general scene of Miami Beach, and the boat can also serve as the storage headquarters for all our communications equipment."

"It won't work, Gordon," I interrupted. This was the Sandwedge "headquarters" nonsense pumped up to Hollywood proportions. It was outright extortion, and it was absurd as well. "How in the world is some whore going to compromise these guys at the convention? They're not that dumb."

Gordon shot an irritated look at me to underscore the fact that he was addressing Mitchell. But he was ready with his answer. "John, these are the finest call girls in the country," he said. "I can tell you from firsthand experience." This broke the tension, as everyone laughed except Liddy, who waited

92

impatiently. "They are not dumb broads, but girls who can be trained and programmed. I have spoken with the madam in Baltimore, and we have been assured their services at the convention."

As Liddy went on, I caught Mitchell's eye and shrugged my shoulders. He winked and puffed several times on his pipe, and the corners of his mouth turned up into a hint of a smile. It relieved me to see signs that he was not taking the theatrics seriously.

The chart changed again. Operation Crystal. Liddy began telling us that the best intelligence could, of course, be obtained by electronic surveillance. He had consulted specialists—"one of the world's leading experts"—and solved the problem of finding untraceable equipment. Then he launched into an extremely technical description of microwave telephone communications, speaking of relay stations, routing frequencies, and the difficulties of intercepting noncabled signals. His point became clear when he said there was equipment capable of intercepting all communications between an opposing candidate's airplane and the ground. The intercepting equipment was required to be near the airplane, but not within sight, of course. So Liddy proposed hiring a "chase plane" to follow Democratic campaign planes and make transcriptions of all airborne communications. It would be expensive, he said, but he stressed how much of a candidate's time is spent in the air, and how large a volume of sensitive communications went over the air microwaves. Then came the heart of Operation Crystal—wiretaps. Liddy told us he could intercept any conversation we wanted, if he were given the target.

On he went to another chart, Operation Sapphire, which detailed plans to sabotage the campaigns of our opponents. They ranged from harassment and false demonstrations to far more ambitious schemes. "I have managed to obtain a copy of the architectural design of the Miami Beach Convention Center," he said, "and it includes a detailed diagram of the

93

ducts and electrical switches for the air-conditioning system. It is possible, I believe, to shut down the air-conditioning system alone in an untraceable, nonrepairable fashion at an opportune moment. Imagine all those Democratic delegates sitting there sweating in one hundred degree heat in that hall on national television." He passed on through plans to have his own hippies harass the Democrats, and then flipped up the final chart.

"This diagram shows how all these independent components fit together into one apparatus," he said. "The organization is cellular. Personnel can be moved about at will from one operation to another without risking security, because the men will not need to know anyone but their immediate superiors. They have been trained to work that way. All the cells will be removed and insulated from the Committee. Untraceable. The operatives are all experienced and will not themselves be identified. But even if an error is committed at the operational level, it is *still* untraceable." Liddy pointed to the operations along the perimeter of the chart and to the lines connecting them all with one central figure. "These components are designed to function together with only one central control. Here. I have assigned code names to the components after individual gems, and I have called the overall apparatus Gemstone."

Liddy paused. "This type of operation is expensive, of course," he said, driving toward his conclusion. "But I have carefully checked and rechecked the budget to make sure there's no fat in it. All of this can be done for a million dollars."

He took his seat. The show was over. We all waited for Mitchell to react. I knew he was offended by the wilder parts of the act, but I also knew he would not say so to Liddy's face. He disliked confronting people directly. It was a trait I had noticed in myself and felt was a weakness. Mitchell usually had other people express his blunt feelings; it was Kleindienst who had dressed me down about Huston's memo. I waited for an oblique response.

"Well, Gordon, that's all very intriguing, but not quite what I had in mind," he said mildly, looking at the last chart. "Frankly, I'm more concerned about demonstrators and police cooperation than some of the things you've mentioned."

"I understand, General," Liddy answered.

"And we can't spend that kind of money, either. I suggest you go back to your drawing board and see what you can do."

"Yes, sir," said Liddy.

As Jeb helped him hastily disassemble his charts and easel and carry them out, I went over to Mitchell's desk. "Unreal, and a little frightening," I said in a low voice.

Mitchell grinned. "I'd say that's a fair statement."

Liddy, obviously disappointed, asked Jeb and me for our assessment of the meeting. Jeb told him the whole thing was too expensive and would have to be toned way down. I hoped Mitchell would never reconsider the plan, but I did not tell Liddy so. I did not know exactly what Mitchell wanted, although I was certain he would reject the carnival tricks and the muggings. In a way, I felt sorry for Liddy. All the tickler's pressure for massive campaign intelligence was now falling on his shoulders, but everyone was reluctant to give him the guidance he clearly needed. Including me. I did not feel he was my responsibility, and, for that matter, I wanted to stay as far away as possible.

"Gordon, you ought to destroy those charts right away," I said finally, which somehow eased my conscience. "I really think you ought to focus on demonstrations. That's our real problem area."

I accepted Jeb's offer of a ride back to the White House in his chauffeur-driven Committee car. No one spoke on the way.

A week later, on February 4, Jeb called and left word that there would be another meeting in Mitchell's office, at four that afternoon. Liddy had revised his plans. I was encouraged by the speed with which life had moved; I hoped it meant that Mitchell had sent a dousing message through Magruder. I wanted to skip the meeting. I didn't want to know what Gordon Liddy was doing, so I let the time for leaving slip past. Then I had second thoughts. If everything turned out as I hoped, I would look foolish for not going. Also, if Liddy stuck to his plans I could be held responsible for not informing the White House. It was still my job to know about intelligence. Reluctantly, I decided to go.

When I arrived the meeting had started. Everybody was hunched over copies of a revised budget that Liddy had prepared. I sat down and listened. They were discussing figures and making cuts. I heard no mention of the expensive and exotic items like the chase plane or the Chinese pleasure yacht, but there was talk of "targets" and "surveillance." I was surprised, and it came to me that Mitchell was perfectly capable of approving a scaled-down version of the Liddy plan. In retrospect, I am grateful to Liddy. If he had brought in a modest, straightforward wiretapping plan, Mitchell might have approved it on the spot, and I would not have crossed him. I would have been in the middle of criminal conspiracy.

As it was, I was worried about the direction of the conference. I studied Mitchell's face for his mood; he did not look happy. He was involved in the conversation, but he was wincing a lot. If he had looked pleased, I would not have seized an opening to protect both him and myself.

"Excuse me for saying this." I cleared my throat. "I don't think this kind of conversation should go on in the Attorney General's office."

All talk immediately ceased. I was surprised that I had the courage to speak out at all and gratified that no one ignored me. Magruder looked as if he'd been stopped by a policeman, Liddy looked perplexed, and even Mitchell seemed surprised. His blank expression changed to one of deep thought, and then he began nodding his head. I was relieved. My old boss felt he had been protected by a good staff man, I figured. The meeting broke up almost wordlessly, and we all left quickly, like doctors vacating the operating room after a fatal mistake.

In the hall outside Mitchell's office, Liddy, Magruder, and I stopped before ringing for the elevator. I was on the spot, but I had the upper hand. "Gordon, you shouldn't deal directly with the Attorney General on stuff like this," I said. "You should talk with Jeb first, and let him talk with Mitchell."

"I understand what you mean," Liddy replied. "Hereafter, I will communicate through Jeb to the Attorney General."

I knew Liddy did not understand what I meant; but then I had not *said* what I meant. I wanted him to take my remarks as a general disapproval of all of his illegal plans, but I could not say it, and he was concluding that, like a good lawyer, I was merely protecting Mitchell from illegal knowledge, building in deniability and insulation. He might even interpret my sense of urgency as a sign that his plans were *important*—that they were not out of the question. Liddy was more knowledgeable than I about the world of clandestine security precautions, where an action like mine might be a sign of high priority. I was troubled by my unwillingness to confront Liddy or Magruder directly. I decided I should add something, to indicate that I didn't want any part of it.

"And, Gordon," I said, "I don't think you and I should ever talk about this subject again."

"I understand," he assured me, "and we shall not." I thought he had picked up my distaste for this business, but, again, I had been ambiguous. He might interpret that remark as a security precaution. I left, annoyed by my weakness but thinking positively about what I had accomplished.

Now, I determined, I had to see Haldeman. As I walked into his office, I flashed back to my meeting with Ehrlichman on the Brookings break-in. I was upset and uncomfortable. I did not want to bring bad tidings to Haldeman, especially when I knew he was absorbed in his work on the President's trip to China, only a few weeks away. He had a half-dozen books on China on his bookshelf, which he was hoping to read.

I floundered at first, not knowing where to begin. I told him in detail about the two meetings. I knew Haldeman had never seen me troubled. "Bob, this stuff is incredible, unnecessary, and very unwise," I protested. Since I assumed Haldeman and the President were part of the pressure on Mitchell and Magruder to do something, this amounted to saying that *he* had been unwise, but I had to extricate myself some way. "We don't need buggings, muggings, and prostitutes and kidnappers to handle demonstrations. No one at the White House should have anything to do with this."

"You're right," he said instantly. "You should have nothing further to do with Gordon Liddy."

I felt better as I left his office, thinking that at least I was out of the campaign intelligence business. And I was. Even the tickler stopped tickling.

I had not scored any points for bravery, by Haldeman's standards, but nonetheless I felt good about having protected myself. I was jaded by my life in politics, especially in the White House, and I had certainly ignored the canons which politicians profess to live by but which few have found as the path to success. Several times I had stopped short of a hazy line that kept me off the first team, where men like Haldeman, Ehrlichman, Kissinger, Colson, and even Bud Krogh trampled the rules, believing that their power kept them from danger. I was not sure whether it was fear, timidity, some shred of morality, or a lawyer's caution that held me back, but I accepted it.

While I was personally out of the intelligence business, the business itself did not stop. Pressure kept coming down through the tickler, and the ITT-Kleindienst scandal that erupted a few weeks later renewed interest in Larry O'Brien, who was given much credit in the White House for initiating our woes. He was second only to Jack Anderson as a target of ugly thoughts—bitterly resented, even feared. For O'Brien was a seasoned pol who campaigned, we thought, with more than simply lofty moral sentiments.

Shortly after the ITT scandal subsided, I approached Haldeman at the end of a staff meeting for a rare bit of political gossiping.

"Bob, who do you think McGovern will select as his campaign manager?" Senator George McGovern was going to be the Democratic nominee.

"I don't have the foggiest notion," he answered.

"How about Larry O'Brien?"

"God, I hope that's who he picks. We can nail O'Brien," said Haldeman, leaning back in his chair, grinning smugly and enjoying something privately.

I went off on another trip abroad, and again I was called back by a crisis. This time, all the forces the President had set in motion with his dictation machine—the O'Brien investigation and the intelligence tickler—had come together. This time the firefighting would not be so easy, but I would at last make the first team.

CHAPTER FOUR:

LINCHPIN OF CONSPIRACY

MANILA, PHILIPPINES, June 19, 1972 (Monday). I was heading back to Washington. The four-day round trip, including a day in Tokyo, had been rushed. Pigeon, octopus, and turtle delicacies from a native Philippine restaurant challenged my digestion on the flight. Tomorrow, when I crossed the international date line, it would be yesterday. I arrived in San Francisco on Sunday, June 18, and decided to stay over. I was tired, and the exotic cuisine was still sending distress signals. I called Fred Fielding to tell him I would not be in the office Monday morning as planned. "Listen, Fred, I'm wiped out. There's no way I can sit on a plane for another five hours. Also, nobody should be expected to have two Mondays in one week. I'll see you Tuesday."

"I think you'd better come back, John." His voice was unexpectedly serious.

"Why?"

"There's a story in the newspaper that's going to cause some problems."

"I don't really give a damn, Fred."

"You'd better." He told me about the *Washington Post* story on the arrest of five men in the Democratic National Committee headquarters at the Watergate office building. Allegedly they were attempting to bug Larry O'Brien's office. Fred was persistent. He wanted to talk to me, but not on the telephone.

Halfway across the country, I was stretched across two seats when a stewardess approached.

"You look awful," she said. "Got a hangover? 'Cause I've

100

got the cure."

"What's the cure?"

"Oxygen. "

"Why not," I told her, and she produced a canister and a face mask and warned me not to smoke. A few hefty snorts revived me. I felt groggy but respectable when I landed in Washington after twenty hours in the air. Fred was waiting for me at my house.

"What's so damned important I have to jeopardize my mental and physical health to hear it from you?" I asked testily.

"Caulfield called me about that story, about the DNC break-in."

"Did Jack do it?" I interrupted, trying to be funny.

Fred wasn't in the mood. "No, damn it, John, just listen. Jack said a guy named McCord, from the Reelection Committee, was arrested with some Cubans in the DNC. McCord told the police his name was Ed Martin."

I knew that was James McCord. He was security coordinator of the Committee to Reelect the President.

"But here's the clinker," Fielding went on. "They found a check on one of the Cubans from Howard Hunt. How about that?"

"Shit, I've always told you Colson is crazy." This sounded like Colson, who was about as subtle in pursuing political intelligence as a pig hunting truffles.

"What else?" I asked.

"That's all Jack told me and all I know."

I sat and thought, all that crazy screwing around has finally caught up with us. No one can help now. "Well, Freddie, there's not a damn thing I can do tonight. I'm bone tired.

Leave it to Colson to blow the election. I'm going to bed. I'll talk to you tomorrow."

It was a good night's sleep. The best I would have for years to come.

The White House, June 19, 1972 (Monday morning again). I walked into the office and made a few cracks about the octopus in my stomach. It would be a bad week, I told Jane, because it had started with two Mondays. This didn't register. I acknowledged a few welcome-home waves from my staff and went on to my desk, preoccupied. I had hardly begun sorting through the pile of paper in my in box when Jane buzzed. Caulfield was on the line.

"Johnny," he said, "I'm worried."

"Yeah, I thought you would be. Fred tells me Jim McCord got picked up at the DNC. Are you sure?"

"Yep. The Secret Service boys told me. They got it from the police."

"Do they know who McCord is yet?"

"Jesus Christ! It's in the paper this morning. He gave them an alias, but it didn't even last through the weekend. Listen, I'm the guy who put Jimmy over there at the Committee. But I didn't know he was mixed up in this business. I had no idea."

"Well, Jack, I don't think you have anything to worry about if you're not involved."

"Rest assured, John, I'm not involved." He tried to sound solemn, as if he were taking an oath, but his voice quickly gave way to panic. "Not at all. Believe me!"

"Well, then, just sit tight and don't worry."

"I've got to worry. This thing could go all over the place."

"Is that stuff about Howard Hunt's name being on one of the Cubans true?"

102

"Yeah, it's true. That's what I mean."

"It figures. Look, Jack, the best thing you can do is to hold on, and don't call people about this thing. You'll be all right. Okay? I've got to go."

"Okay, John."

I reached for the morning paper. Caulfield was right. It had not taken long for the press to smoke out McCord's identity. Headlines: "GOP Security Aide among Five Arrested in Bugging Affair." The story, written by two *Washington Post* reporters I had never heard of, Bob Woodward and Carl Bernstein, included a statement from John Mitchell denying any relationship between McCord's job at the Reelection Committee and the break-in. It was meant to sound as if Mitchell had never heard of McCord. That won't hold, I thought.

While I was still reading, Jane buzzed again. Jeb Magruder was calling. He needed to speak with me urgently.

"What's going on, Jeb?"

"We've got a real problem, John. I think we can handle it, but, well, it's a hell of a problem. Mitchell told me to get hold of you. Get your help. We've issued a statement. Mitchell issued it in California yesterday. He's still out there. Did you read the paper this morning? Basically the thing is going to be a tough PR problem. But I think we can handle it." Jeb's sentences came at me in a rapid staccato. He was on a thin edge between bravado and loss of control. His voice jumped up in pitch every now and again as if he had swallowed a gulp of helium. He was flailing, I thought—throwing Mitchell's name around, looking for my help. Then he hit me.

"Listen, John, this is all that dumb fucking Liddy's fault. He blew it. The stupid bastard. He should have never used McCord. He never told us he was using McCord. It was stupid. This mess is all his fault...."

103

Oh, shit! I lost the next few sentences. Prickles swirled up and down my back. The octopus juice bubbled ominously. I flashed back through the Liddy meetings. My mind sped through its guilt file in an instant and retrieved every seamy entry. I had put Liddy over at the Committee. I saw Mitchell huddled over his budget. Faint hopes against the worst vanished. I was falling off a ledge, and my instincts grabbed for something. What do you mean, we've got a problem, Jeb? I thought. You've got a problem, baby! I recovered a bit. The first thing I had to do was get Magruder off the phone.

"...I think you should talk to Liddy, John." He was still going. "I can't talk to him, because he hates my guts. But he'll talk to you. And you can find out what else went wrong. And what else we've got to worry about. Okay?"

"Uh, I just got back in my office, Jeb." I was trying to conceal my reactions. "I've been out of the country, and I'm trying to figure out what happened—"

Ring-ring-ring. It was my I.O. (interoffice phone line). Someone in the White House was calling. Salvation. Magruder could hear the ring, and he knew what it meant.

"I've gotta go, Jeb. I'll get back to you. I'll find out what I can."

"Thanks, John. Listen, Liddy's over at 1701 [the Committee headquarters, 1701 Pennsylvania Avenue]. You can get him there."

"Yeah. Okay."

I clicked Magruder off the line and leaned forward in my chair. I took one deep breath and exhaled. The signals from my body were all bad, but stable. I punched in on the I.O. It was Ehrlichman.

"How's the world traveler?" he asked with facetious calm.

"I wish I hadn't come back, to tell you the truth." Ehrlich-

104

man's reaction would be a telling signal, I thought. He knew almost everything, and I knew he was not offended by the idea of wiretaps. I flashed quickly back a few months and saw Jack Caulfield, raconteur, pacing around my office like a happy cat burglar, telling me how he had tried to bug the home of columnist Joseph Kraft on Ehrlichman's orders: "...You wouldn't believe it, Johnny. It was a dark night. And here we are in the alley over in Georgetown. And I'm holding a ladder up against the pole...."

"I presume you are aware of the little incident that transpired the other night?" Ehrlichman asked me.

"Yeah, I'm afraid I am."

"Well, here's what I'd like you to do. The Secret Service called me on Sunday morning about the arrests, and had some intriguing details. One of the Cubans had a check in his possession made out by Howard Hunt. That made me think of Mr. Colson. So I called Chuck over the weekend to ask about Hunt's well-being, and Chuck sounded like he hardly knew the man. Said he hadn't seen him in months. Said he couldn't imagine how a thing like this could have occurred. Now, I'm not totally satisfied our Mr. Colson is telling all. Why don't you have a little chat with him and find out what you can, and find out what happened to his friendship with Hunt?"

"I'll try, John, but Chuck isn't likely to tell me anything he won't tell you."

"Give him a call, anyway. And give your friend Kleindienst a call, too. Find out what he's up to. See if you can find out how all this stuff from the Metropolitan Police is leaking to the newspapers." Ehrlichman and Kleindienst had grown almost openly hostile to each other, and Ehrlichman often used others as go-betweens.

"Okay, I'll see what I can do. Uh, listen, John," I went on, thinking of what I had just learned. People were already

105

calling me out of a compulsion to talk, and I too needed to confide in somebody. "Jeb Magruder just called me. He sounded shaky. He said Gordon Liddy was running the break-in. He said it was Liddy's fault. That's pretty strong stuff. Jeb wants me to talk to Liddy and find out what happened. I guess that's a good idea?"

"I think that sounds fine." No reaction. "Find out what he knows and call me back. I've got to gather up a little report for the party in Florida." Haldeman and the President were returning from Key Biscayne that night. Ehrlichman hung up.

I sat back. Suddenly I felt calmer. I had a report to make, top priority, one stop away from the President. Somehow the assignment drove my anxiety into temporary retreat. I decided I would call Colson first, then Kleindienst, saving Liddy for last. The I.O. rang again.

"John, this is Gordon. I need to come over and see you." It was Strachan, Haldeman's tickler, excited. I didn't want to hear it. I was riveted to my job for Ehrlichman, miles above Strachan's level.

"Gordon, I'm tied up right now," I said abruptly. "I just talked to Ehrlichman and I've got to do something for him right now. I'm trying to find out what happened on this Watergate thing. I'll talk to you later." I left him no room to protest, hung up, and dialed Colson on the I.O. before anybody else could call.

"Chuck, I just talked with Ehrlichman, and he asked me to look into this incident at the DNC. Howard Hunt's name keeps coming up, and I wanted to ask—"

"For Christ's sake! I talked to Ehrlichman about it over the weekend," Chuck shouted angrily. He spat out words like a machine gun, giving off so much energy I imagined him running sprints around his office. "I told him I had no idea where Hunt was, or what he was doing! I haven't seen Hunt in months! He's off my payroll. He has been. I can't believe Hunt's involved in that Watergate thing, anyway. That's the craziest goddamn thing I ever heard! I can't believe any of it"

"Well, Chuck," I interrupted, as firmly but mildly as I could, "what's the story on Hunt's relationship to you?"

"I hired him as a consultant for Ehrlichman," he said, stressing the name.

"What do you mean?"

"Well, those guys were all out in California, and they wanted me to bring somebody in to work on the Pentagon Papers. So I sent Hunt over to Ehrlichman. Hell, he wasn't even at the top of my list!"

"Chuck, you sent Hunt out to interview Dita Beard a few months ago, didn't you? We worked on that."

"Yeah, yeah," he said, "and he wasn't even around here then. I had to go find him. That's the last time I remember seeing him. Look, I'm going through my files right now to get all the information. I'll put it all together for you, and I'll let you know what's happening. But I don't know what the hell Hunt's doing. This doesn't make any sense to me."

"Okay, Chuck. Let me know."

"Oh, and, John, I'd like to have a talk with you and Ehrlichman." His tone shifted. He became almost subdued. "I've got some things I'd like to go over with both of you about Hunt. I think we ought to have a meeting later."

"All right. I'm gonna see John later today. I'll raise it with him then. I'll call you."

"Right." He hung up, and I brooded. Obviously, Chuck did not trust Ehrlichman to determine who had sponsored Hunt, and wanted me there as an observer. I called Kleindienst.

"Hello, Junior," he said. "I can't guess what you're calling me about."

"Yeah. Needless to say, there's some interest over here in finding out what's going on."

"That's no surprise. I had a little encounter about that thing over the weekend. The investigation is proceeding as it should."

I had no idea what that meant. Kleindienst was being cool and businesslike. He was the Attorney General. I didn't know whether he was not yet clued in or was already stonewalling.

"I'm sure it is. Say, Dick, my people over here are concerned about all the leaks coming out of the investigation. That shouldn't be going on. Do you have any idea where they're coming from?"

"Whoever's concerned is wasting his time, Junior. It's all coming out of the Metropolitan Police, and there's nothing you can do about it. That place is a sieve."

"I guess so." I decided not to press. "Well, it looks like a pretty strange case. I'll talk to you later."

Now it was time for Liddy, from whom I had learned to expect horrendous surprises. I braced myself and called. He was not in, so I left word. As soon as I hung up, I kicked myself mentally: Real smart, Dean, Liddy's all mixed up in this and you're leaving word for him to call you. How will you explain the call? Wait a minute, I thought. I'm not supposed to know anything about Liddy and this break-in. This can be explained as a perfectly innocent call—legal work, campaign finance laws. I steadied myself, but the fears had already set in.

I summoned Fielding into my office and told him to go to the White House personnel office and pull Howard Hunt's employment records. I would need some hard facts if I ended up refereeing a dispute about when, and if, Hunt had worked for Colson. Fred did not question the assignment. He could feel emergency in the air. There might as well have been air raid sirens going off. He sprang to his duty like a military officer in battle. No questions asked. Lives at stake.

Jane buzzed. It was Liddy.

"Gordon," I said, "I'd like to meet with you."

"I'll be right over," he replied instantly, words clicking. I detected relief. "Have me cleared." He signed off in a hurry.

I buzzed Jane and told her to clear Liddy past the guards downstairs. I sat back to compose myself, and then another wave of self-recrimination washed over me. Another dumb move, John. You're not thinking straight. Liddy has just been involved in a crime, and now you've built a record of meeting with him. I grimly pictured the Executive Protection Service clearance log: "Mr. Gordon Liddy; June 19, 1972; 11:15 A.M.; Northwest Basement Entrance, EOB; cleared by Miss Thomas for Mr. Dean; official business." There was nothing I could do about it now. I finally decided, rather irrationally, that I would intercept Liddy in the hall to lessen the number of people in my own office who would see him with me. I hurried out to the bathroom and then paced slowly in the hallway, trying to look as if I were going somewhere. Just as I was heading for the water fountain, I saw Liddy coming toward me.

"Gordon, I think we ought to take a little walk."

He nodded. He knew exactly what was going on, and he could read on my face that this was a very sensitive meeting. We walked briskly and wordlessly out the nearest exit.

"Let's walk down this way," I said, turning south on Seventeenth Street. We walked toward the Ellipse, with the EOB and the White House on our left, the FDIC building across the street on our right.

This was not the crisp Gordon Liddy I had dealt with before. His heavy beard was no longer shaven to the nubs. The black-and-gray stubble was long enough to glisten in the sun. His usual snappy three-piece suit had given way to a rumpled cord summer suit, the kind I associated with fraternity parties at the University of Virginia. He looks almost disheveled, I thought, he seems flustered, no longer the commanding presence. I noticed lines etched in his forehead.

I began with what I thought were calming remarks. "Gordon, I think I have to... I think you can understand why it's important for me, for the White House, to know exactly what's happened. I've spoken with Jeb, and Jeb has told me—"

He interrupted. "This whole goddam thing is because Magruder pushed me. I didn't want to go in there. But it was Magruder who kept pushing. He kept insisting we go back in there."

"Back?"

"Yes. We made an entry before and placed a transmitter and photographed some documents. But the transmitter was not producing right. I think it was because of the range. The equipment we used was only effective up to an air distance of about five hundred yards. Our pickup was within range, but we got interference from the support girders running up the building. They're steel, and they can deflect a weak signal if they are placed so the transmission passes through their magnetic field. Anyway, it's defective, and the batteries might be weak. So we went in to find out what was the matter. The other thing is Magruder liked the documents we got from the first entry and wanted more of them... "

Liddy was gushing now. We stopped on the corner across the street from the Corcoran Art Gallery. I turned away from the traffic, facing the Ellipse. It was nearly lunchtime. I knew that the buildings would soon emit hundreds of familiar faces, and I didn't want to be seen with Gordon Liddy. I edged over to a park bench and stood there, my back to the sidewalks. Liddy followed me like an awkward dance partner learning a

110

new step. I felt very conspicuous.

"...And, John, I know using McCord was a serious mistake. I accept full responsibility for it. It's my fault, and I don't want to put off responsibility on anybody else. But I do want you to know why I did it. And that's because Magruder cut my budget so much and was pushing me so hard I had to use McCord. I didn't have time to do anything else. Jim's a professional, and I trusted him. He was the only guy I could turn to."

"I understand, Gordon." I had heard enough. "But what about Hunt?"

"Well, Howard Hunt. He was the guy who got me the Cubans."

"You mean the ones who were arrested?"

"That's right. He knew those guys, and he got them for me."

"I see. Well, how about the people in the White House? Is anybody in any way connected with this? I've got to know that, Gordon."

"I don't think so. The only person who might have known about it is Gordon Strachan."

I turned away from Liddy for a moment to absorb Strachan's name. This was the worst blow since Magruder's call. I felt queasy. I really didn't want to know more, because I had to assume that if Strachan knew, Haldeman knew. And if Haldeman knew, the President knew. It made sickening sense. Now I understood why Strachan had called earlier.

Liddy interrupted the silence. "John, I'm worried about the men who were arrested. We've got to get them out of jail. They need bonds and lawyers. We can't let them sit there in the D.C. jail. It's a hellhole."

"Well, look, Gordon," I said, fishing for a clear thought. I

111

wanted to end the conversation. "I can't do anything about that. And I think you can understand why I can't do anything about that."

He stopped for an instant, his eyes narrowing in thought. "Well, that's right. I can understand."

I saw more and more people on the street out of the corner of my eye. "Ah, Gordon, I think I'd better be heading back to my office now, and, ah, I really think this is the last conversation we'll ever have until this whole thing is resolved." I was now more flustered than Liddy, who seemed to feel better after unburdening himself.

"I understand that perfectly, John," he said, straightening himself up. "I'll walk on the other side of the street. That's probably best. But before I go over there, I want you to know one thing, John. This is my fault. I'm prepared to accept responsibility for it. And if somebody wants to shoot me..." My head shot around. His eyes were fixed and hard, his face full of emotion, his words coming out in bursts. "...on a street corner, I'm prepared to have that done. You just let me know when and where, and I'll be there." He ended with a gesture of finality.

"Well, ah, Gordon," I said tightly, flashing back to his burned hand and to Mafia movies, struggling for the strength to calm him again, "I don't think we're really there!"

"Oh, no, no," he said, holding up his hands to hush me. "Look, John, I'm not going to talk about what's gone on. None of these men will talk, you can be assured of that. They're all soldiers. But we know what we're dealing with."

"Okay," I said softly.

We turned and headed back up the street. I was looking at my shoes.

"John, I'll tell you one thing," Liddy said quietly. "Since you've got the responsibility in the White House to find out what's going on, one thing you ought to do is get the 302s from the FBI." He was giving me advice, completely recovered. The drama of the previous moment had already blown away on the breeze.

"What's a 302?" I asked, relieved to return to dull information.

"Well, I'm an FBI man. I know how investigations operate. I used to be a prosecutor up in Dutchess County. What the agents pick up on those raw files will tell you how the investigation is proceeding. Those are the 302s. And the other thing you need is the AirTels. Those are the orders to the agents. They tell the agents whom to interview and what to ask. If you have those, you'll know what's going on."

I responded to his mood rather than to his advice. "Well, Gordon, I'm sorry this whole thing happened." It was the best leave-taking I could think of. "It sure is a mess now."

He didn't say anything, easing away from me with a look of both sadness and determination. I watched him cross Seventeenth Street and break into a brisk walk, and then I went back into the EOB.

I had to get something into my stomach, having fasted since Manila with no good result. I thought of the White House mess and was repelled by the thought of both the cuisine and the company. I wanted to be alone. Soup, I thought, was the answer. I bought a Styrofoam cup full of hot vegetable soup and went to my desk.

I was carefully drinking the soup when I looked up and saw Gordon Strachan at the door. His neck was flushed bright red down to his collar. The splotches stood out in relief against his fair skin and blondish hair. Gordon always looked like a fresh Scandinavian youth; on this day he was a troubled one.

"Have a seat, Gordon," I said uneasily. But he stood.

"John, I just wanted to talk to you about a couple of things.

113

Sorry to drop in like this. I wanted to let you know I had a call from Haldeman. And I've destroyed all the documents in our files relating to that operation over there at the Committee."

"Like what?"

"Well, I think there are wiretap logs we received, I'm not sure. And there's a message there, notes I made, of instructions from Bob to tell Liddy to change his operation from Muskie to McGovern."

I didn't say anything. Strachan continued. "Now, John, Bob's files are clean. I've gone through everything. I've gone through all the political-matters memos, and I've taken out everything sensitive and shredded it. Some talking papers and budget stuff. I don't think there are any problems in there now."

I shoved my soup away and stared. "Well, Gordon, that's pretty heavy."

"I know it is," he sighed.

I sensed he wanted to talk some more, get things off his chest, but I didn't. I cut him short and he left.

Hugh Sloan called. He was upset. As treasurer of the Reelection Committee, he had passed large bundles of cash to Liddy. I asked whether he knew what the money was for, and he said no, but he was worried about a Campaign Act violation for not having reported the expenditure. He was worried about whether fingerprints could be detected on hundred-dollar bills. I told him a campaign violation was minor, there were far larger things at stake. Using my standard line about having just gotten back to the country, being under pressure, etc., I got him off the phone. He was not satisfied.

I told Jane not to take any more calls. I wanted to concentrate on what I would tell Ehrlichman shortly in my report. Fielding came in and out of my office on routine business. He was a blur. I didn't see him. What I was seeing was Jack

114

Caulfield again, several months earlier, whispering to me with conspiratorial delight a story—which Bud Krogh had confirmed—about how Gordon Liddy and some other people had broken into the office of Daniel Ellsberg's psychiatrist in Los Angeles, on a "mission" for Krogh and Ehrlichman: "...They didn't get anything, and tore the place up...It was a bust. But they got away clean." It was not so clean now. This guy Liddy is at a real beggar's crossroads, I thought. He leads to disaster in all directions. Through Magruder up to Mitchell; through Strachan up to Haldeman and the President; through Krogh up to Ehrlichman and the President. I felt way over my head.

I walked over to Ehrlichman's office and found him in his white shirtsleeves, with a note pad before him. He offered me a chair next to his desk and motioned me to get on with the report. He was writing, but I couldn't tell, as usual, whether he was taking notes or doodling. As I recounted my interviews, he was at his unflinching best. I piled up the gory details, receiving only a few raised eyebrows and several uh-huhs. He mustered a drawled "That's interesting" upon hearing of Liddy's offer to be shot on the street.

His interest picked up a bit when I blurted an account of the two meetings I had attended in Mitchell's office on the Liddy plan. Ehrlichman was the only person I could turn to for counsel, but it was only the news of Mitchell's involvement that made him perk up. Here was some leverage over his nearly vanquished rival. Maybe Mitchell could be made to carry some water for the White House on this break-in.

As much as I wanted to tell Ehrlichman everything I knew, I did not tell him about my conversation with Strachan or Liddy's remarks about Strachan. The implications were so gruesome that I believed he should hear those facts from Haldeman or the President. I thought I had already crossed the boundaries of what I should know. At the end of the Liddy tale, I wanted to broach the Ellsberg break-in. It was already on the White House grapevine, a possible threat. I knew I

115

ought to raise the matter with Ehrlichman directly, but I could only bring myself to do so obliquely.

"By the way, John, it looks like the Watergate thing is not the only potential problem we might have at the White House from Liddy. There's also the thing out in California."

Ehrlichman's mouth pursed in a tight circle, his lower lip protruding. I took this as a sign of surprise that I would know of the Ellsberg break-in. He said nothing and looked out over his glasses. I noted his lack of denial and wondered what bells might be sounding off, what strategies were forming behind the impassive eyes.

"I talked to Chuck," I said, anxious to move on. "He swears his innocence. He says Hunt is a figure from his distant past."

"Yeah, I'm not surprised."

"I don't know whether he mentioned this to you, John, but he wants to meet with the two of us later this afternoon. It sounded urgent."

"Okay. Why don't the two of you come back about four-thirty? I've got to send my care package off to Florida."

I went back to my office, called Colson about the meeting, and took care of some routine business. Magruder stuck his head in the door once while I was on the phone, waved, and ran off. He was making the rounds. I called Fielding in and asked him about Hunt's employment records. He reported a hopeless tangle in the personnel office. Clerks were still sorting papers, but the gist of the confusion thus far was doubt that Hunt had ever gone off the payroll. I took this information back to Ehrlichman's office, where I found Colson in a state of vigorously renewed ignorance about Hunt.

Ehrlichman listened to Colson for a while and then knitted his brow mischievously. "Well, where is Mr. Hunt?" he queried with heavy sarcasm.

"I don't have the foggiest notion where he is," Chuck shot back.

"Do you know where Mr. Hunt is?" Ehrlichman asked, turning to me.

"Of course not. I don't have any idea where he is."

He paused and thought heavily. "Well, don't you think Mr. Liddy might talk to him about getting out of the country? Don't you think that would be a good idea?"

Silence.

"Why don't you call Liddy and tell him to pass that message to Mr. Hunt?" he asked, looking at me. Such questions, from Ehrlichman, were commands. He seldom gave orders any other way. So I went to the phone in Ehrlichman's office while the two of them continued their conversation.

"Gordon," I said after fumbling with the phone long enough to reach him, "I have a request that Howard Hunt ought to be out of the country."

"Yes, sir," Liddy snapped. "I understand. That'll be passed on immediately."

I rejoined the meeting, but second thoughts quickly began to plague me again. That order would come back to haunt us, I thought.

"You know, I don't think that was a very smart thing we just did," I said. "Because this guy is obviously a part of what all's happened. I don't know what all the details are yet, and you don't know, but he's gonna be questioned."

Chuck agreed. Second thoughts are contagious.

"Yeah, I guess it was a bad idea," said Ehrlichman. "Why don't you call back and retract that suggestion?"

Back to the phone. "Gordon, what I just said about Hunt. Retract that."

"I'm not sure I can."

"What do you mean?"

"The order's already been passed."

"Well, do your best."

"Right. I'll do my best."

Debate resumed on Hunt's status at the White House. Colson was voluble.

"I've heard all that," I said, "but it's not clear at all from the personnel records, Chuck. Fielding's been down there, and it looks like he's still on the payroll, for God's sake!"

"He can't be!" said Chuck. "He's not been working for me for months!"

Ehrlichman finally waded into the conversation. "I'll resolve this. Let's bring Kehrli [the staff secretary] up here with all the records."

"Well, let's bring Clawson up here, too," said Colson. Ken W. Clawson was the deputy White House director of communications. "He tells me some reporters are on to the Hunt business. They're bugging him about what Hunt did at the White House, and he doesn't know what to tell them."

"Okay," said Ehrlichman.

"While they're coming over," said Colson, with a forced nonchalance, "I want to tell you something else, uh, that we should take care of. And that is that apparently Howard Hunt had a safe here in the White House up in his office."

Ehrlichman became more animated than I'd seen him all day. He leaned forward. "You mean to tell me he even has an *office* here?" His voice rose in bewilderment. He was clearly enjoying demonstrating his ignorance of Hunt's activities as superior to Colson's. Ehrlichman's shock was so well performed I almost laughed to release tension.

Chuck was exasperated. "We just never shut down that office," he explained hopelessly. "No one ever paid any attention to it. It was good office space—I'm surprised our people didn't move in on it."

A little more jousting on this point, and then the conversation focused on the question of how to get into Hunt's safe.

Bruce Kehrli came in, glanced at the assembled faces, and drew a deep breath. He was carrying a bunch of file folders.

"Well," asked Ehrlichman, "what is the status of Mr. Hunt?"

Kehrli was befuddled. He didn't know what to say. He mumbled personnel-office jargon during several intricate sentences, and then managed to conclude that the picture was unclear.

Chuck looked straight at him. "Hunt was off my payroll."

"Okay," said Kehrli.

"I guess," Ehrlichman said, "if Chuck says he is off the payroll, he's off the payroll."

One decision made. Kehrli made a note on his pad, and Clawson entered.

Ehrlichman asked Kehrli to wait while Clawson's press problem was addressed. It was generally agreed to stress the classified nature of Hunt's activities to forestall further inquiry. He had worked on "declassification" projects involving sensitive materials and on "drug intelligence matters." Clawson went off to enlighten the reporters on this point, and to add that Hunt had worked only sporadically at the White House. His work had terminated at some time in the past; old records were being dusted off to determine exactly when.

As soon as Clawson had departed, Ehrlichman addressed Kehrli. "Listen, Bruce, we understand there's a safe in Hunt's office. How can you get into that safe to find out what's in it?"

119

"We have a procedure where we can have the GSA [General Services Administration] open those safes," Kehrli replied.

"Well, why don't you get that safe opened?" asked Ehrlichman.

"Dean should take possession of the contents," Chuck chimed in quickly.

"Yeah, that's a good idea," Ehrlichman said, and added, "and Dean should be present when the safe is opened."

"Okay," said Kehrli, turning to me. "I'll call you when I'm ready."

I hurried back to my office. This is just like the Town House records, I thought. Give the hot stuff to the counsel's office. Double protection—executive privilege and the attorney-client relationship. But I felt no resentment at the notion of having it dumped on me. I was rather curious, in fact, about what Hunt had in his safe.

Jane handed me a note when I walked in the door: "Meeting. Six P.M. Mitchell's Watergate apartment." "You're pretty busy today," she quipped.

Indeed I was. I had dealt with John Mitchell for more than three years as a trusted subordinate, but I had never been invited to his apartment. Swelling with my sudden new intimacy, I rushed off to the Watergate apartment building. It was next door to the Watergate office building, which we would soon dub the "scene of the crime."

Fred LaRue greeted me at the door, wearing his normal warm smile. He was a younger, thinner-looking copy of John Mitchell, which made some sort of poetic sense, because LaRue served as Mitchell's alter ego. A millionaire oil man from Mississippi, he had been serving in the Administration out of curiosity mingled with a sincere desire to be of help. He had no ambitions that I could discern, nor any enemies. LaRue had begun as a dollar-a-year consultant at the White House and had taken a pay cut to join Mitchell at the Reelection Committee. At the endless government meetings, Fred would melt invisibly into the back of the room and smoke his pipe. He held no title. The standard interpretation was that his full-time job was to be Mitchell's friend—a vital service, since Mitchell had little use for the senior officials around him.

Fred led me to the den on the second floor of Mitchell's elegant apartment, where Magruder, Mardian, and Mitchell were already in a discussion. Mitchell rose to greet me.

"Thanks for dropping by," he said warmly, with a handshake.

"How about a drink?"

"No, thanks. I've got a little stomach problem from Manila, and I'm on the wagon." I cast a desperate, longing glance at their drinks and made a useless effort to recall when I had needed one more. But I wanted to have my wits about me in case the meeting introduced some new disaster. I was shell-shocked and nervous.

Within a minute or so, Magruder said he had to leave. He looked remarkably chipper, as if his earlier ashen fear had been only a dream. "Well, I guess I'll leave this crisis to you gentlemen," he said. "I'm almost late." He came over to me and whispered his secret. "I've got a tennis date, John. Guess who?"

"I give up, Jeb. Who?"

"The Veep," meaning Vice-President Agnew. He grinned and waved good-bye. I flinched, wondering if I seemed as ostentatiously juvenile in boasting of my place near the throne. No, I decided. I had the same feelings, but I was more reserved about them. I headed for a vacant spot on the sofa. Magruder's lighthearted departure left me uncertain about what approach was being taken. Mitchell must have sensed this, for he offered me a drink again. This time I accepted. As Mitchell

121

fixed my Scotch, Mardian and LaRue resumed their discussion of another Reelection Committee press release on James McCord. They were taking the same posture toward him that Colson had taken toward Hunt. This struck me as standard press work. The discussion soon lapsed, and an uncomfortable silence ensued. I sensed an uneasiness as to how I would fit into the conversation.

"When did you get back?" I asked Mitchell, to break the ice.

"Just a little while ago, and I'm a little wiped out. That's the last time I'm going to fly all the way across the country in that damned little Gulfstream jet." He took his jacket off and sat down.

"I've just been talking with the President," he said. "I couldn't think of any news to cheer the President up with, but he didn't seem to need it. He was taking it much better than I thought he would. Hell, he tried to cheer me up."

There was a pause. No one would speak until Mitchell relinquished the floor, and no one knew what to say, anyway.

Mitchell went off in thought and then came back to me. "What's happening over at the place where you work, anyway?"

"Well, Ehrlichman's taken charge of—"

"That's terrific," Mitchell interrupted upon hearing Ehrlichman's name. "That's the worst news I've heard all day." The laconic bite in his voice set half the tone for one of the biggest problems I saw down the road for myself. Ehrlichman set the other half.

I felt awkward. John Mitchell was the President's campaign manager and his close personal friend. I was sure he had some criminal responsibility for the Watergate break-in. Any such revelation could be the death blow to the President's reelection, let alone a disgrace to Mitchell's whole life. Mitchell was already in a pressure-cooker, the strain told on his face, and the thought of Ehrlichman made it worse for him. I felt fonder of Mitchell than of any of the bosses in the White House, and I wanted to help. Still, my superiors were in the White House, and I had learned never to breach their confidences. I didn't believe I should tell Mitchell precisely what was going on in the White House. That was someone else's role, not mine, but I knew Mitchell could expect precious little help. I went back and forth in my mind about how to deal with Mitchell. The guilt I felt for having sent Liddy to Mitchell made my dilemma worse. I knew he must be harboring the same dark thoughts toward me for recommending Liddy to him as I was having toward Krogh for recommending Liddy to me.

Fortunately, the matter was largely avoided. The telephone kept ringing. Mitchell's wife, Martha, was still in California, and she was raising hell. LaRue, the only man other than Mitchell who was capable of dealing with Mrs. Mitchell when she was on the rampage, tried gamely for the first few calls, but Mitchell was forced to take over. Call after call—from Committee employees who were with Martha, then from friends of the Mitchell's, and then from UPI reporter Helen Thomas, who called to advise Mitchell of the hysterical outbursts Martha was giving her on the phone. From Mitchell's end of the conversations, I heard talk of doctors, sedation, and alcohol. The pathos and despair of the scene were so immediate they cut through everything else. I knew Mitchell had more to contend with than Watergate, so I excused myself during a break in the calls.

"John," said Mitchell, as I headed for the door, "I'll sure appreciate your help on this thing. We're going to need all the good heads we can put together."

"Thank you, Mr. Mitchell," I said. This was a new kind of flattery from John Mitchell. I felt a sense of importance as I left to drive home.

I was numb. I didn't sleep well, even though I was drained

from jet lag and the day's emotional barrage. An alarm had gone off at the White House, I thought. Almost every important official in the Administration had scurried to the fire poles in panic, and they all landed in the counsel's office. Now I was learning what the job really meant. I felt no danger for myself. In fact, I was proud of having extricated myself from situations that might have left me like the rest—worried. Instead I was a refuge, a shoulder, a brain, a counsel. I was about to arrive.

The next morning I got to my office and picked up the *Washington Post*. I was bemused by the story on the Watergate break-in, which carried the official White House stance. "I am not going to comment from the White House on a third-rate alleged burglary attempt," said Ron Ziegler. "It is as simple as that." He had told reporters placidly that the White House had learned of the break-in from newspaper accounts, and he had deflected all questions to Mitchell.

While I was reading, three workmen in green GSA coveralls and matching green caps wheeled dollies straight into my office and began unloading cartons on my floor. Fielding appeared simultaneously to inform me that these were the materials from Hunt's safe. Kehrli had moved fast the previous night, and Fielding had substituted for me at what he called a "safe-opening party" with GSA safe drillers and Secret Service agents. Kehrli had kept the contents overnight in his office, which was equipped with an ultrasonic sensor alarm system for security. I supervised the unloading, and the cartons were stacked in the middle of my office.

Jane buzzed. I was wanted immediately in Ehrlichman's office. As I left, I told Fred we would go through the material later.

I found Haldeman, Ehrlichman, and Mitchell, seated around Ehrlichman's coffee table. It was the first time I had ever seen the three of them together in one room alone.

"Well, if it isn't our traveling counsel," said Haldeman with a laugh. He had just returned from Florida with the President; there was a new luster to his tan. "Every time you leave the country, something awful happens," he teased, referring to my Paris trip before the ITT crisis. "I hope you're not planning any more trips before the election."

There were chuckles. This group, I thought, is in surprisingly fine spirits.

Ehrlichman leaned over toward Mitchell, smiling. "We thought we should have our lawyer here when the Attorney General of the United States, who is cooling his heels in the west reception room, pays his visit." Ehrlichman loved to stick it to Mitchell and Kleindienst. Mitchell said nothing.

Kleindienst arrived and took a seat. Here they all are, I thought—Haldeman, Ehrlichman, Mitchell, and Kleindienst— with Junior suddenly in their league. I expected some weighty decisions to be made in this company. Wrong. All parties were guarded. The White House faction did not trust the Justice Department faction, and, moreover, no one wanted to acknowledge how serious the problem might be. The Florida weather was discussed, Haldeman's tan, Liddy's personality, Mitchell's political soundings in California. I hardly said a word. Mitchell grunted and puffed. Haldeman dropped a few jolly remarks. Ehrlichman raised the only matters of substance, and even they were marginal. He told Mitchell that the White House would steer all Watergate press inquiries to the Reelection Committee. Mitchell nodded, not happy, not objecting. Then Ehrlichman asked Kleindienst about the Watergate leaks. Kleindienst replied that they were coming from the Metropolitan Police. He said the problem would soon be solved, since the FBI was assuming jurisdiction over the investigation. The conversation lurched down more side avenues, with more half-hearted pleasantries and subtle ribbings, and then the meeting dissolved. I had witnessed the first round of internal stonewalling.

Kleindienst caught me in the hall. "Hey, Junior! What are you doing right now?"

"Nothing. I'm just going back to catch up on some work," I said, thinking of the cartons lying on my floor.

"Come on. Ride back to my office with me." The Justice Department. I followed him to his limousine, and we rode mostly in silence. Kleindienst was seething over the charade we had just attended. Unlike the others including myself, he was not known for masking his inner thoughts.

"This thing is so goddamn stupid I can't believe it!" he exploded when we reached his office. "Breaking in and bugging the damn Democratic National Committee. There's nothing in there but a lot of carp, anyway. Anybody knows that. Dumbest damn thing I ever heard."

Kleindienst walked over to his desk and sat down. He waved his arms to emphasize his dismay. "This fella Liddy must be crazy. He tracked me down at the Burning Tree Country Club on Saturday after my golf game. He said, 'John Mitchell wants you to get the men arrested at the DNC out of jail.' Can you believe it? I told Liddy to get his ass packing. If I'd ever seen a guilty man, it was Liddy. He was rattled and nervous, and I wasn't about to talk to him." So that's the little encounter Dick had with Watergate over the weekend, I thought. Liddy's name had not yet surfaced in the investigation, and I assumed Kleindienst had not reported the incident for fear of implicating both Liddy and Mitchell. Kleindienst was instinctively on the inside of the problem, too. This strengthened my impulse to confide in him.

I watched him change moods as he stared silently at his desk. "If John Mitchell is in trouble," he said gravely, "I'll resign before I'd ever prosecute him." He knew where this was heading as well as I did. I decided to trade worries with him.

"Dick, I don't have all the facts, but I'm worried. I'm afraid this thing could lead right to the President. I don't know if the President is involved, but—"

"God, I hope the President is not involved in this, and that you're not involved."

"I assure you I'm not, but I have no idea where this investigation could lead." I sensed he was backing off. We were being infinitely more candid with each other than anyone had been at the earlier meeting, but we were still playacting, pretending, testing each other. I decided not to tell Kleindienst about my two meetings with Mitchell, Magruder, and Liddy, which had taken place in the same office we were sitting in. The information would squeeze his position even more, and he obviously wanted no ammunition against Mitchell. I withheld it, another small step into the cover-up. I knew Mitchell and the White House would be grateful. So would Kleindienst.

"Listen, Junior," he continued, "those people over there where you work don't understand this place. They think I can take care of any problem they've got. For Christ's sake, John Connally* was over here not long ago trying to get me to handle a problem for him. And when I refused, the President started climbing all over my back."

"I know, I know, Dick. I've tried to tell them a few times, but nobody's ever worked over here."

Kleindienst's thoughts were drifting off again. He was feeling the pressure. "You know, John Ehrlichman may need a friend someday, but I'll be goddamned if it's going to be me. He's like Sherman Adams was in this town.** He's managed to

---

*   [Original Footnote:] John B. Connally, Jr., former governor of Texas, was first Secretary of the Treasury in the Nixon Administration, and subsequently head of Democrats for Nixon.

**   Sherman Adams was White House chief of staff under President Dwight D. Eisenhower. He was pressured to resign for accepting gifts from a businessman.

make everyone hate him, and someday he may regret that."

"I guess so," I said, not anxious to pursue this line. "Dick, if this investigation leads into the White House, I'm afraid the President may not be reelected. There's so much shit going on there." I halted. No need for specifics.

Kleindienst bolted up from his chair. His mind seemed to have been wandering all over the lot. He stopped, picked up the phone, and summoned Henry E. Petersen, head of the Criminal Division. Petersen arrived quickly.

"Henry, Junior here is worried about that Democratic Committee break-in."

"Frankly, I'm worried about this case, too," Petersen replied. "I don't like it. Not one second." He began a cursory status report on the investigation. As always, Petersen had a certain dismantled, harassed look to him. Henry had logged more than twenty years in the Department, working his way to the top through persistence and bureaucratic skill. Now, as the man in charge of all the federal government's criminal prosecutions, he had reached a unique plateau—a Democrat, and a career civil servant, holding a sensitive appointed post in a Republican Administration. It was John Mitchell who had made him head of the Criminal Division. And Henry Petersen had been around.

As he briefed Kleindienst, his craggy face did not break into his usual friendly smile. His expression was hard. My thoughts went back to a conversation I had had with him about a year earlier. Colson, who was trying to win organized-labor support for the President, had become convinced that Mitchell was conspiring against his strategy. Since he and Mitchell had a quarrelsome relationship at best, Chuck had dispatched me to Mitchell's office. Mitchell deflected me to Henry, whom I had known for years.

"Henry, I need your advice, really a little education," I had

128

said. "Colson claims you guys are unnecessarily prosecuting labor leaders, which is making it tough for Chuck to build labor support for the President."

"Shit, we don't have a vendetta against labor," Henry said quickly. "It just so happens there are some goddamn bad men in the union movement, and these labor cases pop up all the time in normal investigations."

"I understand, Henry. Let me tell you what's troubling me. Those folks over at the White House want to halt labor prosecutions, at least till after the election—"

"No, sir," he interrupted emphatically.

"Wait, Henry. I don't disagree. I know exactly what you're talking about. I don't like this, but I need to know what I'm talking about to turn them off, to tell them that that sort of thing isn't possible."

"John, never, I repeat never, has an Attorney General that I know of, as long as I've been here, and that's quite a while now, reversed a major case after an investigation has begun and turned up evidence of a criminal violation." He was firm but friendly. "He couldn't if he wanted to, because the lawyers in this division would walk out." This would weigh heavily against Colson's argument, I thought. "I think you should tell those guys," Henry continued, "not to get involved in any way, shape or form with any criminal case over here. It would have serious repercussions if it ever came out. The only time a case could ever be stopped is before an investigation has commenced. Hell, I've got a recommendation right here on my desk that I authorize an investigation of Lyndon Johnson on some shitty little banking violation down in Texas. Now, I'm not going to authorize an investigation of a former President. This is a case that will never start, and need not start…"

That conversation was on my mind as Petersen reported to Kleindienst on the first stages of the Watergate investigation.

When Kleindienst had to leave for another meeting, Henry and I went to a small lounge in the back of his office.

"Henry, I don't believe the White House can stand a wide-open investigation," I said quietly. "There are all kinds of things over there that could blow up in our face."

Henry looked at me and thought for a few moments. He had to know, I figured. I was fishing for hints on the crucial question of how the investigation would be defined at the beginning. "Earl Silbert's got the case. You know him, don't you?"

"Sure. I know Earl."

"Well, I've instructed Earl on the investigation. He knows he's investigating a break-in. That's the crime we have in front of us. He knows better than to wander off beyond his authority into other things."

I filed these words away in my mind, with some relief. Henry, however, became animated and began pacing. His thoughts turned in a new direction. "John," he said, "I think you ought to go back to the White House and pass the word on to the President that he's got to move quickly on this thing. He's got to cut his losses cleanly and get it over with."

"I couldn't agree with you more," I replied. But I couldn't tell Petersen all the details I knew that would make this charge painful to carry out.

Kleindienst returned. He sighed and said he needed a drink. Petersen joined him, and the two pulled down heavy portions of a midday cocktail. We talked for a few minutes, and I left for my office. White House vulnerability had just diminished, I thought, reviewing the meeting. The prosecutor's authority, which set the sights of the investigation, was limited to the break-in itself. The government's search for evidence would not be programmed on the reasonable suspicion that the incident had grown out of decisions at the White House; the

White House was not a target of the investigators. If we could keep them from stumbling into other areas, which in my mind ran from campaign contributions to the Ellsberg break-in, things might not be as bad as they looked. I was already busily engaged in plotting a cover-up strategy.

It was lunch time. I sat at my desk, waiting for Jane to bring me a sandwich, catching up on normal business. Gordon Strachan dropped in again. Richard Howard, one of Colson's aides, was with him. Both had nonplused looks on their faces. They stood in front of me like guilty schoolboys in the principal's office. I looked at them curiously and waited.

Finally Strachan began a halting confession. "John, I gave some money to Dick [Howard]. For Chuck. For some ads. And they didn't spend all the money. And there may be a problem with the ads. You'd know better than we would."

"What kind of ads, Gordon?"

"Stuff on the war. Things like that." I knew Colson had made a practice of placing newspaper ads to demonstrate support for the President, with titles such as "Tell It to Hanoi." Strachan was worried that some of the ads violated campaign laws requiring explicit identification of funding sources. I didn't reply.

"And here's the rest of the money," Strachan continued, pointing to two white envelopes which Howard held gingerly. "And I thought maybe it should come here. And maybe you could take custody of it."

"Well, how much money is it?"

"Well, I think you'll find there's fifteen thousand two hundred dollars. It was originally twenty-two thousand. And the rest was spent for the ads."

"What do you want me to do with it?"

There was a chorus of hedging noises and coughs. Strachan and Howard looked at each other. "You know," said Strachan. "Hold on to it. For safekeeping. We can decide later."

"Okay," I said. "I'll keep it." I took out a brown envelope and wrote: "$15,200, from GS/RH." I took the money from them. "I'll keep it in my safe for you." They thanked me and backed out the door.

This has nothing to do with Watergate, I thought after they left, but everybody is worried about everything. People are getting religion, I smiled to myself, and they're bringing their sins to the counsel's office.

"I guess we better go through this stuff from Hunt's safe," I told Fielding after Strachan and Howard departed.

We pulled up chairs, took a carton, extracted the contents, item by item, and examined them like archeologists. One box was filled with junk from Hunt's drawers and shelves—pencils, stationery, paper clips, even a blanket. We plowed on into what Fred said was material from the safe.

"Wait a minute," said Fred suddenly. "Wait a minute." He went into deep concentration. "John, this stuff is sensitive. It could be evidence. Don't you think we ought to be careful?"

"Yeah, I guess you're right." It hadn't occurred to me. I had been caught up by curiosity.

"I've got an idea," said Fred, jumping up to leave. "Hold on. I'm going to see Doc Ward."

"Doc Ward?" I called after him. "What are you doing that for?" He was already gone to the doctors' offices across the hall, and I sat puzzling over what he was up to. Dr. Ward was one of the physicians attached to the White House by the Public Health Service. His boss, Dr. Walter Tkach, the President's personal physician, was the butt of many jokes in the White House, where it was fervently believed he had been selected for his pliant personality—because the President did not want to be bothered by an aggressive doctor. Many aides told stories of how the doctor would listen to a complaint and then reach into his bag for little vials marked simply "Headache" or "Flu" or "Diarrhea" or "Congestion."

Fred returned triumphantly with two pairs of transparent rubber gloves, the kind used for rectal examinations. "Here," he said. "Put these on. We won't leave any prints."

I stretched the gloves over my hands. They were powdered on the inside to make it easy, but they were still so tight my hands turned white for lack of circulation. We returned to work. In a metal container resembling a fishing-tackle box we found a revolver, which I pinched between two gloved fingers and lifted carefully, as if holding a dead mouse by the tail.

"Kehrli handled this thing last night with his hands," Fred said disapprovingly. "He was twirling it around like a damn cowboy to check it and unload it. Said he had been in the Marines."

Next I lifted out a stack of documents nearly a foot high. They were classified State Department cables on the early years of the Vietnam War. Fred and I began scanning them. It was apparent that Hunt had been investigating the Pentagon Papers; there was a paperback edition of them under the cables.

The sorting continued with frequent interruptions. Jane walked in several times and looked at us in puzzled, scolding silence. Fred and I tried to ignore her as we sat there struggling with our rubber gloves, surrounded by papers, the gun, and a black suitcase full of bugging equipment and with antennae sticking out of the top. I took several phone calls and decided I could not operate with the gloves on, so I took them off. Fred joked that it was a breach of security.

By late afternoon, we had almost finished. I locked the possible Watergate evidence—the gun and the bugging equipment—in my closet and sent the State Department cables back to David Young to hold in his files. I left the harmless junk in the cartons on the floor and put several folders into my safe. Fred and I considered this last batch to be politically explosive. We had exchanged several low whistles of amazement. There was a psychological profile of Daniel Ellsberg, which I thought might lead to discovery of the Ellsberg break-in. And there was a phony State Department cable, whose obvious purpose was to convince the reader that President Kennedy had ordered the assassination of Vietnam's President Diem. The phony cable was accompanied by several memos between Hunt and Colson on how to leak the contents to Bill Lambert of *Life* magazine.

Jeb Magruder came by my office again in the afternoon, and I walked back with him to a meeting at the Reelection Committee. Nothing of substance was said until we got to the southwest corner of the Pennsylvania Avenue-Seventeenth Street intersection. We stepped off the curb, in the middle of a normal afternoon crowd.

"You know, John, Mitchell approved this thing down in Florida," Jeb said casually.

"No, I didn't know that," I replied, glancing furtively at the people around us. We were stalled in the middle of the street by cars making left turns.

"Well, yeah, after that second meeting, I felt I had to bring it up with Mitchell again because Colson was just pushing me like mad. He kept calling me and asking what's going on. So I went to Mitchell and I told him. I said, 'Listen, if we don't take care of this, Colson's going to take it over!'"

That explains it, I thought. Everything that had happened since the February 4 meeting was falling into place. Magruder had been pressured by Colson in addition to Haldeman's tickler. He knew Mitchell was jealous and leery of Colson, so he had pushed Mitchell's "Colson button."

"So what happened, John, is we were afraid Colson would take it over. And do you believe this?" He turned to me, laughed, and tugged on my arm. "We were afraid Colson would screw it up! Can you believe that?"

I was lost in a fog. Mitchell, the President, Haldeman, Ehrlichman, everybody in the whole Administration was now snugly in the scandal. I was paying no attention to the traffic, and a turning Metrobus almost ran over me. This narrow scrape brought me back to my senses.

When we arrived at the Committee, I ran into Mardian, gesturing wildly like a rug dealer who had just learned his wares were eaten by moths. "I can't talk now," he said, wheezing from his smoking habit, unconsciously lighting another cigarette. "But the shit has hit the fan."

I walked on. There was no meeting, because Mitchell was tied up with something else. But the same cast was invited to his apartment again that night.

Again, everyone was guarded and uncomfortable. No one wanted to recognize, or talk about, the gravity of the situation. Long worried looks were exchanged, but little was said. Most of the discussion centered on public-relations techniques. Such questions took up the time, but the dominant mood was unspoken grief, like a wake.

The meeting soon broke up, and Mardian called me off to the side. He fidgeted. He could barely contain himself and suggested we go up to his apartment for a drink. Like Kleindienst, Mardian is an impulsive man who has great difficulty putting forth a show of composure. I had noticed his impatience during the meeting. He couldn't sit still, and he seemed to be bursting with some urgent discovery.

We walked the few blocks from the Watergate to Mardian's apartment on Virginia Avenue. His wife greeted us in the living room. Mardian muttered excuses to her and hustled me off to his den. He did not live in Mitchell's luxurious style. In fact, the two dens were as different as Bloomingdale's and Alexander's. Mardian's den was filled with photographs, in black frames, of himself with the President and other high officials. I had a smaller sampling of such photographs on the walls of my own home and office. Mitchell didn't; neither did Haldeman or Ehrlichman. The men very close to the President did not need to display his face. If an observer worked down into the middle layers of the staff, where Mardian and I were, he would notice an increasing clutter of ego-boosting badges of intimacy.

I asked Mardian about the photographs of himself in baseball uniforms, and he warmed up with a speech about his semipro baseball career. Then he pulled his desk chair up in front of the sofa where I was sitting. He hunched over close to me, his arms resting on his thighs, his big hands rubbing together.

"Listen, John, we've got to talk about this. LaRue and I had a long meeting with Liddy today. It was incredible."

I raised my eyebrows, trying to look surprised. I didn't tell Mardian I had met with Liddy the day before. He went through Liddy's story, with occasional exclamations of outrage. Then he broke new ground.

"…And then he told me he's done other jobs for the White House. He said he and Hunt broke into Ellsberg's psychiatrist's office. And they took in the same damn Cubans who are in jail now! I couldn't believe it. This stuff scares the shit out of me, John. Hell, I worked on the Ellsberg case. We had men all over it. But I didn't know they were doing this junk over at the White House. No telling what else they've done! They could ruin the President. These guys are a disaster."

"What do you think will happen, Bob?" I asked. "Liddy's crazy, but he sounds pretty tight-lipped to me."

"Well, that's interesting," Mardian went on, trying to calm himself. "Liddy kept calling his men 'soldiers.' Said they won't talk if their fingernails are pulled out. But he said they expected certain 'commitments' to be honored. He said it was traditional to take care of captured spies, you know. Help out with the family and lawyers and stuff. He didn't say exactly what he meant, but I didn't like it."

I didn't like it, either.

"And here's the other thing, John. It's incredible to me. Liddy doesn't think he'll ever get caught. He says his men certainly won't finger him, and he says there's no evidence he was there. He says he's untraceable. So I started questioning him. I said, 'Did you leave your fingerprints in that hotel room over there?' And he said, 'No, I wiped everything.' See, Liddy and Hunt were in the hotel next door when the men got caught, and they scrambled and got out of there. But he says there are no prints. I couldn't believe that."

Mardian lit another cigarette and continued. "So I said, 'Well, Gordon, did you open a window?' And he says, 'No, but if I did, I sure cleaned it.' I asked, 'How about bottles or glasses?' He says, 'I wiped all those.' 'Well, how about the toilet? Did you use the toilet?' Then he says, 'Oh, yeah, I did.' And he gets all mad at himself. But he says, 'I can't believe they'd pick that up. You know, lots of people were using the toilet that night.' He was a little shaken on that, though. I had him on that. Then I asked him about the money. I said, 'Gordon, how about the money? Can't they trace you with the money?' And he says, 'There's no money on me. I made sure. I shredded it all in the office Sunday morning.'

"Now, John, I can't swallow that about the money. This guy Liddy also tells me he took soap wrappers from the Watergate Hotel and destroyed them, too. He took the soap out of the fucking hotel on the night of the break-in! Can you believe that? And then he says he took the wrappers off the soap and shredded them, just like the money. I know the kind of guy who takes little soap bars from hotels. And I'm telling you a guy who takes those things, and then shreds the wrappers and keeps the soap, a guy who does that is not a guy who will shred hundred-dollar bills! It doesn't make sense!"

Throughout Mardian's discourse, I punctuated his monologue occasionally with terse comments, in the manner of Ehrlichman. We talked on into the night, agreeing that Liddy stood almost no chance of escaping clean. Mardian felt somewhat better for having shared his anxiety with me. I felt worse. The commitments to the men in jail sounded ominous. I drove home exhausted. June 20, the second day of the cover-up, was over, and I had no idea there would be over 250 more, all with the same torrid pace.

Although the White House press machine conveyed a media image of Olympian disdain for so piddling a matter as the break-in, the truth could hardly have been more different. The scramble was on. People were worried about fingerprints. High officials were already playing dumb, even to each other, shoveling guilt out of their own offices. A pallor hung over conversations. Cover-up personalities were emerging. Colson adopted an enthusiastic know-nothing posture, unabashedly declaring his innocence, discovering exculpatory memos right and left in his characteristic whirlwind fashion. Haldeman exuded confidence, almost as distant from the mess as the President himself. Mitchell brooded and stewed quietly. Ehrlichman, sensing danger, moved in shrewdly behind a screen of fact-finding agents whom he maneuvered like chess pieces. I had begun as a foil and go-between, but my extensive knowledge qualified me for a major role. From the beginning, I knew that the vulnerability of the Watergate affair spread broadly across the whole Administration. The lesser aides came to the counsel with confessions; the higher aides commenced to behave in a stealthy manner. I simply assumed, both from the facts I knew and from my knowledge of procedures in the White House, that the vulnerability went right into the President's office. Since I was still on the fringes of the inner circle, I did not know precisely how the President was reacting, but I worked from the premise that he needed protection.

On June 20, as Fielding and I were sorting Hunt's papers with our rubber gloves on, the President had summoned Chuck Colson to his hideaway EOB office. "Now, I hope everybody is not going to get in a tizzy about the Democratic Committee thing," the President had told Chuck before he even sat down.

"A little, it's a little frustrating—disheartening, I guess, is the right word," Chuck replied, and he commenced his standard speech about Howard Hunt. "Been off our payroll for three months," he said. "Pick up the goddamn *Washington Post* and see the guilt by association."

The President commiserated with Chuck about the newspaper stories linking him to Hunt, and Chuck continued to protest his innocence. "Do they think I'm that dumb?"

The conversation drifted. Then the President faced the issue squarely. "A lot of people think you ought to wiretap," he said.

"Well, they, I'm, I'm sure most people..." Chuck trailed off, not knowing how to respond to the President's blunt remark.

"Know why the hell we're doing it," the President picked up. "And they probably figure they're doing it to us, which they are." The President strongly believed this rationale for the hardball tactics—that he was fighting back against ruthless opponents.

"That's why they hired this guy [McCord] in the first place, to sweep the rooms, didn't they?" asked Nixon, aware that the Reelection Committee had taken precautions against being bugged.

"Yes, sir," Chuck answered, and he again insisted on his

ignorance. "Frankly, sir, I haven't got into the ultimate details that we want on this, but I assume he was hired to protect our own offices."

The President, displaying more knowledge of the facts than Colson, pursued the matter. He was worried about leaks. "You've got a goddamn person over there that's ratting on us. What do you think?"

Chuck speculated that Larry O'Brien had a clandestine pipeline into the Reelection Committee. The President wondered whether Committee secretaries might be the source. He then turned to "the real question," which he identified as the silence of the suspects in the case.

"Basically, they are all pretty hard-line guys?" he asked.

"Yes, sir," said Colson.

"If we are going to have this funny guy take credit for that..."

"You mean the one with Hunt?" Chuck interrupted. The President had been referring to Liddy, but Chuck was worried about Hunt. "I, I can't believe he's involved. He's, he's too smart to do it this way. He's just too damn shrewd, too much sophisticated techniques..."

"It doesn't sound like a skillful job," agreed the President. "If we didn't know better, you would have thought it was deliberately butchered." The clownish aspects of the Watergate "caper" were being ridiculed in the press, but the President was revealing his opinion that a double-agent theory would not work.

Colson, still anxious about Hunt, offered his theory that the men in jail pulled off the break-in without Hunt's knowledge. "...Then I figured maybe it's the Cubans that did it. Organizing it on their own."

The President warmed to this notion and backed off his

choice of Liddy, who had not yet surfaced in the press, as the culprit. A discussion of Cubans followed, in which Chuck and the President agreed that they are violence-prone and might do anything. "That's, great, great," the President concluded. "Well, and then too, of course, we are just going to leave this where it is, with the Cubans."

Colson, having rescued Hunt, turned to matters of strategy and warned the President against "the ITT mistake." He said it would be a great error to fight the Watergate charges head on, as we had done in the ITT scandal, because doing so would only feed the Watergate coverage in the press. He recommended ignoring Watergate.

"Mistake would be what?" the President asked.

"Mistake would be to get all of them zeroed in on it."

"Oh."

"Make a big case out of it."

"Oh, shit. I couldn't agree more."

"Go after it day in and day out."

"Yeah," said the President.

"Follow the every, uh, I'd say the hell with it, believe me."

The President concurred with the strategy. He endorsed it emphatically to the end of the conversation. "I'm not going to worry about it. The hell with it... At times, uh, I just stonewall it."

The "stonewall" strategy functioned from the very first episodes of the cover-up. It was instinctive, from the very top of the Administration to the bottom. It was also ad hoc, developed in small reactions to the flurry of each day's events. There was not time to take stock of the whole case or to plan a careful defense in the meticulous fashion of trial lawyers. Instead, we found ourselves trying to hold a line where we could. But the line could not be held at the Cubans and McCord; there was too much evidence implicating Hunt and Liddy. Almost immediately, we knew that the money used to pay for the break-in would be traced by the FBI to the Reelection Committee. We conceded that and worked toward two goals: to explain the use of the money by claiming that Hunt and Liddy had diverted the funds on their own for illegitimate purposes, and to keep the FBI from tracing the money backward from the Reelection Committee to its donors. Such a backward trace, we knew, could lead the FBI into what we called "other problems"—Campaign Act violations, unreported contributions, corporate contributions, secret contributions by nominal Democrats, and the like.

I began my role in the cover-up as a fact-finder and worked my way up to idea man, and finally to desk officer. At the outset, I sensed no personal danger in what I was doing. In fact, I took considerable satisfaction from knowing that I had no criminal liability, and I consistently sought to keep it that way. I wanted to preserve my function as an "agent" of my superiors, taking no initiatives, always acting on orders. In the process, I often found myself searching for alternatives that would keep me from taking dangerous steps. When Ehrlichman suggested I "deep-six" the sensitive materials from Hunt's safe by throwing them into the Potomac River, for instance, I delayed for several days, searching for an alternative. I did not want to disappoint Ehrlichman, but I did not want to take responsibility for destroying potential evidence. Finally I came up with what I thought was a clever idea—to give the documents directly to L. Patrick Gray III, the acting FBI director after Hoover's death. By this ruse, we could say we had turned all evidence over to "the FBI," and literally it would be true. At the same time, we felt we could count on Pat Gray to keep the Hunt material from becoming public, and he did not disappoint us.

On such half-truths I sustained the image of myself as a

"counsel" rather than an active participant for as long as I could, but the line blurred and finally vanished. I was too central a figure, and there was too much hasty activity required as the cover-up proceeded speedily along its two main themes containing the Justice Department investigation, and paying the hush money to the defendants. I am still not sure when I crossed the line into criminal culpability, when I failed in my efforts to protect myself, but I know that certain crucial events took place on park benches in meetings as covert as the microfilm exchanges in the spy movies.

Once, I met Pat Gray secretly at his home in southwest Washington. We were both apprehensive about the meeting as we walked to a park and sat down on a bench overlooking the Potomac, discussing my request to obtain the FBI 302s and AirTels on the Watergate investigation. I had remembered Liddy's advice about the 302s and the Air Tels, and I had raised the matter with Kleindienst, Petersen, Mardian, and Ehrlichman before asking Gray himself. On the park bench, I told Gray I needed the materials to keep track of the investigation's progress. He felt the pressure and asked for assurances that the President himself wanted the documents. I told him they would be used "for that purpose"—which was half true and half false, because I knew that the President would not take the time to sift through such documents. Gray gave in, consoling himself with the observation that the President is the nation's chief law enforcement officer and is therefore entitled to reports on all criminal investigations.

Making sure that the FBI did not surprise us was key to protecting the White House. When I learned, for instance, that agents wanted to interview the vacationing Kathleen Chenow, secretary of the Plumbers' Unit, about Howard Hunt's activities in the White House, I dispatched Fielding to England to get her. Fred brought Ms. Chenow back within twenty-four hours. Thus we could say we were actively "cooperating" with the investigation by producing the witness at our own expense.

143

But we were in fact afraid she might reveal damaging information if an FBI agent caught her by surprise. I got to her first and took advantage of the opportunity to advise her not to testify about "national security" matters, such as the Ellsberg break-in.

I met Herb Kalmbach on a park bench. He became the first of several fund raisers for the hush money which was the sustenance of the cover-up. The hush-money issue sharpened the divide between the White House forces, mainly Haldeman and Ehrlichman, and the Mitchell forces. No one wanted to handle this dirty work. Everyone avoided the problem like leprosy. Not surprisingly, the White House thought Mitchell should "take care of" the payments because he had approved the Liddy plan and because Liddy and McCord worked for Mitchell's Reelection Committee. Mitchell, on the other hand, believed just as strongly that the White House had created his dilemma by sending him Liddy and pressuring him for intelligence. Moreover, Mitchell felt the hush money would serve to protect not only himself but also the President from the "White House horrors" that Liddy and Hunt had carried out while working at the White House. I was with Mitchell in his office, looking out the window on Seventeenth Street at the Tax Court building, when he asked me to enlist Herb Kalmbach to raise and pay the "commitments." "John," he said, "you go back over to the White House and check this out." Then, in a low voice, "I think your people over there should be interested in having this problem solved, especially John Ehrlichman." I had no doubt what he meant. Mitchell wanted no part of the hush money—nobody wanted any part of it—but if he were forced to get involved he was determined not to carry the burden alone. He suggested Kalmbach, Nixon's attorney, as the fund raiser, knowing that Kalmbach would never accept the role without the explicit approval of Haldeman and Ehrlichman. I took Mitchell's proposal to both Haldeman and Ehrlichman. Neither liked it, but both approved it. Then I called Kalmbach, and our clandestine meetings began.

Kalmbach gulped and made sour faces upon learning of his assignment, but he accepted it. He knew it was vital for the President's reelection, and he was completely devoted to the President's service. With surprising aplomb, Kalmbach adopted the mannerisms of an amateur spy. After raising the first batch of cash, he called me to arrange a tryst. "Meet me in Lafayette Park," he said, and hung up. The President's personal attorney and the President's counsel met soon thereafter in the park and ambled casually to an unoccupied bench.

"It's done," Kalmbach said simply, sotto voce. We stared off at the feeding pigeons and he reached down to pat his briefcase softly. "I've got it right here." I was distressed at the thought of being so near the actual cash in a public place and quickly adjourned the meeting.

Kalmbach called again a few days later from California to report success—after many initial difficulties—in delivering the money to the defendants. He was calling from a pay phone which was "secure," and he had to interrupt the conversation several times to feed quarters to the operator. The paranoia had caught on.

"You can tell the Brush—" Kalmbach began mysteriously. "You know who I'm talking about?"

"Yes," I said, deciphering the makeshift code. This could only mean Haldeman.

"And you can tell the Pipe. You know who that is?"

"Yes." Obviously Mitchell.

"And you can also tell, let's see, we can call him Brows. Will that do?"

"Yes," I said. Ehrlichman's distinctive furrows made this one easy.

"Well, you can tell them it's all taken care of. The guy I'll call 'Mr. Rivers' has finally made contact with the Writer's

145

Wife. And he is giving her the Script." Translated, this meant that Caulfield's man Tony had given the hush money to Howard Hunt's wife.

"Right, I understand."

"Okay," Kalmbach said. "Good-bye."

The cover-up churned on through hundreds of similar episodes, and did so quite successfully.

I carried messages back and forth between the Mitchell faction and the White House faction. There was no love lost between them in the first place, and the Watergate recriminations made things worse. Neither side wanted to budge. Each side waited for the other to confess and shoulder the cover-up alone. The war of leverage dragged on.

My sense of guilt was to deepen as I lost the few remaining rationalizations that I was acting as a low-level agent. Everyone betrayed a sense of guilt in meetings. I had managed for a while to evade it by contemplating the startling boost that Watergate had given me into the inner councils. My adult life had been calculated blindly and shrewdly, I had always thought. I was now reaching the pinnacle. I was not the source of authority for the cover-up, yet I became its linchpin. I was the only one with the knowledge and personal rapport to reconcile the pitched camps at the White House and the Reelection Committee. I could feel my power growing in every meeting and each conversation as I went back and forth—resolving disputes between the warring factions and unwittingly linking and knitting them together in conspiracy.

146

CHAPTER FIVE:

CONTAINMENT

LATE IN JUNE 1972 I was summoned to Haldeman's office and found Ehrlichman there as well. Ehrlichman asked my advice as to whether Mitchell and Magruder should be removed from the Reelection Committee. I felt a surge of self-importance—unnoticed, I hoped—at the thought of sitting in judgment on a man of such consequence as Mitchell.

"It would be presumptuous of me to pass judgment on John Mitchell, but..." I began, and I cited persuasive reasons for removing both men which rested on a feeling that they might both be indicted.

A few days later Mitchell was gone. I was overruled on Magruder; my superiors feared that if fired he might break and end any chance for a successful cover-up.

I became possessed of the toughness I imagined generals display when called upon to sacrifice divisions and battalions for the overall effort. It is part of the game at the higher levels, I thought. And it is part of the game not to take such decisions personally. I began to take privilege for granted. I began addressing Mitchell by his first name, he was no longer "Mr. Mitchell." I started calling Haldeman regularly on his I.O. instead of going through the White House switchboard. Haldeman's staff switched me into the citadel of the executive mess, where I ate with the select potentates. White House functionaries sensed the new stature of the counsel. They no longer questioned my requests for air-travel expenses or limousine service. I was above the bureaucratic hassles.

Visions of my new role, and the heights it might lead to, extended to my personal life. I broke off with Maureen Biner, the woman I had been living with for the past two years. Our relationship and my love for her had been a godsend to me, but she wanted to get married and I did not. Not now. I was enticed by my prospects as a bachelor; I wanted no hindrances to my career. Maureen went home to California, and I resolved to conquer as many new women as time and power would grant. Henry Kissinger once remarked on power's properties as an aphrodisiac, and I found it true. At the time, it seemed like just compensation for the lonely burdens of state.

As the cover-up progressed through July and August, I was struck by its tremendous political success. Secret White House polls indicated that the Watergate break-in had not made the slightest dent in the President's popularity. Most voters questioned did not know about it, and the few who did said they didn't care. Public consciousness of the Watergate scandal was light-years removed from the reality I lived in the White House, and I conceived my efforts as having helped keep it that way. I was keeping Richard Nixon in office by keeping control of the Watergate investigations. We were way ahead of the FBI and the Justice Department, and, just as importantly, we had prevented their probes from uncovering any of the "other matters" on the fringes of Watergate. We were even further ahead of the press.

The elementary fact that the break-in had been financed with campaign funds did not hit the newspapers until August, and by that time we were prepared with the explanation of "diverted" funds. Hunt and Liddy were not placed at the scene of the break-in until late August, by which time we were prepared to make the claim that they were the ones who had diverted campaign funds to illegitimate uses. Many reporters seemed privately skeptical of this implausible story, and the White House press corps roasted Ziegler with hostile questions each day. I was amazed at how small a part of the hostility that Ziegler absorbed made it into print; the press seemed reluctant to take on the power of a President. The papers had carved up Senator George McGovern, the Democratic nominee, because his running mate had undergone psychiatric treatment. The Democratic campaign had fallen into disarray. I was sitting in an Administration in which a dozen high officials were guilty of criminal violations that I knew of, and I watched the President's lead in the polls climb steadily: roughly twenty points ahead in August and still rising.

On August 29, 1972, I was in San Clemente to report to Haldeman and Ehrlichman on cover-up matters. By then this seemed almost routine. The President was holding a news conference that day on the lawn of his Pacific estate. I was in my hotel room as it went on the networks, and I turned on my television set, listening with one ear as I worked. I remember hearing the President announce that he would not engage in televised campaign debates with Senator McGovern because such debates might be divisive to the nation in a time of delicate negotiations on the Vietnam War. This, I knew, was part of the "high profile" campaign strategy: he would ignore Senator McGovern, as he did Watergate, for as long as possible. The press conference dragged on through other matters of little concern to me. My attention snapped into focus, however, when a reporter asked a very polite question about Watergate: "Mr. President, wouldn't it be a good idea for a special prosecutor, even from your standpoint, to be appointed to investigate the contribution situation and also the Watergate case?"

I shifted quickly to a bed in front of the television. The President explained that a special prosecutor was absolutely unnecessary, because there were no fewer than five investigations already under way. He referred to the FBI "full field investigation," to inquiries under way by the Department of Justice, the grand jury, and the General Accounting Office, and to an incipient investigation by the House Banking and Currency Committee under the chairmanship of Representative Wright Patman of Texas. All these investigations, he said, naming them once more, had received "at my direction" the

149

"total cooperation...of not only the White House, but also all agencies of the government." I was stunned that the President had not ducked the question but had instead plowed into it with such bold lies. These investigations, plus several others, were precisely the ones I was spending most of my waking hours juggling and deflecting, containing them with stories and delay tactics. For a moment, I wondered whether the President might not really know what I was doing. My desire to believe any President, especially my own, was strong. No, I thought, Haldeman and Ehrlichman would never let him make such a strong statement without detailed discussions of its impact. This was hardball, it would probably work. I damn near fell off the bed at what I heard next. "In addition to that," the President continued, "within our own staff, under my direction, the counsel to the President, Mr. Dean, has conducted a complete investigation of all leads which might involve any present members of the White House staff or anybody in the government. I can say categorically that his investigation indicates that no one in the White House staff, no one in this Administration, presently employed, was involved in this very bizarre incident."

How about that? The President was mentioning my name! On national television. That, I thought, was a real vote of confidence. He was saying I could pull off the cover-up. I was ecstatic to be so recognized by the President before the world. I had never been certain the President even remembered he had a fellow named Dean as his counsel, given the negligible contact I had with him. Obviously, he knew how I had been busting my ass to keep this mess from spilling all over everyone, including him.

In a daze, I listened to the President push coolly and brazenly on to bury the Watergate affair as a campaign issue. John Mitchell, he said, had launched his own intensive Watergate investigation before retiring as campaign chairman. Careful, I thought, that might be going too far. He added that

150

Clark MacGregor, Mitchell's successor, was continuing the probe. All these investigations were laudable, said the President, because "we want all the facts brought out." Then he concluded, "What really hurts in matters of this sort is not the fact that they occur. What really hurts is if you try to cover it up."

I turned off the television. What a performance. That's what it takes to be on the first team. I thought of the millions of viewers who must have been nodding in agreement. What a reality warp. I knew its epic dimensions. I also knew that this knowledge was the key to my present success.

The fact that I had never heard of a "Dean investigation," much less conducted one, did not seem important then. I was basking in the glory of being publicly perceived as the man the President had turned to with a nasty problem like Watergate. The President's move suited me fine. Damn shrewd politically too, I thought, particularly the carefully worded touch he had given it by referring to those "presently employed." That was his fallback position in case former employees like Mitchell or Magruder should be indicted. We were trying desperately to prevent that.

The door to Ziegler's office from the hallway to the Press Room was always locked. Atop his other door, the working entrance, he had installed two small lights, one red and one white, mounted on a little gray electrical box attached to the framing. Ron controlled his stop light system with a switch on his desk, and anyone who trespassed through a red light could expect an outburst. I liked nothing better than to stick my head in his door when the red light was lit, wait for him to snarl and paw like a foul-humored lion, close the door, and go on about my business after a good laugh.

Shortly after the President's announcement of the "Dean investigation," I was summoned by a Ziegler secretary and given a "white light" reception. I entered, sat down, and waited for the press secretary to finish his telephone call.

"What can I do for you, Mr. Secretary?" I asked with a smirk.

"You want a drink?" he said, ignoring my sarcasm.

"No, it's against the law to drink in federal buildings," I said.

"I don't give a shit," he retorted as he got up to fix himself a Scotch. He flipped on the red-light switch and then zapped on his two televisions with his remote-control gadget. It was almost time for the evening network news.

"I'm getting a lot of heat out there about your investigation," he said, shaking his head toward the Press Room. "They want to read your report. They want to know when it was finished and who you talked to. Tell me, how did you report to the President?"

"Ron, I didn't."

He nodded. "Well, can I say it's an oral report?"

"Ron, there's no report."

"Well..." he paused. "Can I say there's a report still in progress? Are you still working on it?"

"No, I'm not."

"Well, I don't think I can just keep saying it was an internal study," he declared plaintively. "How should I handle it?"

"That's what you get paid that high salary for. You know as much about this report as I do." I left. Ehrlichman had long ago instructed me to tell Ziegler nothing, and I no longer feared retaliation from Ziegler for curt behavior. A touch of hubris had set in.

But there was a seed of doubt. Ziegler talked with me several times over the next week as he ducked, deflected, and stonewalled a barrage of press inquiries about the "Dean investigation." I began to have second thoughts about being publicly identified as the man who had established White House innocence on Watergate.

I raised the issue with Fielding. "Fred, let me ask you something. You know how this place operates. Do you think I'm being set up on this thing?"

"No," he replied. A perplexed look came across his face. "What do you mean?" Fred had been kidding me about "getting on with" the Dean investigation, and ribbing me about my sudden notoriety. He knew I liked it.

"Well, I'm not sure I like being thrown out in front like this. If something goes wrong, I could be the fall guy." I was thinking of Ehrlichman; I was certain that the President's announcement had been his idea.

"I don't think I'd worry about it, John," Fred said seriously. "It's just a PR move, like the death penalty statement." He was referring to a previous press conference at which the President, when questioned on the Supreme Court's death penalty decision, prefaced his answer by stating he had "just conferred with the counsel, Mr. Dean." He had not, of course, conferred with me and he never did, but no harm had come from the remark. I took Fred's advice and repressed my concern. I had no time for it, anyway.

The cover-up blistered on, with me throwing water on it. Each day brought threats, dramas, and more legal strategies. Clandestine conversations with Kalmbach and LaRue about hush money. Nervous sessions with Pat Gray, during which he would hand me his personal attaché case filled with FBI reports. Conversations with Paul O'Brien and Kenneth W. Parkinson, the Reelection Committee lawyers who were fighting to stall discovery proceedings in a civil suit filed by Larry O'Brien. Constant messages between Mitchell and the White House. Crisis calls from Colson and Mardian. Coaching sessions for the witnesses being interviewed by FBI agents or paraded before the grand jury. Reports from Henry Petersen on the status of the criminal case.

In late August, when the press uncovered the source of the money used to pay for the break-in, and the Reelection Committee's Finance Committee became the target of a long string of stories, its chairman, Maurice H. Stans, was named a principal defendant in O'Brien's civil suit. Treasurer Hugh Sloan was under attack for having passed money to Liddy on Stans's authority. Former general counsel Gordon Liddy was being painted as a wild man, a notion that was not discouraged by the White House. We wanted Liddy to sound like a man strange enough to have pulled Watergate off on his own.* The strategy worked, but the cumulative effect of the critical stories on the Finance Committee created "human problems" among the aides and secretaries. The Finance Committee became tainted. People were ashamed to say they worked there. Many of them grew resentful of the protection given the political people at the Reelection Committee, such as Magruder. Finance Committee workers generally feel trampled upon in campaigns, anyway. They watch the political people spend their hard earned cash like water, taking all the credit, always demanding more. We suspected that most of our adverse press leaks were coming from disgruntled Finance Committee employees.

The resentment boiled over when the President paid his first visit to the Reelection Committee offices. He gave a pep talk to the political employees, thanked them, and predicted victory, and his magic presence lifted their spirits. He did not so much as visit the Finance Committee, whose offices were on a separate floor. Within minutes of his departure, I received an

---

*   When writing *Blind Ambition* I still knew very little about Gordon Liddy. With time I would learn that the suggestion by Mitchell and Liddy, was, in fact, a self-promoting wild man, was strikingly close to the truth. I have addressed this in greater detail, now that I have a lot more information, in the Afterword.

154

angry call from Arden Chambers, Maurice Stans's secretary.

"John, a lot of people over here are outraged," she told me. "And so am I. The President didn't even wave at our door. He excluded us. And we're the ones who are getting all the bad press for the stupid things those people upstairs have done. We're the ones who do all the hard work, and they get all the credit. I think you ought to know a lot of people over here are very upset."

"Arden, I understand perfectly. I know just how you feel." I knew that nothing I could say would allay her anger. I told her I would see what I could do and apologized profusely.

It was time for some firefighting. I called Haldeman on the I.O. It could be explosive, I told him, if the finance people got mad enough to go public. They didn't know many of the Watergate details, but they surely knew what was going on both by instinct and by osmosis. I recommended a Presidential "stroking session." Haldeman agreed and told me to call Chapin and arrange a visit to the White House for Finance Committee employees. The President would meet them personally in the Roosevelt Room, shake hands, slap a few backs, renew their loyalty.

In the midst of this small crisis, and several others, the Justice Department announced the first Watergate indictments on September 15.[*] The fanfare was heavy; it had been preorchestrated. Kleindienst said the investigation was "one of the most intensive, objective, and thorough investigations in many years, reaching out to cities all across the United States as well as into foreign countries." The Justice Department said, "We have

---

[*] [Original Footnote:] A federal grand jury in Washington returned an eight-count indictment against the five men (Bernard L. Barker, Frank A. Sturgis, Virgilio R. Gonzalez, Eugenio R. Martinez, and James W. McCord, Jr.) arrested at the Democratic headquarters on June 17, plus Hunt and Liddy. The charges included tapping telephones, planting electronic surveillance equipment, and theft of documents.

absolutely no evidence to indicate that any others should be charged." * The new Reelection Committee chairman, Clark MacGregor,** called on "those who have recklessly sought to connect others with the case" to "publicly apologize for their unfounded charges." Senator Robert Dole, the Republican Party chairman, said the indictments proved "there is no evidence to substantiate any of the wild and slanderous statements McGovern has been making about many high officials in the Nixon Administration." Congressman Gerald R. Ford, the House Republican leader, said the indictments reinforced his "understanding that none of the people in the White House, in positions of leadership in the party or [in] the Committee to Reelect the President were involved."

I was pleased as I scanned the wire-service reports coming off the ticker machines down the hall from my office. They would be in every paper in the country by the next day, drowning out Larry O'Brien's reported complaint that the investigation had not gone far enough. Phase one of the cover-up was a success. The doors that led to Magruder, Mitchell, and many others were closed, at least for the present. I went back to my office, where Jane greeted me with a startling message.

---

* Remarkably, former Attorney General Kliendienst was never charged. His statement that the Justice Department had "no evidence to indicate others should be charged" was contradicted by his report to me of his meeting with Liddy, who told him that John Mitchell wanted him to release the men who had been arrested at the Watergate headquarters of the Democratic National Committee. In 1980, Liddy wrote his Watergate memoir *Will*, and described his meeting Kliendienst. Clearly Liddy provided the attorney general with hard evidence that Jeb Magruder, if not John Mitchell and the President, were involved. It also defies belief that Kliendienst was not aware of everything that his close friend Bob Mardian had learned, and Mardian—who was indicted and convicted (his conviction was later overturned on a technical matter on appeal)—knew everything.

** MacGregor did not know what had happened, and was smart enough not to ask, which is why he was sent over from the White House to replace Mitchell.

156

"The President wants to see you," she said. "Right now. In the Oval Office."

My stroking session, I figured, and a well-deserved one. As I headed toward the West Wing, I thought of my previous meetings with the President, in which I had been little more than an inert fixture as he signed his tax return, testamentary papers for his estate plan, or other legal documents. I used to joke that I was of far less concern to the President than the little bust of Lincoln he kept on his bookshelf. Other than for legal ceremonies, my contacts with the President had been fleeting and few. The only one I could remember during the previous year had been odd. An urgent call had summoned me to the Oval Office. I arrived, panting, and was ushered in. "John," said the President, "a bunch of long-haired college newspaper editors are coming in here in a minute. You and I will be discussing the budget." Aides were busy spreading budget documents out on his desk as the President fidgeted with his watch. I sat in silent bewilderment, I knew absolutely nothing about the budget.

"Oh, hi," said the President in surprise when the editors filed in. "John Dean, my counsel, and I were just discussing the budget." Then he gave a ten-minute performance on budget priorities and the complexities of government. The editors were ushered out, and so was I.

Later I talked to Haldeman. "Bob, why was I in that meeting?" I asked.

"Because the President thinks you look hippier," he replied matter-of-factly.

"You're shitting me!" I said, but I remembered the jokes about my Porsche and my refusal to wear an American-flag lapel pin when everyone else had eagerly followed the President's lead.

"No, I'm not," said Haldeman.

157

But after the Watergate indictments I was expecting to be treated with more dignity. A pat on the back, staged carefully to seem informal. Still, I wasn't sure. For all I knew, the President might have some garden club in his office.

I was not prepared for what I found. Haldeman was slumped in a chair in front of the President's desk, his yellow pad dangling from his hand rather than poised as usual for note taking. The President was reclining in his swivel chair at what seemed a precarious angle, his feet propped up on his desk to leave the Presidential heel marks. From his nearly supine position, the President looked at me through the V his shoes formed. I paused at the door, feeling like an intruder, and waited for Haldeman and the President to snap back into form. But they didn't, and I walked hesitantly to a chair. I wouldn't have been much more surprised by the atmosphere if the two of them had been wearing dresses. I was flattered to be so collegially received.

"Well, you had quite a day today, didn't you?" the President said cordially, still glancing at me through his feet. "You got Watergate on the way, huh?"

"Quite a three months," I responded, thinking back over the scramble. An awkward silent moment followed, because I didn't know what to add.

Haldeman, noting my uneasiness, rescued me. "How did it all end up?" he began.

"I think we can say..." What can I say? I wondered. What should I say? I thought of the wire-service stories I had just read. "Well, at this point, the press is playing it just as we expected."

"Whitewash?" Bob asked, suspecting the worst.

"No, not yet. The story right now—"

"It's a big story," the President interrupted. He swung his feet to the ground and brought his chair to its upright position.

He had become intent and sounded optimistic. It was important to the cover-up strategy that the press play up Hunt and
Liddy as big catches.

"That's good," said Bob, satisfied that the media were running the story as we wanted. "That, that takes the edge off
whitewash really...which...that was the thing Mitchell kept
saying, that to those in the country Liddy and, and, uh, Hunt
are big men."

"That's right," I agreed.

"Yeah. They're White House aides," said the President.

"That's right," I agreed again.

The President seemed pleased. He sensed his reelection
firmly within his grasp, and he initiated a bull session, opening
it with the use of wiretaps by his predecessors. He was toying
with the idea that a juicy revelation of political wiretapping by
a Democratic President might further bury Watergate, I
thought. He and Haldeman discussed whether to use information we had that President Johnson had ordered the Republican
campaign tapped in 1968. "The difficulty with using it, of
course, is that it reflects on Johnson," said the President.

"Right," I agreed, trying to sound tough and knowledgeable
about such matters. I was busy studying the tone and the mood
of the President.

"He ordered it," the President continued. "If it weren't for
that, I'd use it. Is there any way we could use it without
reflecting on Johnson? Now, could we say, could we say that
the Democratic National Committee did it? No. The FBI did
the bugging, though."

"That's the problem," said Haldeman.

"Is it going to reflect on Johnson or Humphrey?" I asked in
an attempt to offer an acute question. Since Johnson was
retired, I thought, maybe the bugging would reflect on his

Vice-President, who was still quite active.

"Johnson," said Haldeman emphatically. *"Humphrey* wouldn't do it." He intended it derisively.

"Humphrey didn't do it?" I asked.

"Oh, hell, no," said the President quickly.

"He was bugging Humphrey too," cracked Haldeman, breaking into peals of laughter. Bob liked dark humor; the idea of crafty old LBJ bugging his own Vice-President set him off.

"Oh, goddam," chuckled the President. I tried to join in the laughter, too, but I was embarrassed at having been so naive about Humphrey. It was clear the Senator was considered a babe in these woods.

I dropped out of the bugging discussion as the President told Haldeman to seek John Connally's advice as to how President Johnson, his fellow Texan, might react. Then he asked Haldeman if the revelation would also tarnish the image of the FBI. Haldeman said it would, and a brief discussion followed on the dangers of insulting the Bureau. Finally the President dropped the idea. "It isn't worth it, dammit," he said. "It isn't worth—the hell with it."

The rap session turned to other subjects. I reported on the status of the civil suit Larry O'Brien had filed against Maurice Stans and the Reelection Committee. The case looked under control, I said. It had been assigned to Judge Charles Richey, a Nixon appointee, who was sending encouraging signals through our contacts. The judge, I reported, had been so accommodating as to urge Stans to file a counter suit against O'Brien for libel. Stans had done so.

Alexander Butterfield, the President's executive-office manager, interrupted to tell the President he had a call waiting from Clark MacGregor. The President got on the phone and joked with MacGregor a bit before telling him to get on with the "big game," the campaign, now that Watergate was contained with the indictments. Haldeman and I twiddled silently while he was on the phone. I looked out the window at the dusk. This has already been a long audience, I thought. I noticed a greenish light reflected through the windows of the Oval Office and realized it was the effect of the special Secret Service bullet proofing.

My attention snapped back when I heard the President sign off with MacGregor: "...Anyway, get a good night's sleep. And don't bug anybody without asking me. Okay?" He hung up with a laugh. When he had finished signing several papers Butterfield had placed before him, he turned to me but said nothing, apparently waiting for me to say something.

I figured the meeting must be about over, so I tried to wrap it up. "Three months ago, I would have had trouble predicting where we'd be today. I think that I can say that fifty-four days from now [Election Day] nothing will come crashing down to our surprise." A pause.

"Say what?" mumbled the President, as if coming out of a dream. I realized that his mind had been off somewhere even though he had been looking directly at me. I repeated myself.

The President's concentration returned. He leaned back in his chair, said a few words, and propped his feet up on the desk again. To my surprise, the bull session resumed. "Awfully embarrassing," the President continued, shaking his head. "And, uh, but the way you, you've handled it, it seems to me, has been skillful, because you—putting your finger in the dikes every time that leaks have sprung here and sprung there." Haldeman had, clearly filled him in on how busy I'd been. He knew I would relish such praise from the President.

We rambled on about the remaining trouble spots, including the bruised egos over at the Finance Committee, and the proposed "stroking session." Suddenly, the President's mood darkened. He sat up again and set his jaw tightly. "They should just behave, and recognize this, this is, this is war!" His voice was low, but anger spilled out. "We're getting a few shots," he continued. "It'll be over. Don't worry. I wouldn't want to be on the other side right now. Would you? I wouldn't want to be in Edward Bennett Williams' position after this election."

"No, no," I agreed. Williams was representing Larry O'Brien in his lawsuit.

"None of these bastards," the President said, trailing off into a vague but bitter passion.

"He, uh, he's done some rather unethical things that have come to light already," I said, trying to pick up on the President's new mood.

"Keep a log on all that," Haldeman said tersely. The hostile side of his personality fit the President's like a glove.

"Oh, we are," I agreed, hesitating, "on these. Yeah."

"Because afterwards that is a guy..." said Haldeman.

"We're going after him," the President overlapped.

"...that is a guy we've got to ruin," said Haldeman.

The President's brooding anger caught me off guard. It was a Richard Nixon I had seen in the action memos that reached my desk, but that I had never heard personally. I tried to curry favor with him by joining in with the tenor of the conversation. "One of the things I've tried to do," I said, "is just keep notes on lots of people who are emerging as less than our friends." I figured he would like that even though my notes were only mental.

"Great," he said.

"Because," I went on, repeating what he had just said, "this is going to be over someday and there is going to be—we shouldn't forget the way some of them have treated us."

The President leaned forward and gazed at me intently. "I

162

want the most, I want the most comprehensive notes on all those who have tried to do us in," he instructed firmly. He punctuated his phrases by pointing his finger in the air. "Because they didn't have to do it."

"That's right," I agreed.

"They didn't have to do it," he repeated. He paused and looked off for a moment as if genuinely puzzled about why his opponents harassed him. Then he began thinking aloud. "I mean, if the thing had been clo—, uh, they had a very close election, everybody on the other side would understand this game. But now they are doing this quite deliberately. And they are asking for it, and they are going to get it! And this, this," he went on and abruptly stopped. The wave of anger passed over, and the President became suddenly composed again. He started in a new direction. "We have not used the power in the first four years, as you know." He looked at me for a response.

"That's right," I agreed.

"We have never used it. We haven't used the Bureau, and we haven't used the Justice Department, but things are going to change now. And they are going to change," he added to Haldeman for emphasis, "and they're going to get it, right?" Haldeman nodded his approval, and the President glanced at me.

"That's an exciting prospect," I remarked flatly, mustering my hostility toward those who threatened the cover-up. I was trying to sound like a vicious prize fighter and doing a poor job, but I seemed to be pleasing the President. I was taking each apple he handed me, polishing it, and passing it back.

I felt the anger in the room subside. We turned to remaining problems. Congressman Wright Patman's planned bearings on the Watergate money transactions posed the biggest obstacle, I informed the President. Maurice Stans had been

163

calling me regularly to express his fears about being called before Patman's committee.

The President recognized the gravity of this possibility. He informed Haldeman that we would have to lean on Jerry Ford to block the hearings. "This is the big play," he observed intently. "I'm getting into this thing, so that he, he's got to know that it comes from the top and that he's got to get at this and screw this thing up while he can, right?"

His subordinates agreed, and we discussed ways to enlist Ford's aid. When our orders had been made clear, business talk ended and the conversation again meandered. The President lectured me on the intricacies of the Hiss case. It was pitch dark when the meeting ended on a discussion of *Inside Australia*, a John Gunther book I was reading.[*]

My relationship with the President had changed dramatically. He had taken me into his confidence beyond my wildest expectations. I appraised my performance and chastised myself for having seemed naive and guppylike at times, but I knew I was learning. We would make it through the election, I calculated, and then maybe the whole Watergate mess would evaporate in the light of the President's renewed power.

As would be the pattern, I felt at my toughest and most hopeful after receiving a boost from Haldeman or the President himself. Away from them, however, disturbing events cropped up that fed my doubts about the ultimate success of the cover-up. Almost always they concerned the payment of money to the Watergate defendants.

Herb Kalmbach called a few days after my meeting with the President. He was no longer the nervous but willing

---

[*] While long fascinated by Australia, I did not manage to get myself inside until 2002, when I was invited to be the keynote speaker at the Syndey Book Festival. Nothing surprised me more during my visit than the number of people who had read *Blind Ambition*, and wanted me to sign their copy.

soldier, the inventive amateur spy. He was literally wasted. There was no energy in his voice. I knew why. Herb was being investigated by the FBI for his activities as paymaster for Donald Segretti, Dwight Chapin's campaign saboteur, at the same time he was raising and distributing the hush money. The pressures had taken their toll.

"I'm dropping out, John," he told me. "I've cleared it with Mitchell and Ehrlichman. I've had it. I'm coming to Washington, and I'd like to see you and LaRue." Herb was the first casualty of the cover-up, and he was bringing the money issue back to my desk like a bad penny.

"I want to give you fellows my final accounting," Herb told me and LaRue as we all took seats in my office, which by now had become a site for cover-up meetings.

"Herb, I don't think we need any accounting," I said, anxious not to hear the details.

"I know I don't need one," seconded LaRue. At Mitchell's request, Fred was about to assume Kalmbach's duties. He was somber, but less so than Kalmbach.

"Well, I want to clear the decks," Herb insisted. He reached into his back pocket for his billfold, opened it before us, reached with one finger into a hidden compartment, and extracted a tiny accounting sheet. Herb unfolded the paper and squinted unsuccessfully at his own microscopic writing. Then he put on his heavy, dark-framed reading glasses and read off the figures in detail. He had delivered some $220,000 in cash, mostly to Howard Hunt. "That's it," he said finally.

I looked at LaRue, who took his pipe from his mouth and said nothing. He shook his head slowly and seemed as staggered as I at the sum.

"Here, why don't you take this?" said Herb, handing LaRue the tiny ledger sheet.

Fred took it, placed his glasses on his forehead, and

frowned as he strained to read the minute print. Then he passed it back to Herb, saying he had no use for it.

"Well, let's destroy it, then," said Herb tightly, determined to rid himself of the burden. No one disagreed.

Herb reached for the clean ashtray on my desk, tore the note into small bits, and dropped them in. Then he took the matchbook lying beside my pack of Winstons and lit the shreds. The three of us silently watched the paper burn to ash.

"This," said Herb, "will officially end my assignment."

Fred stood up and said he had no idea where or how he would obtain the next batch of cash. On this note, he and Herb walked out of my office like pallbearers. Now Kalmbach was out; LaRue was in.

Such encounters deflated my confidence, but Haldeman usually pumped me back up. A few days after the Kalmbach ceremony, he saw me in the hall and invited me into his office for a chat. Bob had become very friendly and increasingly open. He had to make a few quick calls, so I wandered around his office examining his mementos. He had a beautiful tapestry from the China trip which I admired, but I soon returned to my favorite artifacts: the three dried bullfrog carcasses. They were gifts from Ehrlichman. As always, I picked up one of the mummified frogs to examine it. The bodies were shaped to depict various froglike activities—jumping, smiling, catching flies. I was absolutely mystified as to why Haldeman would have them on display or what Ehrlichman had in mind, although Higby had once said they had something to do with Haldeman's skills as a former campaign advance man.

Haldeman finished his calls and motioned me over to the easy chairs in front of his roaring fireplace. "Listen, I wanted to talk to you about something that came up when we were with the President last week," he began. "And that's these plans for after the election. This is something that's being held

166

very closely, John, and I think you'll understand why. I want you to make sure there's no legal problem in doing it. We are going to ask for the resignation of every single Presidential appointee as soon as the election is over. Every single one of them. And we're going to put our own people in there. Can you check it out for me?"

"Sure, Bob," I replied, swallowing hard. I was astounded. They're really going to do it, I was thinking—take control of the whole executive branch and pull the strings.

"Good," he said. "One other thing. I'd like you to stay on after the election, at least until we get Watergate resolved."

"I'll stay," I said, extending my commitment. My new status in the White House made it easier for me, but I knew I had no choice anyway. After the heavy publicity given to the "Dean investigation," I knew I would be grilled by Congressional investigators the minute I set foot out of the White House sanctuary.

"I'll get back to you on the resignations as soon as I search the law, Bob," I continued, "but I want to check with you about these Patman hearings. It's going to come to a head pretty soon. Patman's got to get his committee to vote him subpoena power, and it's a close question whether we have the votes to kill it. I've been talking to Bill Timmons[*] and Stans and Petersen on this thing, and Mitchell is working on it, too. We think we can give our guys a leg to stand on by telling them that an investigation will cause a lot of publicity that will jeopardize the defendants' rights in the Liddy trial. But that may not be enough. We really need to turn Patman off."

"Call Connally," said Haldeman. "He may know some way to stop Patman. And tell Timmons to keep on Jerry Ford's ass. He knows he's got to produce on this one."

---

[*]   [Original Footnote:] William E. Timmons was the new chief of White House liaison with Congress.

I left and called Connally, whom I'd met before he had been appointed Treasury Secretary. "The Governor," as some called him, had been one of the few high officials to dodge my conflict-of-interest clearance. He had taken a look at our standard questionnaire on financial holdings and decided to handle his own clearance.

"Governor, this is John Dean, over at the White House," I said bravely.

"Oh, yeah, John," he boomed warmly, as though I were an old friend. "What can I do for you?"

"Well, I was talking to Bob Haldeman, and he suggested I might call you about these Patman hearings. We need to find something to help us reason with the Congressman from Texas about how these hearings are not a good idea here before the election."

"Well, yes," he replied. "I believe I can think of something. I understand from the grapevine down in Texas that Patman might have a couple of weak spots, and one of them is he might have some campaign contributions he would not want exposed. Now, I believe I heard the Congressman received some contributions from an oil lobbyist up here. I don't believe Mr. Patman has reported them either."

"That's interesting," I said. Connally was not a man who needed to be led by the nose. "Do you have any idea how we might establish that for the record?"

"No, John, I don't believe I can help you there," he said, obviously not wanting to carry the matter further himself. "Why don't you just check into that and see what you come up with?"

"I will, Governor. Thank you."

"Any time, my boy."

Over the next several weeks, there was a good deal of activity to block the Patman investigation. I asked Ken Parkinson to check into the reported contributions of Patman and the other members of his committee. I was in touch with Mitchell, who told me he was working with "some Rockefeller people" to bring pressure on the New York members of the committee. I continued to urge Henry Petersen to write an official Justice Department letter objecting to the hearings on the grounds that the attendant publicity would endanger the rights of Liddy et al. Henry gave in finally, and soon all the Republican members of the committee began to make civil-liberty speeches about how they wouldn't vote to investigate Watergate because they wanted Liddy to get a fair trial. This was supremely cynical. We were trying to make Liddy, Hunt, McCord, and the Cubans the scapegoats for all of Watergate at the same time that we were blocking Patman with boundless professions of concern for their civil liberties.

Timmons, who met regularly with Jerry Ford, had explored with him Connally's suggestions about Patman. "What do you think?" I asked Timmons. "Do you think we ought to dig into this stuff? Parkinson sent me a file on what contributions these guys have reported."

"Well, John, you know, this is kind of *sensitive*," said Timmons, "and I talked to Jerry about it. Jerry doesn't think it would be such a good idea. And, frankly, I'll tell you the problem is that, uh, Jerry himself might have some problems in this area, and so might some of our guys on the committee. I don't think we ought to open this up."

"I see. I guess that scraps that."

"Yeah, I guess it does."

"Well, how does your head count look?"

"It's gonna be close, but I think we can pull it out. Jerry and Dick Cook [Timmons' aide] tell me they're sure every one of the Republicans is lined up. They're gonna march them into that committee room like cattle, all together. Nobody's gonna be off playing golf that day. But we still need some Democrats to carry the committee. I'm working on the Southerners. I think we can get a couple."

"Mitchell says he's gonna swing Brasco.[*] That's one Northern Democrat."

"Is he sure?"

"I'm pretty sure he is. Put him down. He'll either take a walk or vote with us."

"Okay, John. Let me know if you have any more names for my tally sheet. I'll stay on it. I think we're over the top."

More arm-twisting and back-room politics and Timmons reported we were safe. On October 3, the Banking and Currency Committee voted 20-15 to deny Chairman Patman subpoena power for his Watergate investigation. That ended any chance of a Congressional inquiry before the election, and the White House breathed a sigh of relief. Patman announced that he would proceed without subpoenas, but it was a futile gesture. He held a public hearing on October 10 and lectured four empty chairs with big name plates in front of them marked "Mr. Mitchell," "Mr. MacGregor," "Mr. Stans," and "Mr. Dean."

That day, Carl Bernstein and Bob Woodward broke a story in the *Washington Post* pinpointing Donald Segretti as a central figure in a "massive campaign of political spying and sabotage." This caused another scramble in the White House and more firefighting. Chapin, Kalmbach, and Haldeman had become vulnerable as well as Segretti. After a quick round of investigative phone calls, we assembled our position. On substance alone, we were tempted to fight the story openly. It

---

[*]   [Original Footnote:] Representative Frank J. Brasco of New York.

had portrayed Segretti as the point man of a brownshirt horde, which we knew was grossly inaccurate. Liddy, maybe. But not Segretti. He was a prankster who wore Weejuns, not jackboots. But some of his pranks were tasteless; many were funny, and some were cruel. I searched the statutes and reported that he had broken no laws except some technical and generally ignored provisions of the campaign laws and that these violations were only misdemeanors. But we couldn't use it. If we produced Segretti to rebut, he would lead straight to Kalmbach's financial dealings in other areas. It would lead into the White House through Chapin and Haldeman. Furthermore, if we allowed Segretti to speak openly we would not be able to explain why we were not equally forthcoming in the Watergate investigation. So we had to stonewall the Segretti allegations too; he was told to disappear until after the election.

The Segretti story did not stem the Nixon election tide, but it ruined my wedding. I had grown weary of playing the high-powered bachelor in the limousine, especially as I felt the cover-up tighten the screws. I became lonely and realized that I had made a mistake by letting Maureen go home to California. I loved her. The decision to propose was a difficult one to make. My first marriage had broken up at least partly because I had put my career first. Now I was locked in the White House and it took some mental gymnastics to convince myself I would not repeat the mistake. When I proposed to Maureen on the telephone, I made myself warn her that life with me would be no bed of roses until after the election. If things held together until then, I said, I could probably demand and get any post I wanted in the government. At the time, I was thinking about an ambassadorship to a small French-speaking country somewhere. Certain doubts nagged me to tell Mo that there was a slight chance of rough sledding even after the election, but I minimized the fear and failed miserably to prepare her for what lay in store for her. When Mo accepted, I cleared my plans with Haldeman, of course, and we were married right in the middle of the Segretti chaos. Just as we arrived in Key

171

Biscayne for our first-class honeymoon, Haldeman called me back to Washington for more stonewalling.

As expected, Judge Richey had obliged the White House by ordering a halt in the civil proceedings of Larry O'Brien's suit against the Reelection Committee, citing the same logic we had employed to kill the Patman hearings—the publicity might deprive Liddy and the others of a fair trial. We would be safe through the election, but now we decided to make an effort to use our advantage to get the whole matter dropped. O'Brien was to be the fulcrum. Ehrlichman had pressured the IRS into a tax audit of O'Brien, and it had produced evidence that he had a six-figure annual income far exceeding the salary of the chairman of the Democratic National Committee. The purpose of the audit was both to trace the sources of his income, in hope of documenting his retainer from Howard Hughes, and to find some tax deficiency for which he might be prosecuted. Either success would produce a counterscandal to Watergate.

"I'm going to call Dwayne Andreas* for Maury [Stans]," Mitchell told me. "And I'll tell him to pass the word to Mr. O'Brien that we might find a way to end the nuisance of his tax problem if he can find some way to end the nuisance of his lawsuit. I think he'll recognize this might be a very satisfactory solution to a tough problem for everyone."

I had been trying to pressure O'Brien myself, by urging the Reelection Committee lawyers to inform O'Brien's lawyers that we would seek information about his sources of income in our own discovery proceedings. I had told the President of this fact, aware of his long interest in O'Brien's relationship with Hughes, and he had seemed pleased. But Judge Richey had

---

*   [Original Footnote:] A Minneapolis businessman who had made large contributions to Hubert Humphrey's past campaigns and a $25,000 contribution to the 1972 Nixon campaign. The Nixon contribution had passed through the bank account of Watergate conspirator Bernard Barker.

halted the proceedings before anything could be done. From what I'd learned of the Democratic chairman, I was sure he would not enjoy an intensive discovery proceeding. I was curious to hear whether he would accept Mitchell's offer.

A few days later, Mitchell reported back. "I called Andreas," he said, "and he told me O'Brien is very interested in working something out, but can't do anything. He says the lawsuit is beyond his own control, because he's got so many co-plaintiffs in with him. The Democratic state chairmen and so forth. He can't make a move by himself. So that's out."

After several other legal maneuvers, we decided to let the stalemate ride out. I kept at it furiously, counting down Election Day. The hatches stayed battened down on the FBI, the lawsuits, the Justice Department, the Congress, the GAO, and even the press, everything except the defendants' demands for hush money.

In mid-October, Chuck Colson's secretary stopped me in the hall to complain that Howard Hunt's wife had been calling her at home, demanding that the "commitments" be honored. Colson wouldn't take any calls himself, she said, wouldn't even listen to the messages. He simply told her to pass them to me. I told her not to take any more calls herself and to get an unlisted phone number. I didn't want to hear about the demands either. Still they would not go away. Later in October, I stopped by Fred LaRue's office and found him stewing with Paul O'Brien over how to pass Fred's first payment to Hunt's lawyer. Caulfield's man Tony had dropped out of the picture along with Kalmbach, and Fred was at a loss for a safe way to deliver the money. O'Brien paced the small room, his trench coat flung over his shoulder. I suggested the mails. LaRue asked me to enlist Kalmbach for one more drop. Impossible, I said. Fred finally decided to send "the package" to Hunt's lawyer by commercial messenger.

Finally, Election Day 1972. Oddly, the celebration of the

President's landslide seemed little more than a good excuse to drink with friends. The entire senior staff at the White House assembled droopy eyed and hung over the next morning in the Roosevelt Room, a conference room about the same size as the Cabinet Room. I sat in a corner, one of the few people in the room who knew that the ax was about to fall. We rose to our feet to applaud when the President walked in, looking drawn and haggard, not particularly happy, acknowledging our tribute with a mechanical smile, motioning us to be seated.

"This is a great day," he said flatly, standing with his hands on the back of a chair, "and I want to thank every one of you for your outstanding contributions to the best and most successful campaign I have ever seen. And I've seen a lot of them. Pat and I thank each and every one of you from the bottom of our hearts." Polite applause. The President offered more congratulatory remarks and then served up the heart of his message. "I was reading Disraeli the other night," he said, "and Disraeli spoke of how his administration of the British government lost its spark after being reelected. The campaign took too much out of them, he said. They became a 'burned-out volcano,' fresh out of ideas and energy. Well, I thought about that, and I pledged to myself that no such thing will happen to this second administration. I am not a burned-out volcano, and the second administration will not become one, either. We are going to inject new vigor and new energy into the government. We have no choice but to do that. Our opportunity is too great. Our responsibility is too great. The American people have just spoken and given us a tremendous mandate, a vote of confidence and hope. We can build a generation of peace, with prosperity, in America, and we are going to get on with the job. Now Bob is going to talk to you about some of the specifics. I want to thank you all again." The President smiled and departed, to another standing round of applause.

Bob moved to the head of the table and, never long for

words, went straight to the point. "As the President indicated, some things are going to change around here. I want you all to send me a written description of the responsibilities your office now has, plus a description of the responsibilities you would like to have in the second administration, and the reasons you think you should have them. Now, don't get carried away on the reasons you think you are qualified to handle everything. Make it simple. We can get your flowery reasons later, if we need them." Bob laughed nervously at his joke, coughed when it didn't go over, and composed himself for his important lines. "Now, the President and I are meeting with the Cabinet shortly. We are going to direct them to obtain written letters of resignation from all appointed sub-Cabinet officers in the government and submit them along with their own resignations. And the President has directed that everyone in this room also hand in a letter of resignation. This doesn't mean that you won't be asked to stay on, of course. We will review each situation individually. We just want to show we mean business." And he departed for the Cabinet meeting.

All the President's men and long-time servants had been fired at the post-landslide thank-you meeting. The news hit with a thud, leaving a few seconds of silence before the Roosevelt Room buzzed with shock, complaints and outrage. I slipped out. I was unaffected, secure on the inside.

Ehrlichman stopped me by the elevator. "Well, John, what are your plans for the future?" he asked. I was being tested to find out how much Haldeman had told me.

"Well, Bob's left no doubt in my mind what my plans are," I replied steadily. "I'm going to stay on until we put Watergate to bed."

The eyebrows arched moderately as he nodded a slow affirmative. "I understand."

I hurried back to my office for a strategy session with Fielding. Fred would have to prepare the memo Haldeman had demanded, because I was leaving that afternoon for a California vacation. We scanned the jurisdictional horizons in the White House and prepared a long laundry list of new functions we thought the counsel's office should be awarded. We would not try to take over entire operations, just get a foot in the door everywhere to continue to build the counsel's law firm in our pattern. Riding high from cover-up success, I was not bashful in our requests. We asked for the right to approve the appointment of general counsels to all government agencies and departments, so that we could put our own people in these crucial positions. We asked to be designated the official White House liaison office for all the regulatory agencies. We added a lot of clearance functions, legal powers, and perquisites. We were to get most of them.

As I was preparing to dash to the airport, a fearsome Watergate thought bubbled up. I called Haldeman. "Bob, I've been thinking about those resignations. There's one guy we can't afford to piss off. One guy we need, who's been helpful, concerned, and who's been watching out after our interests. And that's Henry Petersen. I don't think we should let Henry worry about his future."

"Yeah," said Haldeman. "I agree."

"I'd like to call Henry and reassure him he's all right." Haldeman assented readily.

When I called Petersen, he had just gotten his bad news from Kleindienst. "Jesus Christ, John!" he said. "Has the President gone crazy? He can't just throw everybody out in the street like this! Waste everybody's damn career. He'll screw up the whole government. I tell you, he'll regret this."

"Henry, I just want you to know one thing," I said soothingly. "You don't have anything to worry about. I don't know about everybody else, but I know you're not going to lose your job."

"Well, goddam, I'm glad to hear that." I felt a breath of uncertain relief wafting through the line. "Are you sure?"

"Yeah. I just talked to the people over here. Things are all scrambled up here too. But you're solid. You don't have anything to worry about."

"Thanks, John. But I still don't like this. You've got a lot of good people upset over here. Is Dick going to get canned?"

"I don't know about that. It's too early to tell. I doubt it. But you're the only one I've checked on." I signed off. I had chalked up points with both Haldeman and Petersen.

Mo and I flew off to Palm Springs in a second attempt to mix a honeymoon with a little work. Donald Segretti had wound up his elusive travels hiding in the California desert, and I was to obtain a comprehensive report on his activities for Haldeman and Ehrlichman, who now wanted to surface Segretti in the afterglow of the election and then quickly bury him. Otherwise, I planned to bask in the sun for a couple of weeks and forget Watergate. The story had vanished from the newspapers, which were full of the historic landslide.

Segretti came from seclusion to our villa in the Eldorado, an exclusive Palm Springs country club. He was glad to see someone from "the outside world," a bit sheepish about all the worry he had caused but puckish as always. "John, the best idea you had for me was the train trip across the country," he reminisced. "I really enjoyed that. I looked out the window the whole way. But the worst was coming out here to the desert. I ended up in a sleeping bag every night, and every morning I would wake up with the dew soaked through the sleeping bag and all in my clothes. It was miserable. Ugh!" He scrunched up his nose in disgust and then broke into a grin. His ordeal had paid off, and now it was over.

Don and I sat in front of a tape recorder for several hours as I elicited a description of his campaign activities and his

177

relationship with Chapin, Strachan, and Kalmbach. When we finished, he went off and Mo and I settled down to enjoy our honeymoon.

It didn't last long. One of Ehrlichman's assistants called soon after from Key Biscayne to say that Haldeman and Ehrlichman wanted to listen to the tape. Immediately. To Mo's amazed disappointment, we found ourselves in Florida the next day.

Haldeman and Ehrlichman sat through a complete rendition of the recording. "It could have been a lot worse," said Bob as I was packing up the equipment. "In fact, it's not nearly as bad as I imagined. As far as I'm concerned, we could air that thing on CBS tonight and get it over with. Most people think that a lot worse things than that went on."

Haldeman was looking on the bright side, but Ehrlichman was handling the case. "John, the President has decided Chapin has to go," he said bluntly. "He doesn't want this stuff hanging over his head in the second term, and as long as Dwight stays at the White House he's a lightning rod for bad press."

"I'm too close to Dwight to make an objective judgment," Haldeman added painfully, appearing embarrassed not to support his man more forcefully.

I went back to my room, my mind stuck on the decision Ehrlichman and the President had made about Chapin. It seemed callous and unfair. No one, I knew, was more loyal personally to Richard Nixon than Chapin, who virtually worshiped the President. And no one would be more at a loss outside the White House. The high point in Chapin's life had been making the arrangements for the China trip, and now he was on the way out. I had seen and been party to many callous decisions, but Chapin was different to me. He was a friend, and he had done only what was expected of him. His errors were minor. Somehow the decision to can him brought home a fact of life at the White House: everyone is expendable.

Mo accepted the demise of our second honeymoon stoically, and our spirits brightened when Haldeman arranged for us to ride back to Washington with the President aboard Air Force One. On the flight, the First Lady got down on all fours to play with the dogs, and the President himself came back and introduced himself to Mo. She was thrilled that the newly reelected leader of the Western world had taken the time to say nice things to her, and I was proud. The President cuffed me playfully, but a bit painfully, about the ears.

"We're going to keep your husband damn busy," he told Mo.

"I hope not too busy," Mo remarked.

"You may wish you hadn't married him," the President teased.

She smiled. "I'm not worried."

I wasn't, either, flying at thirty-five thousand feet with the President. But I soon would be.

CHAPTER SIX:

CLOSING IN

MONDAY, NOVEMBER 13, six days after the election, I was back in my office, still a bit depressed about the vacation that had been cut short. The papers were busily forecasting Nixon's second term—the negotiations that would be required to end the Vietnam War, détente with China and the Soviet Union. There were long profiles on the President's career and cameos of the First Family. On the outside everything was glowing. I was forcing myself sourly through my mail when Chuck Colson called.

"John, can you come down right away? I've got something to tell you." He sounded excited and happy. I hoped for some good news as I walked down the hall to his office.

He was leaning back in his chair with a big smile on his face. "Hiya, John. Come on in and sit down. I want to tell you about a conversation I just had with Howard Hunt."

It was not a name I liked to hear. I sighed and raised my eyebrows. "You talked to Hunt?"

"Yeah, I really had to," Chuck said, "because the poor guy's been calling and I've been refusing his calls all this time, and I figured I had to talk to him now that the election's over."

"What did he have to say? I hope you didn't promise him a job."

Chuck ignored the parry. "Well, he had a lot to say, but I'll tell you one thing he said. He said I had nothing to do with Watergate." Chuck paused, the smile turned sheepish. "In fact, I felt I had to tape the conversation for my own protection, and I did. Holly's typing it up right now, and I'm going to send it down to you, but you can hear it now if you want to."

"Sure."

I listened apprehensively. The tones were clear as the men exchanged pleasantries. Colson told Hunt straightaway that he didn't know anything about Watergate, that he had stayed out of it at the White House so that he could be an enthusiastic, honest, and favorable character witness at Hunt's trial. "This way the less details I know of what's going on in some ways the better." Old hear-no-evil Colson, I thought. I can't blame him. Hunt didn't deny it. Chuck looked up with satisfaction. "Hear that?"

But Hunt was shrewder than that. He bore in on Colson, demanding a meeting. Chuck's breathy voice sounded exasperated as he turned down the requests, but Hunt pressed on to say what was really bothering him.

HUNT: Well, the reason I called you was to make, to get back to to the beginning here, is because commitments that were made to all of us at the onset have not been kept. And there's a great deal of unease and concern on the part of the seven defendants and, I'm quite sure, me least of all. But there's a great deal of financial expense that has not been covered and what we've been getting has been coming in very minor dribs and drabs. And Parkinson, who's been the go-between with my attorney, doesn't seem to be very effective. And we're now reaching a point of which—

COLSON: Okay. Don't tell me any more. Because I understand, and—

HUNT: These people have really got to—this is a long-haul thing and the stakes are very high. And I thought that you would want to know that this thing must not break apart for foolish reasons.

181

COLSON: Oh, no, everybody—

HUNT: While we get third, fourth-hand reassurances, the "ready" is still not available. That's the basic problem.

COLSON: Okay. You told me everything I need to know, and I can—the less I know really of what happened, the more, more help I can be to you.

HUNT: All right. Now, we've set a deadline now for close of business on the twenty-fifth of November for the resolution on the liquidation of everything that's outstanding. And this, they're now talking about promises from July and August. It has just been an apparent unconcern. Of course, we can understand some hesitancy prior to the election, but there doesn't seem to be any of that now...

Hunt continued to make demands, skirting Chuck's protests. As he upped the ante, he destroyed the thin hope I'd clung to that Watergate would go away. It would get worse, I saw, and it could go on forever. I had suppressed this worry by my faith in the President's immense powers. But Hunt was out there watching his life being destroyed, and he was going to cost the White House plenty. The bottom of my stomach fell out, as it does when I look down from the top of a skyscraper.

I had trouble concentrating on the rest of the tape. "Say no more," Chuck kept telling Hunt, steering him back to safer subjects. Finally he got Hunt to say that Colson had "absolutely nothing to do with" Watergate.

Chuck lit his pipe, looking pleased. "Well, I guess this establishes once and for all that I had nothing to do with this crazy goddam break-in."

I glanced at him. We had been on opposite ends of a see-

182

saw during the last minutes, Chuck up, me down. As with everyone who was thinking, writing, or worrying about Watergate, Chuck's attention was riveted on what had happened before the break-in—who knew about it in advance, who authorized it and paid for it. I was worried about what had happened afterward, and I knew the tape was deadly. I looked at Colson gravely. "Chuck, I don't think you ought to have that tape typed up."

Colson's smile vanished. We both knew Hunt was a time bomb. We had just heard the ticking. Chuck liked to pretend he knew nothing of the cover-up and had succeeded in keeping himself out as best he could. "I understand, John," he said evenly. "Look, why don't you just take the tape for now? It's in your area. But don't lose it, dammit, 'cause I want it back. I want this on record. Okay?"

"Sure, Chuck. I'll get it back for you." I was surprised. The tape exonerated him from one crime and implicated him in another. Neither of us could know that Colson could be indicted on the basis of that conversation with Hunt, and both of us still wanted to think of ourselves as mere messengers.

In my office, I stewed about how I would bring this unwelcome news to the attention of Haldeman, Ehrlichman, and Mitchell. I stared at the Dictabelt record for a long time, turning it over in my hands, trying to figure out what to do with it. Finally I decided to make a copy for myself in case Chuck did ask for it back. I didn't want anyone to hear it, even my secretary, so I made a crude copy by playing the belt onto a recording machine.

I arranged to meet Haldeman and Ehrlichman, and the next day I was in a White House limousine on my way to Camp David, where everybody was busily consumed with plans for the second term. Walter Minnick, a lawyer on Krogh's staff, rode with me and described the reorganization that was being mapped out at Camp David. The executive branch would be controlled from the White House. Working for Ehrlichman, Minnick was trying to find a way to implement the plan without having to go to the Congress for approval. I was peeved, though not surprised, that Ehrlichman had excluded me from the legal work, but Minnick was assuming that I knew the details, and I did not disabuse him. The top Administration appointees were being helicoptered to Camp David, one after another, to be briefed about the President's new tough terms of service. They could keep their jobs only if they agreed to live by the cardinal rule—the White House was to call all the shots.

It all made sense, I was thinking; the flow of power into the White House had been a gradual process during the first term—in fact, during the last forty years. It was tested and proven. Minnick had been part of the pattern in the first term. He and Krogh had run the government's anti-narcotics campaign from the White House, once Ehrlichman had wrested control from Mitchell.

The only time I'd met Minnick before was at an odd meeting a few months earlier when Krogh had called me in and treated me to a mysterious denial that the White House narcotics office had been involved in the assassination of drug traffickers in Latin America. I had puzzled over what this bit of theater meant. No such story had appeared in print, and none ever did. But the episode piqued my curiosity about the drug program. Krogh had described to me how, when he was bored with his desk work, he had carried bars of gold bullion through Asia's "Golden Triangle" in CIA planes and bargained with drug chieftains. There were rumors of bombing poppy fields, and once Bud had asked my office to resolve a dispute among the Pentagon, the State Department, and the Bureau of Narcotics over the legality of kidnapping drug traffickers abroad. If the goal was worthy, the means were secondary, the thinking went, and there was a firm conviction that agencies outside the White House could not be trusted.

Gordon Liddy had received his White House indoctrination

in this very drug program, and he had read the signs clearly. Years later I would learn that the remarkable intelligence force he had described in Mitchell's office was only a part of his dream to build a clandestine police force for the White House. He and Hunt had recruited hundreds of operatives—most had had CIA training—and had promised them service after the election.

As I rode along, I was thinking that the reorganization seemed a quantum leap in the trend toward centralization, but it was obviously also Ehrlichman's consummate power play. He would become, in effect, chief executive of domestic affairs, because Nixon did not interest himself much in such matters and ordinarily deferred to Ehrlichman's judgment.

"Well, this tape is a beauty," I sighed to Haldeman and Ehrlichman when we were alone in the President's Laurel Lodge, an office he seldom used. It was almost bare except for an American flag and a Presidential flag on either side of an empty desk. There were two chairs and a sofa. "I'm kind of surprised Chuck even talked to Hunt, but you might as well hear straight from Hunt how much of a pain in the ass he's going to be. I'm sorry about this recording. I had to do it myself, and I was interrupted by a lot of phone calls while I was doing it. You'll hear some overlaps and repeats, but the gist is here." I was apologizing. I knew how intolerant Haldeman was of any sort of mechanical imperfection. He'd made cracks about my recording of Segretti.

We listened in silence to Hunt's ghostly voice foul the post-election euphoria. Ehrlichman doodled. Haldeman winced during the money talk, smirked at Colson's energetic efforts to parry Hunt's cover-up messages, and laughed aloud as Hunt called Mitchell a perjurer. Then I awaited my instructions. There was no jolly rehash, as there had been after the Segretti tape. No one was eager to discuss the money.

"Well, I can understand why Chuck let you have this tape,"

Haldeman said finally. "It sure as hell's self-serving for him. Colson's no fool."

"Yeah, I know," I replied. "He's proud of it." Haldeman, like Colson, remained fixed on what had happened before the break-in.

Ehrlichman was closer to the point. "Why don't you have our friend John Mitchell take care of Mr. Hunt's problem? He's got a lot of free time up there in New York making money."

"I'm going up to New York this afternoon with Maury Stans," I replied, "and I'll play this for Mitchell. I don't think he's going to be too happy about it."

"Well, he's a resourceful man when he has to be," said Ehrlichman. "Let us know how it comes out."

The conversation ended. I had wanted instructions, some guidance. Haldeman and Ehrlichman wanted to make Howard Hunt go away with sheer willpower. If anything, Ehrlichman was even more curt than before as he tossed the albatross back to Mitchell. He was riding high and was totally absorbed in the reorganization; Hunt was a gnat buzzing in his ear.

"Well, I'll leave it with you fellows," Haldeman said brusquely, rising. "I've got to go talk to our noble Vice-President."

As Haldeman headed for the door, Ehrlichman turned to me. "Your old friend Dick Kleindienst was up," he said, referring to the Camp David shuttle.

"Is he going to stay on?"

Haldeman stopped at the door. "Yeah. We're going to keep him on until some of this stuff is all cleared up. We'll keep him another six to eight months."

"I think that's good," I said to Haldeman, but I was talking to the door. He was gone.

I packed up the recorder, which was all I had in my attaché

case, and Ehrlichman and I got ready to rejoin the others, who were waiting to make a move with Ehrlichman to let him know I would not be so easily left out of the reorganization scheme. "Say, John, I was talking to Walt Minnick on the way up here about the reorganization. It sounds pretty impressive."

Ehrlichman raised his eyebrows slightly and nodded. I assumed he was not happily surprised that Minnick had told me about the project. "I think it will make the birds sing," he said quietly.

"I do, too, but I think you've got some legal problems to deal with that belong in the counsel's office." I hinted at some of the technical points governing reorganizations of the executive branch. I was indirect. I was sending signals: this was my turf. I knew how to solve Ehrlichman's problems, while Minnick was coming in cold.

"Yeah, I think you might be able to help," Ehrlichman replied without enthusiasm.

"Okay," I said, knowing that he had little choice so long as I was carrying his burdens on the cover-up. "What do you think we should tell the others out there about our little meeting in here?"

"Well, why don't we tell them we were discussing the reorganization?" Ehrlichman replied. "Which we were."

We returned to the group and gossiped some. I was satisfied when Ehrlichman suggested that Minnick consult me on the legal arrangements for the reorganization. I had the White House switchboard track down Maurice Stans in Washington and told him I'd missed the flight to New York we had planned on. He said he'd wait for me and we'd take a later plane, and I dashed off to my limousine.

Stans was waiting in his limousine at the entrance to the White House. On the way to the airport, he kept glancing at his watch. Stans is a man who glances frequently at his watch.

His precision had earned him a place in the Certified Public Accountants' Hall of Fame, as well as the standing one-year record for political fund raising estimated at around $50 million.

"Have you ever thought about getting one of those computer watches?" I asked.

"Yes, as a matter of fact I looked at them, but decided against it."

"Why?"

"Because it takes two hands to operate them. When I'm meeting with someone and want to sneak a look at my watch, I don't want to be conspicuous." He showed me how noticeable it would be to press a button on his watch to make the time light up. "And I'm often carrying a stack of papers in one hand, and that would make it tough to check the time if I was on the run."

Stans was the only Administration official who could have tutored Bob Haldeman on efficiency. He was proud of his fund-raising technique, inviting comparison with the work of Herb Kalmbach, his only rival. He would tell wealthy targets that they owed the President a fixed percentage of their income and that he was there to collect. It was insurance, or it was a necessary business expense to keep the right President in office. The ship was sailing, Stans never gave them enough time to think about it. Kalmbach took a seductive, bonhomie approach, loosening his targets by alluding to his intimacy with the President and telling a few jokes. Herb had elevated fund raising to a fine-arts craft. Among his props was a small notebook filled with his joke collection which he consulted before each appointment, choosing items to suit the customer.

As the plane took off, Maury pulled out his attaché case and reviewed his personal reminder list, his own tickler. As fast as he checked one item, he added another. We chatted about the reasons I was along. He was going to see Mitchell to discuss closing down the Finance Committee. He was under pressure to disclose the names of Republican contributors because of a suit by Common Cause, a vigorous citizens' lobby. While Stans talked, I was wondering whether he was going to lay a new cover-up disaster at my door. If so, I knew it would be a whopper. Maury was one person I had never needed to fret about. He could take care of himself. I was relieved when he returned his notes to his attaché case and fished out a copy of *Playboy*.

"You read that?" I asked.

"Sure," he answered with a smile, "and I look at the pictures too." I was embarrassed when he asked me if I wanted to have a look. I liked the pictures well enough, but I didn't have the nerve to display them on American Airlines. I relaxed. Maury eased the tension I felt as I thought about the Hunt tape in my attaché case.

Since Stans had provided our transportation to the Washington airport, I reciprocated in New York. It was now nothing for me to have my secretary call the Secret Service and have agents meet my plane, take me to my appointment, and return me to the airport. I was assigned jurisdiction over the Secret Service in the post-election shuffle at the White House: another score for the counsel's office.

We proceeded to the conference room he had reserved at the Metropolitan Club, a decorous relic from another era. The room was spectacular—high ceilings, faded walls, a huge fireplace with a massive baroque mirror over it, and a conference table that could comfortably handle dozens. When Mitchell arrived, the three of us met around it. Stans ran swiftly through his checklist and then left. His departure spared me an awkward moment; I hadn't wanted him around when I broached the subject of Hunt with Mitchell.

"John, we've got a problem with Hunt," I began. "Now

that the election's over, he's turning the screws." While I opened my attaché case I described Colson's call and how I'd recorded it. "I'll let you hear this for yourself. I played it this morning for Bob and John, and they told me to bring it to you."

Mitchell chuckled. "Hmm, I'll bet they did."

He listened to it impassively, breaking his silence only to protest Hunt's remark that he had committed perjury. "I don't know what the hell Mr. Hunt is talking about on that," he said angrily, and then settled back for the remainder of the tape.

"That's sweet, isn't it?" I remarked, trying to lighten the load I had just dumped on him.

"I'll say." Mitchell rose slowly. "You have any good news?"

"I do, as a matter of fact. Haldeman and Ehrlichman told me this morning that they're going to keep Dick on as Attorney General."

"That's kind of them," Mitchell said with a bite. He was making his way toward a small table near the door, where his overcoat and hat lay.

"Can I give you a ride? I've got a car down in front." I wanted to know what, if anything, Mitchell wanted me to do about Hunt, and I was disturbed by his hasty departure.

"No, thanks." He was putting on his coat. "Our place is just a few blocks from here. The walk'll do me good."

"Anything you want me to report to Bob or John?" I asked plaintively.

"No. No, I don't think so. Thanks for coming up. I'll give you a call later." We both headed out of the room and said goodbye when I stopped at the checkroom. By the time I reached my car, Mitchell was at the corner of Sixtieth Street and Fifth Avenue. His collar was up around his neck, his hat pulled down, and his shoulders were slumped. I watched him cross the street slowly and wondered if this once powerful man felt as burdened by the cover-up as I did. All we had were worries and shady habits, evasions but no solutions.

"Ready to go?" shouted the Secret Service agent.

"Yeah, let's go. Maybe I can make the seven-o'clock shuttle if we hurry." I jumped into the front seat, not wanting the agents who drove me around to think I looked on them as chauffeurs. We took off. "How's it going up here in New York?" I said.

"Fine, thanks. Just fine."

"What kind of cases you been working? Anything exciting?" Some agents had told me spine-tingling tales about breaking up counterfeit rings, a principal function of the Secret Service.

"No. Nothing good recently. I've been on protective detail the last few months." He spoke sourly. Protective details were the bane of many agents' existence.

"Oh. Whose?"

"Sugarfoot," he said. It was Tricia Cox's code name.

"How was it? Pretty painful?"

"I'll say." He fell silent, busy getting through the midtown traffic. But Sugarfoot was obviously on his mind, for he abruptly picked up the conversation about ten minutes later. "Frankly, she's a pain in the ass. She bitches about what we wear, and when she goes shopping she complains if we don't stay a certain distance away from her. I can understand her side of being under protection, you know, but she doesn't understand ours. Shit, we can't do anything right for her. Oh, well, I guess I should keep my mouth shut."

I commiserated with him briefly and jumped out to catch my plane. Mo greeted me warmly at home about eight-thirty and was amazed to hear that I had been to Camp David and

191

back to Washington and then to New York and back in one day.

"Sweetheart, would you fix me a good strong drink? I'm weary."

"Sure."

"I'll tell you—" I called after her, and then stopped. I seldom, if ever, talked about my office problems at home, because I didn't want the unpleasantness to spread into my marriage.

"You'll tell me what?" she asked as she came back with the drink.

"Nothing, really." That's not fair, I thought. "Well, it's just that I'm right in the middle of some nasty decisions that have to be made soon. Decisions that are going to affect the President's second term. It's pretty heavy stuff—on second thought I'd just as soon not talk about it. Okay?"

"Sure."

"Tell me about your day." Which she did as I anesthetized myself with one drink after another. I do not become boisterous or wildly creative with booze. I sink slowly into a solemn, numb catatonia.

A few days later, the middle-level cover-up group filed into my office for a strategy session. Ken Parkinson and Paul O'Brien, who had been the Reelection Committee's lawyers and who were serving as intermediaries with Hunt, reported that Parkinson had received a memorandum from William O. Bittman, Hunt's lawyer. Fred LaRue reported on the tribulations of a secret fund raiser. I referred to the problem that was most constant: Mitchell and the White House were engaged in the perennial war of nerves over who could ignore the problem longer.

"Here, take a look at this memo," said Parkinson. He began pacing around the room. Ken could never sit still when the ugly side of Watergate was being discussed. O'Brien was usually cool and witty, providing comic relief and a clear head. LaRue, who had the toughest job as money raiser, flopped into his chair like a tired basset hound and sat there in quiet mourning. Since I was much younger than the others, I felt the need to prove my worth as the President's counsel. Usually, I would try to act the competent moderator, keeping things going, emphasizing the fact that I was only a liaison between the top and the bottom.

When the Hunt memo was passed to me I looked at it with dread. The money demands of each of the seven Watergate defendants were spelled out: salary, family upkeep, incidentals, and lawyers' fees. Month by month. Due dates for cash deliveries stretching to the early months of 1973. The total was staggering.

"I think I'm going to switch sides," O'Brien cracked. "Any of you guys have any break-ins you want me to do?"

A weak chuckle circulated and died. "What would happen if we refused?" I asked. "Or if we cut the figures in half? Would the whole thing cave in?" No one answered. We all knew the answer.

LaRue was shaking his head. "I can't raise this kind of money," he said sadly. "We can't meet these demands. It's just that simple, so maybe we'll find out what's going to happen."

"You think they'd take it out in trade?" asked O'Brien.

This one never made it off the ground. LaRue looked too forlorn. I turned to him. "Fred, have you had any luck at all so far? What happens when you hit people?"

"Well, Herb and Maury gave me a few names to try," he replied. "But, Jesus, I don't know what to say to the people. I can't tell them we need some campaign money. That won't work. We just won the goddam election, and the papers are full of stories about how much money we have left over. And even if they did cough up some campaign money, I couldn't report it. I don't know what to do. Maury gave me the name of some contact down in Florida who's supposed to be the key to a couple hundred thousand dollars cash. I think it's Arab oil money that Maury wouldn't touch. I don't want to touch it, either. The last thing we need is for some crazy Arab to have us by the balls and threaten to sing if the President doesn't bomb Jerusalem.

"That would be worse than Hunt."

"I'm not so sure," I said. There was a prolonged silence.

"Look," said O'Brien. "We can stall them for a while, but not for long. We've at least got to give them a nibble soon. We can't use campaign money. That's suicide. We've just got to find somebody who'll give some to Fred."

"Right," said LaRue hopelessly. "That's all we need."

As the meeting broke up we were in various stages of distress; the cover-up could well go on forever.

After more inconclusive conversations about money and some routine business, I decided to try to hide again from Watergate. Mo and I went to my parents' home in Greenville, Pennsylvania, for Thanksgiving, but the crisis followed us. The whole family was busy in the kitchen when the phone rang and my sister answered.

"John!" she exclaimed. "It's the White House. John Mitchell wants you." A murmur of excitement went around the room, and my family beamed proud smiles at me. I was pleased, but was caught up short when I realized I couldn't take the call in front of them because Mitchell and I would be agonizing over Hunt's demands. I slipped into the bedroom.

"Where are you?" asked Mitchell, who had relied on the White House switchboard to find me.

"I'm up at my folks' house in Pennsylvania."

"Oh. I'm sorry to bother you, but I was just wondering what happened on the little list that Ken received. Has anything been done?"

"No, John. Nothing's been done. It's the same old problem, you know. We all sit around and worry about it, but no one knows what to do."

"Well, I think Ehrlichman and Haldeman are finally coming down from Camp David tomorrow. So I understand. Don't you think maybe you ought to get back there and see that something's done about this? I don't think we can let it slide."

"I know we can't, but I'm not sure my talking to them will do any good."

"Well, you just think about it," he said, almost pleading.

"I'll see what I can do. Maybe I can handle it on the telephone. What do you think I ought to tell Bob and John?"

"I think they've got a few reserves sitting around down there that they could help us out with. They've got to pull an oar in this thing."

I balked at the thought of using White House cash, even though this "old" money did not have to be reported. I had some of that money in my safe from the day Strachan and Dick Howard had delivered it in the initial panic. There had already been newspaper stories saying that Haldeman had a big slush fund in the White House, and we were all squeamish about it. "I think it would be pretty dangerous to use any of that money, John. There's already been a lot of heat about it."

"Well, we may not have much choice. Think about it."

"Okay. I'll see what I can do."

I walked back into the kitchen, where my family was eagerly speculating on what weighty matter of state had led the White House to call me. "What was that all about?" asked my sister.

"Oh, nothing really," I shrugged. "Just some routine business."

I flew back to Washington the next day and had an awkward meeting with Haldeman and Ehrlichman. They were riding high from Camp David and refused to be bothered with "Mitchell's problem." Each of them offered a few words of encouragement for me to pass on to LaRue but refused to discuss the matter further. I went back to my parents' for the weekend. Things were coming to a head, I knew that, and I wondered whether Mitchell or the White House would budge first.

There was a lot of phoning among the cover-up participants during the following week. The pressure to respond to Hunt was rising. We had not delivered. Mitchell gave the final push in the war of brinkmanship with Haldeman and Ehrlichman when he told me to ask Haldeman for a "loan" from the $350,000 slush fund. He sounded desperate and I didn't argue with him. I called Haldeman on the I.O.

"Bob. I hate to ruin your day, but Mitchell has asked me to see if we could use some of the three-fifty fund. I don't like it. I don't think the White House should have its money used directly, but I don't have any better suggestion. We're all afraid Hunt might blow soon. Things are getting hotter. And Mitchell feels we've got to do something." I sounded like Magruder to myself.

Haldeman seemed remarkably calm as he made a fast scan of the wretched impasse. "Well, if Mitchell says there's no choice and you don't have any better ideas, then go ahead and do it. Just make goddam sure you get that money back, and fast. Make it clear it's a loan."

"Okay. You want me to call Strachan and tell him you authorize giving the money to LaRue?"

"Yep." He hung up.

196

The first bite out of the three-fifty was delivered to LaRue and passed on to the defendants. But the money pressure was not eased. LaRue had to scramble to pay back the White House as well as make the next payment to the defendants. He called or dropped by often, appealing for advice. He looked like a zombie and I began to worry that he might come unhinged. I had seen it happen to Kalmbach; it seemed to me there was an attrition rate for money men. In fact, there was a pattern for all those who worked in the boiler rooms of the cover-up. First came shock, then a burst of dutiful activity, then wariness and stonewalling, and finally the frayed edges began to show. I plotted where each of us fit on the scale. LaRue, I thought, was close to the bottom.

I told Fred I would ask Ehrlichman for advice and did in fact make a lengthy explanation of Fred's difficulties to Ehrlichman in his office, during which Ehrlichman's head moved slowly from side to side in lugubrious tribute to LaRue's dilemma.

"Well, why doesn't Fred go see our friend Tom Pappas?" he suggested after some thought. Pappas was a very wealthy Boston supporter with extensive business holdings abroad, mainly in Greece.

"That sound possible," I replied. "I'll pass it along."

"I think he might be your man. He's discreet. I've got some other dealings with Pappas and, in fact, I'd been thinking of asking him to find some work for young Donnie Nixon, who's gotten himself in trouble down in the Bahamas again."

"Like what?"

"Well, he's got some troubles with some girls this time. I think what I'm going to do is to send young Donnie over to Greece and let Mr. Pappas keep him in some armed camp somewhere over there until he grows up a bit." One of Ehrlichman's jobs, which had started when he was counsel to the

197

President, was to make certain that the President wasn't caused any embarrassment by his brothers. Ehrlichman was telling me about nephew Donnie because he wanted me to assume this responsibility eventually.

I told LaRue what Ehrlichman had said about Pappas.

"He's right, John," Fred declared. "I've already thought of Pappas, but I haven't followed up on it. I've had some dealings with Pappas myself, but I haven't really pitched him. I'm not sure why. I guess I don't want to queer my dealings with him."

"You may have to, Fred."

"We're trying to work on an oil deal together to import crude oil for conversion," he continued, "but we've got a tariff problem. You know, if I could go to Pappas and tell him that this tariff problem could be taken care of, I'm sure he'd be much more receptive."

"Well, Fred, there's nothing I can do about that. Do you want me to mention it to Ehrlichman?"

"Why don't you?"

"Okay. "

Back to Ehrlichman, who listened with interest.

"John, do you want me to become some sort of expert on the oil business?" I asked, pleading for a negative. "I don't know anything about that."

"Nope, I don't want you to get in the oil business. Here's what you do. Tell Fred that when the problem comes up he should call me and I'll have it taken care of."

Back to LaRue. Whatever help he got from Pappas—if he got any he didn't tell me. Not long afterward the pressure became so intense that Haldeman transferred the remainder of the three-fifty fund to LaRue. "Just get all that damn money out of here," he said, weary of being asked for yet "another bite out of the apple."

The money item was rising from the bottom, and at the same time there was pressure from the top. Whenever there was a lull, Haldeman and Ehrlichman suggested I transform the "Dean investigation," the mythological concept, into a historical reality. It would "clear the decks" for the President's second term, they would say; it would definitely establish the White House's innocence in the break-in. The President wanted it: the Dean Report would administer the coup de grace to the investigation, put Watergate behind us. I was the only man who could write the report with credibility and, as the President's counsel, safely.

I didn't much like the idea. A public report with my name attached would associate me even more with Watergate. Moreover, I didn't think a report would work at this stage. It could only raise more questions. I equivocated, raising a host of technical objections with Haldeman and Ehrlichman, which they waved away. My ambitions kept me from saying no flatly.

Finally I thought I had a solution that would satisfy them and protect myself. Instead of stating my own conclusions, I would take "sworn interrogatories" from all those at the White House who were involved and base my report on their answers. If they wanted to lie, fine. I was willing to help them fuzz, ignore, and stonewall, without offering my own versions of the lies. I submitted a draft of this plan to Haldeman on December 5, along with sample questions. It was a halfhearted effort.

A few days later, Haldeman called me into his office. "I've looked over the draft you sent in and it doesn't quite do it."

"Well, Bob, I'm not sure we can do much more."

"I'm not sure about that. I think you ought to go back and try. What we need is just some sort of report that'll put this whole thing to rest and say, 'The White House wasn't really involved.' That's what the President has in mind."

I was being maneuvered, just as LaRue was at the money meetings. I was being pushed toward something awful. I didn't want to do it, and if Bob thought about it, or so I thought, he'd agree. I was confused, but, even so, I hoped that my words carried authority. "Well, Bob, if I go back and spell things out in a report, I'll tell you what's going to happen. This whole thing is going to fall apart. People are going to want to know how I learned all I know. If I say why the White House was not involved, because this was a Mitchell and Magruder operation, then the grand jury is going to open up its doors again and start business very quickly. It's going to call everybody back in there. And none of the stories will hang together and they'll start looking at the cover-up. Then there's going to be a whole slew of new indictments, and I'll tell you who's going to be indicted. Magruder's going to be indicted. Mitchell's going to be indicted. Ehrlichman's going to be indicted. And Haldeman's going to be indicted. And Dean's going to be indicted." By the time I had finished, I was pacing the room the way Parkinson did. I thought my words were clipped and forceful, but I felt near collapse.

"What do you mean?" Haldeman was startled and irritated. "What for? I can understand Mitchell and Magruder for the break-in, but I don't see the others."

"Well, Bob, Mitchell and Magruder know about all these money payments. So do all the defendants and a lot of other people. Everybody's going to have to trust everybody else to commit perjury. If even one person cracks and starts looking for a deal, we're in an obstruction-of-justice situation."

A resigned, slightly nauseated look came over Haldeman's face. "I guess a report isn't such a viable option, then."

"No, I don't think so." I was relieved.

I went back to my office and the calls started to come from

the cover-up principals. There was panic on one more front. Hunt's wife had been killed in a plane crash near Chicago, and $10,000 in bills had been found in her belongings. Was the money ours? Could it be traced? Paul O'Brien reported back that our payments had been in untraceable bills. LaRue said there could be no prints; he wore gloves.

It was time to face squarely what I had rather impulsively told Haldeman about obstruction of justice. I closed the doors to my office and took out a book of criminal statutes. (Ehrlichman had remarked, the first day I met him, how shocked he had been that there were no lawbooks in the counsel's office. When I had succeeded him there were still none, and I had ordered a library.) I was not, am not, an expert on criminal law, but now I took a sweaty tour through the obstruction-of-justice laws. What I found obliterated any notions I might have entertained that I had been protecting myself. Conspiracy to obstruct justice can be proven with evidence of any conversation whose purpose it is to impede or hamper a criminal investigation; the only additional requirement is an "overt act" in furtherance of the conspiracy. My behavior had combined such acts. I stared out the window. It is uncanny, I thought, how the law prohibits all those little acts that had set off my chemical instincts of guilt, instincts which had been quiet as possums during all those meetings. Now that I had read it in black and white, it was clear enough. We were criminals. We had skated this far on the President's power. How had I doubted it?

Haldeman called me again about the Dean Report a few days later, having reconsidered. Maybe I had overreacted, he said. I dodged and made excuses. I was willing to reconsider. I was, in truth, planning how to delay, kill the idea one more time. Ehrlichman has gotten to Haldeman, I thought. Maybe to the President. Or maybe the President has gotten to Haldeman after some coaching from Ehrlichman. Haldeman told me he had scheduled a meeting for December 13—he and I would kick it around again, along with Ehrlichman, Ziegler, and Richard Moore, a Presidential aide who had helped me with my draft. I was not looking forward to it. Fortunately, Ehrlichman ended up boycotting it. At the last minute Haldeman transferred the meeting from his office to Ziegler's, and Ehrlichman refused to descend to Ziegler's office. Without Ehrlichman's skillful advocacy, a consensus was arrived at that a Dean Report would create more problems than it solved. I didn't have to prompt my colleagues overly; the Dean Report went gratefully to sleep. It would return to plague me.

So would Pat Gray. About that time, Earl Silbert, the government's prosecutor, invited Fielding, Bruce Kehrli, and me to the Justice Department to run through the chain of evidence based on the material we had delivered from Hunt's safe. Silbert was preparing his case.[*] We met with him and Henry Petersen in a small conference room off Petersen's office. Responding to Silbert's questions, we described what we had done, omitting not only that we had worn rubber gloves and had had many anxious meetings, but that we had "edited" the contents of Hunt's file. Needless to say, we didn't tell him that we'd given the selected files to Pat Gray.

"That sounds fine," Silbert said. "Except for one thing. Hunt has raised a question about materials he says are missing from those documents. We've had to turn over what we have to him in pretrial discovery. He says there are two Hermes notebooks missing. He claims they are vital to his defense, and his lawyer plans to file a motion claiming we're hiding them if we don't come up with them. It sounds like bullshit to me. You guys know anything about these notebooks?"

"Earl, I don't even know what a Hermes notebook is," I replied apprehensively. Fielding didn't, either. I was afraid Hunt was trying to use what he knew had been there, what I'd

---

[*]   [Original Footnote:] The case against Liddy, Hunt, and the others.

202

first held and then given Gray, to get the case against him dismissed. I cringed at the thought that I was getting caught in the middle.

"Well, they're little cardboard notebooks like clerks use," Earl replied. "And they have 'Hermes' written on them. H-E-R-M-E-S. You remember anything like that?"

"No, I don't," I said. I was trying to call up a mental picture of the material that had gone to Gray, and I didn't remember any such notebooks. This didn't lighten my concern about Hunt's line of thought.

As Silbert pushed, I was called to the phone. I took the call in Petersen's office. It was Krogh. He'd been nominated Undersecretary of Transportation and was preparing for his Senate confirmation hearings. He wanted me to reassure him that he wouldn't be crucified because of what might be known about the Plumbers' Unit or his association with Hunt and Liddy.

Petersen came out of the conference room as I was saying goodbye.

"Henry, I've got to talk to you," I said.

"Sure," he said, puzzled. "What's up?"

"Listen, the only thing I can figure out about why there are some documents missing is that not all the stuff we found was turned over directly to the FBI agents." I was speaking in a low voice.

"What are you talking about?"

"Well, some of those documents were politically very embarrassing, and we sent them straight to Pat Gray. If there are missing documents, he's got them."

"Oh, shit!" Petersen exclaimed. "You're not serious!"

"Yeah, I'm afraid so, and I don't have any idea how to handle that if I get called to testify. I don't really want to get on that stand. Let me tell you what happened."

"I don't really want to hear it," Petersen said in disgust.

"I know it doesn't look good, but that's the way it is."

We went back into the conference room. Silbert was still pursuing the whereabouts of the Hermes notebooks, and a debate was going on as to whether Hunt might have imagined them. Petersen took command and brought the meeting to a close, quickly. He was troubled by my news. I heard nothing more about being called as a witness.

A few days later, I ran into Gray at a luncheon in Kleindienst's office. He pulled me to one side and grabbed my arm tightly. "John, why did you mention that file stuff to Petersen?" He was talking through clenched teeth.

"Listen, Pat, I didn't have any choice. Silbert was grilling me about the goddam stuff Hunt says is missing. I told Henry in private."

"Goddammit, John. You have got to hang tight on that!" Gray spit out each word. "You have got to hang tight. Who else knows about it?"

"Well, the only people I know that know about it are Ehrlichman, Fielding, myself and Petersen."

"Okay. Listen. Let me tell you what's happened. I couldn't tell Petersen I ever got that stuff, because I destroyed those documents."

I gave Gray a determined and reassuring nod. He had made a sticky situation worse and we would have to stonewall that too. I didn't feel very tough.

As the Christmas holidays approached, I began to brood about what all this was doing to my life. Each day I was a whirlwind that covered scores of little Watergate snares: Howard Hunt wanting us to find him a psychiatrist to help

204

prove he was unfit to stand trial; Senator Edward Kennedy looking as if he might launch a Watergate investigation; the Cubans wanting to change lawyers; Judge John J. Sirica making warning noises in pretrial hearings. And business in the counsel's office was skyrocketing, because I was indispensable in the burgeoning cover-up. My empire was developing. I no longer had to ask for fringe benefits. Haldeman had put me on the "A" limousine service, which entitled me to be picked up at home each morning and to have a limousine at my disposal. New partitions went up in my office. I redecorated for the sake of redecorating: new chairs, carpets, draperies. Workmen crowded in; we were expanding... At night, I would go home and feel my spirit evaporate. I would nearly expire on the sofa. Mo knew enough to have the drinks ready and to stay out of the line of fire. I had switched from fifths of Scotch to half gallons so that I would think I was consuming fewer bottles. I spent most evenings at home, escaping with liquor. I asked Mo to cancel our social engagements. We quarreled, our new marriage already under severe strain.

Finally I decided once again to hide from Watergate, and we took off for California on an extended Christmas vacation. For ten days I managed to separate the cover-up from the rest of my life. Mo and I wound up spending New Year's in Palm Springs. Haldeman, Ziegler, Higby, and several other Haldeman staff people were also there, and we played tennis and worked on our tans. Watergate was taboo by unspoken consent. It had dropped out of the newspapers for nearly two months.

On Tuesday, January 2, the Palm Springs party arrived at March Air Force Base. There was a good deal of excited chatter because we were going to fly back to Washington in the new Boeing 707 jet that was soon to replace the current Air Force One. As we milled about in the waiting room, Ziegler told me I had a call from the White House. I went to return it, but before I could get a connection Higby tapped me frantically on the shoulder.

"Hang it up, John," he snapped. "We're leaving. Now. Bob wants to move out."

"I won't be a second, Larry. I've got a quick call to return."

"Make it from the plane. You'll get left if you don't."

Haldeman, always a demanding commander in chief in the President's absence, expected his troops to move double-time. I grabbed Mo and dashed to the plane. It smelled like a new car, and there were sheets over all the seats because the Air Force brass didn't want any passenger to leave a blemish before the President flew in the plane. The ground lines were still connected on the runway, and the White House operator came on when I picked up the phone. She said she had Paul O'Brien on the line waiting to speak to me.

"Where are you?" asked O'Brien.

"I'm out in California, Paul. I'm on my way back, and I'm sitting in an airplane right now."

"Is it safe to talk?" he asked anxiously.

"No, I'm sure we're going through at least two or three switch boards."

"I see. Well, I'll tell you this. We've got some serious problems. One of our boys is off the reservation. It's serious. I need to talk to you as soon as you get back."

The pilot was starting the engines. "Look Paul," I said loudly, we're about to take off. They're going to cut these lines any second now, and we can't really talk anyway. I'll call you tonight as soon as I get back."

The plane was quickly aloft. I wandered up to the cabin where Haldeman was sitting. Everybody was testing out the latest gadgets, including a television that could pick up local stations as the plane passed over them. I stopped Haldeman in

206

the aisle as he was putting on his personal Air Force One flight jacket, one of the highest White House status symbols. "You know, there's no way we can get away from this goddam stuff. I just had a call from Paul O'Brien."

"Oh?" Haldeman said curiously.

"Yes. Apparently one of our boys is off the reservation, and we've got some kind of serious problem."

"You never seem to have any good news, do you?" he said, shaking his head.

I retreated to my seat and picked at my meal. About six hours later, I called O'Brien from my house.

"It's Hunt, John. He's all bent out of shape. He's all screwed up since his wife died, and he doesn't think he can stand trial. He's pissed at the prosecution's psychiatrists. He thinks the government has turned on him by declaring him fit for the trial. He's mad at us for not helping him out more." Hunt thought we owned the prosecutor's office.

"Goddammit, Paul, you know I did what I could with Petersen on that. We did everything we could."

"I know it, but Hunt doesn't see it that way. Bittman says Hunt wants to plead guilty and get it over with, but he's not going to do it if it tooks like he's going to spend the rest of his life in prison. Bittman has been trying to see Colson, but Chuck won't see him. I tell you, he may blow."

"Christ Almighty!" I said, then stopped. "Look, Paul, there's nothing we can do about this right this minute. I'm going to forget about it one more night. Why don't you come see me in the morning, okay?"

"Sure. I'll be there. By the way, John. One more thing."

"What's that?" I snapped.

"Happy New Year."

"Up yours!" I retorted, and then joined O'Brien's laughter in spite of myself.

I needed a drink badly, feeling parched from the long ride with Haldeman. A Christian Scientist, like Ehrlichman, Haldeman regarded people who "used" alcohol as weaklings, so all his courtiers did their serious drinking on the sly. I climbed into my Scotch bottle in the safety of my home. As Mo unpacked I sat alone in company with my own weird thoughts. I heard Fielding instead of O'Brien warning me on a flight back East. Once again, a last night's sleep before the holocaust. I was coming back from Manila again, as I had done six months earlier. This time I felt like an old man.

O'Brien walked into my office the next morning, threw his trench coat on a chair, and sat down in his customary place in front of my desk. The trench coat always reminded me of something he'd said when we were looking for ways to help LaRue raise money abroad. He had said he might be able to help in Greece, because he had a law firm there that served as a front for the CIA. Ever since, I had thought of him as a "spy." He had told me of having been in military intelligence and had tried to enlist my help to get promoted to general in the reserves. Now O'Brien looked pleasant and composed as he waited for me to start the conversation.

"Well, Paul," I said wearily, "you've already ruined any rest I might have gotten from my vacation."

He grinned. "Tough shit."

"Let's get on with it," I said severely. I enjoyed O'Brien.

"John, you're going to have to do something with your buddy Colson, or old Hunt is going to fly off the handle and the whole thing is going to go down the drain. Bittman's got to see Colson. Hunt won't take no for an answer."

"That's going to be tough. I don't think Colson wants any part of meeting with Bittman. He's been avoiding Hunt and

Bittman like the plague."

"Well, time's running out. From what Bittman tells me, Hunt's incredibly unstable now. He's pissed and distraught, like I told you last night. I don't think Colson has any choice. What do you think?"

"Well, I'll see what I can do, but I'm not sure there's anything. I'll talk to Chuck and Ehrlichman and let you know."

"Okay." He smiled. "You'd better make it within the next few hours."

As he turned to leave I said, "Paul, there doesn't seem to be any end to this goddam stuff. Just one day after another. The same stuff."

"Well, maybe if we can get these guys through the trial, we'll have ourselves a little breather."

I called Colson. "Chuck, I've got good news for you. Bill Bittman wants to meet with you as soon as possible, and—"

"I'll be goddamned if I want to meet with him," he interrupted.

"Well, it may be pretty important that you do. Hunt's apparently bent out of shape pretty bad since his wife died."

"I know that. Haven't you seen the letter I sent you yesterday?"

"No, I haven't. I just got back to the office." I reached over into my mailbox and sifted through for Colson's memo. It was one line: "Now what the hell do I do?" Attached to it was a letter from Hunt to Colson, in which Hunt outlined his shaky mental condition and his feeling of abandonment. "Here it is, Chuck," I said. "I guess you're up on this stuff. What do you think we ought to do?"

"Shit, I don't know. You're supposed to be the lawyer."

"So are you, Chuck."

"Well, look, John. I want to stay as far away from this as I can. I don't want any part of it."

"I understand, but I'm going to have to raise this with Ehrlichman and get back to you."

When I met with Ehrlichman, he responded very carefully to what I had to tell him. He said he thought Chuck should hear what Bittman had to say. I called Colson, then O'Brien.

"Paul, it's all set up. Chuck's going to meet with Bittman. So you can tell Bittman to call Colson and make his appointment. But I'll tell you one thing. Colson's damn reluctant to do it, and you better tell Bittman to hurry before he changes his mind."

"Okay, I get you," said O'Brien. "But if there's one guy over there at the White House who ought not to be reluctant to meet with Howard Hunt's lawyer, it's Chuck Colson. That son-of-a-bitch is in this up to his teeth, and how he's staying out of it I'll never know."

I wasn't sure what O'Brien meant, but I assumed Bittman had been feeding him bits of ammunition from Hunt to get Chuck's attention. "Paul," I said somberly, "if Bittman has something to say to Colson, now's the time. Because Chuck's going to play the reluctant lady in this thing, and Bittman better tell Colson what it is that's on his client's mind while he has the chance. Otherwise, ain't nothing going to happen."

"I can assure you that Bittman will make Colson sit up and listen."

Late that afternoon, Colson called in panic. "John, I'm going to meet with Ehrlichman. I'm on my way over. I think you ought to come over, too." The hear-no-evil was gone from his voice. Bittman must have stuck it to him pretty hard. "Right away," panted Colson. "It's important."

In Ehrlichman's office, the three of us sat around his small semicircular desk. Ehrlichman doodled nervously on the desk rather than on his lap. The usual patterns were disintegrating.

Colson spoke in gasps as if he'd been doing his old Marine exercises. His halting report went through the familiar facts of Hunt's near breakdown. "His ulcer," Chuck sighed, "which is a bleeding ulcer, is giving him all kinds of trouble. The guy wants to plead guilty, but he's afraid Sirica will stick him in jail forever. Bittman came at me like a train. The guy's pretty shrewd too. He wants me to give some sort of assurances to Hunt that he's not going to rot in jail. Bittman was cautious in his choice of words, but it was clear what the hell he was talking about. There's no mistaking it. I don't like this, but I've got to say I feel awful sorry for Howard Hunt. The guy's in a terrible mess. With his wife dead and responsibility for all those kids. And they're nice kids, too. I can see why he's on the brink."

Bittman must have pulled out all the stops, I thought.

Ehrlichman, ignoring the sentimental aspects, came straight to the point. "Chuck, I don't want you to get into any specifics with anyone regarding clemency," he said firmly. "I talked to the President many months ago about this whole problem coming up." Ehrlichman's jaw was set as he leaned back. He looked off. "I think it was back in July that I talked to the President about this out in San Clemente, and he told me he didn't want to talk to anybody about clemency for these Watergate people. Here's what I'm going to do. I'll take this up with the President myself. And, Chuck, I don't want you to talk to the President about it at all. You understand? You just wait until you hear back from me."

His words echoed in the room. We all knew the dimensions. Anyone could pay money to the Watergate defendants. Only one man could grant them clemency. I thought, Ehrlichman is shrewd, he's being protective of the President by insisting that he be the only one to speak with him about it; I wonder will he go the extra mile by not raising the matter with the President, assume the burden himself so that he can fall on his sword if necessary? No, I thought, that's not the way Ehrlichman operates. He will raise it with the President. In the unlikely event that he needs to protect the President later, he will say he did not.

Ehrlichman, meanwhile, was glancing back and forth intently from Colson to me, telling us with his eyes that he meant business. Colson and I responded with understanding looks, and Chuck finally said, "Okay, I understand. But Bittman told me he wants to hear back as soon as possible about what we can do. So I've got to get back to him."

Ehrlichman nodded, and the meeting ended.

The next morning, January 4, Ehrlichman called me early. "John, I've been thinking about this Hunt thing and I think it's under control. And I've asked Brother Kleindienst to come over for lunch today to see if we can't find some alternative that'll satisfy Hunt. I'd like you to join us."

"I'll be there."

Jack Caulfield walked in. I hadn't seen him for several weeks, he was now working in the Treasury Department. He was upset; his eyes were bulging. "Did Fielding tell you about the letter from McCord?" he asked.

The question unleashed an unpleasant recollection I had suppressed in the panic about Hunt. Fred had told me that Caulfield had received a letter from McCord, in which McCord had laid down his threats poetically: "If Helms [CIA Director Richard M. Helms] goes and the Watergate operation is laid at the CIA's feet, where it does not belong, every tree in the forest will fall. It will be a scorched desert. The whole matter is at the precipice now. Just pass the message that if they want it to blow, they are on exactly the right course." I had been aware that McCord might be off the reservation, too; furthermore, Paul O'Brien had informed me about McCord's deteriorating

212

relationship with his lawyer. Hunt and the lawyers, said O'Brien, had planned to blame Watergate on the CIA by convincing "those dumb D.C. jurors that they were watching the Mission Impossible show." McCord had balked at this. No one knew why. I wondered whether the Agency had reached him.

"Yeah, he told me about the letter," I told Caulfield despondently.

"When it rains it pours."

"What do you mean?"

"Oh, nothing."

"Well, here's the original letter. I don't understand what the hell Jimmy's up to, frankly. I met with him last summer, and he was all right then."

"What were you meeting with him for?" This was news to me.

"Well, I wanted to keep track of him," Jack sputtered. "I was worried about his family. We've got a code system worked out so we can communicate."

"Well, thanks for this lovely letter, Jack. Let me know if you get any others from your pen pal. And keep in touch, okay? We might need to take some readings on Mr. McCord's state of mind."

I went down to the executive mess for lunch with Ehrlichman and Kleindienst. It was a hurried affair. Kleindienst announced that he didn't have time to eat because he had to rush off to catch a plane.

"Well, Dick, I've been thinking about these Watergate defendants," Ehrlichman said casually, as if the idea had wafted into his mind during late-night reading. "And I just wanted to ask you if there isn't something we might do. Some way the Department of Justice might recommend that these wayward

213

souls involved in this little caper could be treated with leniency when they're sentenced. Some sort of official recommendation to the court to assure that they got leniency. What do you think?"

Kleindienst looked surprised, then puzzled, then uncomfortable. "I don't know," he said quietly. "I don't have any idea about that, John. I'm no goddam criminal lawyer. But I'll check with Petersen and let you know." Now Kleindienst was even more anxious to leave, and he did.

I had just got back to my office when Petersen called. "John, I just rode out to the airport with Kleindienst," he said, his voice rising. "Let me ask you something. Are you all nuts over there? The government can't recommend leniency for those guys. That's stupid. We'd be crucified. I don't understand what goes through Ehrlichman's head sometimes. It's absolutely out of the question. In fact, we're going to do just the opposite. We're going to recommend that the book be thrown at them. And then we're going to take them all back before the grand jury, immunize them, and try to force them to talk. That's what we're going to do. We don't have any choice. And that's what I told Dick, and he told me to tell Ehrlichman."

"Uh, Henry, I don't think it's necessary for you to come over and deliver that message. I'll pass it along."

I called Ehrlichman and told him. The thought of the defendants going back into the grand-jury room broke one more thin straw I had been grasping—that all we needed was to get through the trial. "What do you want to do about Chuck?" I asked.

"I've already talked to him."

"You have?" I was incredulous. Ehrlichman had actually anticipated Petersen's response, I figured, and had acted accordingly. Still, it struck me as extraordinary that he had done anything before he absolutely had to.

214

"Yeah, he's going to meet with Bittman. Chuck's got him a plan."

I went home with all sorts of visions about the Colson-Bittman meeting. The next morning, Bud Krogh walked in. I had long since learned to spot the "Watergate look" on people's faces, and Bud had a bad case.

"I've got a problem, John," he said tersely. "Gordon Liddy called and wants to talk to me."

"That's great, Bud. Why don't we just have a convention of all the goddam defendants over in the Roosevelt Room? We can clear the air. Have a nice lunch and a few toasts." I stopped short, realizing that Bud and I were talking at the same time. This news was a turn of the screw. Hunt and McCord were bad enough, but I had never had any personal dealings with them. If Liddy cracked, he could hit straight at me. I wasn't sure I could bear taking Bud on as a new client in the cover-up. The Ellsberg break-in had been safely buried a long time ago.

"Now, wait a minute," Bud stammered. "I'm not sure it's all that bad. Apparently the Senate Commerce Committee staff has been trying to question Liddy about his work with me. They want to talk to him before my confirmation hearings. I think that's what Gordon wants to talk to me about, but I can't be sure. The thing is, I want to be able to testify that I haven't talked to Liddy since he left the White House a year ago. I think that's important. But at the same time, I sure don't want to piss Liddy off by refusing to talk to him. I don't know what to do. What do you think?"

My spirits rose slightly at the thought that there was a benign explanation for Liddy's call to Krogh. We decided that Bud's secretary should call Liddy. She should be extremely cordial in explaining that Bud couldn't speak personally with Liddy because of the upcoming hearings. At the same time, she should say that Bud hoped Liddy could avoid the Senate

215

investigators altogether. Bud could be hurt by anything Liddy might say or refuse to say about him.

Colson called me in the afternoon for another meeting with Ehrlichman. I was astonished when I found him in almost a festive mood. He seemed pleased with himself and was carrying a stack of his normal work papers under his arm. "Well, I think things are coming out all right," he reported confidently. "I had Bittman over to my office, and I've given him the assurances that I think'll take care of Hunt. But I assure you, John, I didn't give him any hard commitment. I don't think this is going to cause any problem for anybody."

Ehrlichman, as usual, was not taking Chuck's enthusiasm at face value. "What exactly did you tell him?" he asked.

"I told him he could tell Hunt that he indeed had a good friend here at the White House. Me. And then I offered to take care of his children if he went off to prison. I said I would take them into my own home and take care of them like my own. Then I told Bittman I understood it was natural that no man wanted to go to jail. And while I couldn't give any hard commitment, I looked at him square in the eye and said, 'You know, a year is a long time. And clemency is something that's generally considered around Christmas time here at the White House.' Bittman was reading me."

"That's fine," said Ehrlichman, who rarely offered compliments. Colson had conveyed the message clearly but indirectly. He had never mentioned the President's name.

"You think Hunt's going to plead now?" I asked Colson.

"Yep." We shared a satisfied pause.

I turned to Ehrlichman. "John, there's one other thing. I think we should assume the word will get out from Hunt to the other defendants that he has some sort of clemency. They're going to want the same thing. McCord's already making threatening noises. Even Liddy might be shaky. What are we going to do with the other guys?"

"Well, I think we should be fair about this," Ehrlichman said. "We'll give them the same assurances in the same way, if necessary."

Colson and I walked together from the West Wing to our offices in the EOB. On the way he stopped me, looked around to make sure there was no one approaching, and confided, "John, I want to tell you something. Listen, Howard Hunt is a friend of mine. And I decided I couldn't give him any assurances unless I thought I could back them up. This is too serious. So I felt this was something I had to take up with the President himself. To make sure I was on firm ground. And I did. I talked to him, despite what Ehrlichman said. I thought I had to."

Chuck was fishing for approval. "I understand," I said. He put his hand on my shoulder and leaned on it a little as he pivoted to head toward the EOB entrance. As we walked in I listened to the lawyer in me tell me that this act alone put the President directly into the cover-up.

I had scarcely sat down at my desk when Bud Krogh arrived with a report of his secretary's conversation with Liddy. He was distressed. Liddy had been rather abrupt with her and was upset that Bud had refused to talk to him. Bud asked me if I would call Liddy to soothe him. I said I would have to think that one over.

The next morning, Saturday, I paced about my kitchen, debating whether to make the call. Finally I did. "Gordon, I think you'll recognize who this is when you hear the message I have to pass on to you," I said guardedly. I was afraid there might be a tap on Liddy's home phone. "I just wanted to tell you that Bud is very sorry he can't talk to you right now. It's the timing. He's worried that any conversation now might cause him a problem in his confirmation hearings. I just wanted you to know that's the only reason he didn't return your call."

"I understand perfectly, John," Liddy replied. "That doesn't bother me. But I want to say one thing, John, and I hope you don't take it the wrong way. My attorney hasn't been paid, and that's unfair to him. I don't want any money for myself. But I've got to be able to pay my lawyer."

"I understand, Gordon. I'll pass that along," I said, anxious to get off the phone. I told him I wished him well at his trial. I felt small.

Two days later the Watergate trial began, with Judge Sirica presiding. I watched the papers, wondering whether this new public exposure could conceivably make the cover-up any more harrowing than it had been during the past two months. My reserves were running low. I felt ground down.

The trial went as we expected. Hunt pleaded guilty and assured the court he knew of no "higher-ups" involved in the break-in. The press and TV enthusiastically reported Judge Sirica's open skepticism, but it didn't lead to anything. We figured we could weather skepticism as long as no one got a hook into Magruder or Mitchell or any of a dozen "principals" who could rip the cover-up apart.

Then, one week into the trial, *New York Times* reporter Seymour Hersh wrote a front-page story alleging that at least four of the defendants were being paid for their silence. LaRue, O'Brien, Mitchell, Ehrlichman, Haldeman, and I exchanged a blitz of phone calls to find out who had leaked this story. We settled on Henry Rothblatt, the attorney for the four Florida defendants. We knew Rothblatt was strongly resisting his clients' desire to follow Hunt's lead and plead guilty. We were relieved when they fired him and pleaded guilty anyway, assuring Judge Sirica in open court that they had been paid no money by anyone for anything.

The "hush money" story vanished, but it gave me a foretaste of the panic that would follow if any investigators ever touched this rawest nerve of the cover-up. If, in fact, they ever focused attention on what had happened after the break-in instead of before.

One weekend during the trial, I was alone in my office and I decided to search for those Hermes notebooks Silbert had inquired about with such assurance. I still couldn't recall them, but I was troubled by the possibility that they might somehow turn up. In one of my safes, down under the President's estate papers, I found them—two Hermes notebooks and a metal pop-up address book. I leafed through them. Paul O'Brien had told me they contained the names of people Hunt had recruited for the Ellsberg break-in and his "other" White House operations.

I went through a tumble of nervous calculations. These documents were no longer relevant to the trial after Hunt's guilty plea, I rationalized. But they were certainly dangerous to the cover-up. I would have to get rid of the goddam things, as others had gotten rid of evidence. I put them into my new shredder. The machine tore through the pages but choked on the cardboard covers, and I was afraid it might break down. I felt a wave of paranoia. I glanced at the microphone-like devices attached to the ultrasonic alarm system on my walls. I had asked for the sensor system, as I had the shredder, after I had seen new ones in Ehrlichman's office; they were part of the status race. At this moment I worried whether the sensors would "hear" the shredder choking. Finally it ate the last of the documents with a loud growl.

Destroying the notebooks was only a small addition to a whole string of criminal acts I had committed, but it seemed to me to be a moment of high symbolism. This direct, concrete, and sweaty act had also shredded the last of my feeble rationalizations that I was an agent rather than a participant—a lawyer defending guilty clients, rather than a conspirator.

Toward the end of January, the outward signs were still

good. The Watergate trial ended without major mishap, all seven defendants convicted. The President negotiated a settlement in Vietnam; his popularity in the polls rose to a high of sixty-eight percent approval. These were bright spots that helped me hold together an optimistic front. Inside, I was dying.

I closed my office doors for long stretches during the day to escape in daydreams. I flashed through all the weak spots in the cover-up, projected an everlasting series of hurdles for the future. I reflected on my career and listed my talents: an organized mind, an ability to read the desires of my superiors, a capacity to anticipate. Deep down, I knew I was a meek, favor-currying staff man, not hardboiled enough to play the game I had watched Ehrlichman and Mitchell play. The same mental predilections that had propelled me to the White House and into a leading role in the cover-up now made it impossible for my mind to ignore the grave weaknesses of our position, I thought sourly. No one else was focused in on what had happened after the break-in. I pondered my criminal acts, pushing at them like an aching tooth. At times, I thought of myself as a contemporary Raskolnikov, paranoid, schizoid, wanting to get caught, and, for the first time, I thought seriously about the prospect of going to jail. I thought I was not as bothered by the prospect as I had been. Sometimes it actually seemed perhaps the only way to end the lies that had ruined my private life even as they had made me a superficial success. Still, there was no way I could think of to end the cover-up cleanly. One could not just walk out of it. It was ridiculous, I thought, to think about going to jail as I sat there in the White House. Round and round in circles, always the same ones. I drifted on.

February drove some new spikes into the tire. The Senate voted unanimously to establish a committee to investigate Watergate and we were staring at a new hurdle. We retreated to those strategies that had delayed the Patman hearings:

strategies to emasculate the planned hearings; to keep key Administration witnesses from testifying. I began reworking the President's position on executive privilege—the doctrine by which we hoped to keep White House aides out of Congressional hearings.

Late in February, Pat Gray went before the Senate Judiciary Committee for confirmation hearings on his nomination to become permanent director of the FBI. These hearings provided the first opportunity for the senators to question an Administration official on Watergate publicly, and they took full advantage. Gray, trying desperately to sound sufficiently candid to be confirmed, but not so candid as to destroy himself, got into immediate trouble as he testified that he had given Dean the FBI reports on the Watergate investigation, and that he and Dean had met repeatedly during the previous summer. I was in the headlines for the first time: "Dean Monitored FBI Watergate Probe;" "Dean Refuses Senate Testimony;" "Nixon Backs Dean."

I became a public Watergate target. I directed the ugliest possible thoughts at Gray and kicked myself for not having protested his nomination more vigorously. It was an idle regret; we had no choice. We couldn't afford an angry Pat Gray loose on the streets. It was just one more example of the Watergate tar baby: the only thing worse than nominating Gray would have been not nominating him.

Just as the hearings began, I had my first Watergate meeting with the President since the September 15 stroking session. Now, all of a sudden, I was meeting and talking with the President almost every day in my final quantum leap toward intimacy with him. There were complicated reasons behind this new relationship. For one thing, Haldeman and Ehrlichman were swamped with the new Presidential appointees and the reorganization. Both, particularly Ehrlichman, were less and less tolerant of the Watergate problems I kept bringing to them. They were happy to have someone else carry Watergate to the President. And, more importantly, we were all worried that my claim of executive privilege might not hold up in court because I had had negligible contact with the President. This had to be remedied.

On February 27, the first day of a series of private meetings with the President, he called me into the Oval Office and offered me a cup of coffee, which I declined. When he offered it again, I accepted. I was too timid to tell the President that I hate coffee and never drink it, it does terrible things to my body. So I drank black coffee with him as we launched into Watergate.

The President, dealing privately with me for the first time, quickly broke down restraints, confiding his feelings on countless subjects, ranging from the "assholes" in his Cabinet to the "boobs" on the Supreme Court. But the bulk of our conversations dealt inevitably with aspects of Watergate—the Ervin Committee,[*] the Gray hearings, executive privilege.

Although I still went home to Scotch each night, my new status with the President temporarily revived my confidence that I could endure as the ringmaster of the cover-up. I could go no higher: I had become the junior member of the select group that met almost daily with the President. Occasionally he would tell Haldeman, Ehrlichman, Ziegler, or Kissinger to wait while he finished a meeting with me. I would pass them going in and out of the Oval Office, and we would exchange brotherly glances in tribute to our membership in the most select fraternity we could imagine. Kissinger joked in passing that he was happy to read my name in the gruesome Watergate headlines, instead of his own.

---

[*]   [Original Footnote:] On February 7, 1973, the Senate established the Select Committee on Presidential Campaign Activities, composed of four Democrats and three Republicans, to investigate the Watergate break-in and related 1972 campaign improprieties. The committee was chaired by Senator Sam Ervin of North Carolina.

No one had given me pointers on how to conduct business with the President of the United States. I listened to his questions and responded, never volunteered sensitive information unless asked. I was determined not to tell the President anything that might draw him into an obstruction of justice. I had watched Ehrlichman protect him during the clemency discussions. From the beginning, however, the President asked me detailed and knowledgeable questions. Could Magruder's testimony sink Colson? Could Hugh Sloan damage Magruder? His inquiries loosened me up somewhat, and at the end of the first meeting I was hinting to him that I myself had Watergate vulnerabilities. He dismissed my remarks abruptly on the ground that I had not known of the break-in in advance.

In subsequent meetings, the President continually asked questions I had already answered. This disturbed me. He would have bursts of lucidity and logical thinking, but mostly he was rambling and forgetful, and as I grew used to talking with him I nursed the heretical thought that the President didn't seem very smart. Either that or he was carrying a mental overload. His desk was as neat and spotless as my own, but his thoughts and actions were far from organized. Whenever he wanted to make a note to himself, he would go through a long and awkward ritual. First he would put on his dark-rimmed glasses. (To my surprise, I thought they made him look much better.) Then he would reach into a vest pocket to fish for an envelope or a scrap of paper. Simultaneously, he would reach into the opposite vest pocket with his other hand to find his pen. The required objects would often elude his grasp, leaving the President struggling, his arms crossed in front of himself. Finally he would pull out the fountain pen, bite off the top, and hold it in his teeth as he scrawled with some difficulty on the scrap of paper he clutched in the palm of one hand. I would sit silently and watch the effort.

Such episodes, plus the obtuse conversations, gradually humanized Richard Nixon for me. The President still intimidated me, but I had lost a great deal of the romance. I also began to lose faith that the President could overcome the Watergate scandal by infinite power and wisdom. He seemed as enmeshed in it as the rest of us. I soon began to stop looking forward to these meetings; they no longer offered me confidence—about anything. The power fix, the high which I had pursued all my adult life, was wearing off. I was coming down.

Three themes dominated my conversations with the President until mid-March: his desire to launch a counter-scandal against the Democrats, his reminiscence of the Hiss case, and his determination to find a strategy to handle the upcoming Ervin hearings. Each of these topics bothered me. The President was never satisfied with the evidence I brought him of buggings and surveillance by previous Administrations, even though I thought it was impressive in a grisly way. He kept sending me out for more, and I developed a feeling that he was grooming me as his new hatchetman, his new Colson. (Chuck had left the White House.)

The President was famous for reliving the Hiss case, but it unsettled me when he did so for my benefit. He would wax eloquent about how he and his investigators had overcome incredible odds and all sorts of government obstructions to catch Alger Hiss in a crime. Even the power of President Truman hadn't stopped him, he would say. His constant analogies between the Hiss case and Watergate baffled me; I thought the President had everything backward. I identified with Hiss, not the investigators, and I winced whenever the President talked about how he had finally "nailed" him.

The President's emerging strategy for the Ervin hearings was most troubling. He warmed to the idea of taking the steam out of the Senate investigation with a "comprehensive" Dean Report. He never gave me the feeling he was setting me up to take the blame for Watergate, but I began to suspect that Ehrlichman had simply not clued him in on what he had in

224

mind. I squirmed, I raised all sorts of objections, but I couldn't bring myself to say no.

I wrenched myself out of bed late on the morning of Saturday, March 17, and decided to go to the office and struggle to compose some kind of innocuous Dean Report for the President. I had just arrived when the White House operator called and said the President wanted to see me in the Oval Office. I went immediately, wearing casual weekend clothes. It was the first time I met with the President without a necktie.

Manolo Sanchez, the President's valet, was just taking the lunch tray away as I entered, and the President leaned back in his chair, brushing crumbs off the front of his dark suit. He was wearing a shamrock and a green tie in honor of St. Patrick's Day.

He greeted me and asked where I lived. I told him, somewhat startled by the question.

"Any time that you need to get away from town, remember that my Camp David place is very conducive to that kind of awful work," he said, referring to the Dean Report. He knew I was resisting the idea, and he was trying to make it more palatable by offering a sojourn at Camp David.

"I think that might be a good thing," I replied, and proceeded, as usual, to praise him—this time by complimenting him on the effectiveness of his recent press conference on executive privilege. I went on to say I was trying to devise some way we could force Senator Ervin to hold his hearings in executive session, behind closed doors.

The President sat up. "I always hark back to the Hiss case," he said. "We did that on the Hiss case."

"You went into executive session?" I asked, knowing it full well.

The President described in detail how he had lined up the testimony of Alger Hiss and Whittaker Chambers in private

225

sessions before nailing Hiss in public. Then he launched into a long, rambling monologue on the benefits we could derive from a Dean Report. I knew he was leaning on me in his own way, which I had learned was usually indirect. The President was uncomfortable telling aides to do things they didn't want to do. That was why he had Haldeman.

The President waited for my reaction to his speech. We had been down this road before. I didn't like the idea of any Dean Report, but I was determined not to write one that would make me alone responsible for false conclusions. I coughed nervously and mumbled before trying to steer him toward my old "affidavit," that is, the interrogatories idea. "Let me just take you one step further," I said. "It might be a very interesting approach. Ah, if Ervin were to be called down here and given sworn statements that were given to you. That's after I have prepared my report on Haldeman, Ehrlichman, Colson, Dean, everybody."

The President heard me out, seemed to waver, but reverted to his idea of a report—one without the affidavits I wanted in order to protect myself. I decided to try a new approach: if I couldn't sell him on my version of the Dean Report, I would try to make him see that his version would prove unpalatable because I would have to include enough facts to invite disastrous scrutiny. We were jousting subtly so that neither of us would have to acknowledge that there was an argument between us. As a preview of his kind of Dean Report, I conducted him on a tour through the origins of the break-in. He interrupted me when I was recounting the discussions in Mitchell's office of the campaign intelligence plan.

"You heard discussion of that, but you didn't hear any discussion of bugging, did you, in that, your meetings?" He paused. "Or did you?"

He's testing me, I thought; he knows about those discussions, he wants to see how I would handle them. I looked

226

nervously at the floor. "Yeah, I did. That's what, ah, distressed me quite a bit."

"Oh, you did," the President said quietly.

"Uh-huh."

"Who raised it? Liddy?"

"That's right."

"Liddy at that point said we ought to do some bugging?" the President asked.

"Right. Mitchell just sat there and puffed on his pipe and said nothing. He didn't agree to it, and I, at the end of the meeting—"

"Well, you won't need to say in your statement about the bugging."

"No," I said, backing off. I realized that this tack had failed to move him off the Dean Report.

Haldeman interrupted the meeting with some routine business and phone calls. When he left, the President rambled on about other subjects. He struck me as quite lonely. The White House was nearly empty. The President was by himself, the business routine suspended for the weekend. He seemed just to want someone to talk to. Finally he returned to Watergate and brought up the counter-scandal idea, asking my progress in discovering wiretaps that had been ordered by his predecessors. For starters, he thought we should leak a story about how President Johnson had ordered him bugged in 1968.

"You need it very much," he said firmly. "I want it." Then he leaned back and brought up my report again. "Now, you were saying where this thing leads, I mean in terms of the vulnerabilities and so forth. It's your view the vulnerabilities are basically Mitchell, Colson, Haldeman, indirectly, possibly directly. And, of course, the second level is, as far as the White House is concerned, Chapin." He looked at me. I hoped

227

he was getting the message about how bad an idea the Dean Report would be.

"And I'd say Dean, to a degree." I was telling him again about my own vulnerability.

"You?" asked the President incredulously. "Why?"

"Well, because I've been all over this thing like a blanket," I replied, dismayed that this message never seemed to sink in.

"I know, I know," said the President irritably, waving his hand as if to shoo the thought away. "But you know all about it, but you didn't, you were in it after the deed was done."

"That's correct, that I had no foreknowledge—" I replied, but the President cut me off before I could make another run at the cover-up.

"Here's the whole point. Here's the whole point," he said emphatically, shaking a forefinger. "My point is that your problem is, you..." His concentration faded. He stopped. Then he returned with force. "You have no problem. All the others that have participated in the goddamned thing, and therefore are potentially subject to criminal liability... You're not. That's the difference."

"That's right," I agreed, although I was thinking just the opposite. I couldn't bring myself to contradict his strong assertion.

There was a long, uneasy pause, before the President resumed ticking off the Watergate liabilities. He brought up Magruder, then Strachan. I told him that Strachan had pushed Magruder for intelligence "on sort of a tickler basis." After a discussion of how interwoven all the testimony might become if we tried to have just one "higher-up," like Magruder, take responsibility for the break-in, the President looked at me directly and rejected the idea. "Can't do that," he declared.

"No," I agreed. I knew it would be impossible to get one

person to take the fall without implicating others. That was the fundamental weakness of the entire cover-up.

"I think what you've got to do, to the extent that you can, John, is cut her off at the pass." The President was quite intense again, making cutting motions through the air with a flat palm. "And you cut off at the pass. Liddy and his bunch just did that as part of their job."

"They were out on a lark," I echoed, picking up the standard cover-up line.

The President now seemed to be back on the idea of a Dean Report that would cut things off at Liddy. I decided to try to work in certain grisly things that could come out if I got into specifics. I mentioned Ehrlichman and the Ellsberg break-in. The President asserted that he had never heard about it, but then immediately assumed the attitude that Howard Hunt had done the deed. I didn't for a moment believe his show of ignorance. I already suspected he often held things back from me.

We had been playing cat and mouse with each other for nearly an hour; I was the mouse, but I was becoming a little braver. Haldeman came in, and the President announced that he had to get some kind of report to Ervin quickly "so that I appear at least to be making a statement." He looked at me, then at Haldeman, and summarized the meeting for Haldeman as I listened closely. "Now, I'd simply say," the President began in a practice speech to Senator Ervin, "'Now, look, I required from every member of my staff a sworn statement. Here's one from here. Here's one from here, here, here.'" The President was handing out imaginary statements. I was elated. My message had gotten through after all.

"That's good," I said. "That's great."

"The sworn statement, Bob, is much better, rather than giving a statement by Dean," the President told Haldeman.

"That's right," I said.

Haldeman nodded and the meeting broke up. I went back to my office. I had headed the President off for the moment, but I knew he was waffling. Once Ehrlichman talked with him again, I figured, he would be back on the Dean Report. I fiddled away the afternoon until Mo called to remind me of a dinner engagement we had that night with Dick Kleindienst. We couldn't back out. Kleindienst was thinking of joining John Connally's law firm in Washington, and he was entertaining one of Connally's law partners. Mo and I went to the dinner, but I was silent most of the evening.

Kleindienst sensed my mood and commiserated with me about the rash of bad publicity I'd received. As we were preparing to leave, he pulled me aside. "I know it's tough being out front like you are, John," he said in a friendly tone, "but you've got to hold together. And think before you do anything. If things get to you, you can always come talk to me. Remember that."

"Thanks, Dick," I replied, thinking I must be telegraphing my instability. "I'd like to do that, but I don't think we should talk right now."

Marney Kleindienst, Dick's wife, had always been very kind and supportive of me. As we were saying goodbye at her door, she cracked an innocent joke to try to cheer me up. "John," she laughed, "if they send you to prison, I'll bake cookies for you and come visit you every week."

A look of terror must have crossed my face. Marney, Dick, and Mo were halfway through a tension-breaking laugh when they noticed. I tried to force a smile, but I had no control over my facial muscles.

When Marney sensed how badly she had hurt me, she went ashen. "Wait here a minute," she said anxiously. She went off and quickly returned with a folded cloth in her hand. "Here,

John," she said, "this will help your spirits."

I thanked her, but did not stop to look at the cloth. Mo hustled me out the door as if I were a mental patient.

"What's that?" she asked as we headed for the car.

I unfolded the cloth and discovered a hand-made art poster with a huge red caption: "KEEP ME GOING, LORD." Under it, a big red fireball was rolling down a green mountainside. I gaped at Mo; she gaped at me.

I shrugged. "Think this would look nice in my prison cell?"

"Really, John," she said, disgusted with my sarcasm. We rode home in silence.

After a miserable Sunday, I went to the office on Monday, March 19. Paul O'Brien came in, looking edgy, his normal wit and swagger notably missing.

"John, I've been trying to get in touch with you all weekend."

"I've been available."

"Well, I don't know why I couldn't get you." He seemed flustered.

"What's on your mind?"

"I've got some pretty heavy stuff here that's not such good news," he said. I braced myself. I was used to bad news from O'Brien, but he usually delivered it lightheartedly. "Bittman called me last Friday and asked me to meet personally with Hunt. So I went over there. And Howard Hunt's not a very happy man." He paused.

"What's new about that?"

"Well, hang on. I think you're going to find a lot new. Hunt said he was going to meet with Colson too, but I'm not so sure that's going to happen. I think Colson may send his law partner. Anyway, what Hunt was pressing me on was this. He said sentencing is coming up for him. And he's got to get his life in order pretty damn quick. He said, 'I get sentenced next Friday, and by Wednesday I want to have this whole matter resolved of these payments.' I asked him what the problem was. And Hunt said, 'Well, I've got to get things in hand well in advance of my sentencing.' And then he said what he really had in mind. He said, 'I've got a message I want you to deliver over at the White House, if you can.' And I told him I thought I could."

O'Brien is dragging this out, I thought. Here comes the money again. I quit looking at him and stared out the window. I could see myself banging back and forth between Mitchell and Ehrlichman again like a clapper in a bell.

"And I've come with Howard Hunt's message for you, John," O'Brien continued. "He said, 'You tell John Dean that I need seventy two thousand dollars for support and fifty thousand for attorney's fees—"

"Why me?" I shouted as my head shot around toward O'Brien. "Why the hell did he send the goddam message to me?"

O'Brien gave me a helpless look. "I don't know, John. I asked him the same question, and he just said, 'You tell Dean I need the money by the close of business Wednesday. And if I don't get it, I'm going to have to reconsider my options. And I'll have some seamy things to say about what I did for John Ehrlichman while I was at the White House.' And that's the message."

"You're shitting me! He sent that message to me?"

"He sure did."

I sat back and grabbed my forehead with my left hand, pressing my temples between my thumb and forefinger. Hunt

232

was dragging me directly into his extortion loop. He must have learned that I was the one who had carried the money messages before, and now he figured he had a hold on me for more. I could see Hunt extorting me, milking me, for the rest of our lives. This was it. I knew it. I felt a sickening fear, and then a boiling anger at Hunt.

I stood up and started pacing. "Listen, Paul. There's no sense bringing that message to me, because I'm not going to do a goddam thing with it. I'm out of the money business! Ever since that three-fifty went over, I'm out of it. And I plan to stay out of it. And Hunt can shove it up his ass!"

O'Brien seemed taken aback by my reaction, which was out of character. He tried to soften the blow. "Well, look. I don't think it's a message directed at you, John," he said softly. "I think it's a message he wants passed on."

"Well, I'll be goddamned if I'm going to pass it on. Both of us, as you well know, are up to our teeth in an obstruction of justice. You and I have been passing these fucking messages back and forth, and now we're in trouble. And someday we could face an awful lot of problems. And I don't want to compound mine any more. This thing has gotten bad enough for me. I'm out of it."

"I know we've got problems, John," O'Brien said. He seemed unhappy that I had mentioned his criminal liability. "Listen, I'm just passing the message along. I don't like it, either." He waited a moment for me to calm down. "Well, what are you going to do?"

"Nothing."

"Well, what the hell should I do?"

"As far as I'm concerned, you can take this back to Mitchell. This is out of my ball park. I don't want anything to do with it, Paul. And I'm not inclined to pass it on to Ehrlichman." I hesitated. "But I may have to mention it to him. I just

233

don't know."

This last comment cracked the door a little bit, enough for O'Brien to feel he might not have to carry the whole weight. We lamented a bit about how we had both gotten into this monster as message carriers and then been eaten up by it, and O'Brien left.

I went home early, canceled out on a going-away party that night for Chuck Colson, and pulled out the Scotch bottle. I had no idea what I was going to do. I was going to do something.

CHAPTER SEVEN:

BREAKING POINT

I SLEPT LATE THE NEXT MORNING, March 20. I stayed home to avoid the office and debated with myself how I could get out of this thing—deal with Hunt's extortion and protect the President at the same time. The President. I felt myself rising instinctively in salute. I thought of aircraft carriers, battles, strong men reverent at the mention of his name, a communications network that flashed each utterance around the world. This was my life's nourishment. I felt tall for having made it so close to the shadow of the Presidency. Then I contemplated the crimes and the cover-up meetings, the blackmail, and I shriveled to a midget. Alice in Wonderland.

Strategy, I told myself; we needed a strategy, and that was what I was good at. Somebody would have to walk the plank to end this; somebody would have to fall on his sword for the President. I thought of a dozen appropriate phrases, but none of them had the romantic ring I remembered from my college literature courses. Mitchell and Magruder. They were the logical candidates. They had authorized the break-in, and that was what everyone—the press, the prosecutors, the politicians, everybody—wanted to hear about. After nine months, the hot torch of skepticism had finally burned through our story that Liddy had done it on his own. Even the President could no longer lie about it convincingly, and it was eroding his power. Mitchell. That would be convincing. The first Attorney General ever to go to prison. It would end it. No one would show the slightest interest in a cover-up; no one had. Would Mitchell go it alone? I doubted it. And Mitchell had hooks in Ehrlichman, in the cover-up, in me.

I sank even lower. But what if Mitchell did take the blame for the break-in? A public orgy. Sackcloth in some quarters, glee in others. The Watergate case cracked and ended. But what would that do for Howard Hunt? Nothing. He would still demand clemency from the President and money from me, and from Ehrlichman, and from the whole cover-up network. It was a spider web. To save the President, we would all have to go together. En masse. What were the chances of that? Nearly zero. Only the President had the slightest chance of making it happen, and he seemed miles from any such decision. It could ruin him. Was I ready to do my part? Go to jail? Yes, I thought. Then, no. There had to be another way. My thoughts, I realized, were no longer measured or rational. Every breath I drew in seemed cold, and the chill latched on to my thoughts and dragged them down into my stomach, then around up my spine. My cool, my detached calculation, was dissolving in fear. I went to the office.

The President called shortly after I arrived. He wanted to meet with Dick Moore[*] and me about a letter we were preparing to send to the Senate Judiciary Committee. It was a miniature version of the Dean Report; we hoped to answer some of the questions Pat Gray had raised about my role in the Watergate investigation. I had struggled to write the letter in such a way that it would not raise more questions.

As Moore walked back to my office with me for a postmortem, I was thinking that the current draft placed me very close to perjury, and this awareness didn't help my mood. Moore tried to cheer me up.

"John, you're meeting an awful lot with the President these days, aren't you?" he said.

"Yeah, I am."

"Well, you know, this is pretty historic stuff. You're in there with the President himself. Have you ever thought about

---

[*]   Richard Moore, special counsel to the President, who worked on public-relations projects at the White House.

taking notes on those meetings? You might be glad someday."

I looked at him coldly. "Dick, frankly I wouldn't even want to write down what's going on in there right now."

Moore looked startled at the idea that anything transpiring in the Oval Office wouldn't wear golden wings in history. I noticed the discomfort my remark caused him and decided to let him know why I was so morose. Moore had recently come into the hush-money business as an extra White House courier to Mitchell.

"Look, Dick, things have gotten pretty bad the last few days," I said. "Hunt sent a message to me yesterday that he's going to blow it if he doesn't get a hundred twenty thousand dollars by tomorrow. He sent it to me personally. And he said he's going to shit all over Ehrlichman too. Said he'd have seamy things to say about what he did for Ehrlichman in the White House."

"You mean like the Ellsberg thing?"

"Yeah, like the Ellsberg thing," I replied, surprised. "How'd you know about that?"

"Oh, I picked it up around here."

"Well, he could blow that and a lot of other things. Pretty picture, isn't it?"

"Yeah. It's extortion. That's what it is," Moore said, shaking his head.

"I know, and I'm fed up with it. It keeps going on and on, and someday it's going to blow. People are going to keep committing perjury. More and more people know about it. The money payments are chewing people up. It just keeps growing and growing. You know it's bad, and I'm telling you it's even worse than you know. Bigger and bigger." I was gushing.

The white-haired Moore looked kind and grandfatherly.

He shook his head slowly, sadly. "It's like some sort of tumor, I guess. It's like a cancer."

"That's right," I said, struck by the image. "And the President's got to do something to sever it. I tell you, I think he's being ill-served by his aides. All of us. It can't go on like this."

Moore and I agreed we would have to think harder about how to extricate the President. Then he left. I sat down at my desk, freshly aware of how much bigger the stakes were than I felt equipped to handle. Hunt's demands kept rearing up in my mind, and I decided I couldn't simply sit on them. I would have to pass the message along to Ehrlichman at least.

I went over to his office and found him on his way to the Oval Office.

He was in a hurry. We stood in the middle of his office, and I told him about my meeting with O'Brien. The demands coming straight at me. The implied threat to Krogh. The direct threat to him.

"That's interesting," he replied simply, heading for the door.

I followed him, once more amazed by his composure, worried that he could see how totally I'd lost mine. But I didn't really care. "Well, John, what are you going to do?" I asked as we walked down the West Wing stairs.

He turned to look at me over his glasses. "Have you raised this little sugarplum with Mitchell yet?"

"No, I haven't."

"How about Chuck? He's supposed to be holding Mr. Hunt's hand these days. What does he say?"

"I don't know. O'Brien told me Hunt was sending the same message to Chuck, but I don't think there's a damn thing he can do."

"Well, why don't you have a little chat with Mitchell? And get back to me, okay?"

Ehrlichman turned down the hall toward the President's office. I stopped. This man is made of iron, I thought. I was envious, then furious. I watched him stride down the hall, and then I headed toward the EOB.

I reached Mitchell at his New York apartment. "John, have you heard about our latest demand?" I asked, to make sure O'Brien or LaRue had filled him in.

"Yeah, I've heard," Mitchell sighed.

I heard a noise on the line. My paranoia rose further. LaRue had warned me to take extreme care in speaking with Mitchell at home, because Martha had a habit of listening in on the extension. She might call the press. "Well, ah, John," I said, "can I report any progress? Is the Greek bearing gifts?" I was referring to Tom Pappas.

"I can't talk about it now," said Mitchell. "I'll call you tomorrow." Click. I stared at the phone. Same old back-and-forth. I was determined not to get back into it. Sure, I said to myself, but that's what you said yesterday.

Bud Krogh walked in. He was the Undersecretary of Transportation, newly confirmed by the Senate, and he looked the part. He had a wardrobe full of new suits, and he had lost a great deal of weight from a vigorous jogging program. He sat down and began commiserating with me over all the bad press I was getting from the Gray hearings. He was trying to cheer me up, being very solicitous of my feelings.

"It's a lot worse than the Gray hearings, Bud," I told him after we had talked awhile. "That's peanuts. And while you're here, I think I should tell you that you might be in jeopardy yourself. Hang on. This is rough. Howard Hunt's blackmailing us, Bud. He's holding us up for everything we've got, and then some. And his latest threat is that he's going to blow the

239

Ellsberg thing on Ehrlichman. If he does, I don't see how you could get out of that. I'm sorry to lay that on you, but I thought you should know. This whole goddam mess is at the breaking point."

Bud got up and walked over to my window. It was dark outside. He looked out for a couple of minutes and turned back to me. He looked more resigned, and less resistant, than I had expected. "What are the chances Hunt's going to talk?" he asked.

"I have no idea. The whole thing's up in the air right now, and I don't really want to get into that. But you've got to understand something else. If there's an investigator who's worth his salt up on the Ervin Committee, there are going to be some rough problems."

"What do you mean?"

"Well, during the Watergate trial the Justice Department got a file on Hunt and Liddy from the CIA. And the file included some pictures, and they're incredible pictures, Bud. Some of the goddam pictures are of Liddy standing out in front of this Dr. Fielding's office in California. He's standing there proud as a rooster. And any investigator who sees that picture is going to want to know what's happening. And he's going to plow right in and find out that Dr. Fielding is connected to Ellsberg and that there was a break-in at his office. Ehrlich-man's been trying to have me get those documents back from Justice and over to CIA so no one will run into them. But the CIA's not about to take them. Those guys are playing this pretty damn smart, and they don't want that stuff. And Henry Petersen can't do anything with them, either, because he's got this letter from Mansfield[*] telling him to hold on to all the

---

[*]   [Original Footnote:] In early January 1973 Senate Majority Leader Mike Mansfield informed all the relevant executive departments and agencies of the impending Senate investigation, and requested that all documents that might relate to 1972 campaign practices or to Watergate be carefully maintained.

stuff. That's another way the whole thing could unravel. And there are more. A lot of people seem to know about it."

Bud looked at me stoically. "Listen, John, if the damn thing's going to come out, it's going to come out." Bud had been a tough cookie at the White House; now he looked like Sir Thomas More facing the executioners bravely. "I'll tell you something. I haven't really had a good day since I went over there to Transportation. I'm troubled by my confirmation hearings up in the Senate. I think I may have crossed the line up there. I tell you, I thought about saying this was all national-security stuff, but I decided just to sort of dodge it. I don't even like to read back over my testimony."

He's worried about perjury, too, I thought. I decided to get him off the subject. "How strong is Hunt's hand on this, Bud? Did John approve this Ellsberg thing?"

"No," he answered. "I don't think John knew much about it."

His reply caught me off guard. I suspected Bud might be trying to protect Ehrlichman, his mentor, and then I worried that Hunt might know even more "seamy things" about Ehrlichman. "Well, how in the hell did it happen, then?"

Bud glanced over toward the West Wing. "That one came right out of the Oval Office, John," he said gravely.

"You're kidding," I said, sinking back in my chair. There was a pause.

"Goddammit, I hope this thing never comes out," said Bud. "But if it does, I'm ready for it. I've talked to my wife about this whole thing, and we're together. If the curtain comes down, I'll just have to stand up. I tell you, I'm not eager for it, but sometimes I'd just as soon get it over with."

"I've been feeling that way, too," I said. "If this thing isn't put to rest soon, the President's going to have some big problems. I don't think we've advised him very well on this whole

241

mess."

Bud and I rambled on and then parted as if we were leaving someone's death bed. Fielding came in as I was leaving the office, and I gave him my pitch about how the cover-up was coming to a head. He seemed taken aback, as much by my attitude as by my words.

As I walked in the door of my house the phone rang. Pete Kinsey, one of my staff lawyers, who was over for dinner, answered it. "John! It's the President!" he said, between a whisper and a shout. He almost dropped the telephone.

It was the first time the President had ever called me at home. As I went to take the call I motioned to Mo to bring me a drink.

"You are having rather long days these days, aren't you?" he asked, almost tenderly. "I guess we all are."

"I think they will continue to be longer," I replied, surprised that I didn't snap to my usual optimism for his benefit. My mind was sprinting ahead, trying to figure out why the President was calling me. Then, when he launched into a sales pitch on the Dean Report, I knew. Ehrlichman had gotten to him and charged him up about the report again. He'd probably also told Nixon that I seemed shaky. That would make sense. I had revealed my fears to a lot of people that day; such news would travel fast. This was a stroking call, mixed with a little pressure on the report.

As the President talked, I assembled the strands of my courage and asked him for a private meeting, the first time I had done so. "I would think, if it's not inconvenient for you, sir, I would like to sort of draw all my thoughts together and have a, just make some notes to myself so I didn't—"

"Could you do it tomorrow?" the President interrupted.

"Yes, sir," I said. I had wanted more time to prepare, but I would take what I could. "Yes, sir."

"Well, then, we could probably do it, say, around ten o'clock."

"That would be fine, sir."

I had gulped down my drink by the end of the phone call, and I kept up the pace afterward. I avoided Watergate conversation all evening, until Mo and I were going to bed. Then I told her I was going to lay it all out for the President the next day. And I also said that my fears about going to jail were real and growing, but she dismissed the idea and I didn't press it.

The next morning I called Haldeman and told him what I was about to do: I was going to tell the President that the Dean Report was a bad idea, and I was going to tell him that the cover-up couldn't go on. To my surprise, Haldeman didn't protest at all. He wished me well.

As I was composing my thoughts for the meeting, Fred LaRue walked in. He sat down in the chair in front of me without taking his coat off. "John, what are you going to do about the message Hunt sent?" he asked.

"Nothing, Fred."

"Well, what do you think I ought to do?"

"I think you ought to get your directions from Mitchell on that."

"Okay," he sighed. "That's all I wanted to know."

I was far more nervous than I had been that first time I'd met the President at San Clemente, nearly three years ago. It seemed like a very long walk from my office to the Oval Office. I sat in the waiting room as Ehrlichman met with the President. I went in as he came out. Ehrlichman had left a chair directly in front of the President's desk, on the blue rug. I sat down in it instead of in my usual chair off to the side.

The President seemed in remarkably good spirits. We exchanged pleasantries and comments on the morning's news. I sat up on the edge of my chair. The President put his elbows on the arms of his chair and clasped his hands together, resting his chin on his fingers. He looked at me intently, studying me. I felt like an actor on stage for a big performance, with a bad case of butterflies.

"Uh, the reason I thought we ought to talk this moming," I began, "is because in our conversations, uh, I have the impression that you don't know everything I know." This opening was partly true and partly false. Like a good staff man, I wanted to give the President "deniability," just as I had been indoctrinated to do since my first day in the White House, even though most of what I was telling him now was not new. Also, I wanted to give him room to respond with shock and drastic action.

"That's right," said the President.

I warmed up to my first blast to grab his attention; I had settled on Moore's "cancer" metaphor. "I think there's no doubt about the seriousness of the problem we've got," I said. "We have a cancer within close to the Presidency—that's growing. It's growing daily. It's compounding. It grows geometrically now, because it compounds itself. Uh, that'll be clear as I explain, you know, some of the details of why it is. And it basically is because: one, we're being blackmailed; two, people are going to start perjuring themselves...to protect other people and the like." I had my hands out in front of me, ticking these vulnerabilities off on my fingers. Then I stopped. "And that is just... And there is no assurance..." I hesitated.

"That it won't bust," the President concluded for me.

"That it won't bust."

"True," said the President, nodding, his chin still resting on his hands.

"So let me give you some of the basic facts," I continued, and I began a long narrative on the origins of the break-in. I wanted to make absolutely certain he knew what I was building on, because he so often forgot from one day to the next what I had told him. My worries on this point diminished as I went along. The President was with me. I could almost feel his concentration. Each question he asked was acute, and he didn't ask many. Most of his interruptions had to do with Haldeman's vulnerability for the events before the break-in, which was understandable. Haldeman was so close to the President that his vulnerability was nearly indistinguishable from the President's own. I picked up the pace of the story, encouraged by the President's state of mind, and ran on to the day of the arrests.

"Now..." I drew a deep sigh. "What has happened post-June seventeenth? Well, I was under pretty clear instructions..." I succumbed to a short, nervous laugh. I was about to tell the President that the "Dean investigation" was a lie, which he knew, but it wasn't easy to say "...uh, not to really investigate this. That this was something that just could have been disastrous on the election if it had all hell had broken loose. And I worked on a theory of containment."

"Sure," the President said.

"To try to hold it right where it was." I was seeking his approval, and I got it.

"Right."

"There is no doubt, I, uh, that I was, totally aware of what the Bureau was doing at all times. I was totally aware of what the grand jury was doing—"

"You mean..."

"I knew what witnesses were going to be called. I knew what they were going to be asked, and I had to. There just—"

"Why did Petersen play the game so straight with us?" asked the President suddenly. He had dropped his hands from his chin and was looking at me with genuine curiosity.

245

"Because Petersen is a soldier," I replied. "He kept me informed. He told me when we had problems, where we had problems, and the like. He believes in-in you. He believes in this Administration. This Administration had made him. I don't think he's done anything improper, but he did make sure the investigation was narrowed down to the very, very…"

"Right," the President overlapped, nodding.

"…fine…"

"Right."

"…criminal things, which was a break for us. There is no doubt about it."

"He honestly feels that he did an adequate job?" the President asked incredulously. I responded in a way that I hoped would get him off the subject of Petersen, who had nothing to do with the message I was trying to deliver. Besides, I was afraid he was about to start identifying with the investigators again, as he had done so often when he reminisced about the Hiss case.

I dispensed with Petersen, and quickly brought the President to the raw nerve—money: "All right, so arrangements were made through Mitchell, initiating it, in discussions that—I was present—that these guys had to be taken care of. Their attorneys' fees had to be done. Kalmbach was brought in. Kalmbach raised some cash. Uh, they were obvi— uh, you know…" I was hesitating over whether I could be so blunt as to say that the defendants had clearly been going to blow if we didn't pay them. The President interrupted me.

"They put that under the cover of a Cuban Committee or something, didn't they?"

The question stunned me. The Cuban Committee was a technical part of only one of our payment schemes. A committee had been set up to collect defense funds for the Cuban defendants, and we had planned it; the committee would be flooded with anonymous cash. As it turned out, Hunt had preferred to have the money delivered directly to him and his wife, and the committee had never been used. If the President knew about such monetary details, I could not be revealing much to him. I acknowledged the existence of the Cuban Committee, and told him about the payments to Hunt's wife.

"Maybe it's too late to do anything about it," he replied, "but I would certainly keep that cover for what it's worth." He laughed nervously.

"I'll—"

"Keep the committee," he repeated.

"After, after—well, that, that..." I was sputtering. The President's cognizance of the committee, and his wish to keep it alive, punctured any hope that he would recoil in shock from whatever I might tell him. I tried to recover; if I couldn't impress him with details of the cover-up, I'd hammer in the implications. "And that's the most troublesome post-thing," I went on, "because: one, Bob is involved in that; John is involved in that; I am involved in that; Mitchell is involved in that."

I was counting on my fingers again. "And that is an obstruction of justice."

The President sat back, as if I had breathed into his face. "In other words, the fact that, uh, you're, you're taking care of the witness."

"That's right," I stated.

"How was Bob involved?" He was worried about Haldeman.

I described the transfer of the three-fifty fund and that Haldeman had approved the payments. Feeling that I was making progress, I mentioned the assurances of clemency that Caulfield had offered McCord. "As you know," I said pointedly, "Colson has talked indirectly to Hunt about commutation." I stopped to clear my throat. This was tough. I began to lose my nerve. "All these things are bad, in that they are problems. They are promises. They are commitments. They are the very sort of thing that the Senate is going to be looking most for. I don't think they can find them, frankly."

"Pretty hard," the President said.

"Pretty hard," I agreed. "Damn hard. It's all cash."

"Well, I mean, pretty hard as far as the witnesses are concerned." Nixon was focusing on the issue of clemency, the single fact that only two or three witnesses, and they unlikely ones, could testify against him. I regretted that I had given him an opening to see the cover-up as solid and tried to regain momentum by getting back to Hunt's money demands. "Now, the blackmail is continuing," I said. I told him of the latest threats, including a threat directly to Ehrlichman. We rambled on about the Ellsberg break-in, until I intruded to tell the President that Hunt had been unstable since his wife's death.

"Great sadness," he said. He turned in his chair and looked off. "As a matter of fact, there was some discussion over there with somebody about Hunt's problems after his wife died." He cleared his throat. Both of us seemed to do so whenever we had to raise something particularly bothersome. "And I said, of course, commutation could be considered on the basis of his wife, and that's the only discussion I ever had in that light."

"Right," I said. The President was confirming the Colson conversation to me and at the same time he was offering the humanitarian reasoning he would use in order to pardon Hunt.

I returned to the money. "Uh, Mitchell's been working on raising some money, feeling he's got, you know, he's one of the ones with the most to lose. But there's no denying the fact that the White House, and Ehrlichman, Haldeman, Dean are involved in some of the early money decisions."

248

"How much money do you need?" the President asked suddenly, breaking off my recitation of criminal liability in the White House. He seemed impatient with that line.

I paused. I had no idea what kind of figure to put on the future blackmail, but I had to pick a number. "I would say these people are going to cost, uh, a million dollars over the next, uh, two years."

"We could get that," he declared firmly.

"Uh-huh," I mumbled. The President was moving in the opposite direction from the horror I badly wanted him to express, and I was softening.

"If you need the money," he continued, "I mean you could get the money. Let's say..."

"Well, I think that we're going to—"

"What I mean is you could get a million dollars. And you could get it in cash. I know where it could be gotten."

"Uh-huh." I thought that the President was almost boasting about his ability to lay his hands on a million dollars of loose, untraceable cash.

"I mean it's not easy, but it could be done," he stated. He was leaning forward, his hands folded on his desk. "But the question is, who the hell would handle it?"

"That's right," I said. I brightened at the prospect of running through another litany of troubles.

"Any ideas on that?" He was asking for positive ideas on how to deliver money, I realized, not evidence of how the task had broken both Kalmbach and LaRue.

"Well, I would think that would be something that Mitchell ought to be charged with," I replied. The President had turned me around—it was the first of many reversals—and I was back on track, the standard White House cover-up line addressed negatively, hostilely toward Mitchell. I ran down some of the problems LaRue was having in raising money. "People are going to ask what the money is for," I said. "He's working, he's apparently talked to Tom Pappas."

The President nodded. "I know."

This comment, like the one concerning the Cuban Committee, set me back. Only four people knew about the Pappas contact: LaRue, Mitchell, Ehrlichman, and myself. I figured then that Ehrlichman had not been protecting Nixon from such details, since he seemed to know everything. The conversation sailed around the money issue before I brought myself to make another run at the President with still another weakness in the cover-up: Krogh was haunted because he'd perjured himself before the Senate committee that had confirmed him.

"What did he perjure himself on, John?"

I was in a bind. Krogh hadn't told me exactly how he had testified.

I faltered, then made a guess. "His... Did, uh, did he know the Cubans? He did."

"He said he didn't?"

"That's right. They didn't press him hard. Or that he..."

I was attempting to drum up another possible way Bud might have perjured himself, when the President interrupted me. "He might be able to—I am just trying to think. Perjury is an awful tough rap to prove. He could say, 'I...'" He was beginning a perjury defense for Krogh. He stopped and waved the problem away as if it weren't worth the effort. "Well, go ahead."

I coughed several times to give myself a space to think. The President was returning each of my volleys like a backboard. Each time, I backed off before hitting again. "Well, so that's, that's the first, that's one perjury," I said, thinking maybe a whole list might have more impact. "Now Mitchell and Magruder are potential perjurers." I went down the perjury list, but I thought I saw the President's concentration drifting for the first time.

He shifted in his chair and looked straight at me. He was back now, and frowning. "Don't you—just looking at the immediate problem—don't you have to handle Hunt's financial situation..."

"I think that's...damn soon? That's—I talked to Mitchell about that last night."

"Mitchell." The President nodded approvingly.

"And, uh, I told—I was getting set to tell him about my problems when he interrupted."

"Might as well," he said firmly. "May have to rule you've got to keep the cap on the bottle that much."

He would not welcome any contradiction, and I didn't give him any. "That's right. That's right."

"In order to have any options."

"That's right," I said. I was turned around again. Maybe he is right, I began to think. After all, he's an old pro at this sort of thing; maybe I'm just nervous. In any case, my acquiescence seemed to reduce the tension in the room.

My steam was down. I rambled about Kalmbach and lesser weak spots until he broke in to change direction.

"But what are your feelings yourself, John? You know pretty well what they all say. What are your feelings about the options?"

I twisted inside. Surely, the President must know what my feelings were after all this. I suspected that he was testing me now, taking his own reading on how reliably I'd stay on course. I didn't want him to think I would be all that reliable. "I am not confident that, uh, we can ride through this," I confessed. "I think there are, I think there are soft spots." I felt as if I was one of them.

"You used to feel comfortable," he said quietly. The remark hung in the air. It cut into my exposed emotions—guilt and loyalty. Guilt. He was drawing my attention to my loud enthusiasm about the cover-up, calling up memories of the September 15 meeting, making me feel that my tough demeanor had contributed to the dilemma. Loyalty. He was implying that I was abandoning ship. I felt beaten down. I felt I had lost his confidence by admitting to a certain weakness. My rise in the White House was over.

We meandered, but the dynamic did not change. I had been on the offensive, with the President battening down my cover-up woes. Now he was on the offensive, drawing me out, testing options. "All right," he said, starting down a new path. "Now go on. So what you really come down to is, is what the hell will you do? Let's suppose that you and Haldeman and Ehrlichman and Mitchell say, 'We can't hold this.' What then are you going to say? Are you going to put out a complete disclosure? Isn't that the best plan?"

I couldn't rally to this idea any longer. I knew the President didn't intend to disclose the rat's nest we'd just clambered through. The question was insincere. He was probing, I thought, to see how far I might defect. But I figured I'd at least give him my best thinking on this option. "Well, one way to do it is to—"

"That'd be my view of it," he interrupted.

"One way to do it is for you to tell the Attorney General that you finally, you know, really this is the first time you are getting all the pieces together."

"Ask for another grand jury?"

"Ask for another grand jury," I said. And I told him how

252

best I thought it could be done. "But some people are going to have to go to jail. That's the long and short of it, also," I concluded.

"Who? Let's talk about that." The President was leaning toward me again, intent.

"All right. I think I could, for one."

"You go to jail?" he asked in disbelief.

"That's right."

"Oh, hell, no," said the President, shaking his head as if the idea were absurd. "I don't see how you can." Later, when I had explained to him that I was vulnerable for the obstruction of justice, he replied, "Well, I don't know. I think [that] that, I feel, could be cut off at the pass. Maybe the obstruction of justice..."

"It could be a—you know how—one of the—that's, that's why..." I was sputtering again, I couldn't bring myself to agree or disagree. I gave up in a sigh.

The President asked how I might be construed to be guilty of obstruction.

"Well," I responded wearily, "I've been a conduit for information on taking care of people out there who are guilty of crimes."

"Oh, you mean like the blackmail."

"The blackmail. Right."

"Well, I wonder if that part of it can't be, I wonder if that doesn't, let me put it frankly: I wonder if that doesn't have to be continued?" The question was declarative.

Back to the Hunt demands. I cleared my throat to avoid having to say anything.

"Let me put it this way," he continued. "Let us suppose

253

that you get, you get the million bucks, and you get the proper way to handle it, and you could hold that side."

"Uh-huh."

"It would seem to me that would be worthwhile."

I cleared my throat and again said nothing. I looked at the floor to avoid the President's eyes, which I knew would be seeking agreement.

He didn't press. Instead, he went to other subjects. Then he asked who else might have to go to jail. I decided not to try out any more notions about perjuries or obstructions. I simply said Ehrlichman might have to go.

"Why Ehrlichman? What'd he do?"

I drew a breath. "Because of this conspiracy to burglarize the, uh, Ellsberg office."

"You mean, that is, provided Hunt breaks," the President said, qualifying the danger to Ehrlichman.

"Well, uh, let me say something interesting about that. Within the files—" I was getting ready to clue him in on yet another route of discovery.

He interrupted. "Oh, I saw that. The picture."

Jesus Christ, I thought, the President knows as much about all this as I do. He not only knows about the Liddy picture, he's seen it. If he knows all this, surely he can't think this cover-up will hold. I laid out a few other ways the Ellsberg break-in might come out, and then I made one more run at my original thrust: "But what I am coming to you today with is: I don't have a plan of how to solve it right now, but I think it's at the juncture that we should begin to think in terms of, of how to cut the losses, how to minimize the further growth of this thing rather than further compound it by, you know, ultimately paying these guys forever."

"Yeah. "

"I think we've got to look—"

"But at the moment," the President intruded, leaning forward again, "don't you agree that you'd better get the Hunt thing? I mean, that's worth it, at the moment."

"That's worth buying time on, right."

"And that's worth buying time on, I agree." He had agreed quickly, as if it were my idea. I was turned around again and I had very little spirit left. Ehrlichman must have whispered in his ear about Hunt's demands.

Soon the President buzzed for Haldeman and summarized our meeting for him accurately and succinctly: we had to buy time by meeting Hunt's immediate money demands; he listed almost all the "soft spots" in the cover-up that I had identified.

"The point is," said the President, turning to me, "your feeling is that we just can't continue to pay the blackmail of these guys?"

"I think that's our greatest jeopardy," I agreed.

"Yeah," said Haldeman.

"Now, let me tell you, it's no problem," said the President. "We could get the money. There is no problem in that. We can't provide the clemency. The money can be provided. Mitchell could provide the way to deliver it. That could be done. See what I mean?"

"But Mitchell says he can't, doesn't he?" Haldeman asked me.

"Mitchell says that— Well, that's an interesting thing. That's been an interesting phenomenon all the way along on this. It's that there have been a lot of people having to pull oars, and not everybody pulls them at the same time, the same way, because they all develop self-interests."

"What John is saying," Haldeman told the President, "is that everybody smiles at Dean and says, 'Well, you better get something done about it.'"

"That's right," I said, grateful to him for stating it far more bluntly than I dared.

"And Mitchell is leaving Dean hanging out on a... None of us." Haldeman paused. "Well, maybe we're doing the same thing to you," he confessed.

"That's right," I agreed.

The meeting went on through the same points over and over, although I was not much of an advocate for my position any longer. Haldeman wound up by saying that the Watergate erosion was now hitting directly at the President and had to be stopped at any cost.

It finally ended, after nearly two hours. I went back to my office feeling as if I had been squeezed in a vise, experiencing all the unpleasant emotions pressure can bring to bear. My head ached from the mental effort of trying to keep up with all the nuances going on behind the dialogue with the President. There was some relief, however, in having unburdened myself of my doubts about the cover-up. Those above me were now fully aware. Maybe the cover-up was in more capable hands. And I had the solace of having gone through an entire meeting without hearing the Dean Report mentioned.

But even that comfort vanished the same afternoon. Ehrlichman joined Haldeman, Nixon, and Dean, and he lost no time in advocating the Dean Report as the needed solution. Ehrlichman was clever and blunt. He came out directly and said that the Dean Report would give the President a public alibi if the cover-up were to collapse. As always, I wondered how much he was motivated by devotion to the President as opposed to his own protection. I figured—perhaps generously—about fifty-fifty. This meeting accomplished nothing; we simply went round and round. I mentioned the cancer again, Ehrlichman countered with the Dean Report. The only new development was a consensus that Mitchell should be summoned to Washington; he would be cajoled to step forward, own up, walk the plank.

When I went home on the evening of March 21, I avoided Mo's questions. The day seemed to have lasted forever, and I tried to stretch out the night's reprieve with alcohol. I found myself searching for something to look forward to—anything. The search was fruitless, until I began meditating sardonically about the Mitchell meeting which was set for the next day. It would be a real Armageddon. Haldeman, Ehrlichman, and Mitchell in a shootout. Lives and empires at stake. I visualized it as something like the Napoleonic Wars—bluffs, frontal attacks, and mass slaughter—and drifted off to sleep with such thoughts.

The four of us gathered the next morning in Haldeman's office, and I waited for the first missile to blast off. It didn't happen. Once Mitchell said, in code, that Hunt's immediate blackmail threat had been "taken care of," the drums stopped beating. The communication reached new heights of internal stonewalling. I was astonished. It was dominated by nervous pleasantries and indirect ribbing, but with no confrontation, not even an acknowledgment that a cover-up, a Presidency, and criminal prosecutions might be hanging in the balance. It was as if four men were discussing adultery: each knew the others were cheating, each was reluctant to admit it first.

In the afternoon, we four met with the President and there were more jokes and further evasions. At one point, the President asked me what I really hoped to gain with the idea of opening up Watergate, lancing the boil.

"What it's doing, Mr. President, is getting you up above and away from it," I replied seriously. "And that's the most important thing."

"Oh, I know," said the President. "But I suggested that the other day, and we all came down on—remember, we came down on the negative on it. Now what's changed our mind?"

"The lack of alternatives, or a body," I said, meaning that no one was willing to risk jail, alone or in company. The whole group broke up in laughter—this time not nervous, pressured laughter, but guffaws.

"We went down every alley," said Ehrlichman, and he peered over his glasses at each of us in a mock search for a volunteer. More laughter.

"Well," said the President, "I feel that at the very minimum we've got to have the statement, and let's look at it." He meant some kind of Dean Report. "Whatever the hell it is. If it opens up doors, it opens up doors, you know."

"John says he's sorry he sent those burglars in there, and that helps a lot," quipped Ehrlichman, looking at Mitchell.

"That's right," said the President.

"You are very welcome, sir." Mitchell took his pipe from his mouth and bowed graciously. More laughter.

"Just glad the others didn't get caught," said Haldeman.

"Yeah." The President smiled. "The ones we sent to Muskie and all the rest. Jackson and Hubert, too."

So much for the idea of someone stepping forward, I thought as I went home that night. I had other things to worry about. Pat Gray had testified that day, in his endless confirmation hearings, that I had "probably lied" by telling FBI agents right after the break-in that Howard Hunt had no White House connections. I was furious at Gray. Ziegler told me I would be in the next day's headlines, and the next morning I awoke to find my house surrounded by TV cameras, news reporters, a whole army. There was a banner headline in the *Washington*

Post: DEAN PROBABLY LIED.* I retreated to the kitchen to consider my choices, feeling like an outlaw; I could wade into the reporters and tell the truth, which would mean calling Gray a liar; I could really blow my stack and tell the reporters to ask Gray what he had done with the documents from Hunt's safe; or I could go out and say, "No comment, no comment," like a Mafioso. I rejected all the alternatives and decided to hole up at home, pulling the curtains, drawing the blinds.

Then my private White House line rang. It was Paul O'Brien, with big news. Judge Sirica had just read in court a letter from James McCord in which McCord charged that there had been perjury committed at his trial, hush money paid, and higher-ups involved in the break-in. There was a rapid round of phone calls to assess what damage McCord might do, but we concluded that he knew nothing but hearsay, though his charges would give reporters a hook for stories they had been longing to write. The dam was cracking.

The President called later in the morning. I offered my judgment of what harm McCord could cause—lots of heat, little foreseeable legal effect. The President said that I had been right when I'd told him something would break, and that McCord was a hell of a lot better than Hunt. I agreed. He took me by surprise by suggesting that I needed a vacation. He said he wanted me to go up to Camp David for a few days' rest. I protested that Mrs. Nixon and Tricia were up there. Mo and I would be in the way. The President insisted. I wondered what the purpose behind this stroke was, but I gave in. In fact, I was

---

*   The most fundamental problem with Gray's speculation, not to mention the accuracy of whatever information he was relying on from the FBI agents who had asked about Hunt's office, was the fact that they never asked if Hunt had an office. What, in fact, occurred was the agents had asked if they could *see* Hunt's office. I said I would have to check because another Colson aide now occupied the office, which was true. Also, by the time I was asked about Hunt's office, I knew that the contents of Hunt's safe had already been removed.

259

eager to get away. When the press finally gave up and melted away from my house, I called my limousine driver and we headed straight for Camp David.

As we rode, I sank deep into thought, far removed from Mo's excited chatter about the thrills of being a guest at the Presidential retreat. I almost wished I were alone. I was, for all practical purposes, because Mo refused to let her gloomy husband dampen her anticipation. I looked out the window at the brown mountainsides of the Catoctins, and for the first time I thought about escaping from it all, be free. I would not have to go to jail or testify against anyone. The cover-up could be blamed on me, and what had happened earlier on Mitchell.

I could imagine Mitchell huddled with the President, plotting it out: the President calling his old friend General So-and-So and making a secret deal; a helicopter snatching Mo and me at Camp David and taking us to some little-used Air Force base, then on to Latin America; living in grand splendor as guests of some Latin businessmen, waiting for it all to pass. Maybe Bebe could help. What would Mo tell her mother and what would I tell my folks? How would our disappearance be explained? Would they say we had been killed in an accident? What kind of name would my son inherit?

Now our White House driver announced that he was lost. The main road to Camp David was closed for repairs, and Mo was giving him advice, based on instincts, about which back road was the right one to a place she had never been. My thoughts settling back into reality, I suggested that the driver use his radio to ask for directions. But he was embarrassed to be lost and didn't want to admit it on the radio. Mo might be right, he thought. In fact she was, and we soon arrived, were checked through, and shown our cabin.

The phone rang even before the driver could bring our suitcases in—long, irregular rings that told me the operator had an important call. When I answered, she said it was the President, but Haldeman came on the line. This meant that the President had placed the call but that Haldeman had suggested he do the talking. "How is Camp David?" he asked, as if calling for a social chat.

"Fine. The sun's out, and there are a few buds on the trees. It's very quiet and peaceful after being surrounded by those goddam newsmen at my house. Thank God they won't be allowed up here."

"While you're up there, the President would like you to take a shot at writing up the report we talked about on Watergate." I wasn't surprised by this old and unwelcome charge, but I hadn't expected to hear it from Haldeman, who had not pushed the Dean Report since I had spelled out the consequences to him.

"Bob, are you talking about a report for internal use or for issuing publicly?"

"Don't know yet."

"Well, it makes a big difference in how I write—" I started to explain, when he interrupted.

"Give it your best try and we'll decide later," he said.

I assured him I would begin in the morning.

I was sure Haldeman knew it was a setup, and I thought he felt some discomfort in doing it to me. I was bitter that he was beginning to turn on me. Yet if it would help the President, maybe it was the right thing to do. I escaped into a martyr fantasy. Everybody except the President was expendable, including me, and I knew exactly what would happen when it all started to crumble in toward him. With my report in hand, he would go before the cameras to report that his counsel had given him all this information, that he had believed him, and trusted his investigation, but that obviously he had lied, had misled and deceived him. Only Haldeman, Ehrlichman, Mitchell, and the President would know I was making a sacrifice to keep the Nixon Presidency from being consumed by Watergate, and I would go to jail a disgraced scoundrel. I was sure financial arrangements would be made for Mo while I was in prison. Or was I? Probably Howard Hunt had been sure. Would LaRue add me to his list?

It was not the time to try to sort all these things out. Mo was enjoying Camp David. Before I'd finished talking to Haldeman, she had donned one of the navy-blue Camp David windbreakers with the Presidential emblem and was modeling it for me. Now she was exploring our luxurious rustic quarters. It was too late to explore the grounds; it would be dark soon. It was time for the network news, but I didn't want to hear it. I knew what it would be: McCord's letter to Sirica would lead all three networks.

The next day I began making notes of the pre-June 17 activities—notes that could incriminate no one other than Liddy. As I jotted down the highlights of the planning meetings in Mitchell's office, I was able to make everyone at the White House come out well. What I wrote was true as far as it went, which wasn't very far. When I arrived at the point where the "Dean investigation" was announced by the President on August 29, 1972, I was stuck. I went to find Mo.

"I'm bored," she said. "There isn't even anything on television, and I didn't bring a book with me. The books up here are all so dull."

"I know, sweetheart, but I've got to work on this damn report."

"Why right now?"

"Well..." I didn't have a good answer, so I suggested we tour Camp David in the electric golf cart that had been parked near our cabin for our use. It was chilly, so Mo bundled well and snuggled beside me as we drove about the woods. We soon arrived at the perimeter road, where we sped along under

262

the watchful eyes of the sentries.

"I've got the feeling someone's always watching us up here," Mo said.

"Probably so," I grunted.

"Stop. Stop, John. Look over there," Mo said, grasping my knee. A graceful long-eared fawn was standing at the chain-link fence, staring at us. "Isn't she beautiful?" Mo asked, excited.

"She sure is. I bet she's wondering why that fence is in her woods."

As we talked, the fawn quickly disappeared into her part of the woods.

Mo moved closer to me on the golf cart's seat. She wanted to talk about what was in my head. "Why do you think you're in such serious trouble?"

"Well, sweetheart, it's awful complex and I don't really—"

"You didn't have anything to do with that stupid break-in, I hope."

"Not directly. That's not my problem. It's what happened after those guys got arrested."

"Is the President in trouble? I thought you were going to warn him."

"I did, but I was like Caspar Milquetoast going in to the boss for a raise. I went in there Wednesday and tried to paint a picture of what the problems were. I tried to be as dramatic as I could. He listened, but by the end of our meeting he had turned me around again. Out I went, almost thanking him for not listening to me. Just call me Mr. Milquetoast, dear."

"Are you afraid of the President?"

I paused to think about the question. "Yeah, kinda. I'm not

really afraid of the man who is President of the United States anymore. He's really no different than anybody else. That was something that I had to realize slowly. But I'm afraid of who he really is and the power he commands as he sits in the Oval Office. If this cover-up goes on, he's going to be in really serious trouble, and I can't believe he doesn't recognize that. He knows he's got a problem, and he knows there is no easy answer, because I'm not the only one working for him who's got a serious problem."

"You mean Haldeman is involved, too?" she asked.

"Yep, and Ehrlichman and Mitchell and others."

"That's awful, John. What are you all going to do?"

"Let's talk about it after I sort it all out. I'm thinking of getting myself a lawyer, some guy who really knows the criminal law, and having him tell me how serious my problem is."

As we came out of the woods near the helicopter pad, Mo asked, "That report you're writing— is this what it's all about?"

"Not exactly. In fact, not at all. It's an idea of Ehrlichman's to protect the President by giving him a report that says everything is okay and no one in the White House has any problems. It says everything is just hunky-dory."

"That's not true, though, is it?"

"No, it's not."

"Then, John, you shouldn't write that report. That's not very smart."

She was right, but her innocence annoyed me. She seemed so far removed from all the shadings of lies that make up political life. How could she possibly understand the pressure to just do something when the President wants it, regardless of whether you think it's dumb or wrong? Or that my doing such things had enabled her to enjoy Camp David and countless other White House privileges? Still, even though she knew

264

nothing of the details of Watergate, or the rationale behind the report, or all that had gone on before, she had hit the mark intuitively.

When we returned to our cabin I called Fred Fielding, told him I had been asked to write a report, and asked him to go through my files, pull out anything he felt might relate to Watergate and arrange to have Jane come up on Monday to do some typing. That evening I turned again to work on the report, but the assignment was increasingly repulsive. I went out to get some fresh air. The clear night air smelled sweet after the room I'd filled with smoke, puffing one cigarette after another.[*] The paths were dimly lit at night from the scattered building lights. I headed out in no direction.

My mind turned to another decision facing me: what would I do when called upon to testify? I couldn't predict where or when, but I was sure it would happen. The President had tucked me under the wing of his office and said his counsel could never be called upon to testify in a Senate committee investigation. It would be different, however, should a grand jury call me. I wasn't sure executive privilege or the attorney-client privilege would apply before a grand jury. Colson had already given testimony before the Watergate grand jury. Also, the fact that others had appeared before the grand jury would increase the sense that my refusal to testify was designed to hide something, which it would be. Mitchell and Kleindienst had lied to protect the President during the ITT hearings. Maybe he expected the same of me. Maybe I could take the Fifth Amendment.

I walked deeper into the woods, thinking about the Fifth Amendment. It made you sound so damn guilty. PRESIDENTIAL COUNSEL TAKES FIFTH. It was worse than the headline from the Gray hearing: DEAN PROBABLY LIED.

---

[*]   After Watergate, I would give up both smoking and drinking permanently in the 1980s.

The thought started my blood boiling anew. Goddam that Pat Gray, up there lying to get confirmed, calling me a liar to help himself. I shouldn't have let him get away with it. One thing I had not done was to lie and—

"Excuse me, sir, are you lost?" a voice from nowhere said, startling me. I turned. It was a young Navy enlisted man, wearing a heavy Camp David parka, with the Presidential emblem on his jacket and deck cap.

"No, not really, just out for some air. In fact, I might have just found my way."

"Fine, sir, have a pleasant walk." He vanished as my thoughts finally beaded down the path I knew I had to explore. The path of telling the truth if I was called upon to testify. Whatever else happened in the days, weeks, and months ahead, I was not going to lie for anybody, even the President. Despite what I'd done for him, I would not take that step. I might go down the drain as Watergate burst its dams, but I would hang on to one piece of myself at least.

By the time I reached the lodge, Mo was playing pool by herself, so I joined her. I decided I would not write the phony report. I would have my secretary type up an innocuous portion so that I could tell Haldeman and Ehrlichman I was working on it. What I would do would be to start preparing an honest report to the President. I had given him the highlights on March 21; now I'd give him the bloody details. Then no one could say I had lied to the President. To the contrary, I'd have told him what had gone on. In fact, the truth might persuade him, once he saw it written down.

Early Sunday afternoon I began making notes. When I sat back and read what I'd written, I realized I was sticking the problem on everybody but myself. I was coming out as nothing but the simple tool of higher-ups. I was protecting myself, passing blame to others. I asked myself whether I should open up more and include my own involvement.

I thought for some time and decided that it was time I started calculating my moves carefully. It was foolish to believe that Ehrlichman or Haldeman or Mitchell or Magruder would admit to anything wrong. If my notes should fall into the wrong hands, I would have confessed my own involvement in the cover-up. There was something else that bothered me. While I could admit in my own mind what I had done, it still hurt to admit it openly, and putting it on paper made it open. This hurdle was one of the most difficult to jump.

My newfound tranquillity vanished instantly with a phone call from Ron Ziegler late Sunday afternoon. Ron told me the *Los Angeles Times* was going to run a front-page story in the morning alleging that Dean and Magruder had had advance knowledge of the Watergate break-in.

"Ron, that's a goddam, outrageous lie. It's not true. I'm speaking for myself, not Magruder."

"I'm not interested in Magruder, and I've already denied the story. The President wants to put out something in the morning. He knows it's not true. So you think about what he should do, and I'll talk to you in the morning."

"Listen, Ron, if they print that story I'll have the first solid libel case to come out of all this Watergate crap. And I'm not feeling very much like sitting back and taking it quietly."

"Well, the *Washington Post* will be running the same story, so you'd better get busy."

I told Mo and began pacing around the sitting room. "Mo, I'm going to get a lawyer to put the papers who print the story on notice that it's libelous. And someday, when this is all sorted out, I'll sue the bastards."

"Why don't you call Bob McCandless and see if he'll represent you?" Robert McCandless was my former brother-in-law.

"No, I've got someone in mind who knows the libel law

better than Bob, Tommy Hogan.* He was a classmate of mine at Georgetown Law. I'll call him." I tracked him down through the White House switch board and explained the situation to him. His response went right to the point.

"John, only one question. Can you prove the story is false? Not that I doubt your word, but you want my advice, don't you?" he asked, a trifle embarrassed at questioning my denial.

"Tommy, ultimately I can. Immediately, I can't. That's why I just want to put the papers on notice. Since this conversation is privileged, I want to tell you something else. The shit is about to hit the fan, and the whole town is going to smell bad very soon. We need to have a long talk, and one of the things I'd like to talk to you about is hiring a criminal lawyer. I'd like to have some suggestions of people that you know who are really good."

"Okay, I've got to get moving to get these papers on notice. I'll report back to you later on how it goes."

Haldeman called the morning of the *Los Angeles Times*/*Washington Post* story. He was pleased by the libel notice and told me the President would be announcing his full confidence in me. He said Magruder was on his own. The White House would not comment. "We've also been kicking around the idea of the President announcing that you're ready and willing to go before the Watergate grand jury and testify about all this," Bob said. "What's your reaction?"

"Well, Bob, I've been thinking exactly the same thing. But here's the problem as I see it: first of all, my testimony will sink Mitchell and Magruder, who have obviously perjured themselves before the grand jury."

"So what?" said Haldeman.

---

* In time, Tom Hogan would be appointed by President Reagan to the U.S. District Court for the District of Columbia, and rise to become chief judge—and a much respected jurist.

So. The President had decided to cut Mitchell and Magruder loose. They were now expendable because they threatened his own position. And I had a second thought: I was also expendable. Or did Haldeman think I might go before the grand jury and lie? "One thing I've got to tell you, Bob. If I am going to go before the grand jury I'm going to tell it exactly the way things happened."

"Well, we've been protecting Mitchell and Magruder too long. And it got us in this damn mess."

"There's another problem with going to the grand jury, Bob. What if they ask me how I have come to have this knowledge and why didn't I report it earlier? That's likely to lead them right into the activities that happened post-June seventeenth."

"Like?" he asked.

I went over the highlights of his own involvement in the cover-up. Bob asked me to repeat several items. It was evident he was taking detailed notes.[*] He was eliciting information from me as to what my testimony would be. I understood why: my testimony would implicate Ehrlichman and him, among others, in the obstruction of justice. He wanted to be prepared for the worst.

It was a painful conversation for both of us. We were walking tight ropes, suspicious of each other, but not overtly hostile. I wanted Haldeman to know I would not lie for him, if questioned, but I played down my conviction that I would be called to testify about the origins of the break-in, and that such questioning would lead into the cover-up. I could hear the prosecutor saying, "Now, Mr. Dean, tell us if you had any conversations with Mr. Liddy after June seventeenth." My answer would open the door to the cover-up. I raised my

---

[*]   Haldeman's notes would later surface in *The Haldeman Diaries* (New York: Putnam, 1994).

cover-up testimony with Haldeman only as a possibility, because I was not willing to tell him directly that I would turn against him—and therefore against the President.

Fortunately, Haldeman was still concentrating on events before the break-in. He was concerned that my testimony might sink Mitchell and Magruder, and that they might turn on people within the White House to save themselves. "What did Magruder and Mitchell testify to before the grand jury that your testimony might contradict?" he asked.

"I don't know for certain," I replied. "Jeb's story, for example, changes from day to day. But if he sees himself going down in flames, I suspect he'll reach out to grab everybody he can hang on to."

"Why don't you call up Magruder, go over the facts with him, get him down on record as to exactly what did happen, and tape him?"

"Well, I don't have any device to do that."

"Call up the Signal Corps. They'll fix up a machine for you."

I thanked him for the suggestion. I decided I would think about it. Before he signed off, however, he asked about my report. I told him I had gotten diverted by the newspaper story. He urged me to get at it and in a hurry. Later that morning, the President announced his support for me. Not a word was said about my going to the grand jury.

I told Mo about Bob's suggestion of taping Magruder, and she said, "I don't think that's very nice."

"Well, I want to get Jeb on record that I didn't have any advance knowledge. There's no telling what Jeb would say someday about my involvement in this. Everybody at the White House tapes people: Haldeman, Ehrlichman, Ziegler, Strachan, Higby, Colson, and probably two dozen more I don't even know about."

270

"I still don't think that makes it sound very good," she said.

"I know. I've never done it before, but I think it's necessary now. What I'm going to do is get that dictating machine that's over there in the office and bring it here to the cabin. I'd be embarrassed to death if somebody walked in on me while I was using it."

After getting the dictating machine, setting it up on the coffee table, and testing it with a call to my office to see if I could hold the microphone to the receiver, I called Jeb. It was a difficult conversation under any circumstances, but Mo's making fun of my trembling hands made it worse. I managed, however, to get Jeb to admit that I had had no advance knowledge. I tried the same procedure with Liddy's lawyer, and later with Mitchell, but I was not very good at getting the information I needed.

As usual, I felt exhausted when I arose the next morning. While showering, I thought again about hiring a criminal lawyer. If I hired a lawyer for myself, went to the prosecutors and told them everything I knew—except about the President—I'd really be dumping on Mitchell and Haldeman. Frankly, I didn't give a damn about Ehrlichman. But as for me, I'd be a squealer, and just to save myself. Then I rationalized that if I hired a lawyer to assess my liabilities, I could also be assessing them for others. That was it: then I could determine what was best to do next for everybody. The contrivance made me feel less a squealer, but I still could not make a decision.

Tommy Hogan called and we talked about criminal lawyers. One name he suggested struck me in particular: Charles Shaffer. I had met Charlie once, on a duck-hunting trip to the Eastern Shore of Maryland, many years earlier. He had once been an assistant United States attorney in the New York Southern District; later he had been selected by Attorney General Robert Kennedy to come to the Department of Justice. Shaffer was tough, experienced, and well respected. Tom seemed to sense my uneasiness, that I was on the verge of some sort of decision, and asked if he should contact Shaffer.

"No," I told him. "Let me call you when I get back to Washington. I'm really not sure I want to do it yet, Tommy."

On March 28, 1973, after I had been at Camp David for five days, Haldeman called to summon me down from the mountain. It was a call that would bring me face to face with the human consequences of the decision I had made not to lie; Haldeman wanted me to meet with Mitchell and Magruder, who were coming over to his office that afternoon to talk about my testimony. I protested. They knew that my testimony would be about those early meetings in Mitchell's office. Bob insisted, "You can't hide up there on that mountain forever."

An hour and a half later I was in his office. Mitchell and Magruder had just left him; they were down the hall in Dwight Chapin's abandoned office, waiting for me. Again I protested having to meet with them.

"I don't want to get involved with this," Haldeman said flatly. He was seated at his conference table, tilting his chair back slightly, and he seemed different. It was not the Bob Haldeman who had always treated me with a degree of warmth, had often quipped when things were tense, and had never borne down on me as he did on other subordinates. Now he had detached himself from me. "I want you to work this out with Mitchell and Magruder," he said. "They tell me you all agreed on this"—the testimony we would give if it came to that— "a long time ago."

"What?"

"That's what they say. I'm not involved in this and I don't want to be involved in it, but I want you to go down there and talk with them." He brought his chair to the floor, and stood.

John Mitchell's face looked long and gray as he pulled slowly on his pipe. Magruder, nervously clasping and unclasping his hands, spoke for both of them. He was desperate, his voice jumpy. "John," he said, " remember we met over there at Mr. Mitchell's office to discuss my grand-jury testimony on those meetings? You agreed you would testify the way we had. That Liddy had come to those meetings to talk about the election laws. In fact, you suggested that idea. And also that the second meeting was canceled. Bob says that isn't the way you remember it now, but that's what you told us."

Jeb was pleading. I was miserable. If I testified truthfully, I would provide evidence against Jeb both on the break-in and on his perjury. I had never agreed to support his perjured testimony with false testimony of my own, but I had certainly condoned his story and even coached him to help make it convincing. He considered me his partner in the cover-up. I had helped throw him overboard, and now I was yanking back the lifeline. Only my anger at Magruder saved me from feeling like the lowest rat. Jeb was the one who was most responsible for the break-in, who had got us into this whole mess. True, I had helped him save himself by helping him to commit perjury. But I had never agreed to lie for him. Now he was threatening me. I latched onto my anger for dear life.

"Jeb, the question is moot right now," I said. "I haven't been asked to testify anywhere." I was dodging. I couldn't say I would lie, and I couldn't say I wouldn't. I knew they would interpret my hedging as an ominous sign for them.

"Yeah, but what if you do testify?" Jeb persisted.

"I'll cross that bridge when I come to it. Just like you will."

"How do you remember it?" Mitchell asked me. He spoke quietly, not looking at me, staring at the wall across the room.

I couldn't look at Mitchell, either. I felt no animus toward him, unlike Magruder. He had been an uncle to me, and now he was asking whether I would help send him to prison for something I had broken down doors to help him cover up. I felt completely disarmed and wretched. "Well, John," I said, "I recall the meeting with Jeb vividly, and I never heard of the cancellation of the second meeting until after he testified. That was some later refinement I was unaware of. I do recall saying that if asked why I was at the meeting, he could say I was there because I was the election-law expert. Jeb added that he could say the entire meeting dealt with that, and—"

"Yeah, but you agreed you'd go along," blurted Magruder. "It was your suggestion about the election laws that made me decide to testify that way."

Jeb was hurting me, but his aggressive tone was in such contrast to Mitchell's hapless calm that I found it almost easy to brush him off. "There's no sense debating this now, Jeb. I'm just not... No one has asked me to testify."

I turned to Mitchell. I was not certain he had perjured himself, although I would have been shocked to learn he had testified about having heard bugging discussed in those meetings. And I wanted to assure him that I had only hearsay knowledge that he had approved the Liddy plan after the February 4 meeting. "John, I don't know to this day precisely what happened after that second meeting. I've never asked you, and I won't ask now. I can only speculate." I had no intention of speculating, of course. What I was telling him was that I had little or no legal evidence against him on the break-in.

"Well, what is your speculation?" he asked, still looking away.

I was stunned by the question. Why would he possibly ask that? I hesitated, my eyes darting about the room, before deciding to tell the truth. Mere speculation could do Mitchell no harm, I figured. "Well, I have had a lot of theories," I began. "My strongest one is that Colson was all over you on the Liddy plan, and Haldeman was sending down pressure through Strachan. I know you weren't too excited about it, but

I figure you finally said what the hell and approved it to get them off your back. My theory is that you just threw the dice on it."

Mitchell turned to look at me for the first time. He was holding his pipe in his hand, leaning slightly forward in his chair. "Your theory is right," he said quietly, "except we thought it would be one or two times removed from the Committee." [*]

My gut wrenched. I looked in Mitchell's face. This was not John Mitchell the stonewaller, "Old Stone Face," as the President called him. He had just admitted to me that he had approved the Liddy plan, that he was in trouble, and needed help. He had just trusted me with his biggest secret, and if I told the truth I would have to betray this one too. A hundred perjuries are not much worse than one. Deep down, I knew Mitchell had played his best card. He was counting on my feeling for him, laying himself in my hands. My realization was overwhelmed by sentiment. Now I felt the razor edge between the squealer and the perjurer. I had never felt more squalid.

I looked away from Mitchell's eyes. The room was closing in on me. I had to get out. Fast. "Listen, I can't talk about this now," I said to no one, trembling. "I've got to get back to my office. We can talk later maybe."

I turned and walked hurriedly out of the room, down the hall. I did not go to the office. I went straight home. One small lie to stop more lies. My emotions were spilling over in

---

[*] Haldeman would record in his diaries that Mitchell had also told him the same. I had later reported to him on the telephone after meeting with Mitchell and Magruder what had transpired, and among those notes, Haldeman wrote: "Dean says he can't do what Mitchell and Magruder told him to do...Mitchell and Magruder both told him that they had both signed off on the project, which Mitchell told me, also." *The Haldeman Diaries*, p. 618.

all directions. I called Tom Hogan and asked him to arrange a meeting with Charlie Shaffer as soon as possible. I needed help.

CHAPTER EIGHT:

SCRAMBLING

CHARLES NORMAN SHAFFER CALLS HIMSELF a simple country lawyer, but he prosecuted some of the toughest criminals of the sixties and went on to defend many others. Tall, athletically trim, with prematurely graying hair, he strikes a commanding presence in any crowd. Hogan arranged for us to meet at an apartment not far from Charlie's office in Rockville, Maryland. The two of us reminisced briefly about the duck-hunting trip we'd once met on, but Charlie ended the pleasantries.

"Well, John, obviously you didn't ask to meet with me to talk about old times. You're a busy man, and so am I. What's on your mind?"

"Just for the record, Charlie, this conversation is, of course, privileged?"

"Are you here to retain me as your lawyer?" he asked.

"Yes."

"Well, then, whether I take your case or not, this is a privileged communication. You look like a man with some heavy problems," he said.

"I am, Charlie, but I don't want to talk about the President, or matters that might be considered national-security." I was still a long way from telling anyone such things.

"I'm ready to listen. I can give you at least two hours, but I've got something on my schedule for this afternoon. So maybe you better start."

For the next five hours I took Charlie through the highlights of what had happened. He sat silently. Occasionally he shook his head in disbelief and said, "I'll be damned" or "No shit."

Only once did he interrupt, to call his office and cancel his appointment. As I told the story, I felt a great relief in getting the weight of it off my mind, sharing the burden with somebody else. Five hours was not enough to tell him all I knew, so we agreed to meet for another session.

"Well, Charlie, what do you think about what I've told you thus far?" I asked.

"Frankly, I'm overwhelmed. I want to think about it. I'll tell you when we meet next if I can represent you, and we'll talk further. I already think you should minimize your dealings with others as much as possible. Don't talk facts with them. From what you tell me, it looks like this fella Ehrlichman is maneuvering to protect himself at your expense."

Three days later, on the morning of April 3, we resumed our discussion. I realized how much he had absorbed. He asked a few sharp questions "to start separating the wheat from the chaff," and told me he would represent me. I was encouraged. Finally I ended my recital with another "What do you think?"

"John, you're in big trouble. Serious trouble." My heart pounded. I had expected my lawyer to be more encouraging. "But your problem depends on a lot of things, lots of things. For example, who is going to handle this case. Do you know?"

"I assume the U.S. attorney's office here in the District— Earl Silbert, Seymour Glanzer, and a guy named Donald Campbell. They've been on it so far."

"Old Seymour Glanzer is in this case." Charlie laughed. "I'll be damned." I didn't see the humor. "Seymour is a good lawyer, a smart bastard, and one tough prosecutor," he continued. "I know him, know him quite well, I've had a lot of dealings with Seymour and respect him. I think he respects me, too." Charlie was pacing the apartment now. He had taken his suit jacket off earlier, unbuttoned his vest, and had his

278

hands deep in his pockets and his head down as he walked about. "Here's the way I analyze the situation. First, you don't have a problem with what happened before June seventeenth, with the original Watergate break-in. You were a part of that conspiracy, but you clearly withdrew and renounced it to Haldeman. Would Haldeman testify to that?"

"I don't know, Charlie. I would think so."

"Well, it's not really important anyway, because you can make the case against Mitchell and Magruder. I'm not worried about pre-June seventeenth, but post— There, as far as I'm concerned, you're guilty as hell of conspiring to obstruct justice. You may like to think of yourself as just a little guy carrying out orders, but the counsel to the President is no little guy outside the White House. Technically, you're just as much a part of the conspiracy to cover up as Haldeman, Ehrlichman, Mitchell, and whoever." He was still pacing, and he fell silent from time to time, somewhat theatrically, I thought. He was the first of many criminal lawyers I would encounter in the months, and years, ahead whose courtroom mannerisms often became a part of their personality, at least when they were playing criminal lawyer.

"The question I've got to ask you is, what do *you* want to do? But before you answer I want to say this: As far as I'm concerned, you withdrew from the cover-up conspiracy when you came to see me."

"Charlie, it was my feeling that I should go down to see Silbert and Glanzer and lay the whole thing out for them."

"Why?"

"Well, because that's the way to end it all."

"Have you thought about what that will do to the President?"

"I'll say I have. And that's the best solution I've been able to come up with. I figure if I go down there and lay it out, and explain what I've done—"

"I'm not telling you what to do yet," Charlie interrupted. "Or what my advice is. I haven't decided. I'm just trying to see if you know what you believe is the best thing to do. Listen, here's what I want you to do. You have not been subpoenaed to appear before a grand jury. You're just sitting around stewing in your juices right now. I want to find out what is really happening and where the hell we are. I'm going to call Silbert and Glanzer and go see them."

"Hold on, Charlie. If you go to see them, they're going to have to report it to Petersen, who's going to report it to Kleindienst, then to the President. He's going to think I'm doing a number on him."

"Goddammit, first you tell me you want to run down to the prosecutors and be some kind of hero. *You* do that and there's a damn good chance they'll pull you right in front of the grand jury and indict your ass. That's the way the ball game is played. You don't have to run into machine guns to get your story out. I'll talk to them and find out what they're looking for. Let's get this clear right here and now," he said, standing over me and looking me square in the eyes. "If I'm going to represent you, we're going to handle this case my way. You either trust me or you don't. With a little luck and the right moves at the right time, I can keep you out of jail and save your license to practice law. Is that understood? Otherwise you might as well start looking for another lawyer."

I felt comfortable with Charlie's tough manner and I agreed, provided he could assure me he would swear Glanzer and Silbert to secrecy. What I had done by going to Charlie was start a process I had not been able to start alone. Inertia had been overcome. Charlie began meeting with Silbert and Glanzer. His confidence and brashness amazed me. Any hour of the day or night seemed appropriate to Charlie, when he decided to do something.

It was midnight one night when he called Glanzer at his home. He wanted to talk to Seymour privately. I started to protest the hour, but he held up his hand, continued dialing, spoke with Glanzer's wife, and then with Seymour. "Seymour, you need to talk with me. You don't know how badly you need to talk to me," Charlie drawled with relish. There was a long silence as he listened. "Yeah, I know, you've got your problems in life and I've got mine, but I'm going to give you some more." Silence. "You heard me. Now listen, Brother Glanzer, I'm about forty-five minutes from your house. Put some coffee on, because I'm coming over to see you." Silence again. Charlie put his hand over the receiver and said to me, "Seymour can take more words to say less than any man I know, but I'm going over to see him." When he finally ended the conversation, he said he would call me in the morning to tell me the results. "Is your phone bugged at your office?" he asked.

"Maybe. I doubt it, though."

"Well, I'll come see you just in case. I've never been to the White House anyway, and I want to see it." This parting remark struck me as odd. Here I had just told him the awful mess that had happened at the White House, yet he was as awed by it as any American. I remembered that feeling, but it had long since gone.

Haldeman called from San Clemente, where the Presidential party had been astir the last few days over a state visit by South Vietnam's President Thieu. I was not at all happy to hear from him, especially in light of Charlie's instruction to lessen contact with the other cover-up principals. I had my toes in the enemy camp.

"Hi," said Haldeman pleasantly. "Is the press giving you a breather? Things sound a little calmer back there."

281

"Well, yeah, they are. They haven't surrounded the house since I got back from Camp David."

"That's good. I guess with the Gray hearings toned down a little you ought to be able to lead a normal hectic life."

"I hope so," I said. I forced a tiny laugh, but I was wary. Usually Haldeman was all business from the first word. This banter was out of character. He was either stroking me or warming up for something heavy.

"We were talking out here," he continued, "and we decided right now might be the time to put out some sort of statement. Have you finished up that Camp David report yet? We'd like to have it out here."

"Uh, no, Bob. I'm still working on it." So this is the business, I thought. Haldeman is now the heavy on the Dean Report, in spite of what I've told him about the dangers. I could imagine Ehrlichman telling the President that Haldeman would have the best chance of prying it out of me. I scrambled for an excuse. "I've had a little trouble getting at it. Uh, but I'm working at it. And I'll tell you what. Dick Moore has finished the section on Segretti. I've got it right here."

"That's good, but when are you going to finish the Watergate part?"

"Uh, as soon as I can. I'm going to work on it."

"Well, I want you to take that part you've got over to the Situation Room and have it dexed out to me right away.* We want to explore the possibility of releasing it. But I want you to get on that Watergate report."

"Okay, Bob. It's no picnic, but I'm working." I felt my pulse begin to race as I lied. And I felt even worse because I had to tell Haldeman I had retained a lawyer; I couldn't risk his

_____

* The "dex" machine was a pre-facsimile era transmission device that the military used to send documents.

282

finding it out from someone else. "Uh, listen, Bob," I faltered, "I think I ought to tell you that since I've come back from Camp David I've talked to a lawyer. I've talked to him for myself, but I also think he can help me figure out what everybody else's criminal liabilities are. You know, we just don't have a good criminal lawyer around here."

"I understand," said Haldeman.

I felt relief that he hadn't exploded. "I've got a guy named Charlie Shaffer. He's one of the best. And I tell you, Bob, I think it's the only thing to do. I think Shaffer can help us find out how good a case the prosecutors have against Mitchell and Magruder. He might help us with ways to get Mitchell to step forward. That's the only possible way I can think of to end this thing cleanly."

"Yeah. I want to hear about that."

"And, you know, I can already see why John's been checking around for outside criminal lawyers. They can keep us from making any more mistakes. I think John's idea was right." I was trying to make what I had done sound like a suggestion from Ehrlichman, who had, in fact, been gathering names of criminal lawyers; he didn't want to rely on Henry Petersen, which was prudent of him. Ehrlichman had leaned on Petersen, and Henry had not forgotten Ehrlichman's rebuking him for, among other things, calling Maury Stans before the grand jury.

"Okay," said Haldeman. "That sounds okay. Find out whatever you can, but stay on that report."

"Right." I hung up and sat back. First step out of the box. I had been about as honest in revealing motives for wanting a lawyer as Bob had been with his motives for wanting the Dean Report. We were all protecting our flanks, and I was glad Haldeman and the others were out in San Clemente.

Charlie arrived at my office soon after I had sent Moore's report to the Situation Room. He was impressed. Before he reported on his meetings with Silbert and Glanzer, he walked around inspecting the pictures on the wall. He chuckled at the "Many thanks" inscription Mitchell had written for me on the picture of himself. "I'll bet," he mused. Finally he plunked down in front of my desk.

"Everything's okay," Charlie announced. "Here's the situation. Glanzer says they're just trying to find out who authorized the bugging and the break-in. They've reached the brilliant conclusion that someone above Liddy had to be involved. They're tracking on Magruder and Mitchell, and also suspect Colson. Anyway, they're not looking around for post-June-seventeenth activities. In fact, they couldn't care less, from what I could gather."

This sounded encouraging. Maybe I was worrying unduly. "What now?" I asked. Charlie reported the prosecutors had informed him that I was a target of the grand-jury investigation of the break-in. "It's McCord, John," said Charlie, pacing in front of my desk. "McCord says you approved that bugging, along with Mitchell and Magruder. Now, I explained the rules of hearsay to those fellows. I told them McCord doesn't know anything, and that what he thinks is wrong. I told them if they think their ass is in a sling for not cracking this case, they should just wait and see what I'll do to them if they go after the wrong guy. I told them my man is a witness, not a defendant. But I still think they're coming after you. You're going to have to put the finger on Magruder and Mitchell."

"Yeah, I figured. I'm preparing myself for that. And, you know, Haldeman and Ehrlichman actually *want* me to sink Mitchell and Magruder."

"That's good," said Charlie. "They're finally wising up."

"Maybe so. But I can still think of a lot of better ways to spend a day than testifying at that grand jury. What about the cover-up? You think they'll get into that?"

"They didn't ask about it, and I'm sure as hell not going to go down there and tell them what they should be looking for," Charlie said sternly. "I'm not going to volunteer anything to them. Not yet, anyway."

As he would on many subsequent occasions, Charlie began prowling about the room, firing questions at an imaginary Mitchell on an imaginary witness stand. He was playing prosecutor. "I could smoke this guy out. I'd love to cross-examine him and turn that old stone face into jelly," Charlie said, rubbing his hands together.

Charlie's delight at the idea of skewering Mitchell was painful enough to me, but an increasingly troublesome thought began nagging me when I went home at night. Two days later, I raised it with Charlie. "I want to say something to you," I said hesitantly, "and I hope you won't take this the wrong way. But listen, a lot of goddam lawyers have done what I'm afraid you're doing. You're going to fall right into the cover-up trap if you don't start thinking about the implications of this. You know, all these lawyers came into this thing with no worries, and then they started protecting their clients and protecting the President. And the first thing you know they slipped into the cover-up. I'm thinking of guys like Parkinson and Paul O'Brien and Mardian. And me too. We've got to be careful about that."

Charlie stopped pacing, folded his arms, and stared down at me. "Listen, son. You don't have to worry about *me!*" he exploded. "I can take care of my own ass. I'm in charge of worrying about yours. Now, let me tell you what I've done, which may handle your concerns. I've made an arrangement for you to meet with the prosecutors. I've touched on the highlights of your testimony, but only you can really tell them what you know. These facts are damn complex, and they can best judge your credibility by hearing them directly from you. They know I'll never spin them, so they've agreed to an arrangement whereby you can talk to them off the record. They won't use anything you say against you, even if they should still prosecute you later. And they've agreed not to report these meetings to either Petersen or anybody else, because of your concern that it would get straight back to the White House. I think it's a fair deal. These guys may change their minds about wanting to prosecute you after they hear your story. I don't know, so don't get encouraged, but I think it's worth a try." Charlie had gradually calmed down during his monologue. "Now," he said intently, as if he had said all there was to say, "are you ready to go down there and layout the facts?"

"I think so, Charlie." I gulped. He was putting it to me faster than I had expected. "But I don't like it. You know damn well I can't tell them about the break-in without nailing Haldeman, Ehrlichman, Mitchell, me, and God knows who else on the cover-up. I don't want to volunteer that stuff."

"You don't know," Charlie said condescendingly. "Maybe you can stay out of the cover-up. Frankly, I don't give a damn. It's your ass or theirs. Whose do you want to save?"

"Mine, of course, but..."

"Do you think they're going to protect you when the shit hits the fan?"

"No, but I know damn well they won't if they think I stuck the knife in them when I didn't have to."

"You have to, unless you want to keep lying and covering up. You want to do that?"

"No."

"Are you ready to meet with the prosecutors?"

"Yes. Only one thing, though. I think I should first tell Haldeman I'm going to do it."

"Why do you want to do that, for God's sake?"

"Because," I replied irritably. "For one thing, I owe it to him. Not to Ehrlichman, but to Bob."

"Okay. That's your choice. Do it if you want to."

The first "off the record" meeting was scheduled for Sunday, April 8. I procrastinated and waffled on what story I would offer Haldeman until the last minute, when I was already waiting for the prosecutors in Charlie's office. Then I finally called him in San Clemente. "Bob, uh, the reason I called, uh, to talk to you, is that I think I've got to tell you that my lawyer thinks I should meet with the prosecutors myself. He's had some meetings with them, and he really wants me to meet with them directly. They're after Mitchell and Magruder, and they're also after me."

"When does he want you to do that?" Haldeman asked immediately. He was edgy and tense.

"Right away, uh, as soon as possible," I said.

There was silence on the line. I was praying silently that Haldeman wouldn't order me not to.

"Well, listen, John," Haldeman said, "we're on our way back. We'll be in Washington this afternoon. In fact, I'm on my way to the plane right now. And I think we ought to talk about this when we get back."

"Well, Bob, I, I, you know, I can understand that," I stammered, "but I may have to tell my lawyer what I'm going to do here. That's why I'm calling this morning."

"I want to talk to you about talking to the prosecutors," Haldeman said firmly. "Just remember that once the toothpaste is out of the tube, it's going to be very tough to get it back in."

"I understand," I said quietly, avoiding a direct answer. I feared he was zeroing in on what my message really was.

"Look, John, I've got to go," Haldeman said briskly. "You've caught me on the way to the plane. Be careful, okay? I'll talk to you when we get back."

"Right." I hung up with relief.

The prosecutors arrived in the early afternoon. Earl Silbert, whom I had known for years, gave me a sincere and friendly greeting.

He was my age, and cautiously ambitious. He wanted to be United States attorney in Washington. I had met Glanzer briefly in Henry Petersen's office when we were discussing the CIA aspects of Watergate. I had never seen Don Campbell, the least experienced member of the team, who seemed to be mostly a spectator.

Charlie reviewed the ground rules: no notes, nothing could be later used against me, no discussions of my dealings with the President. Considering the fact that I was a target of a grand-jury investigation, everyone was extremely cordial and relaxed. Charlie moved things along. "Well, let's get on with it," he said and turned to me. "Tell these gentlemen what happened and how the Watergate bugging was planned. They don't understand that they've got the wrong man as a target for their investigation. Give them an education."

I took a deep breath and began telling the story from the beginning, moving quickly. I was blowing the whistle gently, using buzz words about "demonstration intelligence" and "campaign coordination," trying not to make it sound as bad as I knew it was. Charlie stopped me.

"Okay, that's enough. Now listen," he said to me, pacing the room. "This is not the Dean Report you're giving these men, with all that self-serving bullshit." He stopped in front of me, hands on hips, glowering at me. The prosecutors couldn't

288

yet understand his reference to the Dean Report, but they seemed to enjoy Charlie's show of pushing me. I did not. "I want you to tell these guys the ugly realities of life," Charlie thundered. "Don't waste their time telling them what a nice guy you are, because they don't feel that way about you. So unless you want them to indict you, lay it out. Understand?"

He had embarrassed me, but I knew he was right. I started going into greater detail, giving a more realistic picture of what had occurred. The prosecutors listened in silence and showed no reaction. I assumed this was how prosecutors behaved. They broke in with only a few questions, one of which rocked me.

"John, are you sure your account of that second meeting is the end of it?" Silbert interrupted. "Since this conversation is off the record, I'll tell you why I'm trying to make sure. Liddy's been talking to us privately. Now, nobody knows about that, but your story is going to have to square with his. You understand?"

Jesus Christ, I thought. Liddy's talking. I couldn't believe it. He had been the rock of the cover-up. If he slipped off the mountain, it was all over. I started to blurt out what Liddy knew, but checked myself. I didn't know how far he had broken. "What did he say, Earl?"

"You know I can't get into that, John," Silbert said firmly. "His conversations are as privileged as yours."

Charlie rescued me. "Goddam, Earl, that's great," he declared. "I don't care what Liddy says. If he tells the truth, you'll know my man wasn't in on this." He turned to me. "You just keep on going with your story, John." [*]

---

[*]   [Original Footnote:] Later I discovered that G. Gordon Liddy had never talked to Silbert on or off the record. This was a prosecutor's ploy.

I did. I had been going at it almost two hours when the phone rang. "It's for you," Charlie said. "You can take it outside."

"That's okay," I said, assuming it was Mo. I reached for the phone.

"Mr. Dean, this is the White House operator. You have a call coming through from Air Force One." Before I could recover enough to tell her to hold until I got to another phone, the Signal Corps operator was giving me the standard military reminder that the call was not on a secured line. Then Higby came on.

"John, this is Larry, do you read me?"

"That's affirmative," I answered in Air Force One lingo.

"Be in Wisdom's office at sixteen hundred hours, for a meeting with Wisdom and Welcome."

"Okay, Larry, I'll be there."

"Over and out."

I stood at Charlie's desk for a moment thinking about the call. It was a mixed blessing. I would surely be confronted by Ehrlichman (Wisdom) and Haldeman (Welcome) about my meeting with the prosecutors. That was ominous. On the other hand, that meeting would enable me to end this one before we got into the cover-up.

"That was a call from Air Force One," I told the curious group. "Haldeman and Ehrlichman want to meet with me at four, so I think we should break this up for now. It'll take me a while to drive all the way back to town."

"Air Force One?" asked Glanzer. "They called you from the air?"

"Yeah."

"How does that work?" he asked, seeming impressed as much by the technology as by the source of the call.

"Well, they send it over the Army's ground-to-air channels and then route the signal through the White House switchboard," I replied casually.

"Do they know we're here?" Silbert asked.

"No, they don't even know where I am." I was thinking, however, that I should stop leaving my number with the switchboard, just in case. I didn't want anyone to stumble on a record of my visits to Charlie.

We agreed to resume the next evening, and I arrived back at the White House just as Haldeman and Ehrlichman were coming in from Andrews Air Force Base. The three of us walked into Ehrlichman's suite, chatting idly about the weather and President Thieu's visit. All of us seemed to have inexhaustible reserves of outward calm, I thought. Haldeman must have reported my call instantly. I wondered if I had the guts to tell them I had just met with the prosecutors in spite of his wish to talk to me first. I hoped I could dodge the question if it arose.

Ehrlichman flicked on the lights in his office, picked up the Sunday *New York Times*, and shook his head at the front-page story about how Colson had taken and passed a lie-detector test on Watergate.

"What do you think about Chuck taking a lie-detector test?" I asked.

"Not much," Haldeman said sourly.

"Well," added Ehrlichman, "I think Chuck's more than a match for any lie-detector machine."

"Maybe so," I said, "but if this idea catches on, we might all have to take those tests."

Ehrlichman tilted his head back and looked down at me over his glasses. "Maybe," he intoned slowly. I took his response as a sign of *unruffled* displeasure at me for raising disquieting possibilities. Haldeman said nothing and flopped down in a chair, with one leg draped over the arm.

I decided to take the initiative in the conversation in an effort to keep them from grilling me about the prosecutors. "Well, I think you all ought to know that my lawyer's been having these conversations with the prosecutors, and he says they're primarily interested in what happened before June seventeenth."

"Primarily?" asked Ehrlichman. "What does 'primarily' mean?"

"Well, they want to find out who authorized the break-in, and they'll do anything to find out. I think they're on the trail. One of the things my lawyer has already found out is that Liddy has apparently been doing some talking."

"Really?" said Ehrlichman.

"Yeah. Apparently he's been giving them some little explanations off the record, unbeknownst even to his lawyer. I don't know what he's said."

"Very interesting," Ehrlichman replied, nodding. His face went blank for an instant, registering surprise; then it returned to normal.

"What I mean by 'primarily,' John, is that my lawyer says the prosecutors are reviewing things like how we handled evidence of the break-in here at the White House. One of the areas I'm worried about, because it's obviously very delicate, is this stuff from Hunt's safe. You know, Gray has opened up that whole FBI area in his goddam hearings, and I don't know how to handle that when they yank me down there."

"What do you mean?" asked Ehrlichman.

"Well, they're going to ask me why we delayed turning that stuff over to the FBI. You know, we've talked about this

292

before. I didn't really know what to do with some of that stuff. And I talked to you about it, and you told me to deep-six that stuff we finally gave to Gray."

Ehrlichman nodded slowly. "Well, I don't think that's going to be a problem," he said easily. "They don't even know about that Gray meeting. I think you can handle it. You can tell them you were making an inventory. I'm sure you'll think of something."

"Well, maybe so." I backed off. "But you know, if Liddy is talking, he may well tell them I passed an order to him to have Hunt get out of the country. And that came out of our conversation when Chuck and I were sitting up here that first Monday. And you wanted to know where he was, and I didn't know, and you thought it might be a good idea, since he wasn't a felon or anything, for Hunt to take a powder."

Ehrlichman began shaking his head slowly from side to side. "John, I just don't remember that." There was the slightest edge to his voice. I knew he was getting angry. "I'm sorry. I just don't remember it that way."

You bastard, I thought. You've been forgetting this stuff for several weeks. Self-protection had set in. Ehrlichman was busily forgetting; Haldeman was withdrawn. I paused and then shot back, "Well, anyway, John, if Liddy blows, he can hit us all. He knows about Ellsberg. He knows about the money. He knows about the whole cover-up."

Haldeman sat up straight. I thought he was going to mediate. "John," he said to me, *"you* haven't told the prosecutors anything about the money, have you?"

"No, Bob," I replied. I had not gotten into the cover-up with the prosecutors, of course, but I was relieved that Haldeman hadn't asked whether I had talked with them at all. Ehrlichman and I parried defensively until the meeting broke up.

I went to Charlie's office the next evening for my second meeting with the three prosecutors. Before they arrived, Charlie gave me a pep talk. I needed it, because we both knew that this session would probably cross the Rubicon into the cover-up. My courage rose and ebbed. I leaned on Charlie for support.

The prosecutors arrived. I took them up through my return from Manila and then skipped to the "Dean investigation," the President's August 29 announcement. "Uh, now, that announcement. There is a problem with that announcement," I said. "I really didn't make a report to the President, as such." I stopped, glanced at Charlie's nobullshit scowl, and went on. "In fact, there was no report at all. I just picked up a lot of stuff through the summer, but I didn't report anything to the President. I sure didn't tell him about those meetings with Liddy, or what I picked up after them."

"Now, stop a minute, John," Glanzer interrupted. "I want to get the chronology on this. *When* did you pick *what* up? Why don't you start on the day you got back from Manila and take it day by day?"

I sighed an assent and started through the rash of alarm meetings. I omitted Liddy's mention of Strachan, without looking at Charlie. Then I sailed truthfully through Ehrlichman's order to get Hunt out of the country; the tension in the room escalated dramatically at the mention of his name. I went on, picking up a little steam, and didn't falter again until I got to the June 20 meeting in Mardian's apartment. "...And Mardian told me Liddy said he expected his men to get some financial support. He said it was only fair." I stopped as I saw Charlie scowl again. "Uh, he said Liddy said we owed support to the defendants."

"And did you give them any?" Silbert asked.

"No, *I* didn't give them any," I said defensively. I looked at the floor. I didn't even need to look at Charlie. "Uh, but I

294

started passing messages back and forth, and uh, I *helped* get them some." I started shifting back and forth in my chair. It was out.

"Who helped you give them money?" asked Silbert.

"Well, I had a lot of conversations. It didn't get really bad until after the election, when Colson got this phone call from Hunt, who was demanding money. And I took the demands to Ehrlichman—" I stopped. "And Haldeman, and Mitchell. And they just shuttled me back and forth on who was going to be responsible for paying, and finally we got somebody to help us get some cash—"

"Wait, John," Glanzer interrupted. "You're way up in November. I want you to go step by step from June. How did this money thing come up? One day at a time. First, Mardian told you, and then what happened?"

I drew a long breath and went back through the June money meetings. When I finished relating, after many pauses, the first involvement of Kalmbach, and the approval from Mitchell, Haldeman, and Ehrlichman, Charlie stopped me.

"That's enough, John," he said. He got up and stalked around. I sank back in my chair, thankful he was taking over for a moment. Charlie walked back and forth across the room a couple of times before saying anything. His timing was exquisite. Then he addressed the prosecutors, still on the move. "I want to stop here a minute to make sure you guys realize the dimensions of the case you are being handed. Now, don't sit there like you know what's going on, because you don't. You've just seen a little peek in the tent. My man has already given you a start on an obstruction case against half the White House staff. When he finishes, you're going to have enough targets to fill up this whole goddam room. You've gotten farther in the last fifteen minutes than you have in the last nine months. Now, I'm telling you my man is a witness, not a defendant. He's going to come so clean you guys will wish you were taking divorce cases. And now you can see why we are insisting that you don't report these conversations. They'll go straight back to the White House, and all those men over there with burdened consciences will cover their tracks before you can get them in. My man is *not* going to hang out here alone. You owe him that. Now, are you ready for Part Two?"

The prosecutors nodded. "Go ahead, John," said Charlie, sitting back down. "Tell them about their FBI director." I was back on stage. It was a little easier now that the ice was broken. When my account dragged out late into the night, I called Mo to tell her I was being delayed. There was no answer. Maybe she's sleeping, I thought. Shortly after 1 A.M., I tried to reach her again. Still no answer. I called Fred Fielding, who usually stays up late, and asked him to look out the window of his house, behind mine, to see if the lights were on. They were, he reported. I called Mo. No answer after fifteen rings. I called Fielding again and asked him to see if Mo was home. He called back shortly and said the car was in the garage, but no one was answering the doorbell. I was very worried now. Charlie and the prosecutors offered to help. Our secret meetings and the gravity of my revelations had made us all paranoid. I told the group I had to get home as quickly as I could.

I rushed upstairs to find Mo seated in the middle of the bed, looking distraught.

"Is everything okay, sweetheart?" I asked.

"No, it isn't," she said curtly.

"What's wrong?"

"You!"

"What do you mean?"

"Just what I said: *you!*" she repeated angrily, and began to cry. I tried to comfort her, but she would have no part of it. I implored her to tell me what was wrong, and she blasted me: "I know what you're doing. You're out fooling around."

"What? You've got to be kidding!" I exclaimed in utter disbelief. I told her where I'd been. "Call Charlie yourself if you don't believe me."

"I don't want to talk to Charlie."

"Well, I'm going to call him now and tell him you're all right. Why didn't you answer the telephone?" She didn't reply. With my own nerves at snapping point, I went downstairs, fixed a strong drink, and called Charlie for sympathy. Then I sat back at the kitchen table thinking. I remembered once before when Mo had fallen into such a state of mind, feeling abandoned. She had threatened suicide, and one night she had locked herself in the bathroom, telling me she was going to slit her wrists. I believed her. I had broken the door down at what I figured was the split second that saved her life. Now her security was being threatened again. She was already depressed and getting more so daily. I had to consider the possibility that she was suicidal, and deal with it.

The next day, April 10, I had my last meeting with John Mitchell. I was in no condition for it, but I had no choice. Ehrlichman called me early in the morning. "John," he said, "before you go see Mitchell, I wanted to let you know he's been putting a lot of pressure on us not to let you testify. He thinks you can claim some sort of privilege against going to the grand jury, and he wants us to take a stand. Go to court if we have to. Now, we've been noncommittal on it. I think it would help if you told him about your duties as a citizen. Feel him out. See if you can move him toward the idea of accounting for his sins." I felt the squeeze. I was paying a heavy price for keeping one foot in the White House. Leaning on Mitchell had always been one of Ehrlichman's ways of using me. "I'll see what I can do, John," I replied, "but I don't think there's much hope. Mitchell's living in a kind of dream world right now. He thinks this whole thing's going to disappear somehow. The incredible thing is that he hasn't even retained a lawyer. He's staring into about a dozen gun barrels, and he hasn't talked to a lawyer yet. I doubt I can budge him."

"I'm not surprised," said Ehrlichman. "But see what you can find out and let me know."

I called Shaffer. "Charlie, Mitchell has insisted on meeting with me, and I can only assume he's going to make one more try to persuade me not to testify against him. I don't want to see him, as you can imagine, but I can't really say no to him. And these guys over here want me to tell him he's sunk already. I don't know what to do."

"Well, you want Mitchell to fess up?"

"Shit, I don't know anymore. A week ago I would have said yes, you know. That's the pipe dream over here—that everything will be okay if Mitchell walks the plank. But now that I've had my little talks with those folks in your office, we're beyond that."

"I'll tell you what to do," said Charlie. "You sit right there and don't do anything until I call you back. I'm going to talk this over with the boys at Justice."

Charlie was back on the phone within thirty minutes. "They say go ahead, John, and I agree," he reported. "But don't tell him exactly how you'll testify. I don't want you to do that with anyone. Just feel him out. Don't give in on anything. I think it would still be good for him to come forward. It wouldn't hurt you any."

"Okay, Charlie. I'm going."

"Hold on a minute. The boys have a lovely proposition for you. They say you can earn a few points for the cause of justice by wearing a wire."

"Doing what?"

"They've got a little hidden microphone they want to put up your sleeve to get Mitchell on tape."

"That's what I thought you meant," I said angrily. "You can tell those guys to go fuck themselves! Jesus Christ, Charlie. It's hard enough for me to turn on Mitchell. I'll be damned if I'm going to set him up like some Mafia informant."

"That's what I thought you'd say. Don't worry about it. Just make sure you write up a memo of everything that is said at the meeting."

Mitchell greeted me at the door of his Washington law office at one o'clock. I was struck by how much better he looked than he had, certainly better than I expected under these circumstances. His normal rumpled gray suit had given way to a smart new one with the cut of a Wall Street lawyer's. His previously chalky complexion had signs of ruddy color.

Mitchell led me over to the sofa and easy chairs in his office. To my surprise, I discovered I didn't feel nearly as shaken by this meeting as I had felt during our last one. I realized that I had already reached bottom with Mitchell; he knew what to expect from me. There was pain in the air, but no electricity. I felt an air of honorable parting. Both of us, of course, were wearing our usual placid exteriors. We chatted amiably about the balmy weather in Washington as opposed to the lingering cold in New York, until Mitchell opened up the business.

"Any indication when you might be called before the grand jury?" he asked.

"No, not really. My lawyer has been talking with the prosecutors. Thanks to McCord, I'm a target of the grand jury. From what I've learned the grand jury is focusing on pre-June seventeenth, which puts me in a very tough spot. John, since I'm surely going to be called before the grand jury someday soon, and they'll likely ask me whom I've discussed my testimony with, I don't think it's a very good idea for us to talk over testimony."

"I agree," he said. "Have you thought about what might happen if you go before the grand jury and how it might affect the President?"

"Well, I have no intention of getting into my dealings with the President."

"No, I don't mean that. I understand that."

"Yeah, I have thought about my testimony and its implications, and I know it's a problem and I don't know exactly what to do. You know, John, when I was up at Camp David I thought about leaving the country. Just taking off. Taking the chicken-shit route and running as fast and as hard as I could so I wouldn't be a problem for anyone."

"Tell me where you were thinking of going, maybe I'd like to join you," he said with a smile, and as we exchanged quick glances it occurred to me that he was, perhaps, not dismissing the idea.

"Well, I don't really know where I'd go, but wherever I went I would not go without Mo."

Mitchell was now laughing warmly, which he had seldom done in any of my recent dealings with him. "I'm not so sure I'd take Martha with me. And I'm not so sure we'd want to have her." We shared a laugh, but his next question cut through the jokes. "How's your new wife holding up under all this?"

"Not very well, John," I replied, subdued. "That's one of my problems. Our marriage has been a disaster. Or should I say I've been in a state of disaster since we got married? I feel sorry for Mo."

"I can understand that. I'm sorry to hear it," he said in a sympathetic tone, which provoked me to open up more. I told him at some length about Mo's potentially suicidal frame of mind, my drinking, the toll I felt the cover-up had taken on me. Mitchell nodded kindly and I spilled over even more.

I wound up looking straight at him, controlled but obviously opening up some of the valves that were deep down. "John, the idea of having to testify against you is not a pleasant thought for me," I said. "You have to know that. But it may come to that if I'm called before the grand jury. And I feel terrible about it. But I don't think I've got any choice. This cover-up has got to end. It gets worse all the time and it could kill the President. It's ruining my life, and I suspect yours too. And I must tell you I feel like I tried to stop this thing in the first place. I think I'm being screwed. Everybody's protecting themselves, and I think I've got to do the same thing. That's why I hired a lawyer. I don't want to be the scapegoat on all this."

"I agree," said Mitchell. He leaned forward intently. "And don't get the impression, John, that I think you should take the rap for others. But I think your testimony could cause a terrible problem for the President."

I leaned back and thought for a moment. Mitchell was shifting gears now, throwing the President between himself and danger, reaching for my loyalty button. "I know that, John," I replied, "and I don't want to do that. But I think we've already caused problems for the President, and they're going to be there no matter how I testify."

"Well, maybe the best thing for you to do is to avoid testifying altogether, then," he said. "Have you thought about taking the Fifth?"

"Yeah, I have. But that looks bad. It would cause more problems for me and for the President. Besides, the prosecutors might turn around and immunize me and force my testimony. That would cause even more problems." Mitchell then suggested other means to block my testimony—executive privilege, the attorney-client privilege. I offered reasons why

301

they wouldn't work: they would cause problems and more problems. That was the word of common currency in the Administration; a "problem" could be anything from a typographical error to a forty-year jail sentence. The word drained the emotional content from tense discussions. It helped us maintain the even, robot-like composure we considered vital to effectiveness.

I decided to make an effort to turn Mitchell around, to get the pressure off me and make him see his predicament. "John, I don't think any of this is going to work. Let me tell you something. I've heard that Liddy has been talking with the prosecutors off the record. Knowing him, it's hard to believe, but he could bring the whole house down. I think people are going to start caving in, causing problems for everybody."

Mitchell nodded at the news, expressionless. "That's always a possibility," he said. "Tell me, John. I understand that Liddy would say you told him he could have a million-dollar budget for his plans. Is that true?"

I was dismayed at the question. Instead of recognizing the damage Liddy could do to him, Mitchell was trying to imply that I might become implicated in approving the break-in. "Well, you know, I know that Jeb has said that," I replied with some irritation. "I don't frankly remember any such conversation with Liddy. If I recall the conversation correctly, I told Liddy one time, thinking about the Caulfield plan, you know, 'maybe a half a million dollars, maybe more.' John, I really don't believe that version, and I don't think it could cause me a problem."

Mitchell thought for a moment, and then made another thrust. "How are you going to handle the activities that occurred after the break-in?"

I looked off at the watercolor prints hanging behind the sofa. Mitchell was going on the offensive, telling me my testimony could backfire on me. For an instant, I suspected he

302

might have been setting me up by drawing out my confessions about Mo's state of mind. I knew that such talk could be used to impeach my testimony, to make me sound like a man unstable enough to say anything. I suppressed the paranoia. Of all the cover-up principals, I thought, Mitchell would be the last to stoop to something like that. My soft spot for Mitchell was still there, although suspicion had turned it into a bruise. My mind returned to his question. I had to show him I was not afraid of it. "Well, John, if they get into questions under oath, I'm just going to have to tell it the way it is. There's no other answer, I'm afraid. I don't have any other solution. And that means I'm going to have to say I was a middleman. I passed messages about the money. There was money. I got into it. I talked to all kinds of people." I turned back to Mitchell and heaved a sigh. "I don't know any other way." Mitchell nodded unhappily. He said nothing. We exchanged quizzical looks and a few shrugs until it was clear there was not much left to say. We'd been talking for more than an hour. "I've got to get back to the office, John," I said, getting up. "But before I go I'd just like to suggest something for what it's worth. Maybe you ought to get a lawyer. I'll tell you, I feel much more comfortable now that I have Shaffer watching out for me."

"Well, I'll see," he replied without enthusiasm. "If anyone tries to charge me with anything, I'm just going to stonewall it." He paused. "Let me ask you this. Could you just keep me advised, if you testify, as to what they ask you and so forth?"

"I don't know. There's some rule about grand-jury secrecy. But maybe something could be arranged. Maybe my lawyer could talk to your lawyer." The phone rang, mercifully hastening my departure. Mitchell walked me to the door and told his secretary he would take the call. "Good luck," he said, shaking my hand.

"Good luck to you, John."

"Thanks. I'll need it." He turned away. I went back to the office and wrote a memo on the meeting. There were others during that week. Under Charlie's instructions, I tried to stay out of discussions about testimony. But rumors of the grand jury's witness list were flying, so I was hardly surprised to find most of the cover-up participants dropping by. My evasiveness put them off. I had become an unknown quantity, straddling, playing secret games with the prosecutors, putting on a show of counsel at the White House.

Even during the strain of my first week of meetings with the prosecutors, the chaos of normal White House business continued. Although I had all but relinquished my title to Fielding because of Watergate pressure, official calls kept coming to me. One of them pushed me over the edge, causing me to buck the tickler for the first time. Higby called on the I.O. "John, what's the latest report on the replacement for the *Sequoia?*"

"You're putting me on, Larry!"

"No, I'm not," he said testily. "I need a report."

I sat back and looked at the phone receiver in bewilderment. Then I seethed, as Higby waited for an answer. For nine months the tickler had been after me to find a replacement for the President's yacht. He had become bored with the *Sequoia,* finding all kinds of faults with it. I had sent aides to obtain blueprints of the best yachts in the world, and several White House offices had spent months going through them in detail, searching for a boat that would satisfy the President's whims. Then there had been discussions with the owners as we bargained to find someone who would donate his yacht for the prestige and the tax write-off.

"Larry, I've turned this damn project over to Kalmbach," I said impulsively. "I don't have any goddam idea what he's doing, and I really don't care."

"You want me to tell *Bob* that?" Higby gasped, as if a priest had just threatened to spit on the Bible. "Tell him whatever you want." I hung up, feeling better. The White House is insane, I thought.

I noticed the cover-up participants reacting to me according to their own plans for dealing with the grand jury. Paul O'Brien was very guarded; I knew he had built ties to Ehrlichman since I had fallen off the first team of the cover-up. Fred LaRue, on the other hand, came in with abject defeat written on his face; he said he would confess to the grand jury and expressed ignorance of the obstruction laws. "You know, John, I really care for John Mitchell. You know that," he said dejectedly. "But I've got to face the fact that he has gotten a lot of people in trouble trying to protect himself. God, I can't believe this. I've been with him a long time, but over the last four months I've watched him disintegrate. I'm afraid of what he might do. I'm afraid he might commit suicide. End it all." Fred and I discussed the possibility of a Mitchell suicide. Highly unlikely, we decided, but possible. Fred asked for legal advice. I suggested he retain counsel.

On Saturday morning, April 14, I went in to the office to hide, meditate, and go through the motions of working on the Dean Report. By now, even Haldeman knew that the idea of any report from me was hopeless, but we discussed it anyway, and I would say simply that I was still working.

Ehrlichman called to say that it was going to be an interesting day. He was meeting with Mitchell and then Magruder in last attempts to get them to take the rap. He asked for my suggestions. I gave him some.

I called Charlie. "I think the shit's going to hit today," I said. "Ehrlichman's bringing Mitchell and Magruder in to lean on them. I don't think anything's going to happen, but I'll tell you what I'm afraid of. Ehrlichman's setting himself up as an investigator. He's going to claim he's just learning these facts.

But he's getting desperate. Otherwise he'd never meet with Mitchell himself. I'll tell you, Charlie, I'm afraid I'm next if he doesn't budge Mitchell. Which he won't. He may try to get Mitchell and Magruder to turn on *me*. If they agree to some phony story about how I gave Liddy the go-ahead, they could all close ranks against me. I don't think Mitchell would do that, but he's sure close to breaking. LaRue told me he's afraid Mitchell might kill himself."

"John, don't do anything," Charlie said urgently. "I'm coming right down there." He arrived soon in his riding habit. Charlie was very much a country gentleman who trained and rode horses in the Maryland countryside. He was on his way to a hunt race when I called.

"I'll tell you what should be done with Mitchell," he said as he walked about my office, looking out of place in his breeches and his well-polished high brown boots. "Mitchell isn't about to tell John Ehrlichman anything. The only person who can smoke out that bastard is the P." Charlie had started using my abbreviated language, calling the President "the P," Ehrlichman "E," and Haldeman "H." "The P should call Mitchell into his office, cross-examine him and get the facts out, and then go down to the grand jury—"

"The *President* go to the grand jury?" I asked. "That's right. He should go down to the grand jury and tell them that this is what his former Attorney General told him. Now, that would put ole Mitchell in a helluva spot. He couldn't later go down to the grand jury and say he lied to the President, nor could he say that the President was lying about him."

"I'll pass that along to Ehrlichman, but I doubt if it will appeal to either him or the President." I paused, almost laughing at Charlie's ridiculous wisdom, but I did pass it on to Ehrlichman when he called during our meeting. Then I continued. "Charlie, I'm going to have to tell the President soon that I've been to the prosecutors. Or I'm going to have to tell Haldeman at least. I think it's time I rattled the cage a little bit and let them know the cover-up is really over. I want to draw up a list of all the people involved and their criminal liability. I want to get the message across that even getting Mitchell to confess isn't going to end the problem." We went over the facts again, and the law, and I drew up a list of those we figured could be indicted by the grand jury. "Charlie, this list is a goddam disaster," I said when I had finished. "It's depressing."

"It sure as hell is."

"You know, what is incredible is the number of lawyers on the list." And I placed an asterisk before ten of the fifteen names.

Pre
*Mitchell,
Magruder,
*Strachan?
Post
H [Haldeman]
*E [Ehrlichman]
*JWD [Dean]
LaRue
*Mardian?
*O'Brien
*Parkinson?
*Colson?
*Bittman?
*Kalmbach/Tony [Ulasewicz]/Sources
    [for Kalmbach's money]
Stans?

We talked strategy, and then Charlie left to get on his horse and hunt foxes. I sat there and fretted about Ehrlichman. I could visualize Mitchell walking into his office looking as if he'd been struck with a month's heartburn. Mitchell would figure Ehrlichman was trying to get an admission on tape, I thought, since taping had been on everyone's mind recently. There would probably be a lot more stonewalling, but I guessed Mitchell would make sure to get in some subtle remarks about Ehrlichman's own criminal problems. That would ruin any tape Ehrlichman might be making.

Mo interrupted my thoughts when she brought some out-of-town guests to the White House for lunch. I took them to the executive mess. While they marveled at the royal service I drifted back to worried musings on what was transpiring in Ehrlichman's office. I excused myself early.

Ehrlichman called. He wanted me right away. I hung up and stared out the window. Then I sighed, picked up my indictment list and started for the door. I stopped. I fidgeted with the list, moving it from an inside jacket pocket to an outside one and then back inside. I wanted to have the quickest and most casual access to it. I felt like a gunslinger practicing his draw. Finally I headed over to the West Wing.

"Well, your old friend John Mitchell didn't have much to say," Ehrlichman reported. He was leaning back in his swivel chair with his feet on the desk, like the President. Haldeman was there, too, seated sideways on an easy chair.

"That's not too surprising," I replied as I sat down. "What do you think of my suggestion that the President march down to the grand jury?" I laughed.

"I don't think too much of it," Ehrlichman said.

"That's not surprising either."

Ehrlichman began ticking off the major points from his notes on the Mitchell meeting. The telephone rang. "Yes, sir," said Ehrlichman. The President, I thought. Ehrlichman listened briefly and then seemed to break in. "Uh, he's right here. Yes, sir." He hung up.

The President is in on whatever they had planned for me, I thought. Ehrlichman seemed momentarily distracted by the interruption. I reached for my list.

"John, this is—what I did this, uh," I began unsuccessfully. "My lawyer was over here this morning, and we went through everybody's involvement. And based on, uh, *his* conversations with the prosecutors, *his* knowledge of the criminal law—and he's a damn good criminal lawyer—we drew up a list of everybody who could be potentially indicted. Uh, both for the pre-June seventeenth and the post-."

"Isn't that nice," Ehrlichman remarked dourly.

"And here's what we came up with." I held up the list as if to hand it to him, but he showed no interest. "It's a disaster," I said, and I began to read off the names. I went through all fifteen, slowly at first, then faster, as I wanted to have it over with. Then I read the offenses with which they could be charged.

Ehrlichman sat bolt upright, his feet dropping to the floor. "John, I wonder if someone might be slipping something putrid into your diet. I don't believe that damn list. I just don't agree with your lawyer's analysis."

I drew another long breath. "Well, John, write down these citations, because I think you ought to pull the statutes yourself if you have any doubt." I looked down at the notes on my list. "They're both Title 18. You ought to look under Section 371, which is a conspiracy statute. It carries five years and ten thousand dollars maximum. And Section 1503, which is an obstruction statute. It carries five years and five thousand dollars maximum. They're pretty serious offenses." I made another motion to hand over the list, but there were no takers.

Ehrlichman was jotting down the citations. Haldeman was gazing off.

Then Ehrlichman turned back to me. "Well, I notice almost all the people on your little party list are for the post period. Why's that?"

I cleared my throat. "Well, let me tell you something else. You've got to know it. Based on my conversations with Shaffer, who's been down there with the prosecutors, they're looking at post too. They're very interested in that. And you're a target of the grand jury on that. I'm a target. Bob's a target. All these guys are."

Ehrlichman protested. His eyebrows, which normally rise vertically, scrunched together laterally over his nose in a frown. "No, sir," he said firmly, shaking his head. "That's not what the grand jury is doing."

"What do you mean? My lawyer's just been down there talking to the prosecutors."

"Well, *I've* just been talking with Kleindienst. And I've told Kleindienst to keep me informed about what is going on down there. And Kleindienst hasn't said a *word* about anything like that. He says the grand jury's going after the people who might have known about the break-in beforehand. So I think your lawyer's misinformed."

"Well, I think Kleindienst is misinformed," I replied evenly.

Haldeman finally sat up. "John, we'll see what we can find out about this. In the meantime, I want you to keep that damn list to yourself."

"All right," I said. The meeting broke up with no farewells. I drove home, thinking of Ehrlichman's meeting with Magruder. If Magruder agreed to plead guilty and testify against Mitchell on the break-in, as I thought he might, Ehrlichman would not worry so much about the cover-up message I had just delivered; its impact would be diluted in hopes that Mitchell's demise would end Watergate. I felt relieved about rattling the cage with Haldeman and Ehrlichman on the cove-rup, but also concerned that I might have severed my White House ties so cleanly as to encourage Ehrlichman to try to implicate me in the break-in. At home, I hid from our guests and pulled out the Scotch bottle.

Charlie called late that night. "John, I just got a call from Glanzer!" he shouted. "Everything's falling apart. Those goddam guys are breaching our agreement!"

I felt a chill. "What do you mean?"

"Well, Magruder went in there and gave them a case against Mitchell, along with your evidence.[*] And they've got the U.S. attorney, and they're going to tell Petersen what we've been talking about. Tonight!"

"Oh, shit! Are they going to say I was in there meeting with them?"

"Yep."

"Are they going to tell Petersen about the goddam cover-up?"

"That's what Glanzer says. Everything. And then a whole pack of them are going to troop over to Kleindienst's house in the wee hours."

"Goddammit, Charlie, they promised us!"

"I know. I've *reminded* Glanzer of that several times, but there's nothing I can do."

"Goddammit, Charlie! They can't do that! Do they think they have a case on the cover-up yet?"

---

[*] I had Shaffer call Magruder's attorney to tell him off-the-record that I was talking to the prosecutors, and that I strongly urged Magruder do the same. It was advice that they took and acted on.

"Hell, no, they don't have a case yet! Seymour says they just can't sit on what they have anymore."

"Jesus Christ! The President will know all this by morning. And I tell you what's going to happen. Ehrlichman's going to go in there, and the President's going to say, 'Goddam Dean. He's a fucking rat!' And he'll close ranks with Haldeman and Ehrlichman. And there won't *be* any cover-up case, except maybe against me!"

"I know," said Charlie. "You don't have to tell me. Seymour thinks they may already have a case against you on the break-in."

"I'll bet. Listen, Charlie. You've got to call Glanzer back and get him to hold off on this thing! Especially my story to them on the cover-up! Tell them to hold off. Tell them they don't understand what they're doing. Tell them to wait just forty-eight hours! I've got to tell the President about this first. I've got to give him a chance to get away from this thing. Otherwise we'll just have a brand-new cover-up at a higher level, and I'll be the goddam scapegoat!"

"Okay. Okay. I'll try. Sit tight."

I prowled like a cat, and drank, until Charlie called back five minutes later. "It's no use," he sighed. "They've already started the ball rolling. The best I could do was to arrange another meeting with them tomorrow."

"Goddammit, Charlie. I don't want to meet with those bastards."

"Listen, John, we don't have any choice," Charlie said firmly. "The cat's out of the bag. We've got to pump them full of the cover-up now. I've got to up the ante with them to have a shot at immunity. That's your only chance not to be the fall guy."

I argued with Charlie for a few more minutes, then gave up. When he hung up, I raced through some calculations and then called the White House operator. I asked for Rose Woods. The operator said she would have to call me back. I planned to tell Rose that I had an urgent matter to take up with the President. I couldn't call the President directly, because the call would automatically be routed through Haldeman. Maybe Woods would be understanding. She had been no fan of Haldeman's ever since he tried to remove her as the President's private secretary.

The phone rang and I leaped to answer it. The operator told me Rose Woods could not be reached temporarily, because she was at a funeral in Pittsburgh. I left a message to have her call me, saying it was urgent. There was no other way to reach the President. By three in the morning I had drunk myself to sleep.

I drove to Charlie's office the next day; adrenalin bathed away my hangover. "I think your strategy of getting immunity is more important than ever now," I told him. "Ehrlichman and Haldeman are sure as hell going to deny ever talking to me about anything, and I'm going to be out there alone. Now, look. You said we have to up the ante, and I've brought something to do it with." I opened my briefcase, took out a copy of the Huston Plan and handed it to Charlie.

He stared at the marking on the cover—"Top Secret: Handle via COMINT Channel Only." "What the hell does that mean?" he asked. "It's a classification a couple of steps higher than Top Secret. It means you have to have official couriers carry it around in locked briefcases and stuff like that."

Charlie handed the document back to me with a look of disapproval. "I don't want to see this," he said. "Look, John, we agreed not to get into national-security matters. I'm willing to play rough for you, but I'm not going to get myself prosecuted for receiving stuff like this without a clearance. And I'm sure those bastards in the White House would love to shove it to me. I'm a Kennedy Democrat, and I bet they'll figure I put you up to all this."

"Okay. I just wanted you to know that national security is like executive privilege. It's vague, and you can use it for anything. Because I'm going to tell you another thing that's considered national security at the White House. Hunt, Liddy, and those same Cubans who're in jail broke into Daniel Ellsberg's psychiatrist's office out in California. They wanted to get some dirt on Ellsberg to destroy him in the press. How's that?"

Charlie stopped and put his cigar down. "Who knew about that?"

"Well, Bud Krogh told me he approved it," I replied, "but Bud works for Ehrlichman and I'm sure it's an Ehrlichman operation. That's what everybody who knows about it assumes, including John Mitchell." [*]

"So that's why Ehrlichman carried so much water for Mitchell in the cover-up," Charlie said in excitement. "I confess I wondered about your story on that, John, since the two of them hate each other so much. Now it makes sense."

"That's *one* of the reasons, Charlie."

"Christ, I don't need any more now. I've got to figure out how to lay this one on Earl and Sy before they get here."

"Well, I have something else on that one." I explained about the CIA pictures of Liddy in front of Dr. Fielding's office in the Justice Department's Watergate files. Charlie put his cigar down again in amazement.

"Does Petersen know about this break-in?" he asked.

---

[*]   In fact, Krogh had told me it came from the Oval Office, but I was still keeping the President out of things.

"I don't know, Charlie," I said. "I never asked him. If he knew, it would just put him on the spot. If he didn't, I didn't want to volunteer it. It's been in the files since last July, and most people are curious about stuff from CIA. I figured Henry didn't have it investigated. You know, he put limits on the investigation—Watergate only—and Liddy wasn't standing in front of the Watergate in that picture. I doubt he knows much about it."

"Well, these prosecutors soon will," said Charlie. "You have an obligation to report this to the government. Otherwise you're going to be involved in a continuing obstruction of justice. We should do that this afternoon."

"What do you mean? I don't really understand, Charlie."

"Ellsberg's on trial right now. The government has information in its possession that could affect the outcome of that trial, and your not reporting it could be construed as an obstruction."

The prosecutors arrived, and Charlie quickly began a pacing lecture to them on their breach of our agreement. He was much tougher than he'd been before. He told them they had panicked; he called their honor into question. Silbert and Campbell just listened, but Glanzer began to argue.

"Look, Charlie," he interrupted, "we had an obligation to inform Petersen. And he had to brief the Attorney General. Who do you think we all work for? I didn't like doing it. But, dammit, you understand why we had to do it as well as I do. You would have done the same thing."

"Bullshit I would. When I make an agreement, I stick by it."

"We informed you beforehand, and we never promised that we would *never* report on our meetings with Dean," Glanzer continued, annoyed with Charlie's manner.

315

"Well, we had a damn good reason for not wanting to have that information reported to Petersen," Charlie retorted. "Now you've not only made it more difficult for us but you've hurt your own chances of making a case."

"Charlie, I'm tired of hearing about this great obstruction case your client is supposed to have for us," Glanzer argued. "His story is jumbled and disjointed.* We can't do anything with what he's told us. Why haven't you brought us a straight, chronological statement of his evidence? Why haven't you given us something we can really sink our teeth into? Like lists of when he found things out, and corroborating witnesses, and supporting documents? If we had had stuff like that, maybe we could have reconsidered."

"You guys," Charlie said, walking in front of them, "remind me of a bunch of horses going to the starting gate. You want to run before the bell is sounded. We plan to take this thing one step at a time. And I'm not even sure if my client wants to cooperate with you anymore." Shaffer was beginning to escalate his negotiating leverage. He moved about his office, raising and lowering his voice, pointing fingers and pounding tables, letting them know that they should not expect any picnic in dealing with him. Earl Silbert watched him carefully and then started smiling and shaking his head. Charlie turned to him and asked, "What are you smiling about, Brother Silbert?"

---

* Glanzer was correct because I had only provided hints about what had occurred after June 17th, and Charlie and I had deliberately left gapping holes in the story—particularly anything that related to the President. Just as Charlie was trying to figure out how to protect his client, I was still trying to figure out how to protect mine: the President. Indeed, I had not told Shaffer anything that would implicate the President for I remained hopefully that as the cover-up fell apart, the President would do the right thing. Also, I thought Haldeman and Mitchell might come clean and the story would remain mostly locked in grand jury secrecy until Nixon left office. These would prove to be naïve beliefs.

Earl kept grinning. "Charlie, you're something else. I've heard about you for years, and I can see that everything I've heard is true."

"Thank you," said Charlie with a slight bow. He seemed pleased by the compliment, and then he was spurred on to even greater performance. "I need everything I've got to get through to you guys. Sometimes I don't think you listen to me. Now, I'm about to send you another little signal about what my man knows. But before he tells you, I want to say it is probably going to be labeled some kind of national-security thing. I'm not sure what that means, but I do know it's sure as hell related to this case. It's almost as important to this cover-up I've been throwing at you the last week as the Watergate break-in itself. I don't want to get into too many specifics, but I'm instructing my client to tell you about it right now. Someday you guys are going to learn how little you know, and how much my client knows, about this cover-up at the White House. Go ahead, John."

I prepared myself while Charlie sat down. "The Department of Justice has in its Watergate files," I began, "information pointing to the fact that there was a break-in at the offices of Daniel Ellsberg's psychiatrist. His name is Dr. Fielding. Charlie doesn't want me to get into details now, but it shouldn't be hard to find." I paused and turned to Silbert, who was a friend of Bud Krogh's. "And, Earl, when you learn who's involved in this, you're going to be as upset as I am in telling you. He is a mutual friend of ours, and I'm sure he'll tell you the truth about it."

"Come on, Charlie," said Glanzer impatiently. "Quit playing games with us. What's this all about? And what the hell's it doing in our files?"

"My man's got a lot to say to you fellows today, but not anything more on that little gem," Charlie replied. "I want you

317

guys to learn that when we tell you something, it's right. When we send you signals, they mean something."

"We're working on a case, Charlie," said Silbert. "I don't see the relevance or significance of this."

"You don't see the significance?" Charlie asked sarcastically, shaking his head in exaggerated bewilderment. "Do I have to teach you guys the law too? Have you read *Berger versus U.S.* recently? It deals with a prosecutor's duty of fair play in conducting a fair trial. If you fellows want to obstruct justice, that's your business. We've met our obligation by informing you. But I suggest you go back, look around in your files for what my man has told you, read a few law books, and then come back and tell me you don't understand the significance." Charlie paused and shook his head to dismiss the subject.[*]

"Enough on that. Now, John, let's give them another dose of cover-up. Let's go heavy on the money this time. We've already got everybody introduced. Why don't you start with the meeting when Kalmbach dropped out and LaRue came in?"

I rambled on through the cover-up for several hours. Mo called a few times to tell me the White House operator was looking for me. As I had asked her, Mo had not said where I was. Charlie made me keep going until the late afternoon, when the prosecutors had to leave.

I called the White House when I arrived home, hoping I'd heard from Rose Woods. Ehrlichman came on the line instead. "Hi, John. Could you come over and see me for a little bit?" he asked in a solicitous tone. "I'm going back to the office. I hate to disrupt your evening, but I sure would like to chat."

"I guess so, John," I replied coldly, thinking the bastard would probably try to set me up. I called Charlie, who advised

---

[*]   Twenty days later, Judge Matthew Byrne dismissed the case against Daniel Ellsberg, citing government misconduct.

me not to see him. I tried to reach Woods again. Still out of town. I thought for a long while and then scribbled a note on a pad. I called Higby.

"Larry, I want you to take down a message," I said authoritatively.

"I know this is unusual, but it's important. Are you ready? Okay. This is for Haldeman, Ehrlichman, and the President." I stared at the pad.

"'I do not think it appropriate for me to meet with Ehrlichman at this time. I would like very much to meet with the President, if it isn't inconvenient for him. I want him to know I am not being disloyal. I suggest that the President turn to Henry Petersen for advice.' That's the message, Larry. Got that?" Higby said yes and hung up.

Mo and her house guest tried to persuade me to join them for dinner at a local Alexandria restaurant, but I was watching my world dissolve and I thought I'd better stay home. They had been gone only long enough for me to be fixing myself a first drink when the phone rang. I froze. It was probably the President. I was tired and I didn't really want to face him. I let it ring, thinking I could hide. Soon the ringing stopped.

I carried my drink to our bedroom, plopped down in the easy chair, lit a cigarette, and was about to take a sip when the phone began to ring again. Simultaneously, the red White House signal-line telephone also began ringing. Long rings. I let them go on and on, but the operators were not going to give up this time. I couldn't believe they'd let the phone ring thirty times. It was as if they knew I was sitting there, staring at the phones, counting the rings. They won. I picked up the phone. The operator said the President wanted me to come to his EOB office. I said I'd be there in thirty minutes.

I dreaded this meeting with the President. I was embarrassed that he had doubtless learned that I had turned to the prosecutors before I had told him. For years, the President's office had been the place I most wanted to be. Now it was the last place on earth I wanted to go.

At nine-fifteen on Sunday, April 15, a Secret Service agent outside the President's Executive Office Building office told me to go right in. I found the President seated in his easy chair in the far corner of his large office, both feet up on the ottoman. He had on what appeared to be a smoking jacket. As I sat down near him, on one of the conference-table chairs, I was close enough to notice a smell of liquor on his breath. He seemed exhausted. His usually neatly creased trousers looked as if he had slept in them, and his necktie was stained. This was not the well-manicured Richard Nixon I was used to.

"Would you like something to drink? Scotch? Martini? Anything?" he asked. The President had never before offered me a drink.

"No, thank you, sir."

"Come on, you'll surely have something?" It was almost an order and I didn't feel I could refuse it. "I'll have a Coke, thank you." He buzzed his valet, told him I would have a Coke, he would have coffee.

When the valet left, I told the President what was bothering me. "Mr. President, I don't know if you've been told, but I have talked with the prosecutors..."

"Yes, Kleindienst and Petersen were here to see me today."

"Uh, well, I wanted to tell you I was going to the prosecutors. I hoped to tell you before you learned from somebody else. And, uh, I didn't feel when I went to them that I was doing it out of any disloyalty to you, I assure you, Mr. President. I hope someday you'll know I was being loyal to you when I did this. I, uh, felt it was the only way to end the cover-up. And so I thought I had to tell them what I knew, Mr.

President, and now I think you're in a position where you can step out in front of it."

The President was nodding affirmatively. He seemed quite friendly. "I understand, John," he said. "I want you to know I understand." He paused. Maybe it will work, I thought. "I'd kind of like to review some of these problem areas that have come up. I'd like to go over them a little bit with you." He looked down at the legal pad on his lap. "For example, let's get into a little bit of this money problem. I'm trying to sort it out, you understand. Let's take Ehrlichman. What's Ehrlichman's involvement in that?"

"Well, Mr. President, both Bob and John guided me in this area every inch of the way. I went to John after Mitchell asked for help on the funds, and I asked John if he thought it was all right to use Kalmbach. I went to him several times, and he approved. Both John and Bob. That's what they did. Uh, they saw the need for it, and then I went to Kalmbach."

The President nodded. "I understand. Now, what about Petersen? How deep is Henry in this thing?"

This question surprised me. I hesitated before answering. Maybe the President just wanted to make sure Petersen was impartial enough to be his counsel on the matter, as I had suggested. On the other hand, maybe the President was probing for evidence of Petersen's own involvement, to use it as leverage to keep Henry from pursuing the cover-up. I was between suspicion and hope. I thought the President was, too. "Well, Mr. President, uh, as I've told you, Henry kept me posted on this thing. He did tell me at one point, for example, that Magruder had made it through the grand jury 'by the skin of his teeth.' But I don't think Henry would be what you'd call deep into the thing. I think he's well aware of the problem areas. And I think that you could well take your counsel from him. He knows all the ramifications, and I think he's the best man to help protect you."

321

"Well," said the President, "you know Petersen questions Haldeman for not cutting this Liddy plan off originally. He says that when you came back from that second meeting with Mitchell and you came back and told Bob about this crazy scheme Liddy was planning—uh, what *did* Bob tell you then, John?"

"Well, he said I should have nothing to do with it, and I felt the plan had been killed then. I really did."

"That's right." The President frowned. "That's what I understand the facts are. But Petersen says, 'Well, why didn't Haldeman do something about it?' He doesn't like that."

I could see the President's worry for Haldeman, and was encouraged at the signs that he recognized how seriously Bob was involved. The President went back to Petersen, raising Henry's suggestion that the President encourage Liddy to come forward with the facts. I agreed. The President then called Petersen to discuss the idea, winking at me when he told Petersen I had "stepped out for a minute."

I was encouraged as I listened to the President's end of the conversation. He was telling Petersen that he would urge Liddy to come forward. He was following my counsel. I couldn't tell whether the President was protecting himself with Petersen or genuinely moving to do the right thing, but I longed to give him the benefit of the doubt.

When the call ended, however, the President aroused my suspicions again. He looked down at his pad and resumed his questions about the facts, focusing on my own involvement, my own legal weaknesses. Each time I told him what they were, he would say, "Now, John, I want you to tell the truth about that when you're questioned, understand?"

"Yes, sir," I would reply, but my mind was elsewhere. I was studying him. He is posturing himself, I thought—always placing his own role in an innocuous perspective and seeking

322

my agreement. I wondered if the meeting was a setup. Was he recording me? I noticed a small cassette recorder on the table beside him, but it wasn't running. I glanced around the room, looking for a machine somewhere else. My hopes wrestled my mistrust to a draw. So what? I thought finally. What difference does it make if I admit my involvement?

"Well, John," he said after running through his list of questions, "what's your counsel on whether I should keep Haldeman and Ehrlichman on? I think that's an issue that I'd like to have your advice on. Uh, I've been talking with Petersen about it, and he thinks maybe they should be removed."

I was surprised by the question. The President did not seem to be posturing. Maybe he was seriously weighing this option. My hopes rose again. "Uh, frankly, Mr. President, I would follow Petersen's advice on that. I really can't see any alternative, you know, to protect the Presidency."

The President shook his head sadly. "You think their problems are that bad, eh?"

"Well, I'm afraid so, yes. I think they are at least as bad as my own," I replied, restraining myself. "My lawyer and I have gone over these obstruction statutes, Mr. President, and you'd be surprised by them. They are as broad as the imagination of man, and I'm convinced all of us have serious legal problems."

The President sighed. "What about you, John? Are you prepared to resign?"

"I have thought a lot about that, Mr. President, and I am. I'm not happy about it, but I think it has to occur. I want you to know I'm ready when you say so."

"Good." He nodded. "Good. Let me say this, John. I'm not happy about this, but Petersen has been talking to me about it. It is a painful thing for the President, you know. I don't think it's fair. I don't think it's right. But what can you say?" He looked off helplessly.

"I understand, Mr. President, but I want you to know I understand the important thing is the Presidency."

"That's right," he said.

"That's what matters."

"That's right." The President looked at me, paused, and then spoke in a soft, quiet voice. "John, let me ask you this. Have you talked to the prosecutors at all about your conversations with the President?"

"No, sir, Mr. President," I replied immediately. "I haven't even talked to my lawyer about anything in that area. Those are in privileged areas, as far as I'm concerned."

"That's right," he said, nodding vigorously. "And I don't want you talking about national-security matters, or, uh, executive-privilege things. Uh, those newsmen's wiretaps and things like that—those are privileged, John. Those are privileged. Not that there's anything wrong with them, understand. But they're national security. There's no doubt about that."

"I agree, Mr. President." I knew he was protecting himself with this admonition, but I didn't care. That was my purpose as well.

The President sat up slowly, removing his feet from the ottoman and placing his pad on it. "John, do you remember that conversation when you came in and told me about, you know, the cancer on the Presidency and things like that?"

"Yes, sir." I wondered what he was driving at.

"Well, let me ask you something. When *was* that?"

"Well, let me think. I can't put a date on it off the top of my head, but I know it was the Wednesday just before Hunt was sentenced. It wouldn't be hard to find out."

"Good," he said. "Would you check on that for me? That's when you brought the facts in to me for the first time, isn't it? And gave me the whole picture?"

"Yes, sir, it is." Now I knew he was posturing that he'd known nothing about Watergate until that day. It was a lie, but it was all right with me as long as he didn't do so at my expense. I couldn't tell which way he was going.

The President leaned over toward me, and a mischievous look came across his face. "You know, that mention I made to you about a million dollars and so forth as no problem..." He laughed softly. "I was just joking, of course, when I said that."

I smiled and nodded as the President rose to his feet with some effort and stretched briefly. "Well, Mr. President, I'm not even getting into those areas. You can be assured of that."

"Good," he said, looking down at me. He began walking slowly, circling around my chair toward the window. "You know, John, this guy Hunt has caused us a lot of problems, but I can kind of understand how sad it is for him. You know, with his wife dead, and being in jail like that. Awfully tough. I really feel sorry for him, and it's hard to look at his situation objectively." The President stopped in the corner behind his chair, about ten feet away from me. He paused and looked out the window toward the lights on the West Wing of the White House, his arms folded in front of him. Then he looked over at me. "John," he said in a hushed tone, "I guess it was foolish of me to talk to Colson about clemency. Uh, wasn't it?"

I nodded silently and slowly. The President had just mentioned the two most troublesome areas he had discussed with me. He knew they were his biggest mistakes, but he was telling me that he considered them small ones—jokes, little errors.

His spirits suddenly picked up again. "Well, John, I want to thank you for coming in here tonight. I want you to think

325

about these things, and we'll talk again about them soon, maybe tomorrow."

"Thank you, Mr. President," I said, rising. "I will think about them. I feel a lot better after this conversation." And I did feel better. At least the President had not exploded at me, called me a Judas, fired me, announced a new cover-up.

We started walking across the office together, stopped, and then began heading in our different directions. "Well, John, say hello to your pretty wife for me, okay?" he said brightly.

I had been brooding as we crossed the office. I thought the President was on the brink of a decision that could determine his future. Maybe I had given him the impression it would be too easy. I mustered my courage to give him a parting warning, a last shove in the right direction. "I will tell her you said that, Mr. President. I know she'll appreciate it. Uh, just one other thing, Mr. President." Drifting away from each other, we were now about five feet apart. We both stopped. "You know, uh, Mr. President, I would hate to have anything I have started here by talking to the prosecutors and getting these facts out— uh, I would hate to have any of that ever result in the impeachment of the President."

He gazed off and thought for an instant. I wondered whether anybody on his staff had ever before suggested such a thing seriously. Of course not.

The President shook his head assertively. "Oh, no, John, don't you worry about that. We're going to handle everything right. You can be assured of that. So don't worry about it."

"All right, Mr. President," I sighed. "Good night."

"Good night," he said, heading toward his private bathroom.

I drove home, turning the conversation over and over in my mind. Everything could be interpreted many ways. At least I didn't feel humiliated or repudiated. The cover-up was hanging in the balance.

Maybe the President *would* thank me for what I had done. Maybe he was plotting to screw me to the wall. I knew that was a possibility. For the rest of the evening I wavered back and forth, slowly drowning my worries in alcohol, imagining Nixon doing the same.

The President summoned me to his office first thing the next morning, April 16. As I walked over to the West Wing my mind was nearly blank; I felt as if I were on automatic pilot. The President would give me some sign of the way he was moving, I knew, but I had no idea how strong it would be. On so many occasions I had seen momentous decisions evaded.

Haldeman and Ehrlichman burst out of the Oval Office as I arrived. They were laughing together like college pranksters, but went abruptly straight-faced when they noticed me. The first bad sign. Those were not the looks of men who had been told they had to resign. We exchanged grave nods.

I took a chair to the right of the President's desk, on his left. He greeted me, shuffled some papers nervously. I felt oddly calm by comparison with last night. The President was too worried to explode at me. He now knew what I had done. I thought he was frightened, just as I was.

He came quickly to his point. "You will remember we talked about resignations, et cetera, et cetera, that I should have in hand," he said, waving his hand in an effort to lighten the matter. He paused. "Not to be released."

"Uh-huh," I mumbled, as I always did when the President said something I didn't like. We had talked about resignations, indeed, but never about having to have them "in hand." I waited.

327

"But I should have in hand something, or otherwise they will say, 'What the hell. After Dean told you all of this, what did you do?'

"You see?"

"Uh-huh."

"I talked to Petersen about this other thing, and I said, 'Now, what do you want to do about this situation on Dean, et cetera?' And he said, 'Well, I don't want to announce anything now.' You know what I mean?"

"Uh-huh."

"But what is your feeling on that? See what I mean?"

I looked at the President without expression. He was being sneaky, but he was weak, I thought. Stroking me. Asking for my advice. Hoping I'd volunteer to do what he wanted: resign alone. "Well," I said quietly, "I think it ought to be Dean, Ehrlichman, and Haldeman."

"Well, I thought Dean for the moment," the President replied, but without much force.

"All right," I said, waiting to hear him out.

"Dean at this moment," he continued, "because you are going to be going, and I will have to handle them also. But the point is..." He hesitated as if he had lost the thread. "What is your advice?" Before I could answer, he remembered his next point. "You see, the point is, we just typed up a couple, just to have here, which I would be willing to put out. You know..."

"Uh-huh." Christ, I thought, he's going to ask me to sign a resignation right here on the spot.

"... in the event certain things occur."

Sure, I thought bitterly. Like releasing it about five minutes after the "event" that I sign it. "I understand," I told him.

Nixon was fumbling awkwardly for something on his desk, near the telephone. "To put, just putting..." He faltered, groping for something with his hands while keeping his eyes on me to maintain the visual pressure. "What is your advice?"

"I think it would be good to have it on hand," I replied, "and I would think, to be very honest with you—"

"Have the others too?" he interrupted.

"Yeah, have the others too." The President had anticipated me. I didn't know whether it was because he was genuinely weighing resignations from all three of us or because he backed down at the slightest resistance. I thought it was the latter.

"Well, as a matter of fact, they both suggested it themselves, so I've got that—" The President stopped and looked up. Steve Bull was striding into the room. I turned around in surprise. "I'm sorry, Steve," the President said with a nervous laugh, "I hit the wrong bell." Fumbling, the President had accidentally pushed the button that summoned Bull.

Steve sensed the President's embarrassed agitation, the smell of fear in the Oval Office, and he quickly backed out. I started to laugh, then stopped. I was amazed that the President had come so unstrung.

He had finally gotten hold of what I knew he'd been looking for: my letter of resignation. He had two of them, in fact, and he slid them across his desk toward me with a jerky push. As I scanned the first one, the President kept assuring me, unconvincingly, that Haldeman and Ehrlichman had also offered their resignations.

The first letter stunned me.

DEAR MR. PRESIDENT:

As a result of my involvement in the Watergate matter, which we discussed last night and today, I tender to you my resignation effective at once.

No wonder he's so nervous, I thought. He's asking me to sign a confession. I saw Ziegler reading this letter in the Press Room. I visualized Judge Sirica announcing that since Liddy had gotten twenty years, I deserved no less than forty. I suppressed the thought and read the second letter. It was worse.

DEAR MR. PRESIDENT:

In view of my increasing involvement in the Watergate matter, my impending appearance before the grand jury, and the probability of its action, I request an immediate and indefinite leave of absence from my position on your staff.

The President was suggesting that I sign *both* letters. I was shocked. Mechanically, I discussed both letters as if they were drafts of speeches. And, as I did, a debate raged deep inside me. A voice said, The President is undeniably a devious bastard who'll ruin you any way he can. You should lash out at him, tell him what you really think, tell him how to save himself. He'll probably fall off his chair and agree. Another voice said, The President is your whole life. He is vacillating; he is talking about firing Haldeman and Ehrlichman too; he just needs a little push to do the right thing. The voices canceled each other out. I was just strong enough to resist the President, not strong enough to defy him.

"Uh, what I would like to do," I said, "is draft an alternative letter putting in both options, and you can just put them in the file." Short and sweet.

The President nodded; he backed down as I had expected. "All right. Fine. I had dictated something myself, all my own, which... If you can give me a better form, fine. I just want you to do it, either way. Do you? Or do you want to prepare something?"

"I would like to prepare something," I said quietly, putting off his second feeble attempt to make me sign the ones I held in my hand. I was struck by the President's reiterated claim that he had drafted the letters himself. This, I knew, could not be true. I had seen too many of his dictations; I knew damn well Ehrlichman had written these.

The President and I then proceeded through a long and unproductive discussion on Watergate. My mind was not on the subject; all I wanted to do was get out. And when I did, I drafted a resignation letter and sent it to him. It did not mention Watergate; but it said that I was resigning arm in arm with Haldeman and Ehrlichman. I went home that night satisfied with my resistance and worrying about the President's next thrust.

It came the next day. Nixon could no longer resist the public pressure to say *something* about Watergate; still, his aides were deadlocked, and he was on the fence. He played for time. That afternoon he walked into the Press Room and read an announcement, refusing to take any questions. The announcement said that "major developments" in the Watergate case had come to his attention, and that he was going to get to the bottom of it. He would now permit his aides to testify. Anyone indicted would be suspended; anyone convicted would be fired. This meant nothing. He could not have kept an indicted aide on the staff. The President closed with a surprise edict: "No individual holding, in the past or present, a position of major importance in the Administration should be given immunity from prosecution."

I read the statement and immediately called Leonard Garment, one of the President's advisers who had worked on the draft. "Len, tell me, was that no-immunity position in the draft you worked on?" I asked.

"No, it wasn't, John," Garment replied. "That was news to me, and I saw the draft after the speechwriters finished with it."

"That's what I thought," I said. "Listen, Len. I think I already know the answer, but would you tell me who the draft went to after you cleared it?"

"Sure. It went to Ehrlichman, then to the President. I guess one of them made the addition."

"Thanks, Len. That's what I figured."

Fielding walked in, curious, like most people, about the no-immunity position. "What was that bit all about?" he asked. "Well, Freddie, that's a message to me from the leader of the Western world, who is in the clever hands of John Ehrlichman."

"How so?"

"Well, the President thinks I won't talk without immunity from prosecution. He thinks he can scare me back into the fold. But he's wrong. I don't have any choice now. It looks like the President is choosing his team, and it's going to be me against the big guys. How would you like to be White House counsel?"

"That's not funny."

"I know. Listen, Fred, I'm not going to come in to the office tomorrow. I don't want to be around here, and I haven't been too much help to you anyway."

I called Jane in, and together we gathered a boxful of Watergate press clippings. I needed the clippings to help trigger my memory. Charlie was urging me to begin preparing a detailed chronology of everything I knew—dates and statements I could swear to. The task intimidated me. As I drove home, I decided I would drink that night and begin in the morning.

The President's statement renewed press interest in me, and my house was again staked out in full force. Reporters stayed near my door round the clock. A few had seen Mo leave a day earlier on a trip to Florida. I had devised an elaborate route to avoid the press corps and camera crews—I would slip in and out the back of the house, across a small alley running behind the row of town houses, and through Fred Fielding's house.

I felt like a prisoner in my home the next day. My only link with the outside world was the telephone. Charlie and I spoke frequently. We were both in low spirits. In one particular call on April 18, he drove in another nail.

"John, I've just gotten a report from Glanzer," he said. "It's fourthhand information, but it's serious. The President just told Petersen that you told him you *already* have immunity. At least that's what Petersen's telling Glanzer. You didn't say that, did you?"

"Hell, no, I didn't. When am I supposed to have said that?"

"Sunday night, when you gave the P your little impeachment warning."

"Goddammit, Charlie, the President's lying. I didn't tell him I had immunity. And I wouldn't have told him so even if I did have it. Hell, I was being the good guy that night. I was telling the President I would face the music along with Haldeman and Ehrlichman."

"That's what I thought. But Glanzer says the P claims to have you on tape. He says he can prove you said you have immunity."

"Shit! I thought he might be taping me that night. I even looked around for the recorder. I tell you what, Charlie. You send word back to Petersen to ask for that tape. I guarantee you he'll never get it. But if he does, what the President says on there will burn Henry's ears off."

"That's a good idea," said Charlie. "I'll pass it to Glanzer."

"No matter what, I didn't say that to the President, Charlie. Why do you think he would tell Petersen I did?"

"Well, I'll tell you, John. My guess is that the President didn't clear his no-immunity statement with Petersen. It probably pissed Petersen off, because it's direct interference in the prosecutor's business. It robs Petersen of a way to force testimony. I think the P was trying to justify his statement."

"Maybe so. And he got to call me a liar in the process."

"Yep. For a guy who you say is sometimes a little loose upstairs, he looks pretty clever to me."

"I'll tell you something, Charlie. I've been thinking that maybe I should go public with something. Maybe I should let them know I'm not going to take this lying down. What do you think about a little statement to the newspapers that I refuse to be the scapegoat?"

"I doubt if you want to do that, John. You'll sure as hell burn your bridges if you do that. You could never get back in their good graces."

"What the hell difference does that make? Look, in the last few days the President's tried to make me confess, blocked my chances of getting immunity, and called me a liar. I'm not going to be his buddy again no matter what."

"Okay, okay. I was just testing you. *You're* the one who keeps hanging on to the idea that the P won't screw you. You're the one who keeps thinking the President deserves your loyalty."

"I know, Charlie. I've been thinking about that too. You know, I've always kind of laughed at the people I've seen leaving the White House. No matter what they say, it always

334

rips them up. They come back begging for mess privileges and invitations and stuff like that. They just can't let go. Now I know how they feel. But I'll tell you, Charlie, what I'm hanging on to is this: I still think the President's interests and my interests lie in the same direction. Even if we don't think much of each other personally. If he lines up against me with Haldeman and Ehrlichman, I think he's in big trouble, and I know I will be. Now, I see only two reasons why he's doing it. One is that Haldeman and Ehrlichman have him by the balls so tight that he doesn't have any choice. If that's true, nothing I do will make any difference. But the other possibility is that Ehrlichman and Haldeman have him convinced that he can run over me. If *that's* the reason, maybe a little public notice might do some good."

"Okay, John. I never like to have my clients in public, but maybe you're right. Talk to McCandless about it. Just make sure you don't say anything specific in there about your testimony. Be general, but pretend you're mean and tough like me." Charlie laughed. "I'm going to call old Seymour back just to hear his voice when I tell him to go after that tape." [*]

I called Bob McCandless. He had come onto my legal team when Tom Hogan had been forced to drop out, and he was a good public-relations man. We worked over a number of drafts of a statement until we were both satisfied. I dictated it to Jane the next morning and instructed her to phone it to the wire services, the *Washington Post,* and the *Washington Star.* The message was in the last two sentences: "Finally, some may hope or think that I will become a scapegoat in the Watergate

---

[*] [Original Footnote:] When Henry Petersen asked for the tape, the President backed down, claiming it was only his dictation of the meeting, which had now been misplaced. Months later, after disclosure of a taping system, the Watergate Special Prosecutor's office subpoenaed the tape of this conversation, on July 23, 1973. On October 31, 1973, the President's lawyers announced to the court that it was missing, because of mechanical failure.

case. Anyone who believes this does not know me, know the true facts, nor understand our system of justice." McCandless said it was a little stilted, but I told him I was still counsel to the President and I had my airs. The statement made headlines, and I received signals from the White House that it had made me a permanent *persona non grata* and the object of the nastiest possible epithets.

The next evening, April 20, I went home late from Charlie's office. We had discussed the possibility of dealing with the Senate Watergate Committee, whose chief counsel, Sam Dash, was anxious to meet with me. Reporters were still all around my house, so I had to go home through Fred's. He invited me to stop for a drink.

"Be careful what you say, because I'm worried that my phone might be bugged," Fred said.

"Hell, I assume mine is bugged, and what they're hearing they should find very thrilling. I just came from Charlie's office, Fred. He's concerned about my life, afraid someone might like to eliminate me from the scene. Can you believe that? Charlie doesn't scare easy. He prosecuted Jimmy Hoffa."

Fred looked incredulous. "Why would you fear for your life?"

"Because of what I know—" Fred pointed to the telephone, reminding me of his concern that his house was bugged. Our paranoia made us speak in hushed tones. "Freddie, do you have any idea where this thing might lead?"

Fred shook his head and reached for a piece of paper on a nearby table. I took a pen from my coat pocket and wrote the answer to our shared question: "Impeachment of the President." I passed the note to Fred.

"Enough facts?" he wrote. "Probably so."

"Are you sure you want the historic responsibility for that?"

"No! But I know enough to cause it."

"So be it!" Fred wrote. We stared at each other for a moment as we sipped our drinks, and then we stared at the crumpled note, which Fred had ignited and put in the ashtray. We watched it burn.

With Mo still in Florida, and Charlie pushing me to remember more and more details, I began working late into the night. Saturday, April 21, I worked particularly late, drinking even more than my usual generous quantity of alcohol. I figured I'd sleep off a hangover, and believed the Scotch was loosening up my memory. That night I had recalled in detail most aspects of the cover-up that had been instituted to prevent the FBI from discovering the Ellsberg break-in. About 4 A.M. I went to bed, leaving my clothes heaped in the middle of the floor and piles of papers spread about on the easy chairs in our bedroom.

It seemed I had been asleep only minutes when the phone rang. With the shades drawn and the blackout draperies pulled, I had no idea it was eight in the morning. I tried to ignore the phone's ring, but it didn't stop. The phone was across the bedroom, buried under papers in one of the easy chairs. I rolled out of bed stark naked, made my way across the room, dug through the nest, and picked up the phone.

"Yes," I hissed in a tone that fit my mood.

"Mr. Dean, it's the President. Please hold on," the operator said before I could say anything. I felt awful: my head was pounding, my mouth tasted and smelled as bad as the brimming ashtray I noticed when I turned on the lamp.

"Good morning, John." The President's deep, familiar voice was chipper. "I'm just calling to wish you and your wife a happy Easter." I was still dazed. The President calling me?

337

To wish me happy Easter? I sat down and found a place for the phone in the pile of papers on the ottoman as he continued, "It's a lovely day here in Florida for Easter services."

"Oh, uh, fine. Happy Easter to you, too." This was too confusing, particularly in the condition I was in. Days earlier he had been asking me to resign and I had refused. I had issued my scapegoat statement and had managed to piss off almost everybody in the White House. Now the President was calling me to wish me happy Easter? Given the way I felt after too little sleep, wondering if my pounding head was from an internal hemorrhage, the next thought that came to me seemed logical: I wondered if anyone had ever said to him, "Mr. President, I think you're full of shit!"

The President must have sensed something in my mood; he stepped in to stroke. "John, I just want you to know you're still my counsel."

"Uh, well, uh, thank you, Mr. President." He was looking for my loyalty charge, and he ignited it. He was being loyal to me, I certainly wanted to be loyal to him. As we talked, it seemed as if nothing had happened. He asked my advice. We talked about immunity laws. Then I added, thinking about his April 17 statement on immunity, "Mr. President, I think you should talk to Henry Petersen about obstruction of justice and the statement you issued. You should be very careful, sir."

"Oh, I will," he assured me, and the brief conversation ended as he talked of having to get ready to go to church. "Well, have a nice day, John."

"Thank you, Mr. President, I hope you have a nice day, also."

This was my last conversation with Richard Nixon. I climbed back into bed and thought about it. Was it really a stroking call, or did he still consider me his counsel? Then I felt ashamed of my thought about telling him he was full of shit; that was not the sort of thought one had about one's President. A spark of hope was left to me: the President was really telling me that he knew I was right, that the cancer had to be cut, that he would do it.

This hope lasted only a couple of days. I called Len Garment again*—he was my last link to the President—and urged him to take my arguments to Nixon without mentioning my name. Len said he agreed with me and would do so, but that the signs were adverse. Whatever else happened, it appeared that the President would try to make me responsible for the cover-up. A campaign to discredit me was gearing up.

Newspaper stories with the White House line began appearing. On Thursday, April 26, columnist Jack Anderson presented a comprehensive version to his readers in nearly six hundred newspapers. It was a thumbnail defense of the White House, a broadside against me, and a foreshadowing of what was to come. Anderson spelled it out:

> Our sources state flatly that Dean used his authority to obstruct the FBI and to keep incriminating evidence from the Justice Department. He even ordered Hunt out of the country. White House aide Charles Colson, according to one source, exploded: "Do you want to make the White House an accessory to a fugitive from justice?"
>
> One of the President's closest advisers, John Ehrlichman, wanted to put out a statement acknowledging Magruder's role in the Watergate conspiracy. This was vigorously opposed by Clark MacGregor, who succeeded Mitchell as campaign chairman.

---

*   Garment was many years my senior. He had been Nixon's law partner, and after I left, he would become counsel to the president. Len Garment and I remain friendly to this day, and have talked–long after the fact–about Watergate on many occasions, and at great length, when we were trying to figure out who Bob Woodward's infamous source "Deep Throat" might be.

339

A few Presidential advisers, including Ehrlichman and Colson, warned the President in February that the Watergate decisions must have been approved by Mitchell and Dean. Mr. Nixon replied that both had denied any involvement and asked for proof.

By mid-March, the President's faith in Dean began to waver. He ordered Dean to Camp David to write a belated report on his Watergate investigation. After a few days at the Presidential retreat, Dean reported back to the President that he simply couldn't write a report. Angrily, Mr. Nixon took Dean off the Watergate case.

Colson, meanwhile, took a lie detector test to prove his innocence. Dean was furious. "Now, we're all going to have to take one," he grumped.

Colson and Ehrlichman also put together information that (1) Dean had advance knowledge of the Watergate bugging; (2) Dean had ordered Hunt out of the country; (3) Dean had authorized payments to the Watergate defendants to keep their mouths shut. On Friday, April 13th, Ehrlichman confronted Dean with the charges.

This view of reality was so contorted that I didn't know where to begin to refute it. Ehrlichman and Colson had obviously cooked up the story and fed it to Anderson. I knew that both had lines into him and it was what I expected from Ehrlichman and Colson, a skillful job.

But as jaded as I had become about politics, I was surprised that Jack Anderson, famous Nixon enemy and Watergate sleuth, was offering up the versions of two prime targets in the case without qualification. He offered no hint that Colson or Ehrlichman was his source and opened with a flourish: "The astonishing story can now be told how the Watergate cover-up suddenly tore apart at the stitches." What a whore, I thought bitterly—he was taking all the sides, playing to power like everybody else in town.[*]

A few days later, Charlie called to inform me that I had been subpoenaed to appear before a New York grand jury which was then investigating the dealings of John Mitchell and

---

[*] Many years later I found myself sharing a lecture stage with Jack Anderson. My agent had not told me of the arrangement. Before going on stage I was introduced to Anderson in the Green Room. His journalistic dishonesty flashed in my mind, as did my anger. Seldom do I confront people, but this was an opportunity I could not pass. I told Anderson that he should brace himself because I planned to tell our audience that he was a dishonest journalist who would print anything he was told without checking its veracity. Anderson flinched and flushed. He immediately walked out of the room, and soon returned with the host who was sponsoring the event, who said that Anderson was going to cancel if I insisted on attacking his credibility as a reporter. I explained that that was fine with me if he cancelled, for I would be happy to explain that Anderson was a coward as well as a dishonest journalist. Anderson asked our host to step outside, where they conferred. Soon we headed for the stage, and the host introduced us, and explained to the audience that Anderson had an unexpected conflict so he would give his talk first and take questions, and then he would have to depart before I proceeded. When I had my turn at the lectern Anderson was gone. I took a few mild cracks at him but he had effectively defeated my effort for a head-on confrontation about his ethics and honesty. Indeed, he did not mention a word about me, Watergate, or Nixon in his talk. My agent later told me that Anderson cancelled a second appearance with me that he had arranged. He had put us together because I could draw an audience, while Anderson could not, but he thought it might work for us both and be a good program. I thought it would be a great program to debate his indefensible journalism. See also, John W. Dean, *The Rehnquist Choice: The Untold Story of the Nixon Appointment that Redefined the Supreme Court* (New York: Free Press, 2001) where I explained that former Virginia Congressman Richard Poff withdrew his nomination for a seat on the high court because he worried the confirmation process would reveal that he had adopted one of his sons—a fact he and his wife did not think the child was ready to learn. Jack Anderson was told of this private information long after the fact but while the child was still unaware of his adoption, and over the pleas of Poff and his wife, Anderson insisted hurting the Poff family by reporting the no longer relevant story. I wanted to publicly debate Anderson not only about his misinformation about Watergate but his willingness to harm an innocent child with his column.

341

Maurice Stans with international swindler Robert Vesco. Charlie and I joked that I might be the first person ever summoned who was actually happy about it—the Vesco case would take my mind off Watergate. We left for New York full of black humor about how things could not get worse, but on Monday, April 30, they did. Jane called from my office while I was in the U.S. attorney's office at the New York Federal Courthouse. The two prosecutors who were grilling me asked if I wanted to take the call privately. Not necessary, I said.

Jane sounded shaken. "John, there's a story on the wire services that you've been fired. Fred says it's true."

"Thank you, Jane. Don't you worry. You'll be able to stay at the White House. I'll call you later and talk to you about it. But don't you worry." I hung up and turned to the two prosecutors. Charlie had gone out to get us all lunch. "Well," I told them, "I have just learned I've been fired by the President."

"I'm sorry to hear that," one of them said sincerely. "Would you like to take a break for a while?"

"No, I'm fine. Let's proceed." And we did. They were surprised, both at what had happened and at my lack of reaction. I had expected it. But I did not expect the speech Nixon would give on television that night.

Charlie and I were staying at the Waldorf-Astoria, at his request, until I realized I was paying the bills. It was our last stay at the Waldorf. When Charlie asked me what the President would say on television, I wanted to believe that somehow he would do the right thing. I should have known he could not. He felt the need now to cover up his own involvement in the cover-up.

I was psyching myself up for what I knew was ahead, beginning to want to dislike the President as I'd never been able to in the past. When he announced the resignations of Haldeman and Ehrlichman, "the two finest public servants it has

342

been my privilege to know," I steeled myself. He removed Kleindienst with faint praise. Then he shoved a ten-word sentence into me, twisted it with a brief pause, and quickly stepped away so that all could see whom the President had stuck it to: "The counsel to the President, John Dean, has also resigned."

"That's what loyalty earns you, Charlie," I said.

"Yeah, I see. You don't have to wear that suit anymore," my lawyer and now friend answered.

"I may not be able to afford *any* suit any longer," I said miserably. "And I don't even think I'll be able to afford you, Charlie. I think I have just gone down the tube."

"Cut it out, John," Charlie rebuked me. "I don't want to hear any talk about my fees. You know damn well I'm with you on this one, and we're not licked yet. There's one good thing about that statement. Haldeman and Ehrlichman went, too. Nobody's going to believe that the President fired his two closest and most powerful aides unless there were some pretty heavy guns trained on them. I don't care how many flowers he tossed them. The fact that he got rid of them is pretty damn strong evidence that you are telling the truth."

"That may be, Charlie, but he's thrown in with them on the cover-up. It's still going on and I'm out there alone in the gutter."

"Except for me," Charlie insisted.

I called Mo. It had to be rough having your husband fired on national television. She was distressed, but not about the speech she had just heard.

"John, why didn't you call Jane back? She's frantically trying to reach you."

"What's up?"

"Jane's really upset. She said that just after she talked to you this afternoon a bunch of FBI agents marched into your office. They asked where your files were and then put metal bands around them. They're standing in your office, guarding them."

"Holy Christ, you're kidding!"

"No, I'm not!"

"Sweetheart, this is important. There's a box of documents up in the bedroom. It's not very heavy, and I want you to carry it to the attic. Leave it there until I come home, or until Charlie comes over to pick it up. In that box there's a sealed brown envelope. Take it out and hide it somewhere."

"John, what's wrong?" Mo had fear in her voice.

"Nothing, sweetheart, please be brave. It's very important. Also don't answer the door for anyone. *Not anyone.*" We went over again what she was to do, and I told her to call me back after she had done it.

Charlie was pacing the floor; he wanted to know what I was instructing Mo to do. I told him about my office files and the copy of the Huston Plan. "Charlie, this is like something out of the Third Reich. I'm actually worried that Nixon might send FBI or Secret Service agents out to the house to see what they can find. Nixon, obviously, is playing very hard ball. That's evident from his speech and sending agents to my office. I believe the man is capable of anything. "

Charlie knew me well enough by now to know I was not paranoid. He seldom drank, but that night he did.

"Charlie, all this has got to change," I told him. "This is bigger than both of us, but I'm in a position to do something, I think—if people will believe what I have to say, and that's a big if."

344

CHAPTER NINE:
GOING PUBLIC

CHARLIE AND I WENT BACK TO WASHINGTON the next day, May 1. We didn't say much on the trip; we were in shock. I was now just a private citizen guilty of crime, up against a battery of prosecutors who wanted to nail me. The President of the United States wanted to nail me. All I had going for me was my word that there were bigger people involved.

By the time the plane landed, both of us had to come back to life. I invited Charlie to my home for a strategy session. "If there are reporters around the house, we can slip in the back," I told him in the taxi.

"No sir," he declared. "Those bastards aren't going to make *me* use back doors. If they ask me for a comment on your firing, I'll stop and say, 'Why don't you go fuck yourself? Now print that, and remember my name is spelled with two *f's*.'" I knew this was only tough talk. Charlie did refuse to talk to reporters, but he was too much a gentleman to insult them and he was always polite when he told them to go to hell.

Charlie made himself comfortable in the living room while I went upstairs to reassure Mo that everything was all right. I found her calmly reading. After my "scapegoat" statement I had warned her that I might be canned, but I had really been bracing myself. I returned to find Charlie searching the living room for a match.

"How would you like to get into a pissing match with the President of the United States?" I asked Charlie.

"I think we are already in one," he answered. "It looks like the P is going to keep walking with his German shepherds."

345

"No, I mean directly."

He shrugged. "Why not? What do you have in mind?"

"Well, we've never really talked about the President, but I think you know there is no way I can testify completely about the cover-up without telling you about my dealings with him."

"Right. I'd like to hear about the P if you're ready to tell me."

"Let me begin with some of the things I heard when I first went to the White House." Charlie was still reluctant to hear details of the Huston Plan, but he agreed now that, as my attorney, he had to advise me on what he thought was or was not "national security."

"You mean to tell me you've got memos showing that the President approved illegal taps, mail opening, and break-ins?" he reacted angrily.

"That's right. Mo hid them last night. You want to see them?"

"No, I don't want to touch them. I don't like you having them here in your house, either. You are no longer a government employee, so you're not authorized to have them. You've got to get them back to the White House in the morning. I don't want you to commit another crime accidentally."

"If I send them back, they'll disappear forever. That's why I took them. I figured nobody would ever believe me if I said there was such a plan. It shows the kind of thinking that produced Watergate."

"Okay. I've got an idea. I want you to get a safe-deposit box. Tomorrow. Understand? And put that stuff in the box. Then I'll draw up some papers, and we'll turn the key to the box over to Sirica. He can decide what should be done with them."

"Charlie, I don't have any evidence that the President knew what Liddy and Hunt were up to once they went over to the

346

Reelection Committee. But, goddammit, I know the way that place works, and Haldeman must have told him something. Ain't no one ever going to be able to prove that, though, I assure you." *

I took Charlie step by step through my dealings with the President on the cover-up, from the first meeting, on September 15, 1972, through the last. Charlie's cigar went out somewhere along the line, but he didn't notice.

"What do you think?" I asked finally.

Charlie stood up and walked across the room. He stopped and turned. His head was shaking and his lips were tight, as if they were fighting to hold back the words: "The President is a goddam criminal, that's what I think."

I nodded.

Charlie began pacing. "Now, listen, I want to go back over a couple of points. I want you to tell me again what he said about it being no problem to get a million bucks, and what you told him about laundering money. That's the damnedest conversation I've ever heard. The P sounds like the Godfather, for Christ's sake."

He sat back down in the easy chair beside our fireplace and listened as I repeated the conversation.

"Now tell me about the clemency offers again," he said.

I repeated it.

"The P's in big trouble. Big trouble," he concluded and was off pacing again. Then, as he lit his cigar, "The P needs a lawyer and he better get himself a good one."

"Well, now you can understand why I suggested that Silbert and Glanzer get that tape of my meeting with Nixon on

---

*   After Nixon's taping system was revealed, as I set forth in the Afterword, the evidence has surfaced indicating Nixon did have knowledge.

347

April fifteenth," I said.

"Yeah, I see." Charlie sat down again with a sigh. He was quiet for a long time. When he finally spoke, his mood had changed. "I don't think I ever told you this, but I voted for Nixon last time. Everybody, I guess, figures that an old Kennedy Democrat like me would love to nail Nixon, but I'd figured the bastard would make a better President than McGovern. You know," he continued as he watched the smoke from his cigar swirl up toward the lamp beside him, "it's damn depressing, what you just told me." He was silent again.

"Would you like a drink?" Mo asked Charlie as she came down the stairs to check on us.

"I'll have a little brandy if you've got some, thanks." Charlie waited until she was out of the room and then spoke to me softly. "I don't think you ought to tell McCandless about the P. I don't think this stuff should be leaked to the press.[*] He'll learn about it in due time, but not now. Okay?"

---

[*] Neither Charlie nor I knew exactly what McCandless was up to but we both suspected he was leaking information to the press. His job had been to keep the press away from me so we could address the problems of unraveling the mess. Charlie did not want to be distracted by dealing with the news media. McCandless, however, viewed Watergate as a political fight with Nixon for he had been Hubert Humphrey's campaign aide in 1968 in the presidential race against Nixon. McCandless had begged me to be a part of my legal representation, and said he would work for free. When he later presented me with a bill for his services–about which I had no knowledge–I was stunned and it ended our relationship. He wanted twenty percent of my future earnings for five years. It was absurd. We did not speak for almost three decades, and when he did seek me out, he told me that he met regularly with the press but never told me because he did not think I needed to know or should know. I mention it here because McCandless would complain to columnist Robert Novak that I had stiffed him for his fee in representing me. I have never stiffed anyone, including McCandless. If McCandless had not offered to work for free, I would never have let him become involved, for Charlie was the only attorney I was interested in listening to.

"I agree."

Charlie sighed again. "You against the President. Shit, I can't believe it. I knew you were carrying a load around in your head, but I didn't realize it was a goddam atom bomb. I want to think about this for a while. We're going to take this one step at a time. It may be your word against Nixon's and the rest of 'em, and that doesn't make me very comfortable."

"It doesn't make me very comfortable, either."

"Not that I don't believe you," Charlie reassured me, and I knew he meant it.

He had said the same thing to me a few weeks earlier, at a time when he had had doubts. It had been an awkward situation for him and most uncomfortable for me. I had gone to his office to meet with him and had found that something was bothering him. "I had a talk today with Silbert and Glanzer," he had said. "John, they don't believe your story about Gray destroying documents, which makes them very leery of what else you told them." Charlie's worried tone upset me. He always sounded confident, about everything. "They say Petersen talked to Gray, and Gray has denied ever receiving any documents from you and Ehrlichman, let alone destroying them." Charlie shifted in his chair. "Now, I believe you," he added hastily, "but..." He was struggling for the right words. I knew my face must be registering my concern, and Charlie was trying to comfort me, but his words didn't offer solace. "...but I'm not the prosecutor in this case."

"Charlie, I'm telling you the truth. Gray told me he'd destroyed those documents. I'd swear to it under oath," I pleaded, looking for stronger assurance than the mere fact that my own lawyer believed me.

"Here's the problem. They say, 'Why should we believe Dean?' You see, it's your word against his, and just because I tell them Gray's a damn liar doesn't help us a bit. We've got to

convince them, and I've got an idea I'd like to run by you."
Charlie was more fidgety than I'd ever seen him. He spun a
pencil with his hand as he spoke.

"Sure," I said, but I felt desperate. I'd been trying to convince myself that if I said what had happened I'd be believed.
Now even Charlie wants more, I thought.

"Here's what I'm thinking. You don't have to do this if you
don't want to, but it might be a good idea if you took a lie-
detector test. If the results don't come out right, we'll put the
goddam report in the bottom drawer and bury it." Charlie was
testing me.

"Hell, Charlie, I'm ready. Gray's lying, and if that's what
I've got to do to prove it, fine."

"Terrific. That's terrific. I'll set it up for you as soon as we
can do it. I've got the man." He was smiling for the first time
since I had arrived, which made me feel better.

Charlie called a private investigator and made the arrangements. The next day I would "get on the box," as he called it.

Charlie's investigator friend and the lie-detector expert
were waiting for me in the uninviting back room of a sterile
prefabricated office building in suburban Maryland. What if I
fail, I kept thinking; then I'm going to be in really big trouble.
I had nearly convinced myself that no machine could register
anything about me because my central nervous system was
carrying more voltage than it was built to handle. The tester
tried to put me at ease. The purpose, he explained, was not to
trick or surprise me. We reviewed the questions carefully.

There was no way to get comfortable in the hardwood
chair, with terminals attached to my fingers, a blood-pressure
tourniquet around one of my arms, and a rubber belt around my
chest. Wires ran behind me to the "box." The tourniquet cut
off the circulation in my arm. I felt a tingling feeling as my
fingers fell asleep, then pain. This was normal, the tester said

when I complained. He kept asking questions: "Did you turn documents from Hunt's safe over to Pat Gray? Did Mr. Gray tell you he had destroyed the documents from Hunt's safe you had given him?"

"We're almost finished," he said. "But I want to do one more test. Please select a card." He held out a fan of half a dozen playing cards. "Now, remember the card you selected. I'm going to call off all the cards, and I want you to lie to me about which card you selected." He read off the cards and I picked the wrong one. He peered at his instruments, laughing. "That's a good sign. You damn near broke my machine when you lied." I felt better as he unhooked me from the straps and wires.

Charlie called when he received the report the next day. He was riding high again. "Son, from now on whenever there's any doubt about who's telling the truth, you're going to get on the box. I already called Silbert and told him to get Gray on the box, because my man passed with flying colors." Gray, of course, never took a lie-detector test; he finally confessed that he had destroyed the documents.

The polygraph test was not wasted. It led us to an important decision: I would testify only to facts on which I was prepared to take a lie-detector test. Often when we were preparing testimony in sensitive areas, Charlie would lean over, smiling, and ask whether I was ready to go on the box about it. It would give us a boost as we squared off against the President.

Now Charlie quickly decided what to do with the new information about the President. "We're going to see how serious those fellows downtown are about seeing justice done," he told me, dialing Silbert's number. "I want to put a little more coal on the fire we've got under them."

"What do you have in mind?"

351

"I want to find out what those bastards are made of," he said as he let the phone ring. "And I may want you to tell them of your dealings with the P, at least those I don't believe are privileged." Charlie had decided that any dealing I had with the President in furtherance of a criminal conspiracy would not be subject to attorney-client or executive privilege.

"Hello, Earl my boy, how's my favorite prosecutor?"

Silence. Laughter.

"Of course. That's why I'm calling. I think you should talk to Dean one more time, before I meet with Sam Dash, up there with that Senate committee. Dash sure is interested in talking to us."

Silence. Charlie's eyes were smiling as he listened.

"Right, and I think you guys should come out here, particularly because of what I want my man to tell you about."

Silence. Then Charlie put his hand over the mouthpiece and told me Silbert was bucking a private meeting now that our dealings were known.

"Listen, goddammit, he's going to tell you about the P," he said into the phone.

A very brief silence and Charlie erupted. "The P, goddammit. The Man. Your top boss who lives down the street in the big house. You know now?" Silence. "Good. I always knew you were a bright fellow. I want to find out if you fellows plan to really prosecute this case. Otherwise, I don't want my man to throw in with you. I know a lot of U.S. attorneys around the country that would love to talk to my man, and I—"

Silence. Now Charlie could not keep from smiling. Again he covered the mouthpiece as he nodded and said to me, "They'll meet with us. I've got poor Earl so high in the air he's afraid to come back down." Then to Silbert: "Okay, I'll wait to hear back from you. But don't waste our time if you're not interested in taking this case all the way."

Charlie hung up. He stood up, stretched, and plopped back down.

"They want you to plead guilty to a one-count felony—"

"What?" I exclaimed.

"Don't get excited. I refused to even discuss it with them. I've just upped the ante, but they're almost afraid to talk with you. They're damned if they do and damned if they don't. Earl can't make a move, I suspect, without talking to Petersen now. I want old Henry to know this is the biggest fucking case he's ever touched. Earl's going to have to meet with us, and I want you to tell him of the highlights of your dealings with the P, the money, and clemency stuff."

"You think that's wise? Petersen's going to pass it right on to the President, I suspect."

"That's fine. I think Nixon should get the message that you're not going to lie for his ass. He'd better fess up before he's in jail."

Earl called back, and a meeting was arranged for May 3. But it was different from what Charlie and I expected. The prosecutors listened to my details on the President's complicity as if I were talking about something of historical value rather than immediate interest. At one point, I thought Earl might fall asleep. Only Seymour Glanzer seemed to be absorbing every word, his eyebrows rising and falling. He seemed to be plotting how the facts I was relating fit with the law.

"John, I want you to listen to me," Glanzer said as I concluded. "We need more details, more facts, more specifics, more proof. Not impressions, opinions, and conclusions. This information is amazing, but it is not strong enough."

"I understand, but—"

353

"Hold it, son," Charlie interrupted. "You don't need to give these fellows any 'buts.' You've already given them enough. Maybe too much. Now if they want to do their jobs they know where to come for the information. If they're not interested, well, the United States Senate is very interested. I suggest we adjourn. If you guys want to talk further, you've got my phone number."

I didn't know where we were now. Charlie was playing the heavy negotiator, and I relied on him to handle it. He knew how prosecutors thought and acted, I didn't. Charlie reported to me almost daily, but gave me few details. I was growing less convinced they would grant me immunity, but the negotiations gave us time to figure out what I should do, and Charlie was more optimistic than I was about the prosecutors. He felt that Seymour Glanzer was far ahead of Earl Silbert in analyzing the situation. Glanzer had told Charlie privately that I should be granted immunity because I was telling the truth and would make a key witness for unraveling the entire mess. He seemed to understand my position—it was my word against Mitchell, Ehrlichman, Haldeman, and the President. Glanzer had asked a private law firm to prepare a brief on whether a sitting President could be indicted. Clearly he saw where all this was headed, but he was not in charge.

Charlie's bargaining put the prosecutors in an awkward spot. They didn't know what to do with me, while Sam Dash, the chief counsel of the Senate Watergate Committee, had no doubts: he wanted my testimony. But he told Charlie he was worried that the members of his committee, who were reading heavy doses of anti-Dean material in the newspapers, would need more detail about my testimony in order to make a decision about whether to grant me immunity.

Charlie continued to play the Senate committee against the U.S. attorney's office for my testimony, and the negotiations dragged on. Each conversation I had with Bob McCandless and Charlie ended up at the same point: it was inevitable that I

354

would soon testify somewhere, but my story was anything but organized. "Goddammit," Charlie said. "You've got to quit worrying about everything else and focus on that testimony. You let McCandless worry about the press, and let me worry about your legal problems."

When I protested that daily distractions made it impossible for me to focus, Bob McCandless arranged for Mo and me to use a beach house in Bethany, Maryland, that belonged to a friend of his. Late on the night of May 7, as neighbors turned off their lights to darken the alley, we slipped from our house through Fielding's house and into Pete Kinsey's waiting silver BMW, while Pete went in the other direction from Fred's house through our house and down to our garage, revved up my Porsche and took off. The reporters scrambled to follow him as he roared up the street into his own garage, closed the door, and went to bed.

The oceanfront house was marvelous, even in gusty, over-cast weather. There were no televisions or newspapers or reporters. The beach was deserted. Mo looked happier than I had seen her for weeks, and I began the task I had put off so long: recapturing nine months of complex detail. The high-lights were easy, so I began with a rough outline. Reading old newspaper clippings helped call to mind what had been going on simultaneously inside the White House. My memory operates something like a movie projector when I hit the right switch. I knew I had to be very careful. Sometimes the pictures in my mind were out of focus, and sometimes I could not hear the accompanying words; when I tried to force my memory, it resulted in greater confusion.

The process was slow, but I made good progress for the next two days. Then McCandless called. "Johnny, I hate to bother you," he began, "but I told you things were going to get a lot rougher, and it's happened. Daniel Schorr is going on CBS tonight with a story that the reason you're fighting for immunity is that you're afraid to go to jail for fear of homosex-

355

ual attacks."

"You're shitting me! Aren't you?"

"Nope. I tried to get him to kill the story. I told him it was the most preposterous thing I'd ever heard, but he's still going with it."

I was stunned, then angry. "For Christ's sake, Bob, I can't believe Schorr's going with that garbage. He's been around a long time, and he sure as hell must know a smear when he sees one."

"No way to turn him off. I've tried. He's attributing the story to one of your lawyers. Shaffer may choke the son-of-a-bitch, if I don't do it first."

"Well goddammit, try once more, Bob," I said. "Tell him I'm not any more afraid of getting raped in jail than any other man. But I know enough to know that those guys in prison watch the news. If Schorr runs that story, they'll lick their chops to test me my first day in prison. You tell Schorr that's the dirtiest goddam stunt I ever heard of." I hung up, fighting a small suspicion that Bob himself might have faked the story in order to force me out in the public with my story.

"Mo," I said, as she watched a stray dog wander down the beach, "how do I counter the image of an unethical, President-deceiving, fag fearing squealer whose wife, it is rumored—and according to Bob it's still only a rumor—has quietly left him because she unwittingly married the scum of the earth?"

"That's really sweet," she replied.

Daniel Schorr's story was one of a mass of similar tales— all seemed designed to frighten me or impugn my motives. I knew that the White House was behind most of them. It was a rough game. The White House was taking advantage of its power, and betting that millions of people did not wish to believe a man who called the President a liar. It played upon emotions: no one likes a squealer, a Judas, an informant, a tattletale, especially one who is also guilty. Every base motivation was attributed to me: I had turned on the President for money, for publicity, for spite, because I was a perverted character. More commonly, it was stated that I was lying about the President to save my own skin.

The stories stung me. I kept reminding myself that I was not lying, and that my loyalty to Richard Nixon had died a long, painful, and justified death. But I winced defensively when reasonable commentators said that my record cast doubt on my right to accuse the Nixon White House of anything. I exploded in anger when I was called a liar. The statement that most infuriated me was columnist Joseph Alsop's public declaration that I was a "bottom dwelling slug." I didn't even know what a slug was, so I went to the dictionary: "any of various slimy, elongated...gastropods related to the terrestrial snails." Slugs live in mud, under rocks.

McCandless called two to three times a day with rumors and intelligence he had picked up from reporters, and I soon had an unhappy baptism into the ways of the Washington press corps. Reporters who swore publicly that they'd rot in jail before revealing their sources were calling McCandless with stories that the White House was trying to plant on them. Some wanted to trade them for my stories on the White House. Colson was peddling a story that I had lied to the President about Howard Hunt. What dirt did I have on Colson? Pat Buchanan was putting out the word that I had taken part in wild sex orgies. What did I have on Buchanan? Maxine Cheshire, the *Washington Post* gossip columnist, was about to write a story that I had bought a new Mercedes, the implication being that my disloyalty had brought me ill-gotten riches. (I had been seen driving Charlie's Mercedes.) Did I have a better story that we might offer for the one about me?

McCandless called me in the wake of the Daniel Schorr story. "John, I know you're working on your testimony, but you've got to stand up and punch back at these bastards in the

White House. They're killing you in the press, and the reporters wonder why you're hiding."

"Talk to Charlie, Bob," I replied. "He's all over me to pin down my whole story, and it's going to take months this way. I'm getting subpoenaed all over the place. I can't focus on it. I can't remember. I just don't have time to deal with reporters. Nothing else matters if I can't testify truthfully. When I go on the box and under oath, people will believe what I say."

"Come on now, John," Bob said impatiently. "You know better than that. I know your testimony is important, but this truth stuff is not worth a damn if you don't have any credibility. Goddammit, you've been around long enough to know that. Christ, John, LBJ lied through his teeth about Vietnam in 1964 and won in a landslide. McGovern told the truth about Watergate last year and got his ass kicked. You've got to start fighting to build an image! You've got to give these guys something to convince them."

"Okay, Bob. I tell you what. Why don't you draft up a statement to denounce the malicious stories about me? Something tough, but general?"

"All right. That's a start. But these guys want to see you in the flesh. Get a feel for you. They say their asses are on the line about believing you."

"Well, let's start with the statement. I'll talk to Charlie."

Through early May, I stayed isolated at Charlie's insistence. Bob had to handle the reporters himself in the "great war of leaks" after Watergate began to break open. I would see bits of my testimony like Liddy's offer to be shot or Ehrlichman's order to "deep-six" the things from Hunt's safe on the front pages. I thought Bob had leaked them, but I never asked him. Charlie wanted me to be able to testify that I had not "tried my case in the press." I could say under oath that I had not leaked stories and had not been told who did.

Tension inevitably developed between Charlie and Bob, since their functions were almost diametrically opposed. Charlie protested whenever a story appeared that looked as if it had come from me; it hurt his negotiations with the prosecutors, who wanted my testimony kept secret with them. On the other hand, Charlie's tough demands that I be granted immunity hurt Bob's relations with the press; they made it seem that I was trying to get off scot-free, and they worsened my squealer image. I felt pulled and tugged between my two lawyers.

On May 11, I had my first interview with a reporter since the White House had turned its guns on me. Bob had finally convinced Charlie that I had to go public. It would be a test, and only a brief diversion from my work constructing testimony. Bob arranged a clandestine interview with *Newsweek* correspondent John Lindsay at the Tidewater Inn in Easton, Maryland, halfway between Washington and my hideaway.

Lindsay arrived accompanied by photographer Wally McNamee and immediately struck me as friendly, informed, and understanding. "Your old friends at the White House are doing their damnedest to ruin you," he said sympathetically. Then he smiled. "Of course, I'm not about to give up any of my sources, but I hope you don't labor under any illusions that Chuck Colson, Ken Clawson, and Ron Ziegler are still friends of yours."

"I don't," I said.

"Okay. Now, Bob tells me that we can't get into the areas of your testimony. I can see your reasons. But would you be willing to go off the record on a few points?"

"John, I really can't," I told him. "Someday I'm going to be under oath and may be asked about my dealings with the press. Any statements I make I would like to be on the record."

"I understand perfectly," he said immediately. I answered his questions guardedly, trying to skirt testimonial areas.

Between questions, I found Lindsay telling me more than I was telling him. He told me the prosecutors had put out the word that they had concluded that the President was not involved in either the events before June 17 or the cover-up. He informed me that Sam Dash had been saying I was telling the truth and would be the most important witness the Senate could call. Lindsay felt that my best forum would be the Senate. I had thought it would be the grand jury. After several hours, I felt I had given him little of news value and learned much, including his prediction that a special prosecutor would be appointed as a result of Senate pressures, and that Nixon would find himself hinging his defense on national security.

As we parted, Lindsay told me that he felt confident I would be pleased with his story and that maybe it would help reverse the tide of negative news about me. When I saw it three days later, I was horrified. The story was hostile in tone, and laced with derogatory tidbits:

> ...Federal investigators let it be known that they were less than impressed with Dean's story...he seemed ready to offer at least tentative solidarity with anyone whose testimony has damaged the Administration...reports cast doubt on his value as a pivotal witness whose testimony would be needed to hook bigger fish in the White House... He had refrigerant blood," one former associate recalled last week.... He declined to say...he made it perfectly clear...he observed tartly...his story remained transparently designed to enhance his bid for immunity.

Lindsay called to say that the *Newsweek* editors in New York had rewritten his story, and that he would understand if I never spoke with him again. When McCandless confirmed his account, I liked Lindsay even better, but Charlie did not miss the opportunity to make choice remarks about Bob's press strategy.

Although the press was now bearing down on the Watergate story, I found it difficult to trust even the most dedicated reporters. McCandless called with a proposition from Carl Bernstein and Bob Woodward, the investigative reporters who had already won fame and prizes for their pursuit of the scandal.

"John, the wonder twins from the *Post* are on me again. This time Bernstein's got something that scares the shit out of me," Bob said in a grave, low voice. "He said they're picking up serious rumors that there may be attempts to rub you out, get rid of you."

"That's nice," I said dryly. I had been struggling to control my paranoia about this possibility.

"Well, they've been right before," Bob kidded.

"Who does he say is thinking about that, besides a bunch of kooks and Ehrlichman? Are they going to run the story?"

"No, I don't think so. It doesn't sound hard enough."

"Well, tell them I appreciate the warning even though it's not very helpful," I said wearily. "What do they really want, Bob?"

"I thought you'd ask that. Carl says it's a remote possibility, but one you should consider. Just in case, he says you should put everything you know on tape and give it to them for safekeeping. He promises they won't even listen to the damn thing unless you pass on. He makes a pretty persuasive case about what might happen if you can't ever testify. Anyway, I thought I would pass it along."

"Yeah, well, you tell them thanks for the suggestion." I could tell that Bob wasn't offering the idea with much enthusiasm. "Christ, Bob. Can you imagine what would happen if it got out that I had given my testimony to those guys on tape? I can just see myself explaining that the only reason I did it was because I was afraid the President of the United States would have me bumped off."

"Okay, okay. Like I said, I was just passing it along."

"You tell them I'm trying like hell to get everything I know down on paper, okay? And tell them to keep digging."

While Bob continued his campaign to rally reporters to my side, Charlie shuttled between the prosecutors and the Senate Watergate Committee. He arranged my first meeting with Sam Dash for the night after my interview with Lindsay. Dash took elaborate precautions to insure secrecy and came to Charlie's office late at night. As was his custom, the first thing he did was to call his wife and leave a number.

Despite his years as Philadelphia's district attorney, Dash is more professor than prosecutor. Soft-spoken, scholarly, relaxed but intent, he viewed his undertaking as a complex and difficult research project. He wasn't out to prosecute anyone, but he had strong gut feelings about where the facts would take him—and he saw Richard Nixon standing at the end of the corridor that he wanted most to travel down.

"Only Chairman Ervin and I know about this meeting," Dash began. "We were afraid to tell anyone else. It would get to the minority members, who would leak it and give us hell for negotiating with you. The chairman trusts my judgment, and I'm here to review your testimony. I have to make a recommendation to the full committee about whether to grant you immunity."

"You aren't getting him without it," Charlie said.

"Look, Sam, I'm taking a hell of a beating about this immunity thing," I said. "I agree with Charlie that I shouldn't stick my neck out without some protection. You know from what Charlie's told you that I'm going to confess to crimes when I testify. My own words will hang me. The others aren't going to confess to anything, and it'll be my word against the President, Haldeman, Ehrlichman, and Mitchell. That's a tough

362

case to make, and if I'm not believed."

"I understand all that, John," Sam interrupted. "That's why I'm here."

"Okay. But I want you to know something off the record. I know Charlie doesn't want me to say it, but I'm inclined to testify before your committee with or without immunity. I wanted to testify before the grand jury, where my testimony would come out in trial, but now I tend to think it's better to go public. Otherwise, what I say is going to get distorted as it leaks out bit by bit."

"I'm still pushing for my man's immunity," Charlie insisted.

"I understand," Dash replied to both of us. "I think you're going to get it. But I'm glad to know you're considering testifying without it, John. That's important to me for personal reasons."

I leaned over and looked straight at Dash, deciding to try to get off on the right foot by leveling with him. "I don't want you to get me wrong on this, Sam. I'd love to get out of this damn thing without going to jail. It's already ruined me. I've been ripped up by it. But I'm getting eaten up by the idea that all I want to do is save my own ass. The press has seized on it. The public seems to lap it up. I'm beginning to think about down the road, and I don't want to be known just as the snitch of Watergate. You may not believe this, Sam, but I've been thinking about going to jail since last January and February. I'm beginning to think it's worth it." Charlie gave me a warning look, somewhere between sympathy and toughness, for being so emotional. "But I'll be goddamned if I'm going to sit down and be the only one to go and take the whole rap for this thing. That's where I want to know if you can help me."

"I think so, John," Dash said sincerely. (Charlie had told me he worried that Dash was too sincere to be quick enough and tough enough to help me.) "But I've got to know how

363

strong a witness you'll be, and we don't have much time. Our hearings open next week." Dash was in a hurry, but then he launched into a long story about his troubles with the senators on the committee, especially Howard H. Baker, Jr., of Tennessee.

"Tell the man your story," Charlie interrupted to prompt me.

"Okay," I sighed, and launched into the highlights once again.

Dash and I talked during several more sessions, and the idea of going before the Ervin Committee grew increasingly attractive. I mulled it over with Charlie and Bob and listed the advantages. For one thing, I was not as uncomfortable with a Senate forum as with grand juries and courtrooms. Capitol Hill was familiar ground from my days on the staff of the House Judiciary Committee. I had testified there many times, and I knew how hearings worked. Also, the televised proceedings would give me a chance to lay out my whole testimony before millions of viewers. I was not faring well in the written press. I could use a piece of the President's own philosophy against him and "go over the heads" of the written press straight to the public. Finally, I was drawn to the technical ramifications of the Senate's immunity powers. The Ervin Committee could grant me only what is known as "use immunity," which meant that nothing I confessed to them could be used as evidence against me in court. But I could still be prosecuted on the evidence of others. Charlie was negotiating with the prosecutors for total immunity, known in the trade as "bath immunity," which meant that I could not be prosecuted. I was familiar with the difference, because I had helped write the law establishing use immunity. The squealer image would be muted somewhat if I were granted use immunity by the Senate. There would still be a strong possibility I would go to jail; I would not be guaranteed a free ride. It might make me a more credible witness.

Bob had leaned toward the Senate committee from the beginning. It would enable him to cease playing games with reporters: he could tell them I would be going public soon. It would give me a chance to pump up my credibility, about which he was rightly concerned. Also, Bob had a string of contacts in the Senate, having once worked there, and he could help behind the scenes. Neither of us had to be reminded how much maneuvering would go on off camera.

Charlie also warmed to the Ervin Committee, even before I did, for hard, practical reasons. He knew that while use immunity in the Senate would not make it impossible to prosecute me, it would make it more difficult. The government would have to prove it got none of its evidence from my testimony. He could still fight to keep me out of jail. Also, by threatening to go to the Senate, Charlie knew he could increase the pressure on Silbert to give me total immunity. He made speeches to the prosecutors about how he didn't need them anymore, because "my man" was going to the Senate. Charlie was turning the screws. The increasing likelihood that the President would be forced to appoint a special prosecutor gave him even more leverage on Silbert. Earl knew he was in danger of being taken off the case soon if he didn't move fast. Charlie enjoyed reminding him of it.

The negotiations with Silbert and Glanzer were extremely complex, largely because they involved questions of trust. The prosecutors had a genuinely strong reason for not wanting to give me total immunity: it would make me a much less believable witness against Haldeman, Ehrlichman, and Mitchell. We suspected they also had another reason: their bosses were in the Justice Department and the White House might jump down their throats. The President had prohibited grants of immunity. He could appoint Silbert a U.S. attorney; I couldn't. The prosecutors said they would move quickly against higher targets as soon as I pleaded guilty. We suspected they might merely claim triumph for having broken me and then find insufficient evidence for other cases. Charlie's negotiations with the prosecutors boiled down to close judgments about strength and motivation, and we were both inclined not to cast our lot with them. After all, for nine months I had considered them partial allies in the cover-up, or at least not implacable enemies of it. In mid-May, as Charlie fired up his blowtorch under Silbert, I began to have doubts about whether I even wanted him to succeed. I pondered whether I would welcome total immunity if it came. It was close, but I admitted I probably would.

As our preference moved toward the Ervin Committee, it became more important than ever that I organize my presentation, and I was a long way from being prepared. We all knew I would be roasted for the slightest error. I coaxed my memory. Had I met with Kalmbach on June 28 or 29? Had O'Brien said that at this meeting or another one? Was I sure it was LaRue who said that, and not Parkinson? Was I exaggerating? Was I sure enough to say all this under oath? Was I ready to go on the box?

The job was made more difficult by frequent interruptions. Judge Sirica wanted me in court for a hearing on what to do with the copy of the Huston Plan I had placed in a safe-deposit box. Another court scheduled me for depositions in the Common Cause suit against the Reelection Committee for failing to disclose campaign contributors. Sam Dash wanted to meet me at night. Back and forth between Washington and Bethany. Bob wanted me to talk to more media people. He thought he could get me a television interview with Walter Cronkite. I told him to go ahead, and he arranged for Cronkite to come to my house for a CBS News Special interview on May 17, the day the Watergate hearings opened. Mo and I watched it that night and I jotted a list of criticisms of my television manner. One of my worries about the Ervin Committee option was insecurity about how I would come off on television. Would I look too cocky, too nervous, too mousy, too young?

I went back to work at Bethany, but the interruptions continued. Now the House Commerce Committee was calling me to testify about the handling of ITT documents between the Securities and Exchange Commission and the Justice Department. Secret Service investigators wanted to meet with me about one of their senior officials who had passed information to Chuck Colson through me about Presidential candidate McGovern. Everyone wanted to talk about something, and McCandless was also pressing me to have further meetings with the press. I returned to Washington and appeared before the House Commerce Committee, met with the Secret Service investigators, and, as Bob requested, met with Hays Gorey of *Time* magazine.

The day before, on May 22, the President had issued his four thousand-word defense against the Watergate charges that had been accumulating against him. Gorey brought me a copy of the statement. He was disappointed when I refused to comment on it, but he asked if Mo and I would permit a *Time* photographer to take a few pictures.

Bob pulled me aside into the kitchen of his apartment. "You ought to give Hays something. I promised him. He is a good man; he hasn't made any judgments about you, one way or the other. I think he'll give you a fair piece."

"That's what I thought about Lindsay."

"That wasn't Lindsay's fault, be—"

"I understand, but why will it be any different with *Time*?"

"I explained what happened with Lindsay to Gorey, and he said he'll get it in as he writes it, in a separate piece. You really should do this. It's important for your image."

I was half persuaded and returned to the interview. "What will you say for me about the President's defense?" he asked.

"It's a public-relations statement. Some of it is not quite accurate. Some of it is not accurate at all."

"Off the record, what's not accurate?"

"Well, Hays, I don't like to go off record, but I will say this much, the damn thing is filled with lies."

Gorey took a copy of the document from the coffee table in front of us, took off his glasses, and studied it for a moment. "I won't quote you, but I'm curious for my own information. What about Nixon's claim he had no prior knowledge of the Watergate operation?"

"Off the record, that's probably true."

Gorey was now paraphrasing from the document. "He took no part in, nor was he aware of, any subsequent efforts to cover Watergate up?"

"Not true."

"He didn't authorize any offers of executive clemency, nor did he know of the offers."

"Bullshit."

"He didn't know until his own investigation, and I guess he's referring to the so-called March twenty-first investigation, of efforts to pay off Watergate defendants."

"Cleverly worded, but a lie."

"What do you mean?"

"I'd rather not be more specific, but he never initiated any investigation, for openers."

"What about his statement that there was no attempt, or authority from him, to implicate the CIA in Watergate?"

"I don't know firsthand, but I've got to assume that Haldeman and Ehrlichman did not act without his approval. Probably it's a lie."

"He says he didn't know about the break-in at Ellsberg's psychiatrist's office until his own investigation, and then specifically authorized the report of this fact to Judge Byrne, who was sitting on the case."

"Lies. He knew, and he was forced to report it."

"Finally, this document says, and, John, this is very helpful to me, that he didn't authorize or encourage subordinates to engage in any illegal or improper campaign tactics."

"Complete bullshit, if you'll excuse my French."

Hays sat back. "If you're right, this really is some public-relations document." He had recently interviewed Senator Barry Goldwater, he said, and Goldwater had told him that if Nixon had lied and were to get caught, he'd be in serious trouble. He was telling me that if my testimony destroyed Nixon's defense the President would fall. It was a sobering observation; I'd been flip as I offered my off-the-record reactions.

After meeting with Gorey, I went to see Senator Goldwater at the home of his son, Congressman Barry Goldwater Jr., my old high school roommate and friend. The Senator had been much more than another politician to me for a long time; I looked up to him as a friend who would be honest with me. And because he was a vital element of the President's public support, it was risky for him to meet with me at all. He knew I wouldn't ask for the meeting unless I considered it urgent. I was about to charge the President of the United States publicly with offenses that might ruin him; and I was ready for that, but I was unnerved by other thoughts: What if my testimony undermined negotiations on a nuclear treaty? Caused a military flare-up somewhere in the world? Jeopardized a national-security matter I didn't even know about?

"Frankly, Senator, I'm a bit frightened," I told him. "I don't want to get into details about my testimony with you—I don't

369

think we should, since you've got to judge it for yourself—but I'm worried about my testimony."

"Hey, Barry," he shouted to his son, who had gone to the kitchen to find some food, "have you got any bourbon? I think I'm going to want a drink."

I continued as Barry returned with a sandwich and a glass of bourbon. "I just felt that I should talk to someone about this, because it's bigger than me. Do you see me causing any problems, if for example my testimony weakens Nixon as President?"

"No, even though I don't know what your testimony is about, I don't see that problem," he said.

"Senator, have you read the President's May twenty-second defense?"

"Yep. It raises more questions than answers."

"Well, it does something else, also. It makes him a liar. The thing is filled with lies, it's nothing more than a public-relations document, and I'm going to tell the full story of what happened."

"Hell," Goldwater said hoarsely, "I'm not surprised. That goddam Nixon has been lying all of his life."

The Senator is known for his frankness. I asked him if he felt the public could accept one of the President's aides charging him with being not only a liar but a criminal.

"John, you just march your ass up there to the Senate, and in front of those cameras, and tell 'em what you know as best you can. Sure a lot of sanctimonious people are going to say they're shocked to hear about their President doing these things. But don't think it's going to surprise anyone, really. Don't you worry about the consequences."

"Well, that's exactly what I plan to do, Senator."

"Good," he said. He took another sip of his bourbon, and the conversation about Watergate ended.

When I went home, there were no reporters at the house, but a letter from the U.S. attorney's office was waiting for me.

"I'll be goddamned!" I shouted after reading it, so loudly it brought Mo running in from another room.

"What's wrong now?" she asked.

"This is the damnedest letter I've ever seen," I said furiously. "Silbert and Glanzer are demanding that I plead guilty to a one-count felony, as usual. But now the bastards are saying the train is moving out, and it's my last chance."

"What does that mean?"

"It means those guys are desperate, that's what it means," I steamed. "They're trying to protect their asses now that the Special Prosecutor[*] has come in. This letter reads like a goddam press release! They sound like they had had the case all wrapped up until I blocked them, when those bastards know damn good and well I handed them the cover-up on a silver platter. This is the most hypocritical piece of shit I've ever seen. Listen to this." I read her the last paragraph in a tone of mock piety, still in a rage:

> If at this late date, you are sincerely sorry for your participation in the sorry picture of corruptions; if at this late date, you wish to make amends and let the truth be told; if at this late date, you are genuinely interested in advancing the public interest and the ends of justice, then you should demonstrate this in a meaningful way by providing testimony which could facilitate the successful prosecution of others who are also guilty in this matter.

---

[*] On March 18, 1973, Attorney General-designate Elliot L. Richardson picked former Solicitor General Archibald Cox as the Special Prosecutor for the Watergate case.

The letter triggered queer images. I could see myself sitting on my cell bunk in prison denim, hunched over a broken-down radio, listening to the President: "Good evening, fellow Americans. There is a reason I am wearing a big smile tonight. I have good news. Less than an hour ago a jury of twelve American citizens, people just like you and me, returned a verdict that has vindicated a President. Two of the finest men and most outstanding public servants it has been my privilege to know have been found not guilty of participating in this disgraceful Watergate cover-up which has plagued you—and, of course, me. As you can see on camera now, these men are here with me. With this pen I am signing the papers to reinstate them to their vital jobs, and of course I will give them back pay for the time they have spent unfairly away from their desks, defending themselves against the groundless charges of the self-confessed scoundrel responsible for the cover-up. A man who deceived everyone, then struck out to save himself by maliciously implicating others. Ladies and gentlemen, young and old, there is justice in America. I never doubted it for a moment. Even my dog, King Timahoe here, a very smart dog, used to bark at the man who has wronged me. Well, I want to say I have tonight directed the Attorney General, Mr. Earl Silbert, to immediately prosecute John W. Dean for one hundred and eighty-six counts of perjury, which represents the number of lies he's told against Bob Haldeman and John Ehrlichman here. There will be justice! Good night, and God bless you all."

I called Charlie. "You're not going to believe what I just got in the mail—"

"Yes, I am," he interrupted. "I already got the damn thing. In fact, I just talked to old Seymour, bless his worried little ass. He said he drafted it. I'll be damned if I understand why he's proud of writing that self-serving piece of bullshit, but he is. I told him the fucking letter didn't even deserve a response, and it won't get one. Put on your Jimmy Stewart clothes, boy.

372

You're going to the Senate!"

I began desperately drafting my testimony. It was past the hour when I should have put pen to paper, and I knew I had a groaning labor ahead. I had watched some of the previous witnesses before the Ervin Committee; most of them had just taken the oath and begun answering questions. I couldn't do that, I knew. My testimony would be picked apart if it emerged in disconnected bits. I decided Seymour Glanzer had been right about one thing: the only way to understand the complexities of Watergate was by absorbing a day-to-day account of the events. The reality I wanted to convey was too distant from what most people imagined about how the White House operated, and I had laid down my own restrictions on my testimony—no personalities, no subjective judgments, no "color" about how the White House really worked. Just dry legal facts.

I had now amassed a stack of notes that would help me put events in order, but the events would be comprehensible only if I wove them into a narrative. The amount of detail was the key. I would have to offer my own corroboration by filling in exact particulars. Building from small to big, I hoped to give my testimony credibility by sheer weight of concrete detail. The massive statement would give me a reassuring point of reference; those who attacked me would have to counter a statement I was completely comfortable with.

On June 11, I was summoned to the U.S. attorney's office at the Federal Courthouse in Washington for a grand-jury appearance, a last-ditch effort by the prosecutors to protect themselves before I proceeded to give my Senate testimony. As Charlie and I were waiting outside Earl Silbert's office, one of the new members of the Special Prosecutor's office, James Neal, came walking out.

"Well, if it's not old Shaffer," Neal said with a big smile, extending his hand in greeting.

"Hello, Jimmy," Charlie answered, obviously pleased to see him.

"You've really been ripping up the pea patch down here," Neal said sarcastically, referring to Charlie's dealings with Silbert and Glanzer.

"Isn't that what you taught me?" Charlie asked. Charlie and Neal had been special assistants in Robert Kennedy's Justice Department. They had tried many cases together, including the Jimmy Hoffa prosecution. Neal had settled in Nashville, Tennessee, his home town, after serving as the United States attorney there. He had recently left his lucrative private law practice to assist the new Special Prosecutor, Archibald Cox.

In the grand-jury room I had to bite my lip to keep from saying something I would regret. The prosecutors knew damn well I had to take the Fifth Amendment rather than confess to the crimes I had laid out for them. It was a humiliating, useless exercise. The grand-jury room was intimidating, and I cringed each time Silbert's questions forced me to utter the words I had snickered at so often when others said them: "Upon advice of counsel, I must respectfully decline to answer, on the grounds that it may tend to incriminate me." Over and over. I shot hostile glances at the prosecutors, and tried by my manner to communicate to the grand jurors that I wanted to tell them what I knew. My refusal to testify, I knew, would produce one more round of stories that Dean was out to save himself at others' expense. Was it the element of truth in those stories that bothered me the most? Maybe so, I would think; then each time I looked at Silbert. He was putting me through this empty gesture just so that he could console himself with dreams of how tough he'd been, I thought, building a record to protect himself—he could say he'd called me but I'd refused to talk. I tried not to take spiteful pleasure in the fact that he was soon to be removed from the case under a cloud of suspicion. But I failed.

With only five days to complete my draft, I rushed my pace considerably. If there were going to be any mistakes, they had better be on the side of omission. I was clear on the main points of my meetings with the President, but I figured I had to take two things into account: the possibility that the President had recorded our conversations, and my commitment to be willing to take a lie-detector test on anything I said in my testimony. I would tell only what I knew for a fact. To cross that line by an inch would be foolhardy.

For example, I believed that the President had probably known that Liddy was operating an intelligence program at the Reelection Committee long before the June 17 break-in. I could not imagine that Haldeman had kept anything of such magnitude from him, nor could I believe Bob had not known, though I had never asked him directly. Nothing that cost that kind of money, or that raised that kind of risk, or offered a potential for the type of intelligence so beloved of the White House could have escaped Haldeman's attention. Still, I could hardly hazard such a speculation in my testimony.

As I was drafting the sections on my last meetings with the President, I wondered whether to mention my sensation that I was being taped. The President himself had raised the issue by telling Henry Petersen he had me on tape, but when Charlie had pressed Petersen to get a copy, the President had deflected Henry, claiming it was a Dictabelt of notes which had been misplaced. Later, when I was going over my records at Bethany, I found this notation on a list of things to discuss with Charlie:

Information re tapes of JWD conversation with P
determine if Oval Ofc is wired:
Butterfield (now FAA Administrator)
Bull (W/H staff)
Gen. Albert Redman (WHCA)

Translation: Alexander Butterfield, Steve Bull, and General Albert Redman, head of the White House Communications Agency, should be questioned about whether the President's office was bugged. Later I had mentioned to Dash that I thought I'd been recorded, and he had expressed but passing interest.

Now, as I was drafting my testimony about the April 15 meeting, should I insert my suspicion about being recorded? It would violate the rule against speculation; on the other hand, my suspicion had been real, and the President's claim to Petersen made it more than pure speculation. I resolved the matter by deciding to mention my sense of being taped only in the course of recounting the conversation during which it had occurred to me. I mentioned the leading questions the President had asked and my dismissal of the thought that he might be taping me. Then I wrote:

> The most interesting thing that happened during the conversation was, very near the end, he got up out of his chair, went behind his chair to the corner of his Executive Office Building office and in a nearly inaudible tone said to me he was probably foolish to have discussed Hunt's clemency with Colson.

I added that I felt that the committee should seek such a tape if the conversation had indeed been recorded. I thought the mere suggestion of taping would produce cross-examination. It did not.[*]

Charlie and Bob came to the house to review my draft when I finished it. They liked it; but Charlie had some strong criticisms.

"This is your testimony, I understand that," he began, sit-

---

[*]   When I did testify, a disbelieving Senator Howard Baker did ask for elaboration, but he was the only member of the committee to do so.

ting on the living-room sofa with a stack of the testimony beside him. "And it's good. In fact, it's a great statement of what happened. But you're asking for trouble in some places."

"What do you mean?"

"I mean that goddam self-serving crap you've got in there."

"I don't think the statement is self-serving, Charlie. I confess a lot in there," I replied defensively.

"Well, generally that's true, but you've got a self-serving twist here and there," he persisted. "And listen, you're not going up there to win friends, or a popularity contest."

"Specifically, what are you talking about?"

Charlie flipped through some pages and read: "I had never heard Mr. Magruder's story in full detail until just before his Grand Jury appearance, in mid-August 1972 when he asked me if I would be a devil's advocate and question him before he went before the Grand Jury. Magruder came to my office, as I recall, the day before his second appearance before the Grand Jury."

Charlie looked up and took off his reading glasses. "Now, listen, the next sentence is the kind that's trouble. This is what I'm talking about: 'When he came in I told him I could not tell him to lie before the Grand Jury.'"

"That's true, that's exactly what I told Jeb." I was getting very defensive; this was exactly the kind of self-protective statement I'd been so careful to construct all through the cover-up.

"I don't give a shit if it's true or not," Charlie declared. "You might have told him to consult with his wife, his conscience, and the Pope himself before he lied. But so what? You sat there with him and helped him prepare the lie. You helped him practice, didn't you?"

"Yeah," I sighed.

"Well, that's what's important, dammit. So say it, and don't try to make it look like something nice you did. Otherwise they're going to tear your statement apart up there."

We worked our way through the statement, knocking out most of the apologies. I met the next morning with the staff of the Watergate Committee for a preview of my testimony. I had decided not to give them anything from my prepared statement; instead, I just answered questions for five hours, mostly from Republican staffers.

That night I got a call from one of my new friends in the press. "John, those guys you met with today are passing out your executive session testimony to any and all takers."

"Who's doing it?" I asked.

"The minority staffers. They damn near put out a press release on it. They're trying to destroy it before you even give it. What they are really pushing is the stuff you gave them about your using the money that was in your trust for your wedding and honeymoon expenses."

"It figures. I'm glad I refused to talk about the President. I think that pissed them off."

"I know it did, but you were smart not to do it."

"Did they mention what I told Baker?" Senator Baker had opened the session and then left, but not before I had given him a little message.

"What did you tell Baker?"

"Well, I don't think I should get into the details right now, but someday I'll tell you about Baker's secret dealings with the White House. I mentioned it to him in the session today. Baker was shocked that I knew about his meeting with Nixon, but he played it cool as a cucumber. He's a damn slick fella." I had reminded Baker that I knew the Watergate Committee was a political proceeding, and that I knew how the White House had tried to influence the senators. I had worked that side of the street myself.

On Monday, June 18, 1973, I was scheduled for a private session with all seven senators. On Tuesday I would present my public testimony. As the time drew closer, I began veering wildly from one state of mind to another. I have never been an emotional person—quite the opposite—but I found myself trembling at odd times for a few seconds, feeling that I might be on the verge of breaking down, and then I would swing back to a lucidity and calmness I had rarely known. I felt as conflicted as I had during the worst moments of the cover-up, but in a different way. At certain moments I would dread the ordeal by national television so much that I would stop writing and ponder running away. At others I would actually look forward to it, yearn for it. I would swell with the confidence that I could remember every fact, every small detail—what people were wearing on certain days, where everybody was seated at a meeting—like a computer. Then one fact would slip out of place and the whole edifice would crumble. One moment I would dismiss my fears with the thought that I would simply be telling the truth. My mind would lock on the facts, and I would recite them as easily as people recite their names or birthdays. I had no cover stories or complicated lies to keep straight. I thought of the ordeal that someone like Mitchell or Ehrlichman would endure, and counted myself lucky. The next moment I would freeze at the thought that I was the guy who had given his heart, body, and mind to be treated as little more than an artifact in the Oval Office. Wasn't I still that person deep down? It was impossible that I would go alone in front of millions of people and call the President a criminal. Anger, duty, fear, guilt, truth. The emotions blew hot and cold. I had risen so high and fallen so low. If I were believed, I might put myself back together, I would have something to start with. If I were not, if I were rolled over by the power and deceit I had seen in politics, things could get even worse. I would begin to crack up, maybe go crazy. I was not only playing for the

379

Presidency and the Congress and the networks and the respect of millions of people, I was playing for myself, and the odds were against me. I would feel the little trembling again. Back to details, calculations. What did the President say next? Return the call to Charlie. Run back through the virtues and hypocrisies of each senator on the committee: this is politics. I've got the strategy. Finish the sentences, think of everything. What should I be thinking of at the last minute? How should I look? Cosmetics are important for something like this. I've got everything else under control. On track.

I thought about how I wanted to look. I had watched some of the others testifying, seated at the witness table, flanked by lawyers who whispered in their ear. I decided to sit alone—to dramatize the fact that I was comfortable with my own words. Neither Bob nor Charlie argued with this decision, although both of them seemed disappointed that they would be out of the spotlight.

I reviewed the notes I had made on my interview with Cronkite.

"Eyes blinking." I had been oblivious to the fact that my eyelids were flickering in a nervous twitch, but I found that my contact lenses had scratched my right cornea badly. I stopped wearing the lenses and fished out an old pair of horn-rimmed glasses. Sam Dash said he liked what they did for me: "You look more studious and distinguished."

"Voice inflection and gesturing/trying to impress people." It would be easy to overdramatize, or to seem too flip about my testimony. I knew from speech-making and from appearances before Congressional committees that there was a lot of ham in me. I would, I decided, read evenly, unemotionally, as coldly as possible, and answer questions the same way. When I told Mo I was going to use a monotone, she worried that I would put everyone to sleep.

"Laughter sounds insincere." No forced laughs. If some-

thing funny did happen, which I doubted, a genuine laugh might push its way to the surface. Laughing to be polite, or to make light of something, as I had tried to do on the Cronkite show, was bad. It looked and sounded insincere, and it was. People tend to think that somebody telling the truth will be calm about it.

"Too many 'you knows.'" These came from starting to answer before I had thought out what I was going to say. "You knows" are sound fillers. Think, I told myself. Don't answer a question until you know the answer you're prepared to give.

"Shaggy look." I needed a haircut when I did the Cronkite interview. I always needed a haircut, it seemed. I would have to get my hair trimmed.

The executive session on Monday, June 18, was held in a Capitol office. We had just started over procedural matters when the buzzer signaled a vote on the Senate floor, and the senators had to leave. Charlie, Bob, and I waited in a small, windowless hideaway office. Thirty minutes later the session resumed, but we were soon asked to step out of the room again. Another thirty minutes passed as Charlie, Bob, and I took shifts pacing the floor. Then Sam Dash called Charlie and Bob out of the room and explained that the committee was voting to postpone my appearance for a week. Leonid Brezhnev, the Russian head of state, was coming to Washington, and the White House had passed word to the Senate leadership that my appearance might not be convenient for the President.

Suddenly the postponement seemed very attractive. I was ready for the inevitable, but I did not want it to happen. That night I took Mo out to dinner, to a restaurant near our home, something I hadn't done in many months. Bob used the extra week for more press-relations work, and I did several on-the-record interviews. Charlie discussed with his friend Jim Neal a worry that he did not wish to discuss with me. Then he asked if Mo and I had any objections to having U.S. marshals live in our house and guard me during my testimony. It was not until they arrived that I thought about the implications of protection. I would live with the marshals night and day in the years to come.[*]

Late Saturday, June 23, I remembered the haircut. After scouting out three different shopping centers in suburban Virginia, I found a barbershop.

"Cut it nice and clean, please."

"Yes, sir." The barber busied himself at the task as I sat silently. "What do you think of these Watergate hearings?" he finally asked.

"They're pretty interesting, but I haven't been able to see much of them."

"I'll say they're interesting. I'm bringing my TV set to the shop next week. I want to see this guy Dean get his butt kicked."

"Yeah, that's going to be something," I said. "We'll find out what the squealer has to say for himself."

"Right. You know, I can't imagine a guy lying that way about President Nixon. The guy is crazy, maybe?"

"Could be."

The barber finished the haircut. "See you soon," he told me in a friendly manner.

"Sooner than you think, probably Monday!"

---

[*] I was placed in the U.S. Marshal's Witness Protection Program–at the request of the Watergate Special Prosecutor, Archibald Cox, and Sam Dash, the chief counsel of the Senate Watergate Committee. I never was given much information about the threats believed sufficiently serious that I be placed in this program, but I was later asked if I thought Nixon would encourage "taking me out." I said I did not.

CHAPTER TEN:

ON CAMERA

CAPITOL HILL POLICEMEN LED US IN a processional through the subway passage that joins the two Senate office buildings—Sam Dash and his deputy James Hamilton first, Mo and me right behind, then Charlie and Bob, flanked by two marshals from my protection detail, with a plainclothes police officer following. We walked silently and in formation, like soldiers. I felt as if I were being led to the electric chair.

When we arrived at the old Senate Caucus Room, shortly before ten o'clock, it was packed with people, television cameras, and klieg lights. A buzz passed through the room as we entered. I tried to block it out. I heard my heart pounding hard and I felt that tingling sensation run up and down my spine; it was alternately pleasant and excruciating. I was worried that I would have to go to the bathroom every five minutes. Behind my plastic smile, I had to keep reassuring myself that the first day would be easy. All I had to do was read a short book—my 245 page opening statement. The work was already done. I was thankful that I would not have to do any thinking.

Senator Ervin administered the oath, and it was time to begin. I had planned to offer a few ad-lib remarks before diving into the dry narrative, but the words did not come easily. "First of all, Mr. Chairman and Mr. Vice-Chairman and members of the committee," I said, scanning the faces of the seven senators before me, "I sincerely wish I could say it is my pleasure to be here today, but I think you can understand why it is not." I had intended this as an ice-breaker, and I waited for a senator to make some lighthearted welcoming comment, but there was no reaction, not even an understanding look. Sam Dash leaned forward soberly and told me to speak louder into the microphone.

I started again, haltingly. "It is a very difficult thing for me to testify about other people. It is far more easy for me to explain my own involvement in this matter. The fact that I was involved in obstructing justice. The fact that I assisted another in perjured testimony. The fact that I made personal use of funds that were in my custody. It is far easier to talk about these things myself than to talk about what others did. Some of these people I will be referring to are friends. Some are men I greatly admire and respect. And particularly with reference to the President of the United States, I would like to say this: it is my honest belief that while the President was involved, he did not realize or appreciate at any time the implications of his involvement. And when the facts come out, I hope the President is forgiven."

I paused. This time the words had spilled out. I was apologizing for what I would say about the President. The squealer's fear was still very much on my mind, and so was Charlie's admonition against self-serving testimony. I realized, however, how difficult it would be to give a convincing account of my motivation. Even confession seemed self-serving. My conflicting emotions bounced off each other like balloons. It was a relief to turn to the facts, to my prepared text.

Sustained by a diet of throat lozenges and water, I droned on for nearly three hours before the lunch break. Our group trooped through the crowd back to Dash's office, where I lay down and breathed like a fighter between rounds. Dash appeared a few minutes later with a glowing report on the soundings he had taken about my testimony. No one was going to sleep, he said. Several senators' offices had sent word that their staffs had suspended work for the day to listen. Sam was excited. He painted a picture of millions of viewers doing the same thing, as if I were FDR delivering one of his fireside chats. "Everything looks great, John," he concluded, "but I wanted to ask what you were trying to say at the beginning. It sounded to me, you know, like you were—"

"Like he was pulling his punches," Charlie interrupted bluntly. His mouth was full of cheeseburger, which he had picked over like a health inspector before daring a bite. Charlie hates junk food.

"Eat your lunch, Charles," I retorted. Buoyed by Sam's report, I was in no mood for one of Charlie's sermons. "Sam, I said what I felt. It's that simple."

Sam looked skeptical. "You don't mean to tell me you think Nixon didn't know the legal implications of what he was doing, do you?"

"No, I was talking about how he slipped into this mess like everybody else..."

"Get off that pussyfooting line," Charlie snorted again. He was fingering through a box of french fries. I looked at him sourly. He laughed. The lunch break soon ended.

To my amazement, I managed to finish reading the entire statement in one day. Mo and I watched a brief segment of the rerun on public television that night. I assessed my performance against the notes from the Cronkite interview and nursed my aching neck, which had cramped during the hours of leaning over the witness table toward the microphone. Sleep was fitful.

Sam Dash began the cross-examination the next morning. His questions were soft and mushy—long-winded recitals of my statement, with tag lines asking me if I agreed with his summaries. "That is correct," I answered repeatedly. This is too easy, I thought, trying to stay poised for anything. But Dash's friendly probing put me in a thoughtless state, and he caught me badly off balance at the end.

"I guess you are fully aware, Mr. Dean," he said crisply, "of the gravity of the charges you have made under oath against the highest official of our land, the President of the

United States?"

"Yes, I am," I replied softly. But the question struck like a dart. I felt my control loosening.

"And, being so aware, do you still stand on your statement?"

"Yes, I do."

"Mr. Chairman, I have no further questions," Dash announced, and settled back in his chair.

The silence further unnerved me. Dash's summary and his precipitous exit had been too stark, and I felt compelled to say something. "I might add this, Mr. Dash," I said. "I realize it is almost an impossible task if it is one man against the other that I am up against. And it is not a very pleasant situation..." My voice trailed off. I knew I was choking up, feeling alone and impotent in the face of the President's power. I took a deep breath to make it look as if I were thinking; I was fighting for control. I ground my teeth and squeezed the pen I held in my hands, damn near breaking it. You cannot show emotion, I told myself. The press will jump all over it as a sign of unmanly weakness. I thought of how Senator Muskie's campaign had collapsed after he had cried briefly in New Hampshire. "...But I can only speak what I know to be the facts, and that is what I am providing this committee."

"Mr. Dean, do you want to take a break?" Senator Ervin asked in a grandfatherly tone. His question alarmed me. I was sure I had not betrayed my state of mind, but apparently the Senator had sensed something wrong. The chairman's offer was kind, but I fought immediately to resist it. Accepting his offer would be an admission of weakness.

"I am here at the will of the committee," I replied stoically, "and whatever the chair would like."

"We will proceed, then," Senator Ervin said, and he recognized. Fred Thompson, Dash's Republican counterpart, for cross-examination.

"Mr. Dean, you have, of course, made some serious accusations with regard to the cover-up of criminal activities," Thompson began. "And we have heard other testimony about the cover-up of certain criminal activities. And, of course, the responsibility for prosecuting these criminal activities did lie with the Department of Justice..."

This will be my first major test, I thought as Thompson drawled on. I had still been in the White House when he was selected minority counsel, and all we had been able to learn about him was that he had handled a lot of moonshine cases as an undistinguished assistant U.S. attorney in Tennessee. He was a young political crony of Senator Baker, and Haldeman had been irritated at our failure to obtain a more experienced Republican counsel to help keep a lid on the committee's investigation. That failure was a comforting thought now, but I was still apprehensive about Thompson. Where was he going with his speech about the Justice Department?

"I would like to ask you a few questions based upon some of your testimony yesterday," he continued, "concerning contacts with Mr. Petersen." He started grilling me on my dealings with Henry during the cover-up. Instantly my back went up. I realized how shrewdly Thompson had chosen his line of questioning: he wanted me to accuse Petersen of crimes, because Henry would be in an excellent position to destroy my credibility. A man widely respected by both Republicans and Democrats in government, Petersen was as yet unsullied by Watergate. He was, as well, in charge of the Criminal Division at Justice. If I angered him with my testimony, he could make things more difficult for me in the criminal cases ahead. I was already standing alone against the President, Haldeman, Ehrlichman, and Mitchell; I wanted no part of Henry Petersen. Thompson knew this; I figured he was trying to push me out on a limb.

From the thrust of his questions, it seemed to me that Thompson had interviewed Petersen and was fishing for testimony that might cause Henry to accuse me of perjury to protect himself. I sparred with Thompson evasively, volunteering nothing. Fortunately, he did not know the precise questions to ask. Henry, I gathered, had understandably failed to tell Thompson of areas in which he might have compromised himself during the cover-up. I was able easily to deflect the questions, but I worried about appearing vague and uncooperative. Thompson had me on a tightrope, and he seemed to know how to shake the wire.

Suddenly he switched targets and started asking me about Ziegler. Had I lied to Ziegler? Was he involved in the cover-up, too? Another attempt to pull a marginal figure into my charges, I thought. He wanted me to overstate my case. Or at least he wanted me to look as if I were reaching out to drag everyone in the Administration down. I wanted to stick to the charges in my prepared statement. They were more than enough. Again I parried his questions. And again I thought I was successful because Thompson did not know the right ones to ask. I imagined Haldeman and Ehrlichman grinning at their television sets somewhere, watching me squirm, applauding Thompson's efforts to push me into vulnerable territory. Thompson had me rattled already.

Then he switched directions. "Mr. Dean, let me ask you a few questions about your actions after the Watergate incident by asking about your own personal involvement," he said. "I hope that I am not appearing to be badgering you in any way..." I flinched. Now he is going to bear down, I thought. "...But I'm sure you understand that your actions and motivations are very relevant?" He looked to me for an expression of agreement, and I looked back at him across thirty feet of television lights. All the sentimentality of the Dash interlude had vanished, and my survival instincts allowed me to concentrate solely on Thompson. They also told me I had to strike back or Thompson would trip me up disastrously.

"Yes," I replied firmly. "In fact, if I were still at the White House, I would probably be feeding you the questions to ask the person who'd be sitting here." I stared straight at him. Now he flinched.

"If I were here—as I am—" Thompson said, scrambling to regain his equilibrium, "I would have responded as I have responded. That I do not need to be fed questions by anybody." I had put him on the defensive. Good.

"Don't get cocky just 'cause you hit the guy pretty good," Charlie whispered from behind. He was right. I eased off, and so did Thompson. He brought his questions to a close without doing further damage. I figured he would save his ammunition for his final round of cross-examination.

Senator Ervin recognized Herman E. Talmadge, the easy-going Georgia Democrat. I knew that Talmadge's colleagues in the Senate considered him one of their brightest members, but I did not expect him to be a skilled interrogator. I had pegged him as a behind-the-scenes man without great forensic talent. Wrong. Talmadge seemed to have a divining rod pointed toward all the questions I had trouble answering, and he bore in on them relentlessly.

"What makes you think that your credibility is greater than that of the President, who denies what you have said?" he asked.

I floundered. "Well, Senator, I have been asked to come up here and tell the truth..." I hesitated and sighed. I was winging it. "You are asking me a public-relations question, really, in a sense. Why should I have greater credibility than the President of the United States?" I repeated his question. I couldn't say what I was thinking: Nixon is a goddam liar, and if you put us both on the box you'd find out who's lying. All I could add was, "I'm telling you what I know. I'm telling you just as I know it."

I felt that my answer had been inadequate, and, by the look on his face, so did Talmadge. He pressed on. "Now, you are testifying, I believe, under use immunity that this committee has granted you?"

"That is correct." I braced myself for an attack on my motives.

"You would not be here testifying today had we not granted that use immunity, would you?"

"I would probably be before the prosecutors downtown," I dodged. He would never believe me if I said I would have testified without immunity.

"Now, you refused to testify before the grand jury, I believe, did you not?"

"That is correct." Talmadge was not going to let me get away with anything, including my evasive answer about being "before the prosecutors."

"You pleaded the Fifth Amendment there?"

"That is correct," I submitted.

"You have been bargaining with them for immunity, which has not been granted. Isn't that an accurate statement?"

My mind raced. I felt helpless. I knew I couldn't say I was holding out for immunity because I was unsure whether the prosecutors would go after the others involved. Everything seemed cloudy. I submitted again: "That is correct, Senator."

Talmadge shifted the subject. "Now, there have been various reports in the press. I know nothing whatever about their credibility. Did you see an article in one of the Washington papers that you were kicked out of a law firm here for violations of the canon of ethics?"

"I did, sir." I cringed. Talmadge was cutting to the nub.

"Would you like to comment on that?"

As I began to explain the incident, I felt an inner despair about being able to satisfy anyone. The public forum and pressure demanded simple answers. How could I make a complicated matter simple? To explain what had happened on February 4, 1966—the day I was "fired" from my first and only job in private law practice—I would have to spin out a long story about a young lawyer's initiation into a Washington communications law firm. The senior partners were wheeling and dealing in broadcast stocks, and I quickly became bored and unhappy with the work. When a friend at the firm asked me if I would be interested in investing in a television station, I said yes, and soon suffered the consequences. The firm's senior partner, a man who intimidated me by his practice of carrying a revolver in his office, learned of my investment, and was outraged. Since I already planned to leave the firm, I refused to talk about my investment and told him I was quitting. He told me I was fired. Two years after, he accused me of "unethical conduct," but he retracted the charge when I resolved to take the charge before a lawyers' ethics committee.

Now—before Talmadge and the whole world—these old skeletons were coming out of the closet. I could not do justice to the incident in less than an hour, so I said merely that the matter had been investigated by a lawyer responsible for certifying my integrity to the Civil Service Commission. I offered the lawyer's letter, which had cleared me, to the committee.

Senator Ervin broke in to ask me to read the letter. I did so gratefully, but I was stung by the realization that it is impossible to get clean once one is publicly tarred.

Next Talmadge asked a string of specific questions about the early days of the cover-up, which was fine with me. They were easy. I recounted the facts almost by rote. My confidence began to revive, but I couldn't figure out where the

Senator was headed until he arrived: "Now, after all those facts were available to you, why did you not, as counsel to the President, go in at that time and tell him what was happening?" The Senator looked intent as he awaited my answer.

"Senator, I did not have access to the President," I replied lamely. Talmadge's unhappy look told me he was not at all satisfied, so I tried harder. "I was never presumptuous enough to try to pound on the door to get in, because I knew it just did not work that way." I paused, glanced at the Senator's stare, and panicked. I had seen Clark Mollenhoff of the *Des Monies Register* sitting in the gallery. He inspired another feeble answer. "I know of efforts of other White House staff to get in," I stammered. "I have seen, for example, one of the reporters sitting here in this room, Mr. Mollenhoff. I have seen memoranda he tried to send in to the President, and they were just blocked."

Mollenhoff had worked briefly at the White House, and I hoped he would clue Talmadge in on Haldeman's system.

Senator Talmadge looked incredulous. "You mean you were counsel to the President of the United States and you could not get access to him if you wanted to? Is that your testimony?"

My mind went blank. How could I possibly explain in a few words the way the White House worked? How could I explain that my stature in the White House was not all that different from a grounds keeper? I'd be laughed out of the hearing room if I testified that I was not sure the President had known my name then, or if I told of my "meeting" in the Oval Office with the college newspaper editors. There were hundreds of stories I might have offered to show that I could not have gotten a piece of paper into the Oval Office, much less my body. Even later in the cover-up, after my influence had risen dramatically, Haldeman had blocked me. Once, when the President was preparing for a meeting with Senator Henry

Jackson, I had written a "talking paper" for him, suggesting ways he might question Jackson about the early talk in the Senate of a Watergate investigation. I had shown how the President might ask Jackson whether it was inevitable and, if so, whether Jackson might lead it; we thought he would be much friendlier to the White House than someone like Senator Ervin. Ehrlichman had approved the talking paper, but Haldeman had cut it off before it reached Nixon. Later, when he handed it back to me with a big line drawn across it, I had protested and mentioned Ehrlichman's okay. Haldeman had said, scowling, "I didn't approve it. Besides, the President's no good at this sort of thing."

Now, facing Senator Talmadge, I gave up. No illustration of White House procedures would be convincing, and I couldn't think of good ones anyway. "I thought it would be presumptuous of me to try," I repeated. I looked at Talmadge. Still not enough. I tried to accelerate my mind, but it was in neutral. "Because I was told my reporting channel was Mr. Haldeman and Mr. Ehrlichman," I added weakly, "and I was reporting everything I knew to them."

Senator Talmadge wasn't buying. "It seems to me after finding evidence of a conspiracy of this magnitude, it was incumbent upon you as counsel to the President to make every possible effort to see that he got that information at that time."

His persistence had worn me down. Forget the White House, I thought. Try another angle. "Senator, I was participating in the cover-up at that time," I said bluntly. This confession, although hardly new, seemed to mollify him. Later, during the lunch break, McCandless reported hearing that this one sentence had gone a long way toward winning the Senator's confidence.

That afternoon, Senator Lowell P. Weicker, Jr., Republican of Connecticut, went fishing all throughout his cross-examination. I tried to figure out what he was driving at with his long speeches and readings from my testimony, but I could only guess. He wasn't asking many questions. From his declarations, he appeared to be particularly incensed about the Administration's political abuse of government agencies like the FBI and the IRS. I decided that his anger might stem from a private encounter I had had with him weeks earlier at Charlie's home, when I had informed him of a White House strategy to "neutralize" him, if necessary, by confronting him with evidence that he had received political funds from Jack Gleason's 1970 Town House Operation. Weicker had stopped me to deny the allegations as if he were making a speech on the Senate floor; he said he had reported every cent of his contributions over his entire political career. Now he was going on about the Administration's unscrupulous use of government information for political purposes. I thought perhaps he was still piqued about what I had told him.

"I apologize to the committee for taking so much time," Senator Weicker said near the end of his allotted period, "but it is a subject that I confess I don't have every last bit of information on. It is a difficult thing to piece together."

I decided to volunteer something that might help him. "I might also add," I said, "that in my possession is a rather—very much down the line as to what you are talking about—is a memorandum that was requested of me, to prepare a means to attack the enemies of the White House. There was also maintained what was called an 'enemies list,' which was rather extensive and continually being updated."

Senator Weicker sat up straight at the mention of this memo and the list. "I am not going to ask who was on it. I'm afraid you might answer," he quipped. "I wonder, are these documents in the possession of the committee?"

No, I explained. They did not fit the description of the Watergate documents Mr. Dash had asked for, but I would be happy to submit them.

Weicker had reeled in a whopper. The press went crazy over the enemies list, and it became an instant status symbol to be on it. In the chaos, I was not asked what the enemies list meant. Colson, whose office had prepared it, defended himself with a statement that the list was nothing more than a compilation of names of people to be banned from White House functions. That much was true, but it was also true that Haldeman had selected some twenty people from the list who had incurred the President's special wrath. These people had been targeted for IRS audits and other government harassment, but no action had been taken as far as I knew.[*]

The furor over the enemies list threw me into another of the uncomfortable situations that I was learning to expect. I thought it was vastly overplayed in the media as evidence of a sinister and repressive machine. Under ceaseless pressure from the tickler, the enemies project had indeed grown from nothing into a list-making effort and could have had repressive effects in the second term, but it hadn't. When the President's political detractors exaggerated its significance and applauded me for revealing it, I felt even more of a squealer as a party to untruth. At the same time, however, I was aware that the hoopla was helping me. Everyone who loved the enemies list developed a stake in my value as a witness. The President's opponents began to defend me more vigorously, almost as if the enemies list were more important to them than my testimony on the cover-up. I felt confused. The interpretations were beyond my control, and the atmosphere was heated. And since no one asked for my opinion about the enemies list, I sat back and privately enjoyed Colson's attempts to explain himself.

My second day at the Ervin hearings ended with cross-

---

[*]   Years later I would discover that Haldeman's staff had written a number of memos to their boss recommending that I be fired for failure to start tax audits on those targeted on the enemies list. Haldeman, who no doubt realized it was illegal to start such audits, did not act on the advice of his staff.

examination by Democratic Senator Joseph M. Montoya of New Mexico, who read prepared questions from index cards, one after another, oblivious to the possibility of pursuing any answer I might offer. The Senator was so friendly that I fell prey to temptation and took the opportunity to bounce back from Thompson's and Talmadge's grillings by making sanctimonious speeches about my good intentions. The nobler my answers, the better Montoya seemed to like them, though I could hear Charlie groaning in the background as I told the Senator what a fine character I was. When Montoya asked me how I thought the committee could resolve conflicting testimony in light of the President's refusal to appear, I obliquely challenged the President to get on the box: "Mr. Chairman, I strongly believe that the truth always emerges. I don't know if it will be during these hearings. I don't know if it will be as a result of further activities of the Special Prosecutor. I do not know if it will be through the processes of history. But the truth will come out someday. As far as any issue of fact...I am quite willing to submit myself to a polygraph on any issue of fact with any individual who says that what I'm saying is less than truthful."

Senator Montoya smiled as he read his next question: "What's really made you change and start coming out with the truth in this matter as you have related it? What motivated you?"

I answered with a lyrical speech about my conversations with Mo on the power of truth and the dead end I saw in the cover-up. Charlie gagged, but I was too far gone to pay any attention.

"Do you have peace of mind now?" Montoya intoned.

"Yes, sir," I replied.

"In disclosing everything that you knew," the Senator repeated, "do you have peace of mind and a clear conscience?"

"I'm not here as a sinner seeking a confessional," I replied, laying it on ever more thickly, "but I have been asked to be here to tell the truth. And I have always planned at any time before any forum to tell the truth."

The Senator rose to new heights. He wasn't even reading from index cards. "What I'm trying to ask you is do you feel better now that you've told the truth instead of hiding it?"

"Indeed I do," I averred. "It's a very difficult thing to hide. And as I explained to the President, it would take perjury upon perjury upon perjury if it were to be perpetuated. I'm not capable of doing that..."

"That is all," said Montoya. "Thank you." And Senator Ervin adjourned for the day.

I was barely out of the room when Charlie accosted me. "Goddammit, John, you sounded like you were running for office in there!"

"What's wrong?" I snapped.

Charlie looked exasperated. "If that self-serving crap makes you feel good, fine. Just forget I said anything." He changed the subject, but his advice sank in.

The third day opened with Senator Ervin in hopeless confusion about a list of questions that J. Fred Buzhardt, my successor as the President's counsel, had sent over from the White House. The Senator thought they were addressed to the committee, and he had started to answer them until he realized they were meant for me. I felt embarrassed for Ervin, but I was enjoying a vision of Buzhardt near apoplexy in front of his television set. Finally Senator Baker rescued Ervin from the tangle, and it was Senator Gurney's turn to question me.

Edward Gurney, the first Florida Republican elected to the Senate since Reconstruction, had spent two terms in the House of Representatives during the time I worked at the Judiciary Committee. I remembered that I had asked why he carried a small cushion to sit on during floor proceedings, and that a Republican congressman had told me that Gurney had been seriously injured in World War II. Unless drinking or under sedation, he could sit without his cushion for only a short while. Now he was sitting on his cushion, so I assumed he planned a lengthy and intense interrogation. I expected no friendship from him, especially since I had drawn attention to the White House opinion of him in my opening statement: "...in a subsequent discussion I had with the President, he also reached a similar conclusion...that Senator Gurney would protect the White House and would do so out of political instinct and not have to be persuaded to do so... The long and short of this morning discussion was that the White House had one friend—Senator Gurney..."

He began with some basic questions about the origins of Watergate, trying to fix me as among those directly responsible for the break-in. Although the answers to his questions were not difficult, I felt myself tensing. I was not sure how to deal with Gurney if he got rough. After serving up some nonsense about how his only desire was to conduct a nonpartisan investigation, he inquired again about the law-firm incident in 1966 and put on his best doubting-Thomas face at my explanation. He pressed the issue, and I did not handle it well. I was off balance again. "When did the matter [turn up] in the Civil Service files?" he asked. "Was that in connection with your employment at the House Judiciary Committee?"

I seized an opportunity to go on the offensive. "No," I said. "It was after I left the House Judiciary Committee. As the Senator knows, the House does not run Civil Service examinations on staff," I added pointedly. I wanted to let Gurney know that I would call him on his errors. I also wanted to let him know I was aware of Congressional foibles like exempting staff from Civil Service-type clearance, which is done, at least in part, because congressmen like to hire friends and political cronies.

Now Gurney wanted to know why so many people in the White House had called me the first day after the break-in if I had not been a conspirator: "Why all these calls if you weren't that closely associated with what they were doing over there in the political field?"

"Well, Senator, I would say that my office was one that, one..." I stopped to think, and then switched to a more direct approach. "I did have some dealings with the Reelection Committee. I did know all the parties involved." I paused again. I was not thinking well. As Charlie had advised me to do, I went back to the first answer that had occurred to me: "My office normally was asked to investigate or look into any problem that came up of that nature. When any wrongdoing was charged, any Administration offense. For example, when the grain deal came up." The words were disjointed; I was busily planning another attack on Gurney. "And I think the Senator will recall, during the ITT matter, my office had some peripheral involvement in that. And I believe we had some dealings with your office on that matter."

"Not my office," Gurney shot back. "I think we met in Senator Hruska's office, the Republican members of the [Senate Judiciary] Committee, isn't that correct? With you?"

It was not correct, and Gurney was understandably sensitive about having huddled with me about a scandal like ITT. I corrected him. "Well, Senator, I recall one time that Mr. Fielding and I came up to your office on the matter, and Mr. Fielding provided some material for your staff." I had added Fielding's name to serve notice that he would have to refute two people. Then I went back to why Watergate had fallen so quickly on my doorstep: "It was that type of thing that would come to my office for assistance and aid."

Senator Gurney was still nettled by my ITT references. "What does that have to do with the Watergate?" he asked defensively.

I started explaining again, and soon he turned to confer with his aides. When he did, Charlie leaned forward and whispered to me. "I don't mind you dumping on Gurney, but be careful."

"What do you mean?" I thought I had Gurney on the run and was now debating whether to drive him home by describing the material Fielding had given him. It had been impressive, but not uncommon a few hundred questions we wanted Gurney to submit to Jack Anderson about his ITT disclosures. Before Charlie spoke to me, I had been entertaining ironic thoughts about how I was then trying to nail Anderson for being tough on the White House, whereas I was presently furious with him for toeing the White House line on how Dean had engineered the whole cover-up.

"You've got to remember you can't really win anything up here," Charlie explained. "He's the one asking the questions. You've already established his bias, and he's doing a damn good job of showing it."

"Okay," I sighed, "but I can't let the son-of-a-bitch roll over me."

"I'm not saying you should. But you can't try to roll over him. You've got to remember where you're sitting."

I nodded. Charlie was right. I was getting dangerously close to branding Gurney as a White House lackey, which, although I believed it was true, I could not afford to say. Charlie and I had decided that I had to stay clear of subjective judgments and characterizations. And I knew it was especially perilous to cast aspersions on the integrity of any senator. My experience on Capitol Hill had taught me that senators band together when one of their own is under attack.

Senator Gurney turned back from his conference and quickly changed the subject. I coasted through the rest of his cross-examination and guessed that he would save his parting shots

400

for the final round.

Senator Daniel K. Inouye of Hawaii was next. "Mr. Chairman, the charges contained in Mr. Dean's testimony are extremely serious, with potentially grave consequences," he announced somberly. "The President of the United States has been implicated, and because of the gravity of these charges, I believe that the witness, Mr. John Dean, should be subjected by this committee to the most intense interrogation to test his credibility."

I leaned forward, wondering what Inouye was up to. He wasn't supposed to be hostile. I felt a chill when he declared that he would use his own time allotment to ask me Buzhardt's questions, which had gotten lost in the morning's confusion.

Almost as soon as Inouye began reading the questions, I realized how clever a show the Senator had put on with his gruff manner. Buzhardt's work was clumsy and naïve, not at all threatening. The exercise provided me another opportunity to recite the cover-up facts for the record. It dawned on me that the President's new team of lawyers couldn't perform effectively because they still had no idea of what had gone on.

Senator Inouye's interrogation carried over into the fourth morning. Buzhardt's questions proved so embarrassing to the White House that Ziegler was to deny that they had official blessing. Charlie, Bob, and I shared a good laugh over the announcement.

Chairman Ervin followed Inouye with a gentle round of questions. I had had an easy morning, but during the lunch break I stumbled onto ominous signs. I asked Sam Dash's secretary where the closest lavatory was located, and she suggested that I use the one adjoining Fred Thompson's office. When I walked in, I found Thompson and one of his assistants hunched over a table.

"Excuse me," I said. "Sam's secretary told me to come

401

through this office. She didn't know you were here. I wanted to use the bathroom."

They stared at me as if I had caught them poring over pornographic pictures. Strewn before them were copies of some of my canceled checks and other financial records, which had obviously been subpoenaed. I looked quickly away, not wanting them to know I'd seen.

"The bathroom is right there," Thompson said tersely, pointing to the only other door in the room. I made a quick trip and left, apprehensive about the money questions that were apparently in store for me.

Howard Baker began his interrogation that afternoon with a long speech that rivaled the Dean-Montoya exchange for sanctimoniousness: "...I want to say, Mr. Dean, that you have been a very patient witness, and very thorough. You presented us with a great mass of information...and we are very grateful... The net sum of your testimony is fairly mind-boggling...it is not my purpose now to try to test your testimony. It is not my purpose to try to impeach your testimony, to corroborate your testimony, to elaborate or extend particular aspects of it, but rather to try to structure your testimony so that we have a coherent presentation against which we can measure the testimony of other witnesses heretofore given... It occurs to me that at this point, the central question, and in no way in derogation of the importance of the great volume of material and the implications that flow from it, but the central question is simply put: What did the President know and when did he know it? ."

As Baker went on, I tried to find his tack. I knew that he was foxy and that his purpose would be well hidden. I remembered how boldly he had announced that he had not met with the President about Watergate—in spite of the fact that I myself had prepared the agenda for one meeting, and had been summoned to the President's EOB office in the middle of it. I

402

knew Baker had insisted that no record be kept of his visit. When I had tried to disarm him by informing him in the committee's executive session that I would reveal the secret meeting, he had gone on national television and smoothly reversed his previous public statement. He was playing both sides, I knew: demanding the truth and then exchanging strategy messages with Colson; voting with the White House in private sessions of the Ervin Committee and then switching to the other side in public.

Baker's questioning about the President's knowledge was difficult. This was a critical danger area for me, and I was well aware of it. My head was filled with minutiae that had to do with the President's involvement but which I had omitted because I couldn't be precisely sure of when things had occurred. As Baker tried to pin me down on more details, I became suspicious. Gurney and Thompson had pushed me for the same kind of information, and I assumed they were working in tandem. Gurney and Thompson had tried to badger me to pad my testimony about the President; Baker was trying to seduce me to do the same. Since I feared they were all three seeking to catch me in a major demonstrable error, I tried not to be budged from my prepared statement.*

In the final round of questioning, Senator Gurney said: "Just a few questions, Mr. Dean. I would like to go back to the Kalmbach meeting again, when you and he first discussed this cover-up money."

"On the twenty-ninth, Senator?" I asked.

---

* More than a year later, after the President resigned, a lawyer in the Special Prosecutor's office told me that the President's lawyers had wanted the Watergate Committee Republicans to push me for additional details about the President's involvement. He and Haldeman had been listening to tapes of his conversations with me, and the lawyer reported that the President said he would nail "that son-of-a-bitch Dean" for perjury and "end the ball game."

"June twenty-ninth."

"Yes."

"You're absolutely certain about that date? It could not have occurred in July, could it have?"

"The first meeting I had with him was when I flew in..." I began, and realized I had erred. Gurney made me nervous. "...*He* took the last flight, I believe, out of Los Angeles. We met the next morning." Gurney was playing with me, he must have something, I could sense it in his smug manner. I tried to anticipate him, undercut whatever he had. "The records—he very seldom stayed at the Mayflower Hotel and he was staying at the Mayflower, and I would assume that if the committee investigators would check the records of the Mayflower Hotel, they could confirm that date. That is the best of my recollection, that it was the twenty-ninth."

"This was the June twenty-ninth date?" Gurney repeated.

"Yes."

"Was there anyone else at the meeting?"

"No, sir, there was not."

"And my recollection is that you had a short meeting in the coffee shop, is that right?"

"I was to meet him in the coffee shop and I recall we sat down in the booth. And it did not appear very private in the booth, so we decided to go to his room to discuss the matter."

"And that was there in the Mayflower Hotel?"

"That is correct."

"Well, the committee has subpoenaed the records of the hotel. And I have a letter here from the Mayflower, and also one from the Statler Hilton. I would like a committee staffer to give these copies to the witness."

I looked at the documents. The Mayflower said Kalmbach hadn't been there. The Statler Hilton said he had been there. I had confused the hotels, even though I remembered the meeting vividly and could still see Kalmbach turning on the television in his room so that the chambermaids nearby could not hear us. I remembered it as clearly as the next meeting, when Kalmbach had tapped his briefcase filled with money while we were sitting on the park bench. I knew that Gurney might demolish my entire testimony because I had made one careless error. How could my memory of the President's words be trusted, he would wonder aloud, when I had been proven wrong about something as elementary and as obvious as a hotel name? It was all I could do to keep from leaving the hearing room in disgust. I was overwhelmed by the absurdity. In desperation, I suggested illogically that perhaps Kalmbach had stayed at the Mayflower under another name.

"Well," the Senator countered, "it also occurred to me that that could be the case, that he was using an assumed name, but it just does not make sense. If he was coming into the city under an assumed name so that no one would know he was here and no later record could be found, why in the world would he register under his own name at a nearby hotel?"

"I see what you're saying," I conceded. "I have testified the Mayflower, and I am never sure which is the Mayflower and which is the Statler Hilton. The hotel I recall is the one that is on Sixteenth Street up from the White House. I walked up from the office to his room."

"How long have you lived in Washington?" Gurney wasn't going to settle for a confession either.

"I've lived here about ten years."

"And you don't know the difference between the Washington Hilton and the Mayflower?"

"I continually get them confused, I must admit."

405

"Well, I must say I am reminded of your colloquy with the chairman yesterday, Mr. Dean, when you said what an excellent memory you had right from school days right on down. That is why you were able to reconstruct..."

I interrupted defensively, "That is right, but I confuse some names often. I don't pretend to have a perfect memory. I think I have a good memory, Senator." Gurney was doing a hell of a job on me, I thought. Then I got a break.

During an interruption, Bob McCandless handed me a note: *"The coffee shop at Statler Hilton is called the Mayflower Room."* Bob didn't have to tell me what to do with this little gimcrack. I cleared my throat, got the attention of the committee, and said, "I might go back over one point. The name of the coffee shop at the Statler Hilton is the Mayflower."

The audience applauded. I'd explained my confusion with a plausible answer. The crowd's support, which I hadn't expected, did more to repair the dents Gurney had made in my credibility than anything I could possibly have said or done. Gurney was annoyed and tried to discredit my explanation. When he claimed it had come from my lawyer, Charlie jumped up and grabbed the microphone. "Mr. Chairman, that was Mr. McCandless," he said, smiling and pointing at Bob. "I would like to give him credit for that." This time the entire room, including Gurney, broke out in laughter.

"Bob, thanks for the note," I said at the recess. "I was afraid I was going down the tube over that silly hotel thing."

"Don't thank me. Thank Dan Schorr. He handed it to me and told me he eats there all the time and is positive of the name."

"I'll be damned," I responded. Schorr had run the nasty story, over our strong protest, that I feared going to jail because of homosexual attack. He had done me a dirty deed, but he had just evened the score as far as I was concerned.

406

It is difficult to keep track of time when one is testifying. The windows of the hearing room had been blackened for the television lights. There were no clocks visible, and I'd been busy concentrating on questions. By Friday afternoon, my fifth day, I could think of little else but what time it was. I kept checking my watch. I wanted to get out of there. I was weary, and when you're tired you can make mistakes, I kept reminding myself. It was three o'clock. Four o'clock. Five o'clock. And the questions kept coming. I was getting upset and angry. The senators take a break whenever they feel like it, I thought resentfully; they interrogate only as long as they feel like it. Shit, I have to sit here while they take turns at me. It's unfair. At five-thirty, I turned around to speak to Charlie. Fred Thompson was questioning me.

"Charlie, give Dash the signal," I whispered. "I've got to take a leak, awful." Charlie and Sam had devised a signaling system to use if I needed a break, but I had not yet called for one. I had sipped water all afternoon for my throat, and my bladder was sending a painful message.

"Can't you keep going?" Charlie asked unsympathetically. "I think we can finish up this afternoon, but if you stop now they may call you back Monday for more. Dammit, just keep going." The more I thought about my dilemma, the worse it got. It was interfering with my concentration, and Fred Thompson was hot and heavy after me. He was grilling me about something very embarrassing that I'd volunteered with considerable pain to both the prosecutors and the committee during its executive session—I had taken several thousand dollars of the money Gordon Strachan had given me after the break-in, to use on my honeymoon, and left an IOU in my safe. I had been in a pinch because of a particularly frenetic cover-up week, had failed to get the cash necessary for the trip and the wedding expenses, and had taken an expedient loan. The "honeymoon money" had become a favored topic among my detractors, who were making me out a thief.

407

Thompson: "Did you subsequently get to Miami to spend a few more days on your honeymoon?"

"As I recall, we made several trips to Miami to try to have a honeymoon and were called back."

"Did you leave for Miami on October twentieth, if you recall?"

"That is very possible. As I told you when we started this line of questioning, I have not sat down and tried to reconstruct this. I am perfectly willing to reconstruct it for the committee and turn it all over to the committee for the committee's use. I just have not entered this area of reconstruction and I am sure—"

Thompson interrupted. "You will not test your memory on these particular points. Is that what you're saying?"

Goddam him, I thought. I could take him day by day through my trips to and from Florida, but it would take more effort than I've got left in my condition. He obviously thinks he can show I never intended to go to Florida for more than a few days and will insinuate that I must have taken the money for some other reason.

I had run out of steam and I was in pain. I decided to let Thompson have it his way and renewed my offer to let the committee investigators go over all my finances. It wasn't a very good way to handle him, I knew, but I no longer cared. Thompson, feeling sure he'd scored well, started toward the finish line. Chairman Ervin apparently thought Thompson had scored well also, and intervened on my behalf.

"If I could ask a question or so here, I might shorten some of this," Ervin interrupted, exercising his chairman's prerogative. "Mr. Dean, did anybody know that you had taken the $4,850 out of this money, except yourself?"

"No, sir, they did not."

"If you had wanted to deceive anybody about it, what would have prevented you from getting $4,850 and replacing it?"

"Nothing."

He was offering me the chance to say that I could have hidden it. In fact, the IOU was still in the safe when I told Charlie of the loan, which I then immediately redeemed.

Finally the chairman turned to the other members of the committee and asked if there were any further questions. Nobody asked anything. I was elated. It was over. It had been a wretched week. Now all I wanted was to get first to a bathroom and then out of Washington for as long as I could.

Mo and I talked about where we might go. We had to be careful with money, because I didn't know when I would be able to work again. We decided to accept the invitation of Lance Cooper, an old prep-school friend, who had a beautiful little house on an isolated stretch of beach near Melbourne, Florida. It was so private that the deputy marshals who met our flight in Orlando felt they could leave us alone.*

The trip to Florida made me appreciate the privacy all the more. People now recognized me instantly, and I didn't like being infamous. I was ashamed to be who I was, even though people said nice things to me. I didn't feel I could explain my new thirst for privacy to Mo. When we were packing I had ignored her question about why I was carrying *Inside the Third*

---

* One of the most memorable moments of all the events associated with Watergate occurred on the trip down to Florida. When we changed planes in Atlanta, the U.S. Marshals in my protective detail had me exit the door of the ramp to the terminal, rather than going into the terminal, and walk over to our connecting flight. As Mo and I came down the stairs we heard applause, shouts, whistles, and cheers of approval from about thirty to forty mechanics and bagging handlers who had lined up to express their approval of my testimony. It was the first sign I had received that people understood I had been telling the truth, and it was greatly appreciated.

Reich, by Albert Speer. I wanted to know how Speer had coped with guilt.

After a week of my refusing to go to the grocery store (except once disguised in sunglasses and a pulled-down tennis hat) or to restaurants or window shopping, Mo was getting annoyed. She wanted to get out and do something. I wanted to hide. To ease the tension, we invited some friends down. When Heidi and Morgan arrived, the party started. It went on day after day, almost nonstop. For the first time in years, I was having fun.

When Sam Dash called on Friday, July 13, 1973, I wasn't surprised. He'd already called several times to ask me about John Mitchell's and Richard Moore's testimony before the committee.

"Can you come back to Washington?" Dash asked. The request took me aback.

"What do you need, Sam?" I moaned. "Can't we handle it on the telephone?"

"Not really. It's important, very important, John, that you return, so we can talk. I need to see you. Something has come up."

"I should have known your call would be bad news today. Okay, I'll make reservations and call you back," I said unenthusiastically.

Sam was excited and a bit nervous. Most unlike him, I thought. I wondered what was up. Was he going to recall me as a witness? Whatever it was, it made me nervous, because he wouldn't tell me. I hated the thought of leaving Melbourne. Mo had been enjoying herself more than I could last remember. This would not sit well with her. The taste of relaxation had made us both crave more. As I called to arrange a flight back, I decided I would not leave until the next morning. I was determined to have one more day off. Mo took the bad news

410

without comment, and we all decided we would not let it spoil the last night. Out came the Monopoly board, the booze, a run to the grocery store by Morgan, and the barbecue was stoked up, and we all assembled at the dining-room table for the first event of the evening.

"I'm going to build another hotel on the boardwalk," I announced well into the Monopoly game. "But I'd like to make a small loan from the bank," I told the banker. It was Morgan.

"You can't do that," Mo protested.

"Why not?" I asked.

"You're already overextended," she said, glancing at some of my choice properties, which had been costing the others dearly.

"Sure I can, if Morgan thinks I'm a good risk. Also I can mortgage some of this stuff."

"Don't you dare," Mo said threateningly, "or I'm quitting!"

"I'm going to start dinner," Heidi said, getting up from the table. She sensed what I knew—that Mo's anger had nothing to do with the game. Both Heidi and Morgan knew we had serious financial worries. Lawyers' fees and living expenses were eating our savings. Mo was worried about how we were going to make it. So was I, but I refused to admit it to her.

"Morgan, I'd like to borrow one thousand dollars for another hotel and I'll give you a mortgage on the two existing hotels, which are worth double my loan." I had decided to confront Mo's threat; I was really telling her that our finances were my worry.

"Well, I don't know," Morgan said, stroking his chin. "Maybe we could work out a private deal and I'd give you a little loan myself." He was being diplomatic.

"Oh, no. No, sir," Mo said. "No charity for the kid over here."

411

"Now, that's an ugly attitude," I told her, steering away from a clash with a mocking smile.

"I tell you what. After you take your turn, I'll consider a bank loan," Morgan announced. His strategy was good, both for the game and for the incipient argument between Mo and me. If I could survive a roll of the dice on the heavily owned board, I'd be in good shape.

"Okay." I rolled. Eleven. I started counting as I moved my race car around the board. GO TO JAIL! Everybody cracked up, including me.

The game quickly ended, and Mo chided me with a dig that was fair game: "That's why you're a bad risk, sweetheart."

After dinner it was backgammon time, and we played on two boards, until Heidi mused aloud, "I wonder if the turtles are out tonight."

"Let's check," Mo said, but no one moved. "Who's going to brave it?" she asked, excluding herself, since she'd been injured in earlier battles with the mosquitoes.

"I've got an idea," Heidi said, and she disappeared. She returned soon with an armful of jackets, broad-brimmed women's hats, and other apparel. We all began bundling up. Mo, who refused to go out and risk another bite, assisted us. All exposed areas had to be covered. Rubber dishwashing gloves and potholder mittens served to cover the hands. Silk scarves, worn under our hats, served as mosquito netting.

Dressed like Arctic scarecrows, we three headed out of the air conditioned house into the humid night air, off for the beach to see if we could find any turtles. Not fifty feet from the path leading to the beach, we found the flipper marks of the enormous female tortoises. I shone the flashlight along the tracks coming from the ocean toward the sand dunes. There we came upon a huge turtle digging a hole for her eggs. We watched in appropriate awe. She seemed oblivious to us and to our light.

412

Soon she had dug a hole at least five feet in diameter, climbed in, laid hundreds of eggs, climbed out of the hole, and covered it again with sand so that the eggs could incubate during the warm summer days. Then she started back to sea.

"How much do you think she weighs?" I asked Morgan as she dragged her enormous hulk before us.

"I don't have any idea," Morgan responded.

The turtle stopped right in front of us. She looked at us as if to say, "See for yourself." Without moving, she waited patiently as Morgan and I tried to lift her. We could not budge her an inch.

With that, the tortoise resumed her march to the sea without our help. We headed on down the beach, finding tracks but no more turtles. In the excitement of our pursuit I had paid little attention to the distance we'd walked in the soft sand, but we'd gone about a mile. We turned to head back and with the wind now behind us I realized how heavily I'd been perspiring under all the clothing. I also was short of breath. I had to stop.

"Here, Morgan, you take the light and go on with Heidi," I said, and they walked on. I walked into the water, shoes and all, up to my knees, to cool off. I still couldn't catch my breath, and I loosened my shirt. My chest was pounding. Heavier that it should be, I thought. I was glancing down the beach, after the flashlight with Heidi and Morgan, thinking I'd better get along after them, when—wham! A sharp pain, like someone had just pounded on my chest with a hammer. Jesus Christ! I'm having a heart attack! My lungs gasped for breath as some reflex took over. My mind raced and said, Get out of the water so you won't drown if you faint. Slowly I staggered out and sat down. Maybe I should call for help, I thought as I glanced again at the light. I took a few more breaths, slow and easy. No pain, but the muggy sweat had turned cold. What in the hell's wrong with you? I asked myself. A few more deep breaths, and I decided, nothing. No chest pain. My pulse seemed normal. I'd decided that it was not a heart attack, but that nature had sent me a warning.

I got up, took off the jacket I was wearing over a sweater, then the sweater. Who gives a damn about mosquitoes, I decided. Testing myself, I started down the beach, staying near the water, where the sand was hard and easier to walk on. I could hear Morgan and Heidi exclaiming about new tracks down the beach. Take it slow, make sure you're okay, but get back to the house, I told myself. As I walked I decided there was no need to alarm anyone with what had happened. I would get a physical checkup as soon as I got home. I was nearly thirty pounds overweight from nervous eating and excessive drinking. I had been living under intense stress for several years and hadn't exercised in a long time. I smoked like a potbelly stove and slept poorly.

Sam Dash came to the house within an hour of my return to Washington the next day, Saturday, accompanied by Jim Hamilton.

"What's on your mind, Sam?" I asked as he wandered about the living room. I had sat down on one of the sofas, assuming that Sam would do the same. He always did. Obviously he was stirred up; neither he nor Jim sat. Sam paced; Jim stood in front of the fireplace, gazing at us.

"Something's come up" Sam said. That was obvious. He had a very serious look about him. "John, let me ask you this. Do you think it's possible Nixon could have taped all of his office and phone conversations?"

"Sure it's possible. You know my testimony about the—"

Sam cut me off. "I know, but you were talking about one conversation. You think he could have taped all of them?"

"Sure. I wouldn't be surprised if he had."

"Well, if he did," Sam said, standing over me, arms folded, "how could we find out?"

"Find out if he taped his conversations?" I repeated, as I mused over something I'd thought about several times and had a ready answer for. "Sam, if he did, I'll tell you who would probably know." I suggested several names: General Al Redman, head of the White House Communications Agency, Steve Bull, Alex Butterfield, Haldeman, and Ehrlichman.

"Who's Redman again?" Dash asked. I explained that he had been assigned by the Army Signal Corps to head the White House Communications Agency, which provided communication support for the President.

"This fellow Butterfield. Would he know?" Dash asked.

"He might, but I think Redman would be more likely. Also Redman would not lie to you. He wouldn't want to risk losing his—"

"Would Butterfield lie?"

"No. Never. Butterfield's a no-bullshit-type guy. You ask him and he'll tell you."

"Interesting," Sam said, walking about again.

I wondered what all this was about. Certainly Dash could have asked me these questions on the telephone, and I would not have had to return.

Sam came back and stopped in front of me. "John, what would you say if I told you that we've learned from Butterfield that Nixon did tape all his conversations?"

"You're kidding!" I said. I was on my feet: "Listen, Sam, that's fantastic! Absolutely fantastic! Can you get the conversations?"

"You think Butterfield would know what was going on, do you?" Sam asked, ignoring my question.

"If Alex said the old man recorded his conversations, you better believe it. Sam, do you know what this means, if you

415

can get those conversations?" I went on excitedly. "It would mean my ass is not hanging out there all alone. It means that you can verify my testimony. And I'll tell you this, you'll find out that I've undertestified, rather than overtestified, just to be careful. I always figured something like this could happen." I was ecstatic.

Dash swore me to secrecy; he was going to put Butterfield on as a surprise witness on Monday, interrupting Kalmbach's testimony. When Sam was ready to leave, I walked with him to the door. Standing on the front stoop, he reached out to shake my hand.

"John, I think I should tell you I came out here to test you. We weren't sure how you'd react to the idea of a record that might contradict your testimony. I'm on my way to see Chairman Ervin right now and tell him that—you passed the test with flying colors."

"Professor, I don't give a damn what kind of test I passed, but I do hope you can get those recordings." Dash had been clever in his examination, I was thinking; better than when he questioned me before the committee.

Charlie called me later that afternoon and came on strong. "What in the hell do you mean meeting with Dash without your lawyer present?" he shouted into the phone.

"I didn't have time to find you. You were off riding in some damn steeplechase or whatever it is you do as a country gentleman," I answered, not falling for Charlie's phony bluster. "How did you find out about the meeting, anyway?"

"I know everything about my client," he said, shifting tone. "Listen, I called to tell you that Sam called me. He and Ervin met this afternoon after he left your house. Dash told me all about the meeting with you, and you damn near floored him when you told him to get the tapes. You know, I don't think old Sam totally believed you, but now he and Ervin sure as hell do."

"Charlie, it's a new ball game now. If they can get the tapes of the President's conversation—" Before I could finish Charlie interrupted.

"What do you think Nixon's going to do when Butterfield reveals this?"

"I don't know for sure. He'll probably say it's true. In fact, he'll have to admit it, because I'm sure a lot of people had to be involved in putting such a system in. But he'll say those are conversations protected by executive privilege. He sure as hell isn't going to turn them over. That's what I told Sam, that Nixon would probably go to court, and Sam said he was ready to go to court after them."

"Who'll win? You're supposed to be an expert on executive privilege."

"Who knows, Charlie? There's really no law on it. But what worries me is Nixon might screw around with those tapes—change them, splice them or something."

"Naw, how in the hell could he? Who would do it?"

"Some technical expert."

"Yeah, and that some technical expert and everybody between him and the President would own Richard Nixon for life."

"I guess you're right. I hope you're right."

"Yeah, but it's still your word against Haldeman, Ehrlichman, and Mitchell, as far as your dealings with them."

"Well, I suspect they're on the tapes, too."

"Don't get too encouraged, son. You've got a rough road ahead."

But we both knew it would be different. Now, as far as the

President's fate was concerned, I was no longer the sole accuser. The tapes themselves were the best evidence, and I began long and complicated calculations on whether they could ever be obtained. There was, at least, a glimmer of hope that my own future was not so closely intertwined with the President's. I felt the pressure ease as the battle for the tapes began, and I began to focus more closely on a settlement for my own crimes.

JOURNAL

July 1973-January 1975

Late July 1973

Mo and I went to California to be near her mother, who was dying of cancer. I ignored the Ervin hearings. I was worried about my own health, and that I was becoming an alcoholic. I quit drinking, cold turkey. Twenty-five pounds came off my body with a crash exercise regimen and a diet. I jogged around the UCLA track in sunglasses and a floppy tennis hat.

Early August 1973

Charlie called long distance from Washington. "How is my favorite health nut? I guess you're fit as Tarzan by now."

"Totally reformed," I joked. "It really feels good, Charlie. I only wish I could be about three thousand more miles away from Washington."

"Well, don't you forget about us back here. I need your help, I'm having trouble getting in to see the P. He won't return my calls."

"Try Rose Woods," I suggested. "Tell her Jimmy Hoffa wants to give the Teamsters' yacht to the President. Maybe that'll get you in."

Ever since Butterfield had revealed the Presidential taping system, Charlie had been declaring that he wanted to see the President eyeball-to-eyeball in the Oval Office and demand all the tapes of his conversations with me. It was a running jest. Charlie's rehearsals of those confrontations were executed with his usual flair.

"Listen, John," he said when the fun had died down, "I was

down to see those fellows at the Special Prosecutor's office today."

Here comes the business, I thought. I went on guard. "Did you talk to Cox?"

"No. I ran into him, but I met with Neal and a young fellow by the name of Richard Ben-Veniste. He's a bright little kid from the Southern District up in New York. And I tell you, Ben-Veniste and old Neal are really something together. They're as different as molasses and vinegar. I wanted to see what's on their minds down there, so I went into Neal's office and said, 'Jimmy, I guess maybe you've lost track of my man now that you're all balled up trying to get those tapes.' And he laughed and said, 'Shaffer, I never lose track of you.' He said he'd been thinking about calling me, because he wants to know what we're going to do. He says he can feel it in his bones that you're going to plead guilty."

"Maybe he's got pretty good feelings," I said quietly.

"Maybe so," said Charlie. "We've got to talk about that. But I decided to ruffle his feathers a little bit. I told him it makes no sense for my man to plead, because the government can never get a conviction against him. I told him he's got a big bag of problems, and the first one is that we'd destroy his case with a taint motion."

"What did he say about that?" Charlie was convinced that Silbert and Glanzer had made extensive use of the evidence I had given them in our off-the-record meetings. He thought the government could never prove that its case against me was not "tainted" by my confessions.

"Well, he said he's not worried about any taint motion," Charlie replied. "But he's bluffing. He knows he's in trouble."

"Charlie, do you really think a taint motion would prevail?"

"You're goddam right I do!" Then he paused, sighed, and lapsed into a less confident tone. "But who knows what will

420

prevail in this kind of case? I just think we've got a good shot. I don't risk predictions."

"But Neal's worried, you think?" I became unsettled whenever Charlie's bravado waned.

"Yes, sir," he replied firmly, his spirits reviving. "And I gave him another reason to worry. If he indicts us I'll put a motion for the tapes right on top of the taint motion. I told him there's no way you can get a fair trial without those tapes."

"It sounds like you leaned on him pretty hard."

"I did, and let me tell you why. These guys need you as a witness, and they need you bad. They still want you to plead to a one-count, five-year felony for the cover-up. They're leaning hard, too. I want you to put down your barbells out there and do some thinking. If you want to go to trial, fine. I'm ready. It will cost you a couple hundred thousand bucks, but I'll give you as long as you need to pay me. We might win, we might lose. If you want to plead, on the other hand, that's fine too."

"What do you think I should do?"

"That's not my decision. It's yours. And you should start deciding."

September 1973

Mo was opposed to my pleading guilty. People beat raps in Washington all the time, she argued, and I should give myself a fighting chance. Charlie waxed hot and cold, and so did I. When he leaned in one direction, I leaned in the other. We stayed on the fence. But in my mind the question was more which than whether I would plead.

421

October 1973

Charlie called one afternoon. "Big news today, son," he began. "A little good and a little bad. The Court of Appeals finally had to bite the bullet. They upheld Sirica's order to hand over the tapes. What do you think Nixon will do now?"

"There's no question what he'll do," I said. "He'll fight it. He'll take it to the Supreme Court. That's where he wants it, anyway."

"Well, if he does I think Cox is going right up there after him. It looks good for Cox."

"I'm pulling for him." I paused, caught between hope about Cox and anxiety about the other part of Charlie's news. "What else, Charlie?"

"You've got to come back to Washington right away," he said tersely. "If you're going to plead, it's now or never. And if you don't plead now, they're going to the grand jury and have you indicted." There was finality in Charlie's voice.

"What's the rush all of a sudden?" I stammered. "Why right now? Why can't we wait until the tapes case is settled? Christ, Charlie, Nixon is still a long way from giving those things up. Can't you get Neal to hold off? What's eating him?" I felt panicky and off balance. Frightened. I would have given anything for a week's delay.

"I don't know what's going on for sure. Neal kind of hinted that Cox and the White House are going after each other pretty hard now, and something's going to give. Neal says it's vital that you plead now. He's getting his horses in the gate. It's post time. I can't budge him, John."

"Charlie, that's what Silbert said in his goddam letter," I protested. "I could be walking into a trap.,,"

"Cox is not Silbert," Charlie replied. He was being gentle but firm. "This is a new game. Look, I can delay all sorts of

422

things, John. Afterwards. But you've got to decide whether you're going to throw in with Cox. And if you are, you've got to come back here right away."

"How soon?"

"Tomorrow. The next day at the latest. Neal says they're going to wrap it up this week, one way or the other. They're going to court with your plea or they're going to the grand jury without it."

There was a short silence. I felt my throat tighten. "Okay, Charlie," I sighed. "I'll fly back in the morning. And I'll bring Mo back with me so I can break it to her. I don't think she thought this day would ever come, either."

"I'll make the arrangements," Charlie said briskly. "I'll call Neal and set up an appointment. We still have some leverage for the details. He's got to give us some room. We're not going to cave in right off the bat. But you've got to understand that Neal will know damn well what it means that you're showing up." Charlie was nervous, jumping right into the arrangements to avoid the tension.

"All right, I'll call you when we get in."

"I'm with you, John. And for what it's worth, I think you're doing the right thing.* You know that."

"I know, Charlie. Thanks." I fought against a swell of emotion. "I think it's the right thing to do, but so did Custer." I laughed weakly.

---

* Shaffer also truly believed that if I wanted to "beat the rap," that I had the perfect case to do it. He was confident that because the government had granted me informal immunity, first the prosecuters and then the Senate, that I could not be prosecuted. Because this was still speculative, I did not write about it when working on *Blind Ambition*. Now it is the law. And to this day Charlie has enjoyed reminding me that I had Oliver North's case before Oliver North made his case to avoid prosecution. But I was not interrested in "beating the rap," because I felt that under the rules we are supposed to play by, I had to pay for my mistake.

"Those were less civilized times, my boy. If you get scalped, you'll have due process and the best damn lawyer money can buy. I'll talk to you soon." He hung up.

I made several runs at telling Mo what had happened. It came out hesitatingly, in bits and pieces. We latched on to distractions. That evening we avoided the subject by watching a political spectacular on television. With great fanfare, the President announced his choice of a successor to Vice-President Spiro Agnew, who had resigned in the face of criminal charges.

"That's very shrewd," I said when Gerald Ford's name was pronounced. "The President just bought himself an insurance policy."

"What do you mean?" Mo asked.

"Well, he's just made sure there won't be any Republican groundswell for him to resign. There won't be a big push to put Jerry Ford in the White House."

"Why not?" she protested. "I like Jerry Ford. He was very nice to me over at Pat Golubin's. Remember? He didn't know me at all, but he said nice things."

I remembered. Ford had been on crutches that evening, recovering from some sort of accident. "I know, sweetheart. He's the kind of guy who's a nice neighbor, but that doesn't mean he's the kind of man Republicans will want as President. He's not well known, and everybody in Washington considers him a lightweight. Christ, Mo, you know more about foreign policy than he does."

"Well, he's still better than Agnew and Nixon," she insisted.

"Maybe you're right," I admitted. "I'm just worried that he'll strengthen Nixon. And anything that strengthens Nixon hurts me."

October 19, 1973

"Mr. Dean, you have heard the charges against you, how do you plead?" Judge Sirica asked, peering down at me from the bench.

"Guilty, your honor."

It was over. And I felt nothing. Or refused to let myself feel. Maybe it was easier because there were no immediate consequences, I thought, as Charlie, Mo, and I walked out of the courtroom.

"Well, I'm not going to be with you the rest of the way," Neal said. He was announcing his resignation. "You're my best trophy, and now that I've brought you to Archie, I'm going back home and make some money."

"I look forward to talking with you, Mr. Dean," Archibald Cox said to me in the elevator as we rode down from Judge Sirica's courtroom. "I'll give you a call early next week, and see if we can arrange a meeting."

"I'd like that, Mr. Cox," I said. When the elevator door opened, he stepped out briskly ahead of me, his briefcase tucked under his arm. Boy, do I wish that was filled with the tapes, I thought. I visualized Cox walking down the courthouse corridor with me under one arm and a briefcase of tapes under the other, like two big loaves of bread, heading for the grand-jury room.

October 20, 1973

The evening news had been heavy: reactions to my guilty plea; the President's compromise proposal to have a summary of the tapes verified by Senator John C. Stennis of Mississippi; Cox's refusal to accept the compromise. I was delighted when Mo found a variety show on the television. Time to tune out.

WE INTERRUPT THIS PROGRAM FOR A
SPECIAL ANNOUNCEMENT.

NBC reporter Carl Stern flashed onto the screen. He was standing in front of the White House, breathless. His voice was filled with emotion, which was highly irregular. The President had fired Cox! The Special Prosecutor's office had been abolished!

"My God, what in the world...?" I shouted at Stern, who continued, oblivious to my protest.

Attorney General Elliot L. Richardson had resigned. Deputy Attorney General William D. Ruckelshaus had been fired. The FBI had been sent to seal off the files in Cox's office. The FBI had also been dispatched by the White House to seal Richardson's and Ruckelshaus' files. Stern said he'd report any further developments, and disappeared from the screen. I was motionless.

"What does that mean?" Mo asked with a frightened look that mirrored my alarm.

"It's bad. Nixon's fighting back. He's going to play rough." I got up and started to pace. I brought the telephone over to the ottoman in front of the television, sat down, got up again.

"I'd better call Charlie." I sat down again. My hands were trembling as I dialed. It felt like the night Nixon had fired me.

"Is Charlie there?"

"No, sorry. He's over at some friends' house at a party," his daughter told me.

"This is John Dean. Could you get a message to him, and tell him to call me? It's very important." As I put the receiver down, the phone rang. I was so jittery it felt like an electric shock. "Hello."

"John, this is John Lindsay," the *Newsweek* reporter said.

426

I assembled my composure. "How are you?"

"Well, that's not very important. I guess you've heard what your former leader has done."

"I sure have. I can damn near hear the boots of marching FBI troops. It's a little terrifying," I said.

By the time Charlie called, I'd settled down. I told him what I was thinking about. "Listen, I've given up everything by pleading, and I got nothing. All I've got is a letter from Cox saying I can still be prosecuted for perjury. And if it's my word against everybody else's, what's to stop Nixon from telling his next Attorney General to prosecute me? Charlie, I've been screwed."

"Maybe."

"Can I withdraw my guilty plea?"

"Nope. You voluntarily pleaded. It doesn't make a damn bit of difference that you pleaded because you like Cox. Let me think about this. I can't really talk now, but I'll call you tomorrow." Charlie had little comfort to offer, and I badly needed some. Rick Ben-Veniste had given me his unlisted number. I fished it out of my wallet and called him. He had replaced Jim Neal as the assistant special prosecutor in charge of Watergate.

"What are you guys going to do now?" I asked Rick. "I've got, or I had, a lot riding on your office."

"I don't know what's next."

"Have you talked to Cox? Or have you all met or something to see about blocking Nixon's move? Or is it over?"

"I'll give you a call tomorrow," he said. Rick seemed preoccupied, and as stunned as I. I continued calling people. And I drank more Scotch than I had drunk in months.

October 21, 1973

It had been a sleepless night. Rick called early.[*]

"I think we're going to be absorbed into the Department of Justice. We just don't know, but the reason I called is we'd like to meet with you tomorrow, about one-thirty. I'll call you tomorrow morning and give you the details. Please don't mention this to anyone, other than Charlie, of course. Okay?"

"Sure."

October 22, 1973

Monday morning I tried not to stare at the telephone as I waited all morning for Rick's call, so I read and reread the newspaper. At 11: 04 he called.

"Can you come downtown to the Statler Hilton at twelve-thirty?"

"You bet."

"Remember, that's not the Mayflower," he quipped.

I laughed. "I'll never confuse them again in my life. But where in the hotel? The coffee shop?"

Rick laughed, too, which made me feel better. "No, we'll wait for you in the lobby."

An hour later, I followed Rick and three of his colleagues to the elevator and on to a room they had taken. After checking to make sure no one had followed us, we went in separately, as if we were conspirators going to a cell meeting.

"It's going to be announced today that Henry Petersen is

---

[*]   After Watergate, Richard Ben-Veniste stopped using the nickname Rick, and asked friends and colleagues to call him Richard. To those who knew him first as Rick, this required a moment of thought.

now in charge of the Watergate investigation," Rick began. "We're going to be under the Department of Justice. How do you feel about that?"

"I think it shits," I said.

"We're not exactly overwhelmed, either. Why don't you like it?"

"I think that's obvious. Henry Petersen has been marching into the President's office every time Nixon wants a look at the evidence, and he tells the President what it is.[*] I doubt if Petersen will go after the tapes. So, if that's the situation, you're looking at all you're going to get—me."

"Didn't you recommend Petersen to the President?"

"Right. I told the President that I didn't think Henry would want to hurt the Presidency and he should take his counsel from him. It looks as if he's following my advice. I like Henry, but he's sure as hell not going to be very happy with me as a key government witness. I talked to him throughout the cover-up. How in the hell can he be the prosecutor when he's had all those dealings with me?"

"We have some problems with that, too. Was Petersen part of the cover-up? We need to know."

"Well, I don't think I ever compromised him to the extent that he could be considered a co-conspirator. But he had to know why I was always calling him for information. Henry had to look the other way on some things, like when I told him Gray had received documents from Hunt's safe before the first

---

[*]   Tapes would later confirm what I knew in my bones to be the situation, and Petersen provided evidence to Nixon, who in turn gave it to Haldeman and Ehrlichman, who began recreating the record, particularly Ehrlichman, who taped people responding to his leading questions unaware of what he was doing. The House Judiciary Committee would later include Nixon's passing on evidence to Haldeman and Ehrlichman as part of their charge that he had obstructed justice.

429

Watergate trial."

November 1, 1973

In the wake of the now-famous firestorm, the fierce public reaction to the "Saturday Night Massacre," and with an array of impeachment resolutions in the Congress, the President was forced to back down. He appointed a new Special Prosecutor, Leon Jaworski. He announced that he would comply with the Court of Appeals' order on the subpoenaed tapes, although he continued to fight against turning over others.

"Christ, Charlie," I moaned, "we're on our third set of prosecutors. I can't tell whether we're going backward or forward."

"Look on the bright side," Charlie advised. "If Jaworski goes down the tube, we'll just get another one, by God! Same disease, same medicine! Nixon's getting eaten alive."

November 16, 1973

During one of my frequent meetings with staff members in the Special Prosecutor's office, I inquired about Jaworski.

"It's still too soon to tell, but Leon seems all right so far," said Ben-Veniste.

"We're keeping an eye on him," echoed Jill Vollner. "We guarantee you we won't keep quiet if he walks away from this thing."

January 16, 1974

"Who do you think erased the tape?" Jill Volner asked.

I was reading the report of the technical experts on the

430

eighteen-and-a-half-minute gap that had been discovered in the tape of the President's conversation with Haldeman on June 20, 1972; they had concluded that the gap was the result of five separate and intentional erasures.

"Somebody who is not very good mechanically," I answered.

"Like?"

"Maybe someone I know who had trouble taking the top off his fountain pen, or somebody who hasn't driven a car in years..."

"Yeah, but how do I prove it? I couldn't break Rose Woods, even if she knows anything."

February 13, 1974

Ben-Veniste's office was crowded with the other members of the Watergate Task Force: Jill Vollner, George Frampton, and Peter Rient. A chair had been placed in front of Rick's desk for me, and another chair sat ostentatiously empty. Rick explained.

"We've invited Leon to sit in on this meeting," he said smugly. "He's got to go down to court tomorrow and vouch for your credibility."

"I thought we were going to go over my conversations with the President for my grand-jury appearance tomorrow," I said.

"Well, we are. But since Leon has never really dealt with you, he thought he ought to sit in as we go over this material."

"Fine with me."

Rick was grinning. "We want to show Leon how a prosecutor operates. You can give us a few of your 'I don't recalls' to show him we don't push you around."

"We want him to see your credibility for himself," Frampton added in a more serious tone.

"I'll be happy to perform for him," I said sportingly.

"After this show, you can vouch for Leon's credibility in vouching for your credibility," Jill cracked as the telephone rang. It was Jaworski's secretary. He was tied up, but we were invited to his office when we'd finished. The prosecutors mumbled their disappointment. It was clear from their remarks that, while they trusted Leon, they didn't think he understood what was happening.

Special Prosecutor Jaworski's office was almost bare, certainly not furnished to the standard of his Texas law-firm offices. Rick, unaware that Jaworski and I knew each other, began to introduce us. Jaworski stopped him and came around from behind his desk to greet me.

"I haven't seen you since I was in your office at the White House," he said with a smile, extending his hand. When he was president of the American Bar Association Jaworski had visited me to argue against the nomination of Congressman Richard Poff to the Supreme Court; on another occasion he had come to lobby against no-fault auto insurance, which took business away from trial lawyers.

Adjusting the vest of his three-piece suit, Jaworski helped Jill with her chair and then seated himself. "I've managed to get myself dragged into this fight with the White House over your credibility," he said. "Judge Gesell wants me in his courtroom tomorrow because of my statement on the television that you were a very believable and credible witness."

"I want to thank you for your support," I replied.

"Well, I felt I should. I'd said the exact same thing in court. Those reporters on the TV show were really grilling me, so I thought I might as well say it there. I don't think it was fair of St. Clair to jump on me over that statement." The statement

432

had resulted in a motion by Dwight Chapin's attorney to dismiss the case against Chapin in Judge Gerhard Gesell's courtroom, and it had brought Jaworski a public blast from the President's lawyer, James D. St. Clair of Boston.

"I thought you were very careful in not going beyond what you'd said in court," Jill added, in a tone and manner that recalled to me how I used to try to please the boss.

"Thank you, Jill." Jaworski smiled graciously. "I think the judge will understand it when I explain. I had a long-standing commitment to be on that show."

"I've heard St. Clair is a pretty good lawyer," I said. "Is he?"

Jaworski let my question pass. "The *Los Angeles Times* hit him hard for criticizing me. And his very own *Boston Globe* lambasted him. Even his home-town newspaper didn't like it." He repeated that several times.

"So St. Clair isn't as good as they say?" I asked.

"Jim is in an impossible position over there. Buzhardt listens to all the tapes, knows all the problems."

"So Buzhardt's still running the show?"

"Yes, sir. In all the meetings I've attended over there, Buzhardt has made the decisions. He just blurts them out, and St. Clair goes along whether he agrees or not. I don't think St. Clair knows what he's supposed to be doing." Jaworski shook his head with pity for St. Clair's fix.

"Well, Buzhardt got there first and learned the ropes," I suggested. Jaworski nodded his agreement.

"I told those people over at the White House not to try to destroy you," he continued. "I told them they were asking for trouble with me, and I feel I made the point very strongly. I raised this with someone above Buzhardt, and—"

433

"Haig?" I interrupted. General Alexander M. Haig, Jr., had replaced Haldeman as White House chief of staff.

"I'd rather not say, but I went to the top." This confirmed my feeling that it must be Haig. "I'll tell you this," Jaworski said. "He assured me he was personally not involved in those efforts. I think I did some good in raising this matter with them. We'll see."

He sat thinking about what he had just said. Then he assumed a rather formal pose, as if he were sitting for a portrait, and told a story in his best Texas drawl. "Last Sunday I went to the Presbyterian church up on New York Avenue. It's convenient to where I stay in Washington. As I went in for the service, I stopped to say hello to the deacon, who was greeting people at the front door. The deacon stopped me and said, 'Mr. Jaworski, President Nixon is coming this morning.' I told the deacon that was fine and went along to my seat. I opened my program and saw that the sermon was on 'Moral Courage,' which made me chuckle to myself." Jaworski paused. But before going on, he erased the smile from his face and slowly shook his head. "During the service I prayed to rid myself of hate. Hate's one of those evil things we've learned," he said squeezing his eyes tightly and shaking his head hard, as if dispelling evil from his mind.

He relaxed. "When the minister began his sermon he was very nervous, and he had a rough time getting it together for about ten minutes. But once he got going it was a good sermon. I guess he was worried about what he had to say with the President there. Anyway, I kept thinking if the President only had the moral courage to admit his wrongs, this thing wouldn't have gone as far as it has."

Amen. We all agreed, and the conversation rambled on about the tapes, my grand-jury appearance, his able staff, my memory. Finally Jill said she had to get back to work, and the meeting ended. On the way back to Rick's office, I asked him whether Jaworski often used hip phrases like "getting it together." Rick only rolled his eyes. I asked whether Jaworski would permit the grand jury to indict President Nixon.

"What do you think?" Rick retorted.

"No."

He smiled. "You know I can't discuss that with you, but you've got a pretty good batting average for predicting what'll happen."

February 14, 1974

The deputy United States marshal stood near attention in front of the door to the grand-jury room. Usually he dozed in the chair beside the door. Something was happening inside. After about ten minutes, Jaworski emerged and nodded a greeting, but walked quickly by. Shortly, I learned what had happened. He had been concerned that the testimony I was to give concerning the President would precipitate the grand jurors into hasty action—a runaway grand jury, out of the Special Prosecutor's control, that would indict a sitting President.[*]

March 9, 1974

"I think you ought to have protection again," Charlie said.

"Why? Have you heard more threats?" I asked.

"Not directly. I don't believe in that fortunetelling crap. But some woman who claims she's never been wrong, which I

---

[*] [Original Footnote:] There had been an intense debate in the Special Prosecutor's office. Jaworski was convinced that such action was unconstitutional. Finally he persuaded the jurors to name Richard Nixon as an unindicted co-conspirator, along with Haldeman, Ehrlichman, Mitchell, Strachan, Colson, Mardian, and Parkinson, who were indicted.

doubt, wrote a letter to her senator telling him that your life is in serious danger. I don't have the details, but I talked with the fellows down in the Special Prosecutor's office. They would like you to have some protection, too, because you're going to be back in the public eye when you testify in the Mitchell-Stans trial in New York and the Chapin trial." *

"Do you really think it's necessary? It's a hell of a note having a couple of marshals around all the time."

"I do. Otherwise I wouldn't suggest it."

When I flew back to New York for the Mitchell-Stans trial, I was met by two deputy marshals. A protective detail was assigned to me in New York, Washington, and California. For the next six months, two marshals were with me wherever I went: out to dinner with Mo, to the supermarket, to courtrooms and hearing rooms, even to men's rooms.

April 4, 1974

"Excuse me, John," the deputy marshal said, "there's a girl at the door who'd like to talk with you."

"Who is she?" Mo and I had sold our house, and I was packing for the move to California. "Is she with the press?"

"I don't think so. I've never seen her before, and I know most of those press people. I should have asked, but I figured she must know you."

---

* [Original Footnote:] On May 10, 1973, John Mitchell and Maurice Stans were indicted by a federal grand jury in New York for conspiring to obstruct justice and for perjury in relation to a $200,000 campaign contribution from financier Robert Vesco. Later they were acquitted on all charges. On November 29, 1973, Dwight Chapin was indicted for lying to the Watergate grand jury about his knowledge of Donald Segretti's political sabotage activities in the 1972 campaign. He was found guilty and went to prison.

I went down to the front door, where an attractive dark-haired woman whom I didn't recognize was standing silently. Another deputy stood guard. As I approached, she became visibly nervous and began biting her lower lip.

"Can I help you?" I asked.

She seemed stunned. Her eyes blinked, and she could not get out whatever it was she wanted to say. Finally she asked me haltingly, "Are you my mummy?"

"I beg your pardon?"

"Are you my mummy?" she repeated.

What in hell was she talking about? She looked perfectly normal, but she was either crazy or putting me on. I wasn't sure. I answered politely, "I'm sorry, you must have the wrong house."

"No, I don't," she said, slightly peevish, then turned and walked away.

The deputy marshals didn't like what they'd just heard and seen. They followed her. She got into a late-model car and drove away. It was too dark to get her license number. They were agitated. "John, you've got to watch out for the nuts like her," one said. And for a few weeks the marshals tightened security. Such weird episodes dotted the months ahead.

April 15, 1974

"Have you seen this, John?" asked the assistant U.S. attorney excitedly. I was in New York preparing for my testimony in the Robert Vesco influence-peddling case against Mitchell and Stans. The prosecutor handed me a newspaper, which was opened to an article on the latest Harris poll. Harris had sampled public opinion about the conflicts between my Watergate statements and President Nixon's. Overall, he found

437

twenty-nine percent support for the President, forty-six percent for me, with the rest undecided.

"Very interesting," I murmured, trying to appear nonchalant. I was noting the breakdown. The President scored highest among Southeners, while I ran away with Jews and young adults.

"Interesting?" he exclaimed. "I think it's fantastic! Hell, you're more credible than the President of the United States! This makes me think you're going to be a better witness than I thought you were going to be. I sure wish I could figure out some way to slip this in on the jury."

My ego was getting a welcome boost.

April 25-27, 1974

Three days spent in Jaworski's office listening to the White House tapes for the first time. I sat down in front of the recorder, put the cushioned earphones on, and closed my eyes. I could see the meetings in my mind; the tapes provided the sound track. My senses synchronized, I floated back through time.

I felt excitement and anger as I listened, but the prevailing feeling was a fierce kind of embarrassment. It reminded me of being a teenager, when the thought of last month's wisecrack made me shudder at how childish and out of style I'd been. I winced when I heard myself brown-nosing the President on September 15, and I was shamed by my weakness in the March meetings.

Several lawyers in the Special Prosecutor's office seemed baffled that I didn't get more of a charge out of the experience.

April 28, 1974

"I guess you've heard," sighed the Southern District prosecutor. He was calling from New York, where the jury had just found Mitchell and Stans not guilty.

"Yeah, it's on the radio down here," I groused. "They're playing me up big. They say the jury obviously didn't believe Dean, star witness. Goddammit, I don't know why they call me the star witness. I hardly knew anything about that damn case."

"Well, for what it's worth, we feel worse than you do," the prosecutor replied. "It's hard to take. The thing is, these juries are used to cops and judges getting cash under the table. We figure the jurors were impressed that Mitchell and Stans put Vesco's money in the campaign instead of in their own pockets. Anyway, we're sorry it didn't work out, John. I hope it doesn't hurt you too much."

"Thanks. I understand." But I didn't. The press had made me the star witness, which I wasn't. Now they were saying that no one believed me.

Once again, the reporters and camera crews staked out my house.

April 29, 1974

I had long ago learned to expect an unpleasant time whenever the President went on television about Watergate, but his speech when he released the edited transcripts of his tapes was the worst yet. It was especially infuriating since I'd just listened to the tapes themselves and knew how phony his version was. I didn't know that I was reaching the apogee of my anger toward him, but I felt I was getting near it. I smirked at the huge display he made of the transcripts, gagged on his quotations from Lincoln, and seethed at his personal attacks on

439

me: "John Dean charged in sworn Senate testimony that I was fully aware of the cover-up at the time of our first meeting on September 15, 1972. These transcripts show clearly that I first learned of it when Mr. Dean himself told me about it in this office on March 21, some six months later. His revelations to me on March 21 were a sharp surprise, even though the report he gave to me was far from complete, especially since he did not reveal at that time the extent of his own criminal involvement..."

June 27, 1974

"You know, I ran into one of your old friends the other day," I told Jim Neal during a break in our session.

I was in Neal's Nashville law office, along with Charlie and Rick Ben-Veniste. The meeting was tense. I knew Rick resented the fact that Neal had agreed to come back to the Special Prosecutor's office and take back the reins of the cover-up case. And I resented having had to come all the way across the country just because Neal was worried that James St. Clair might ruin me as a witness during my upcoming testimony before the House impeachment inquiry.

"Oh, yeah?" Neal drawled, seeming pleased to get into small talk. "Who's that?"

"Jimmy Hoffa," I said. "I've been giving depositions in his suit against the government over his conditional pardon, and he showed up. It was a pretty weird deposition, I'll tell you. Hoffa's lawyer is Leonard Boudin, the guy who defended Ellsberg and the Chicago Seven. They're quite a pair."

"Good ole Jimmy Hoffa." Neal laughed, glancing at Charlie. "God, we had fun with him, didn't we, Shaffer? Well, John, when you see Jimmy again, you just tell him I said hello. And you remind him that you're a good friend of mine and that

440

your lawyer is Charlie Shaffer. And I tell you what he might do. He might have his hands around your throat in about two seconds."

"Well, I guess I won't mention your name if you don't mind," I replied as Neal and Charlie chuckled over the good old days.

"I'll never forget how Jimmy used to come into court," Neal said. "He'd look over every morning and smile and nod good morning to me like I was his best friend. He'd have on that sweet face for everybody in the courtroom. And I'd look over at him and see his hands under the table. He'd be giving me the finger, just jabbing away as fast and furious as he could. Damn, he's too much."

July 11, 1974

After a week and a half of twelve-hour days reviewing my testimony, I appeared before the impeachment committee. It was almost like old home week for me. I was back at the House Judiciary Committee, where I'd had my first government job nine years earlier as chief Republican counsel. Some of the same congressmen and staff were still there, and we joked about how times change.

The testimony was an anticlimax. St. Clair, who had let it be known that he was eager to confront me for the first time, seemed tired, unprepared, and confused about facts and sequence. I felt a new confidence in handling him.[*]

---

[*]   [Original Footnote by Editor:] St. Clair committed a grievous error at the beginning of his examination of Dean. Quoting from Dean's testimony before the Ervin Committee that "the money matter was left very much hanging" in the March 21 meeting in the Oval Office, St. Clair suggested aggressively that Dean himself had removed the President from the chain of events that had led to a payment that same day to Hunt. In fact, as Dean at once made clear, his testimony had referred to a discussion at

441

Mid-July 1974

Charlie demolished my lighter mood with the news that Judge Sirica planned to sentence me, and might send me to prison, before the cover-up trial began.

August 2, 1974

As I entered the courtroom, the clerk was announcing, "The Case of the United States versus John W. Dean. Criminal Number 886-73. Mr. James Neal for the government; Mr. Charles Shaffer for the defendant." The chamber was filled with reporters; their faces were indistinct blurs to me. In fact, no one except Charlie seemed to have a human face. I was numb, the people seemed like machines, the sounds were far away, like echoes. Everyone was a prop, stereotyped for his role. The gravel voiced clerk was straight from Central Casting.

---

that same meeting of an eventual million dollars that might be needed to pay off all the Watergate burglars, and that payment of Hunt's demand of an immediate $120,000 had been authorized by the President. Seventy-five thousand dollars was paid Hunt that very day. St. Clair continued to demonstrate his confusion about sequence and previous testimony. Firmly corrected several times by Dean, he resorted to tactics that led several members of the committee to object that he was browbeating the witness. Finally, demoralized, he relinquished his witness to the members of the committee, and the potential "classic battle between a great cross-examiner and a great witness," as Bob Woodward and Carl Bernstein characterized the White House's hopes, never materialized. St. Clair's failure marked the end of the Administration's chance to break Dean as a witness.

     Author's Note: Because it seemed too self-serving at the time I was writing *Blind Ambition*, I excluded what members of Congress present for my testimony best recall. At one point there was an interruption in the cross-examination, and when it resumed St. Clair could not recall his questions. I could, almost verbatim, and when I recited it back I pretty much eviscerated St. Clair's efforts to impugn my memory.

Judge Sirica was grave. "Mr. Shaffer, you have a motion pending. I will hear the motion first."

Charlie went to the lectern and argued for a postponement of sentencing until the judge could have an opportunity to hear the new batch of tapes that the Supreme Court had just ordered the President to surrender. It was a long shot. We hoped Sirica would grow more lenient toward me with each tape he heard.

Charlie had barely begun to speak when the judge interrupted him testily. The motion was soon denied. Charlie eased back helplessly.

"Mr. Dean, will you step up here," Sirica commanded. I walked forward. "I ask you, Mr. Dean, if you wish to make a statement. I will listen to anything you have to say." He gazed at me sternly.

I had thought about my final words for weeks, written long drafts, rehearsed mentally, and had finally decided that there was nothing I could add that would make any difference. I knew that my sentence was already typed neatly on the paper in the judge's hand.

I felt my knees tremble, but I was surprised to hear my voice sounding quite even and natural. "Your honor, I've just a few words as I stand here at the mercy of the court. The only thing I would ask for is your compassion and understanding." Okay, John, that's enough begging. Now tell him you know you're a criminal. "I came in here last October nineteenth and admitted my guilt. I have done wrong. I realize the wrong I have done. What bothers me most is I was involved in corruption of government and misuse of high office. Realizing to say I'm sorry is really not enough, I have tried for about the last eighteen months to do everything I can to right the wrongs." I stopped. End it. The judge is in a hurry. "And regardless of how this court judges me, I will continue on the same course. Thank you."

Sirica put his glasses on and began reading from the paper in front of him. "In Criminal Case Number 886-73, the court sentences the defendant to be incarcerated for a period of not less than one year nor more than four years in an institution to be..."

Reporters fell over each other running for the doors, and it seemed to me that I heard each comment, each footstep, each piece of shuffled paper. It was as if someone else were being sentenced. Numbers: one and four. I must hear the rest of what Sirica had to say. Maybe he would suspend sentence. But the judge had stopped because of the din. The clerk rapped loudly with his fist on the side of the jury box and called for order.

Sirica continued, "The court will recommend that the defendant serve his sentence in a federal minimum-security institution such as Allenwood, Pennsylvania; Danbury, Connecticut; or Lompoc, which I understand is in Southern California; or in some similar institution...

"As I indicated," Judge Sirica said as he took off his glasses, "the court will grant the defendant until September third, Tuesday, September third, to get his personal affairs in order, at which time he will surrender himself to the United States marshal..."

The judge left the bench, and the courtroom emptied as if there were an air raid. A deputy marshal led me and Charlie through a back door. Charlie asked if I could use a telephone to call my wife. I felt the way I had once after crashing in a small airplane—my mind was racing to figure out what was happening, not realizing that I was in shock.

I collapsed into a chair. "Wait a minute, Charlie. I can't call Mo yet." I was absorbing Sirica's words. "He threw the book at me! The most he could have given me was five years, and he gave me four. Why'd he do that?"

444

"I don't understand it," Charlie said, over and over. He paced the room. "This is my fault, John. I should never have let you plead to Sirica. I'm sorry. I didn't know. I don't understand." Charlie was as shaken by the sentence as if it were his own.

"How can he do that?" I asked plaintively. "I figured I'd get something like Krogh—six to eighteen months, maybe a year at the most. He hit me harder than Magruder. Even Colson didn't get the sentence I got. It can't be, Charlie."

"You've got to be realistic, John," he said. "You've got to realize that you're going to be in jail for a year or two years or maybe three. We've got to be realistic."

"I can't tell Mo that, Charlie. It would kill her."

He stopped pacing, and we exchanged desperate looks. "Listen," Charlie said, "we've got ninety days from today to file a motion for reduction of sentence. Maybe the bastard will reconsider. He knows you're the key witness in the cover-up trial."

With this thread of hope, I called Mo. I misdialed our home number twice. Neither my hands nor my head was working. Finally I got through.

"Sweetheart—"

"How could he do that?" Mo shrieked hysterically. She was sobbing, out of control. It was less than ten minutes since Sirica had pronounced sentence, but Mo had already heard the flash bulletin on the radio in California.

"Wait a minute," I begged. "Wait a minute." Then I raised my voice to try to get through louder than her crying. Conversation was impossible. "It's not as bad as it sounds. We've got ninety days to file a motion to reduce sentence, and Charlie is optimistic..."

"Oh my God, John! How can he do that?"

445

It was useless to talk. "It's going to be all right, swee-theart," I shouted. "I'll talk to you about it when I get home." I hung up. Charlie was looking away.

Deputy Marshal Bud McPherson, still in charge of protecting me, came into the office. He expressed sympathy and warned that an army of reporters was hunting me down. We left Charlie and fled down Judge Sirica's back elevator into the basement garage. Bud drove out at top speed, almost running over a camera crew, and we headed toward Virginia to hide until it was time for my flight to California. Within blocks of the courthouse, Bud realized we were being followed by two men on motorcycles. They were press scouts, equipped with radios. Bud tried to lose them as he sped toward the U.S. marshal's office in Alexandria. He parked the car conspicuous-ly on the street, and we ran into the office. We hoped to duck out the back into another car before the scouts could summon the other reporters.

CBS correspondent Leslie Stahl's car screeched to a halt near the scouts just as we were leaving. The Alexandria deputies delayed her, and we made our escape.

The chase distracted me from thinking about my sentence. We holed up in Pete Kinsey's house and plotted how to get out of Washington without being caught at the airport. We couldn't take our scheduled flight from Dulles Airport, because reporters would be covering all direct flights to California. Bud booked passage on a flight from National Airport to Chicago, with connections to California. I was ticketed under the alias "John West," and, with some stealth, we made our way undetected to National. A half-dozen reporters waited all evening at Dulles and then raised hell with airline officials who they believed had boarded me secretly.

August 8, 1974

With jail approaching, it was time to put some things in order. I worked on our family finances, made out a new will, and had four wisdom teeth removed. Pumped full of painkiller, my cheeks swollen and blue, I watched Richard Nixon's resignation speech on television. Through most of the speech I felt pangs of sympathy for him, which I fought to suppress because I thought they were vestiges of my old loyalty. By the time he had finished, my pity had given way to dismay. He never admitted a damn thing, I thought. He went out with a campaign speech. Oh, well, I thought, at least he's consistent, but why? Why is he taking Watergate with him?

I went to sleep trying to figure it out. The cover-up had been a stupid error. Lying about it had been deadly for him. It was over now. He'd been caught in his lies, so why didn't he confess? Was he really far wiser and shrewder than most would give him credit for? Would history say he'd been unfairly forced from office? Was he planting seeds of doubt? Or did he fear prosecution and jail?

I didn't know, but I found comfort in the fact that he himself had caused his demise. Not I.

Late August 1974

"You're not going to like this," said Charlie uneasily. He was calling from Washington. "The prosecutors want you back here to start getting ready to testify in the cover-up trial. They want to ask you a few thousand questions."

I was livid. "Goddammit, you tell them to go to hell! Those bastards haven't done a damn thing to help me, and I've busted my ass helping them. I can't believe their nerve, Charlie. Here I am staring at four years in prison, and I'm not about to give them my last few days of freedom."

447

"As your attorney, I advise you to calm down," Charlie quipped, trying to take the sting out for me. "Listen, you've got to realize they can do anything they want to you. Start thinking of yourself as a prisoner. You have to. And what a prisoner worries about is when he will get out, not when he goes in. Let's face it, John. Those prosecutors are going to make a recommendation to Sirica on your motion to reduce, and you can't afford not to cooperate with them."

"Charlie, I know all that stuff as well as you do," I retorted irritably. "But I'm tired of sucking up to people. Don't those bastards know I'm going to jail? I can't keep churning this Watergate crap out. I'm tired of turning my head on and off like a light bulb."

"I tell you what," Charlie sighed. "I'll call Neal and play the violin for him, but I don't think it will do any good."

"Thanks. Give it a try. Tell him I'll have a lot of time to work on my testimony as soon as they send me up the river," I closed bitterly.

It didn't work, and I returned to Washington early.

August 29, 1974

"How do you feel, Brother Dean?" Neal drawled when I arrived at his office, which was filled with cigar smoke.

"Okay, I guess, under the circumstances," I said, trying to suppress my resentment. It was the first time I had seen Neal since the sentencing. I didn't trust him, and he knew it. And we had a long way to go together.

"For what it's worth, I want you to know I think Sirica hit you too hard," he said, seeking to warm me up. I nodded my agreement warily. "We wrote an eighteen-page letter for you and filled it with all kinds of facts about how you cooperated with this office and how vital you've been to the case. We only

448

sent a one-page letter on Magruder. But the judge didn't seem to get the message."

I nodded again. "I can't figure it out, Jim. I guess either Sirica just doesn't like me or maybe he believes all that crap the White House put out about how I invented the cover-up and ran it single-handed."

"No, I don't think that's it. He gave you a hefty sentence because he wants to make you a credible witness. I tell you, I think Charlie's going to be in good shape when he files a motion to reduce. He's just got to wait awhile."

I felt a glimmer of appreciation for having been given this hope, but I was still too uncertain of Neat to show any gratitude. He seemed to notice my withdrawal, and a long, uncomfortable pause ensued, during which he lit a fresh cigar.

"John, you and I've got to understand each other," he said finally. "You're going to be my witness on the stand. I've got to get you ready, and you've got to get me ready. You're going to be the first witness for the government. Boom—right out of the box pops ole John Dean.

"You'll lay out the whole case for us, and the tapes and the other witnesses will come in to corroborate your testimony. You're it, Big John."

I smiled at the flattery and remained silent. Neal seemed to be regrouping for another charge, when Larry Iason walked in. He was one of Neal's staff lawyers with whom I'd become friendly. When he expressed his regrets about my sentence, I knew he meant it.

I saw Jeb Magruder strolling down the hall. He was in from Allenwood Prison for trial preparation, and he gave me a thumbs-up sign and a weak smile as he passed by. Iason left, and Neal resumed his courtship.

"I'll tell you something," he said. "Sirica hurt us too when he stuck you." Neal shook his head sadly, took the cigar from his mouth and contemplated the chewed end. "He really hurt us."

"What do you mean? I thought you said my sentence would make me a credible witness."

"Well, it's a long story. A very long story. We've got to get to work now." Neal didn't want to tell me what was on his mind, he was caught up in his own thoughts. He started pacing around his office, lawyer style. "Hell, I'll tell you why," he blurted. "Why shouldn't I? Bill Hundley, Mitchell's lawyer, was in here feeling out a guilty plea for his man when you were sentenced. I think I could have gotten Mitchell to plead if Sirica hadn't hit you so hard. I could feel it. But when you got one-to-four, they figured they'd get worse. So they decided to take their chance with a trial."

"Interesting. I had no idea Mitchell might do that," I commented with understatement. I was surprised both by the revelation and by Neal's candor. After a pause I said, "I saw Jeb out in the hall just now. How's he taking prison?"

Neal looked disgusted. "I'll be honest with you. He's a crybaby. All he does is bitch, bitch, bitch. I don't like him very well. Any man who slants his testimony to satisfy a prosecutor is weak, and I don't have much respect for your friend Jeb."

I had already known that Jeb's testimony had vexed the prosecutors; Jill Vollner had complained often about his eagerness to tailor his story to the prosecutors' needs. But I was struck again by Neal's frankness. His judgment was harsh but understandable, and it seemed to come more from disappointment than from malice. This guy doesn't pull his punches, I thought. He's a pro who thinks about sending people to jail the way I used to think about sending off a memo. I was beginning to see why Charlie and Neal were such good friends: they both acted out a flinty, free-swinging role, but there was much more underneath it. Neal was winning me over.

450

"I hope I can deliver for you as a witness, Jim, but I want to be straight with you about it. I don't know how I'm going to adjust to prison. I'm no Gordon Liddy, and testifying is a bitch. I'm going to miss all those Scotch-and-waters."

"Ah, you'll do fine," Neal said, waving his hand as he headed toward his desk. "I'll put you in a motel room with a bottle of Scotch every night if I have to. Lubricate your memory. We have a very flexible prison system." He was grinning. "I'm not worried about ole John Dean. Let's get to work."

"It's your wife," Neal said as he handed me the phone. "Tell her you're behaving. I'm willing to vouch for you."

"When are you coming home, John?" asked Mo. "You've been there all day."

"I can't answer your question, dear, but I'm sure prosecutor Neal knows he's cutting into our time together. Hold on, and I'll check with him." I was speaking loudly so that Neal could hear. "How much longer are we going to work tonight?" I asked him. I held the receiver toward him so that Mo could hear his answer.

"Eight or nine o'clock!" he boomed. "But tell her I'll spend more time away from my wife in the next year than you will."

I put the phone back to my ear. "That creep," said Mo. "How about the weekend?"

"No problem. Prosecutor Neal tells me he's in a tennis tournament back in Nashville this weekend."

"I hope he loses," she said.

When I turned back to Neal he was unconsciously studying his reflection in the windows of his bookcase. Vanity, I thought. He emerged from his reverie and grinned at me. "I'm going to win that tennis tournament," he declared. "I'm one of those little guys who's insecure, so I like to get into tourna-

451

ments with big guys and whip 'em." I smiled at him, thinking how like Jim Neal was to a bantam rooster. I liked him, despite my vicious thoughts of a few hours earlier.

September 2, 1974

Charlie worried that his office doors were open. This was Labor Day, my last day of freedom, and he was still trying to find out where I would be imprisoned. The officials were giving evasive answers. They had merely hinted that I would be put in an abandoned missile site outside Washington. Charlie was expressing his displeasure over the confusion forcefully, but he was distracted by his unlocked doors. He was worried about break-ins and wiretaps.

"I'm going to have a look around," he said, and he walked out the door. Deputy Marshal Bud McPherson waited in the office and watched as Charlie nodded politely to a man walking by on the sidewalk. A few minutes went by.

"You're under arrest!" Charlie thundered. Bud ran to the door. Charlie was crouched like a wrestler in front of a man he'd noticed before. The man was carrying a batch of office equipment under his arm. The veins were standing out in Charlie's neck. "Don't move!" he shouted. "You're under arrest!"

"You can't arrest me," Charlie's suspect sniffed with calm indignation. "Who are you, anyway?"

"That's my office," said Charlie, pointing to the building, "and that's my partner's Dictaphone," pointing to the machine the man was carrying. "I'm making a citizen's arrest!"

The suspect tensed visibly. "You haven't got the power to arrest me."

Charlie shrugged and backed off a few steps. "You're going to be mighty surprised, friend," he drawled amiably,

452

"'cause there's a thirty-eight revolver about seven inches behind your head." Charlie looked thoughtful, then: "Maybe ten inches."

The suspect rotated slowly so as to keep an eye on Charlie, but he was shortly staring down the barrel of McPherson's gun. Bud was in the classic arrest pose, knees bent slightly, feet spread, arms stretched out, both hands steadying the gun. The suspect went pale and limp as sheets in a laundry bin. Later he pleaded guilty to breaking and entering.

September 3, 1974

"John, you're not going to like this, but there's been a change in the plan," Bud McPherson said grimly. He and Terry Walters, his partner, had been protecting me for six months. Their last assignment was to deliver me to prison.

"What's happening now?"

"Well, Marshal McKinney says you have to surrender to his office instead of the Special Prosecutor's office. He ordered us to bring you in to him at the courthouse."

"Goddam, Bud, I don't want to do that. Can we go in the backdoor?"

"Yeah, I think so. We're supposed to rendezvous with two of McKinney's deputies at DuPont Circle. They're making a big deal out of this."

"More bad news," Bud said later as he climbed back into the car at the rendezvous. "Those guys say we have to follow them right to the front door. They won't let us go in the back."

"Oh, no," I moaned. "I don't like any of this. Why do we have to follow those bastards? Can't we just slip in the back when we get there?"

"Afraid not," Terry lamented. "We're from the L.A. office,

453

and we're in McKinney's jurisdiction. He's like the Sheriff of Nottingham in his territory. We can't buck him."

I slumped down in the seat, hiding behind my sunglasses. There was a lump in my throat. My mind was brimming with memories of my leave taking from Mo just a few minutes earlier. A hug and a brief kiss, as if I were going to the office. I couldn't have made it through anything more intimate. I was already daydreaming, I realized, living in memories. Like a prisoner.

"Oh, shit!" cried Bud. "Look at that!"

I snapped up and looked out the window. Several dozen reporters were milling in front of the courthouse. "I knew it," I said. "I'll give you a hundred to one McKinney tipped them off. No wonder he's making sure we go in the front door."

"It figures," said Terry. "His men up ahead have got on their Sunday duds."

"Keep your chin up, John," Bud encouraged. "Let's go. We'll fight our way through."

The horde surrounded us before we could get out of the car. Questions came at me one on top of the other: "What's your reaction to Nixon's resignation?" "You've been vindicated as President Nixon's chief accuser. Any comment?" "How do you feel about going to jail?" I forced a smile and muttered, "No comment." McKinney's men were cheerfully official; I thought they lingered a bit before the cameras. Bud and Terry made a flying wedge for me all the way to McKinney's office, where the District of Columbia marshal was waiting proudly.

"Good work," he said. "You're right on time." He accepted my surrender formally. It took all my willpower to control my temper. But I was McKinney's prisoner, and he could make life difficult for me.

I was spreadeagled against the wall in the cellblock beneath the courthouse, frisked, fingerprinted, and then posed for mug shots. Down the hall into a cell. A huge door clanged shut behind me. "The slammer." Just like the movies. I turned around in panic and looked back at sixteen feet of greenish iron bars.

Only a few minutes—I was talking fast to myself—then I'll be taken to some "safe house" jail. Don't count on it, I cautioned myself. I hadn't counted on this, surrendering at the courthouse and being locked in its basement cellblock, and I still didn't know where I was going, or when. I was learning.

There wasn't much to inspect in the cell. Iron bars, three very solid tile walls, a toilet with no seat, a sink high enough so that prisoners couldn't urinate in it, and a long steel bench. It was clean. I sat down on the bench and read the graffiti. There was no window. I glanced at my watch. I had been there ten minutes. I thought about time. Chunks of it. Ticking sounds of it. Vast clouds of it. Circles, infinite numbers, endless waves.

One of my jailers came to check on me. He handed me the sports section of the *Washington Post* and left. I tried to read. Suddenly, I felt it coming. My pulse began racing. I tried to breathe deeply to relax, but that seemed to make it worse. The stale musty air coming into my lungs was so stifling that I tried to forget about breathing. The room was closing in. Claustrophobia. I kept telling myself I'd always been able to suppress it. I walked around the cell several times. That helped some. I forced myself to read the paper.

The deputy returned with a chair and sat down outside my cell. "Damn hot today," he observed.

"Sure is." I was glad he was there. But I was annoyed that he thought he could just talk at me.

"You remember me?"

I gave a weak nod.

"Up in Connecticut," he prodded. "The big demonstration

455

at Yale."

"Oh, sure." The memory pushed the claustrophobia back a few degrees. He and I had shot the bull one afternoon back in 1970 when I was covering a pro-Bobby Seale demonstration for the Justice Department.

He wanted to reminisce, but I was spent and nauseated. I went over to the tall sink, cupped my hand under the spigot, but there was no water. The deputy brought me a cup of ice water from the cooler. Then he lectured me about how President Ford had vetoed a pay hike for the Marshal's Service. I said enough to keep the conversation going. Each time I glanced at him one of his eyes was cut off by a cell bar. It was disconcerting at first, but then I found a game in it: I would look around the cell quickly and try to guess which of his eyes I would see when I turned back. I was batting just over .500 when he left.

"Hey, Joe! Bring him out!" A guard's yell echoed down the cellblock, and soon my door was rattling open. I was escorted out of the courthouse basement and into a car by more marshals.

"Where are we going?" I asked.

"Fort Holabird."

The Marshal's Service ran a small prison at Fort Holabird, near Baltimore; it was used mainly for Mafia witnesses with contracts on their heads. Magruder, Colson, and Kalmbach had been transferred there in preparation for the cover-up trial. I was surprised to be joining them. Neal had told me I wouldn't be, because he was worried that the defense lawyers might charge us with concocting false testimony if we were together. I hadn't talked with my old colleagues for nearly a year and a half, and I presumed none of them would be happy to see me. My apprehension was overshadowed by relief. Two hours in the cellblock had felt like an eternity. It was a bad omen.

"Dean, I'm the site supervisor," announced a frail, colorless

456

man with a surprisingly strong voice. He avoided looking at me and sat fidgeting at his desk, appearing uncertain about what to say. "We're crowded here," he said. "This is a small place. We can barely handle the twenty-one men who are here, so we have rules that must be followed." He paused again, and then something else jumped into his mind. "Listen, Dean. I don't want you signing a lot of autographs around here. Understand?"

"Yes, sir," I replied. I was bemused and disoriented. The idea of autographs in prison was to baffle me until deputies started asking me to sign copies of Magruder's book; he sold them to all takers.

"Good," the supervisor said. "Now, if everyone follows the rules here, we all get along pretty well. You will be treated fairly. All the men are called 'principals,' not prisoners. Understand? This is a special facility. It's no hard-core prison. All principals are allowed two personal phone calls every week. Collect only. They have to be placed by the supervisor on duty. Understand? Now, you are allowed unlimited calls to and from your lawyer, of course. Your wife is not your lawyer. Don't try to cheat. Okay. Once a week you will be paid a witness fee of eight dollars a day, but half of it goes into our general house fund here for food and supplies. And you are not to keep any of it in your room or on your person. We don't want any trouble, and we've got a lot of fellows in here with sticky fingers. Understand? Just see the supervisor if you want to transfer some money. Okay. Now, the principals are responsible for all cooking, housekeeping, and chores. They assign their own duties. You'll get the hang of it. That's about it. You'll pick up the rest. Understand?"

"Yes, sir." I nodded.

"Now, one other thing. I have been directed by Washington," he declared with emphasis, "that you're to be confined to your quarters and not to talk to anyone here. You will be segregated from the other principals. You will eat your meals in your room, and there will be a deputy posted outside your door at all times. Is that clear?"

"Yes, sir," I replied mechanically. The prosecutors wanted me to have no contact with the other Watergate witnesses. It was just as well.

A deputy took me down to the grimy pit of a kitchen after I'd unpacked the Second World War-vintage supplies in my room, which was in a dilapidated Army barracks. It seemed almost plush after the cellblock.

Kalmbach and Colson appeared, and I eyed them tensely. Then Herb came over, shook my hand firmly, and looked me in the eye. "I'm glad to see you, John." I knew he meant it, and I felt immense relief. Herb had lost weight. I would have thought he looked chipper but his eyes told me otherwise.

"Hi, John," Chuck said nervously. "Would you like to borrow my radio or something?"

"No, thanks. I'm fine, Chuck."

"The food is damn good here." He was making conversation. "We rotate the cooking every day, and some of these fellows are terrific. You'll find beef Stroganoff in the refrigerator from dinner, and I highly recommend it."

"I'll try it, but I'm not too hungry tonight."

"After you get some dinner, I'll take you around and introduce you to some of the men here," Herb said brightly.

"Well, I'm not sure we can do that..." I eyed the deputy next to me. I had already changed my mind about the restrictions on me, feeling miserable that I couldn't talk to Herb and Chuck. They had touched me with their efforts to be friendly. Our old grudges and battles seemed to have happened years ago.

"He can't talk to anybody," announced the deputy, twitching his neck in my direction. "He's on restriction. No contact with the other principals."

"Oh, I see," said Herb with disappointment. I explained the special rules. Herb nodded and then put his hand on my shoulder. "Everything's going to be fine," he said sincerely. "Just fine. Don't worry."

"It doesn't get any better, but you grow used to it," added Chuck.

"Thanks, Chuck," I said. "Thanks." I felt gratitude welling up and I wanted to express it, but I had to keep a grip on myself. I thought about Chuck's last remark. I was loaded down with sensations that were going to take a lot of getting used to. The smell of soured kitchen grease and body odor. The sight of the other principals wearing everything from Bermuda shorts to tailored suits. Thoughts about hoarding my phone calls. An anxiety which I couldn't attach to anything except loss of freedom.

As the deputy and I returned to my room with dinner, we ran into Magruder. "Welcome to the club, John," Jeb said. "This place looks almost like the White House with all of us here." He leaned over and whispered, "But we wouldn't be here if we'd used a few of the guys here to pull off Watergate. They think we're a bunch of amateurs, and they're right. Talk to you later."

"...You motherfucking, cocksucking two-cent bitch! You just wait till I get out of here! Nobody whores around on me with no goddam shit-ass greasers! I'm gonna shoot your ass full of holes and cram your tits down your fucking mouth!..."

It was one of the principals, a Mafia killer, yelling on the prison phone outside my door. I was lying in my bunk, my eyes were rolling around in my head. They felt as big as oranges.

"...What do you expect Richie to do, you stupid slut! He's

459

not gonna give you any dough! How do you think I feel! I've got a goddam fucking hundred-thousand-dollar contract out on me! I'm marked, baby, and so are you..."

For all the rough language I had heard and used in my life, I was still stunned to hear a man talk that way to his wife. The Mafia men tended to have trouble with their "old ladies," who were cut off from the normal financial support the syndicates provided. Holabird was indeed a special prison. It was full of "rats" in big cases. The authorities took elaborate precautions to keep their organized-crime witnesses from being hit in jail. The man on the phone was a tinderbox friendly and humorous one moment, then suddenly maniacal. The deputies tried to keep him pumped full of tranquilizers.

Every sound in the hallway seemed amplified a thousand times, and my mind was racing. Howard Hunt's money demands. My son. Counsel to the President. Nixon going to jail. When the tirade on the phone finally ended, the building quieted down. My ears were then assaulted by a constant squeaking. The deputy posted outside my door was rocking slowly in his chair. I was too intimidated to complain, and I tried to escape by thinking. Then I would see little sparks of light flying about on the inside of my eyelids. Nervous energy. I tried to drive thought from my mind so that I could sleep. When I did, the squeaking returned, as if the deputy's chair were floating toward my head. My thoughts danced around to loud carousel music. The night inched by in a haze.

September 4, 1974

"How you doing?" Neal asked, smiling. "You surviving?"

"I'm okay," I managed, bleary from the ordeal of the previous night. The marshals had returned me to Jim's office.

"You don't look so good," he allowed. "Didn't they treat

460

you right up at Holabird?"

"Well, I'm a little shellshocked. Holabird's no country club, but I'll get used to it. The thing that unglued me yesterday was spending a couple of hours in the slammer down in the courthouse basement. I didn't exactly feel like Jimmy Cagney."

"In the slammer?" Jim exclaimed incredulously. "You're kidding!" He was surprised, and I was surprised that he was surprised.

"No, I'm not kidding. Old Marshal McKinney made Bud and Terry parade me right up to the front door of the courthouse, where he had the press waiting for a big show."

A thundercloud came across Jim's face, and he lurched into his pace around the office.

"Goddammit," he fumed. "This keeps happening. I'm going to have to knock those damn marshals' heads together. First they threw Kalmbach in the county jail in Los Angeles! Then they put Magruder out in the Arlington County Jail—not that I really care where they put him still, they did it, and now you. Goddammit, I'm gonna put a stop to this! I don't want any of my witnesses in jail, 'cause it's gonna rattle the shit out of all you guys! You're not used to it. And until this trial is over I'm not gonna let you get in those hellholes. You've got my word."

"Thanks, Jim," I sighed.

"All right. Now let's get going on the witness book. We've got a long way to go to get you ready."

September 7, 1974

"I used to have trouble reading the Scriptures, too. But I found something that helped me. Start with John in the New Testa-

461

ment. Don't start with Genesis. And get yourself a modern version." It was Chuck Colson talking religion late at night with the deputy outside my door. The deputy was an old man, a Southerner, and he was confiding in Chuck.

"Maybe that'll help, Mr. Colson," he said. "But I don't know. I'm a good, God-fearing Christian, but I've never been able to read the Bible."

"It's hard to get started," Chuck said gently. "It took me forty years. I'll tell you what, though. You can come down to my room and read with me any time you want. Be glad to have you."

"I might just do that, if you don't mind."

There was something real about the new Chuck Colson, I decided after a period of skepticism. He was different, but his faith did not erase his old zest or wit. "Sometimes I don't think there's much ministry for me to do in here," he twinkled one night. "All these Mafia guys say they're already good Catholics."

September 8, 1974

"Boy, have I got some news, good and bad, for you," announced Neal as he swaggered into my working office at the prosecutors' office with Jill Vonner and Larry Iason on his heels. He was trying to look serious, but I saw salty mischief in his face.

"The good part first, please," I said.

Neal put his hands behind his back, rocked in his shoes, looked up at the ceiling, pursed his lips, and then spoke like a town crier: "The former President of the United States, the Honorable Richard Nixon, has announced from San Clemente, California, that you—good ole John Dean—are responsible for the entire Watergate matter. Therefore, President Gerald Ford

462

has seen fit to pardon him for all crimes he may have committed as chief of state." Neal grinned.

"Very funny."

He let out a belly laugh and slapped me on the back in celebration of his performance. "No, no. I'm kidding about what Nixon said, but your wife just called to inform us she heard on the radio that Ford did pardon Nixon. She's damn mad about it. I don't think she likes your old boss."

One glance at Jill and Larry and I knew Jim was serious. "Did he pardon anybody else?" I asked tersely.

"No," Jim growled, the humor draining from his face. "Just the President. The son-of-a-bitch. Presidents are special, you know."

"They sure are," I observed bitterly. "That's what I used to think."

"I can't believe it," sighed Jill. "I really can't believe it. What's happened to justice in this country? I don't see how the citizens will stand for it." Jill paused and looked off. "I wonder if our system is capable of equal justice. This is proof to me it isn't."

"Well, I'll tell you one damn thing," said Jim as Jill's comment hung in the air. "This is going to have one hell of an impact on our trial. Old Jerry has really thrown a monkey wrench in the works."

"I agree," said Jill.

"It's the old empty-chair situation," Jim continued, carried away by his lawyer thoughts. "If I were a defense lawyer in this case, I'd stick a big empty chair in the middle of that courtroom for every juror to see. And I'd point to it every day and make speeches about how my client couldn't get a fair trial because of the absent conspirator, Richard Nixon. The big cheese. The head man. A good lawyer could do wonders with

463

that routine. I can't understand why the hell Ford didn't at least wait until the jury is sequestered." He paused. "But I'll tell you something else. This prosecutor has got him an alibi now."

"What do you mean?" asked Larry.

"If we lose this damn case, it's not our fault. It's Jerry Ford's fault."

Jill looked at me with evident concern. "How do you feel about this, John?"

"Well, I'm not too happy about it," I replied lamely. I looked away, trying to sort out my feelings. One second I felt a surge of anger that Nixon would never have to admit doing anything wrong, and I thought I would be willing to serve an extra month just to see him have to do it. The next second I would swing back: no, I'd rather see Nixon back in the White House if I could trade it for one week off my sentence. I didn't know. "I will say one thing, Jill," I said finally. "I'm sure as hell going to work harder on my testimony. I'll be damned if I'm going to come off as the liar after all this."

"Attaboy!" Jim exclaimed. "Mean John Dean." A new nickname had been born, and "good ole John Dean" began to fade from Jim's vocabulary.

"I guess we all just have to work harder," sighed Larry. Jill agreed. "Well, at least Ford's taken poor Leon off the hook," Jim mused. "I guess Leon is pretty happy he straddled the fence on whether to indict Nixon. He passed the cup to Jerry," he said dramatically as he held out his Styrofoam coffee cup. He paused and then gulped down the coffee. "And Jerry poured it on the floor." Jim grinned and turned the cup upside down.

Mo followed my marshal's car to Holabird from the Special Prosecutor's office, since she didn't know the way. It was our first visiting day, and I had worked late the previous night

464

cleaning my quarters. We rushed into each other's arms. I don't think I had ever felt more emotion, and Mo returned my feelings. We joked about making love in the closet and made nasty faces toward my door. My guard was standing just outside, as always, and he insisted that the door remain open. Rules. Mo and I were full of steam, but we had to channel it. She stepped back, smiled, and threw herself into a kind of birthday ritual, presenting me with all the things I'd asked her to bring—two potted plants, a small rug, an old radio, a soap dish, and new towels from Sears Roebuck.

We made the most of the ceremony, and then Mo brought up her worry about the pardon. "I'm going to issue a statement, John," she said firmly. "Senator Weicker will help. I'm not going to just sit around and take this. The President's got to pardon you. It's only fair."

I winced and decided not to encourage her hopes, or mine. "We've got to be realistic, sweetheart. The President's probably not going to pardon anybody else. It's over for now. Even the prosecutors would recommend against a pardon for me now. They want me in here."

Mo looked shocked and hurt by my response, then angry. We were both strung tight as bowstrings. "Why do you say that?" she exploded, in tears. "Do you like being in here?"

That stung me. I had taken the wrong approach. "No, I don't like being in here," I said gently. "I just don't want you to get your hopes up. That's all." I was trying to baby her, and it backfired.

"Well, you said the time was going by real fast," she sobbed. "You said it was all right. I don't understand you!"

All our emotions were out of sync. We floundered painfully until Mo finally said she was worried that she might not get home before dark. She left an hour before the visiting period ended, and I collapsed on the bunk, feeling as if I were

465

wrenched inside out.

I struggled to my door in response to a loud knock. It was Chuck. He had persuaded certain guards to let him speak to me from the doorway as long as we didn't discuss testimony.

"Hi, Chuck," I sighed.

"Get on your horse." He was sparkling. "We've got work to do! I told Magruder to draw up a game plan. And we should get Patty and Mo to do The Today Show, The Dick Cavett Show, Merv Griffin, and Mike Douglas. One tough and one crying, demanding pardons for their husbands. I'll get a hold of some of the heavies to put the screws to Ford. Jeb can get his old operation going and take out full-page ads urging freedom for the POWS, Prisoners of Watergate! Herb can raise the dough." Chuck was mimicking his old White House locomotive style. Then he roared with laughter, and it was infectious.

"Ah," I sighed loudly, feigning lament. "Those days are gone forever."

"I know." Chuck grinned and ducked away in good spirits.

September 12, 1974

Gordon Liddy walked past me in Neal's office, flanked by two marshals. I was just leaving for Holabird.

"Hello, Gordon. How are you?"

He stopped and peered into my face. His eyes were so glazed that I suspected he was under sedation. After a long and blank stare, he shook his head jerkily as if to throw off a dream. "John!" he exclaimed. "How are you? I didn't even recognize you. I'm sorry."

Liddy was holding a long thin cigar in his right hand. He stuck it into his mouth in order to shake hands. The smoke

466

drifted up into his eyes, and he looked more natural as he squinted. Then he took the cigar out again and the dazed look returned.

"I'm fine, Gordon," I said uneasily. "How are you holding up?"

"As well as can be expected, I guess."

We had a brief formal conversation. I studied Liddy's appearance. It was the first time I had seen him since June 19, 1972, at the moment I had watched him stroll off after offering to have himself shot on the street; he was drawn and hollow-cheeked, but mostly I was struck by his eyes and by his shirt collar. It was worn and grimy. His beard was turning prematurely white. His suit looked like a painted veneer.[*]

Liddy walked off with his marshals. Jim was about to make one last vain effort to persuade him to break his silence. "I'm really sorry about not recognizing you," Liddy called over his shoulder. "You know how it is."

Not really, I thought. He had already spent nearly a year in the D.C. jail, a notoriously vicious and overcrowded inferno.

---

*   Liddy would later fantasize a very different encounter, claiming he had walked into Neal's office only to find me sitting behind Neal's desk. Liddy writes: "I stood stock-still, trying to figure out this development. Here was the perfect opportunity to kill Dean. A pencil was lying on the desk. In a second I could drive it up through the underside of his jaw, through the soft-palate and deep into his brain. Had someone set it up? If so, why now? President Nixon was out of office. I had received no orders to kill Dean and certainly wouldn't be presumed so irresponsible as to do so on my own initiative; his death might hurt, through reaction, the trial chances of Mitchell, Ehrlichman, Parkinson, and Mardian. [Liddy omits Haldeman, who was also on trial, and then continued.] I decided to consider that my being shut up alone in the room with Dean had just been an incredible error." Liddy writes that I "jumped up with a look of stark fear" and then stammered into a brief conversation. It never happened as Liddy depicted, rather writing years after the fact, he twisted this event and many others to his fancy. As I report in the Afterword, Liddy's later distortions are so egregious they suggest psychological problems.

My resentment of Holabird was ludicrous when I thought of Liddy's environment. And I felt even luckier that Jim thought he needed me daily in the Special Prosecutor's office.

Mid-September 1974

Despite the restrictions, I had formed a general idea of the Holabird prisoner population within the first couple of weeks. Since most of the others were imprisoned at Holabird because of threats against their lives, I decided that it was not prudent to pry into the reasons for their incarceration. The knowledge seemed, in some cases, deadly.

As best I could piece it together, the twenty-some prisoners broke down as follows: four "Watergate guys;" two former Baltimore policemen on corruption charges; three members of the French Connection conspiracy; a con artist; a key figure from the Tony Boyle/Yablonski murders; three Latin heroin traffickers; a man who had slit the throat of a female government informant and burned her corpse (Chuck was working with him); a seasoned hit man with twenty-eight murders under his belt; and an assortment of Mafia figures whose crimes ran from murders to heavy narcotics trafficking.

Late September 1974

"How are you doing, Paul?" I asked as I poured milk over my morning Raisin Bran in the Holabird kitchen.

"Fine." He beamed. "Paul" was a professional banking swindler, the last of a group of con men who had been held at Holabird. He was there to brief Senate investigators on the fine art of his profession.

"Why are you smiling so?"

"Well, I'm in the middle of a little project here," he said

468

casually as he bent over a sheaf of papers near the toaster. "I'm buying a couple of banks."

"You're what? I thought you were out of the business." I began backing out of the kitchen with my cereal, fearful of learning about another crime.

"Don't worry, John. It's perfectly legit. I can do it all in correspondence with letters of credit. I don't have to put up a cent. Here, look at this." He proudly outlined complicated financial maneuvers showing how he could buy banks with no money. From prison. "I've got a line on another one in Texas," he said. "You want it?"

"No, thanks," I declined, laughing.

"Nothing to it," he said. "Let me know if you change your mind. I figure it will look good on my parole sheet if I can prove I'm a respectable bank owner."

September 29, 1974

Jim Neal had moved into a new office in the Federal Courthouse in preparation for the trial. He sat behind his desk, looking thoughtful. Suddenly he started chuckling to himself and shaking his head.

"What are you laughing at?" I asked.

"Aw, I was just thinking about old John Wilson," he drawled. "He's a funny old codger."

"What's he doing now?" John J. Wilson, Haldeman's lawyer, had always struck me as fearsome and choleric.

"Well, he was in the other day, and he stopped me after the meeting. And he says, 'You deal a lot with Dean, don't you?' So I say, 'Yeah I do.' And then he says, 'Well, let me ask you a question. After you've been dealing with him, do you have to wash your hands?'" Jim cracked up laughing. I swallowed.

469

"Old John's really something," he went on. "But don't you worry about him. He's not going to lay a glove on you."

I wasn't reassured.

October 5, 1974

"Mr. Dean, you've got an emergency phone call!" shouted one of the security guards in the Special Prosecutor's office. He had caught me walking down the hall between two marshals, on my way back to Holabird.

"What for? Who from?" I asked in panic.

"Don't know. The operator said it's an emergency call."

I rushed to the phone, fearing a tragedy. Mo? My son? My parents? Mo's mom?

"John, this is Junie." It was a friend of Mo's in California. "Mo's okay, but she's in the hospital."

"What's wrong with her?"

"Well, she got real run down. So I sent her to my psychiatrist, and he put her in the hospital. But don't you worry about it. Believe me, John, this is for the best."

Junie told me, as gently as possible, that Mo had suffered a breakdown. I had never felt more helpless. What could I do? Nothing but worry. I couldn't even call her.

The vomiting began about one-thirty in the morning. I slipped quietly in and out of the bathroom without telling the deputy posted at the door. I had eaten no dinner. By dawn I had discovered blood coming up from my stomach. A marshal drove me to a Baltimore hospital, where I was pumped full of anti-nausea serum before being returned to Holabird.

470

October 10, 1974

Mo was released from the hospital on her birthday. She hadn't told me how she was planning to cope with my being in jail, but I soon found out. She tried to pretend nothing had happened. I felt guilty. I felt a void opening between us.

October 12, 1974

The jury was selected. Neal spent the day watching a University of Tennessee football game and then guided me through a dress rehearsal of my testimony. He had trouble concentrating. He was upset. Leon Jaworski had unexpectedly resigned.

Several members of the staff watched the evening news in Jim's office. When it was reported that President Ford would take an active role in the selection of a new Special Prosecutor, Jim hit the roof.

"Dammit!" he roared. "That really burns my ass. I don't know why the hell Leon couldn't have told me what he was going to do! He begged me to come back and handle this case, and now he's walking out on me. Shit, I've got enough to worry about without Ford putting some bastard in over me who might fuck up my case!"

I had never seen him as angry or depressed. The staff lawyers kept their distance.

October 16, 1974

"You're on next, John," whispered Judge Sirica's bailiff. "Uh, excuse me. I mean Mr. Dean."

As I entered the packed courtroom I spotted Mo, who had agreed to come for the first day. I winked at her, and walked to the witness box where I was sworn in. While Neal gathered his papers and walked to the lectern; I watched the five defendants. None of them looked back at me, and I felt I had won the first round.

"Mr. Dean, are you acquainted with Mr. John N. Mitchell?" Jim intoned.

"Yes, sir, I am."

"Would you, for the benefit of the court and the ladies and gentlemen of the jury, identify Mr. Mitchell for the record?"

"Yes, sir. He is—"

Before I could identify Mitchell, his lawyer, William Hundley, jumped up and stipulated that I knew him. I wondered if Hundley was worried about how I might describe the John Mitchell I saw hunched over his table in the back corner of the defendants' area. His wan, expressionless face gazed up at me as if I were a total stranger. At least he was looking, I thought. He had avoided my eyes at the Vesco trial. I still felt sorry for him. He and I both knew he was guilty, and I figured he was rolling the dice again as he had done in the Liddy plan, but they were still loaded against him.

"Do you know, Mr. Dean, the defendant H. R. Haldeman?"

"Yes, I do."

"Would you identify him for the record, please?"

"Mr. Haldeman is sitting right over there with the brown suit on." Bob turned from a stack of papers he was busy underlining with multicolored pens and faced me. He looked much less severe since he had let his hair grow stylishly longer. "Trial cosmetics," the prosecutors had joked. Bob and I exchanged our first glances since I had left the White House. He no longer struck fear in me, nor guilt. Jail and time had healed most of my squealer emotions. I was riveted on the fact that Bob had called me a liar under oath, and that he was about to do so again. Don't waste that innocent look on me, Halde-

472

man, I thought. You and I know better. My stage fright lessened as Jim led me through a description of Bob's duties at the White House.

"Now, do you know the defendant Mr. John D. Ehrlichman?"

"Yes, sir, I do."

"Would you identify Mr. Ehrlichman for the record, please?"

"Mr. Ehrlichman is there in the blue suit, with glasses on." He was seated at the table closest to me and the jury, making notes. He didn't bother to look up. I wondered if he could make it through the whole trial with his armor intact. I thought of Liddy, of myself, and of the other prisoners, and I decided he could never stay unruffled all the way through prison.

When I identified Bob Mardian, mentioning the color of his tie, he whipped off his glasses to face the jury and looked quickly down at his tie to make sure I was right. The same old hyper-animated Mardian. Frightened, but vain and defiant. He was paying for his brief but crucial role in the early days of the cover-up—a corporal in the dock with the generals.

Ken Parkinson, the last defendant, seemed completely out of place. I knew a half-dozen men who had played much larger roles in Watergate than Ken, and who were absent. He had never met Haldeman or Ehrlichman before his indictment. I harbored some suspicion that the prosecutors had included him as "mercy bait." An acquittal of Parkinson would lend an air of even-handedness to the trial.

"Well, how did it feel in there?" Jim was cheerful enough. "You got your sea legs yet?" The postmortems were pleasant, even though most of my time on the stand had been spent listening to legal haggles over the admissibility of my testimony.

"I thought it went okay, but only a few of the jurors looked

473

at me. They're a shy bunch so far, but it's hard to tell about them."

"You did fine, John. Don't worry about the jury. We'll get their attention tomorrow when you get mean. Just stay comfortable."

"I'm getting there, but there is one thing. You went off the witness sheet several times in there and threw those dollar figures about the hush money at me. I couldn't answer those because I'm not ready to go on the box with them. I thought we had ruled those out."

"Oh, hell, I know that," Neal said sheepishly. "That's why I'm throwing you some curves. I want the jury to watch you struggle and then refuse to answer things you're not sure of—it makes you look good. Besides, I can slip the dollar amounts in with questions. You still don't understand how we prosecutors work. You just keep going."

Mo arrived at the prosecutors' office for a brief visit. I wanted to talk about the growing distance between us. She didn't.

"How is it, testifying?" she asked.

"Not as bad as I expected. I don't even miss the crutch of a few Scotch-and-waters to sleep the night before. I was nervous at first, but it went away quickly. You know the anticipation is always worse than the real thing."

"I sat beside Jo Haldeman and her daughter in the courtroom today," Mo said. "She's taking notes like mad."

"That's interesting. Bob is taking notes also. The defendants are probably sharing one copy of the transcript to keep their costs down. Haldeman's note-taking will give him his own transcript. He's like a damn machine, isn't he?"

"I know, I saw him taking them, too," Mo noted. "He looked over at me while you were testifying and started staring real hard and mean at me, and I just stared back. Finally I stared him down!" she added gleefully, which made me chuckle, too.

"You going to come to court tomorrow?"

"I don't know. I really don't like this very much. It's kind of boring, and I feel sorry for all those defendants. I think Mitchell looks pathetic, and Ken Parkinson looks lost. If you don't mind I'd really rather not come tomorrow."

"Sure, I understand." She's escaping, I thought. I couldn't blame her. "I'll call you after court from Holabird and tell you what happened. You may want to come toward the end of the week, because they're going to start playing some of the tapes."

"I'd like to hear them," she said. When she did she was shocked. She told me we sounded like a bunch of Mafia gangsters.

October 17, 1974

Neal led me through an account of the taped conversation between Colson and Howard Hunt right after the election, during which Hunt had escalated his money demands. Mitchell had acknowledged that I played the tape for him—it was the tape he'd listened to at the Metropolitan Club—but said he couldn't remember what was on it, and that, in any case, he hadn't done anything about it. Both Haldeman and Ehrlichman had said they didn't remember that I had played the tape for them at Camp David. They couldn't afford to—the tape destroyed their defense that they had authorized payments for humanitarian purposes only. Mitchell admitted there might be something sinister about the payments, but he swore he had nothing to do with them. The perennial factions were still at war.

I spelled out every admissible detail I could remember. It

475

was a major crunch point in my testimony; either I or the three of them were lying. I looked at Haldeman and Ehrlichman as I described the Camp David meeting. Haldeman listened impassively. Ehrlichman frowned and squinted his eyes into a hate-filled look. If stares could kill, my testimony would have ended abruptly. He was trying to unsettle me, but I found I was able to look right back at him.

John Wilson was working especially hard to bait Judge Sirica into making errors. The two men had been friends and colleagues for decades, but Sirica finally had enough. He put his old friend in his place gruffly. The air crackled with hostility, and soon Sirica called the lawyers to the bench for a conference.

As always, the bailiff led me out of the witness box so that I wouldn't overhear the private discussion. When I returned, all the lawyers had left the bench except the slow-moving Wilson. Judge Sirica stopped him and whispered off the record, "Hey, I didn't mean anything personal when I called you down, you know."

Wilson looked up and smiled warmly. "Aw, John, I understand," he said. "You've got to do that in this trial."

Everyone was doing some acting. I watched Wilson hobble back to Haldeman's table on his stiff, arthritic legs.

October 25, 1974

"Now, Mr. Dean, how many days have you been on the stand, approximately?" asked Judge Sirica when the cross-examination finally wound down.

I was so elated at the thought of getting off the stand that my mind went blank. I had answered all those terrible questions with reputations and prison terms at stake, and now I couldn't even count up my days in the courtroom. My confusion worsened. "Nine days, your honor." I had guessed wrong. It had been eight.

"My advice to you is this," said the judge, with a kindly expression. "You get off this stand as fast as you can, and get out of this courtroom before some lawyer thinks of a question to ask you." Then he actually smiled.

"Is the witness now excused, as I understand it, from testifying in this trial?" Neal asked as casually as possible.

"No! No!" shouted Wilson, jumping to his feet.

Sirica nodded soberly. "He is subject to being recalled."

"Recalled," Wilson echoed.

I walked away with my happiness slightly smudged by Wilson's proviso. Back to Holabird.

November 1, 1974

"Listen, son, I want you to quit moping around out there and get to work on that motion to reduce your sentence. I think you've got old Sirica softened up now, and I want to give him a strong dose of the Dean vitamin before he changes his mind."

"Charlie," I sighed, staring at two other prisoners walking by the phone, "I've already tried. I've written three or four drafts, and none of them is worth a damn. You're going to have to do it yourself. I can't write it. That's what this place does to me. I sit down and start feeling sorry for myself, so I read. I can't do anything else."

Charlie grunted as I spoke, but he had worked his mustard up again by the time I finished. "It will be done by a master of the art, then," he declared. "I'll play Sirica like an organ. That's what you pay me for."

November 12, 1974

Colson made an arrangement with the deputy at my door and brought Herb Kalmbach in to see me. I put my book down nervously. I knew that Herb was upset about the testimony he had given that day. He looked it. Here was one of the most likable men I'd ever met. He was wearing pajamas, a bathrobe, and slippers, and the long bags under his eyes made him look like the saddest basset hound I'd ever seen.

"What happened today, Herb?" I asked. "Pretty rough?"

"Well, John, I don't know," Herb sighed. "All of a sudden it hit me, and I didn't even know where it came from. I was talking about one of the times I had gone out to raise more money, and the prosecutor asked me about that meeting with John Ehrlichman, you know. And I testified how I had looked him in the eye and said, 'You know me and my wife, Barbara, and I know you and your family, John. And I know you wouldn't tell me to do this if it wasn't important.' And I looked at Ehrlichman in the courtroom today just like I did when he told me it was okay, and then I started to go on. And suddenly the tears just started coming up, and I just couldn't keep going. The judge had to have a break for me. And I was so embarrassed. My God, I've never done anything like that before—"

"Herb, you don't need to be embarrassed about that," I interrupted softly. "It's the most natural thing in the world. Hell, I start crying in here sometimes just reading a book. You know all our emotions are much closer to the edge in here."

"Yeah, I know," Herb sighed. "But that's different. I don't know why it had to happen in front of my friends and all those reporters and the judge and everybody. I couldn't stop myself from doing the last thing in the world I wanted to do."

"Herb, it was probably what you most wanted to do," said Chuck. "And you shouldn't feel ashamed of it. Believe me."

Herb cradled his face in his hand and started shaking his

478

head. Just talking about it was upsetting him again. Chuck and I felt lumps rising ourselves. We looked at each other helplessly and then tried to cheer Herb up by changing the subject.

November 13, 1974

"Hey, Jim, what happened with Herb yesterday?" It was the next morning.

"Herb?" Neal's face lit up. He started pacing his office, rubbing his hands together joyously, like a brand-new father. "John, it was beautiful!" he drawled, his eyes rolling in ecstasy. "Beautiful! If I had asked somebody to put on that performance in the courtroom, I couldn't possibly have gotten away with it! I'd have been rightly criticized. I'll tell you, it was something. That jury was so moved by Kalmbach's testimony they'll never forget it! They'll never forget the way he nailed Ehrlichman! It was the best damn piece of testimony we've had in the trial. Better than anything you ever did on the stand, Mean John Dean!"

My jaw dropped at Jim's wild delight. "Well, that's good, I guess," I commented quietly.

Jim looked at me, did a double take, and slowed down his hand rubbing. "No, but I understand, and I feel sorry for poor old Herb," he said, shaking his head. "I feel sorry for him. He's had it tough." Then Jim lit up again. "But, by God, he's a hell of a witness!"

November 27, 1974

"You know, I liked poor old John Mitchell until today," Neal observed during the day's recess in the trial. "That son-of-a-bitch lied and lied and lied! He lied to me, personally! I can understand him lying about you and Magruder and all the testimony, but I would think he'd have the common decency not to lie to me!"

"What do you mean?"

"Well, last spring he told me it was Mardian who told Magruder he should have a little fire to destroy that bunch of documents from the Reelection Committee. But today he testified that no such statement was ever made by anybody. Goddammit, he crossed me up! I liked him until he did that, and now I'm going to crucify the bastard!"

Jim was psyching himself up to cross-examine Mitchell, and he didn't seem to notice that Rick Ben-Veniste had come in.

"Listen, Jim," Rick broke in at the first opportunity, "you've got to hit Mitchell in the cross on the fact that Pappas gave him fifty thousand dollars."

"Are you serious?" I asked Rick. I had informed the prosecutors, and the tapes had confirmed, that Pappas had been frequently mentioned as a potential source of cover-up money, but I didn't know they had followed it up.

"Why do I want to use that?" Jim asked skeptically. He was all steamed up for his own charge at Mitchell, and he seemed irritated at the idea of a last-minute line of attack.

"Just listen, and I'll tell you."

"I don't have time now, Rick. I've got to get ready for Mitchell." He didn't want to lose what was dangling in front of him.

"At least let me explain it to you, so you'll understand," Rick insisted. "You can kill Mitchell with this. Pappas gave him fifty thousand dollars in October, and—"

"Why?" Jim interrupted.

"Mitchell says for his apartment in New York."

"So?"

"Well, he never used it for his apartment. He put it in a bank account at the Chase Manhattan. The account jumped from one thousand to fifty-one thousand, and it's still that way now."

"I don't see what that proves," Jim said tartly.

"It shows Mitchell was collecting funds to pay the Watergate defendants. Or at least you can make it show that in conjunction with other testimony."

"Bullshit," Jim snorted. "It doesn't prove that to me, and I'm not inclined to use it. Write it up and have Tony bring it in to me." Rick nodded and went off to find Tony Passaretti, an investigator for the Special Prosecutor's office.

Rick left, and several other assistants filed in. Jim dispatched them with assignments like a drill sergeant, sprinkling his orders with tirades against Judge Sirica. "As if I didn't have enough problems, now the judge is acting like he just walked into the courtroom off the street. Just as I think he's beginning to understand what's going on, he starts asking Mitchell the dumbest damn questions you ever heard. I couldn't believe it! Like he broke in and told Mitchell he really wanted to know why all this money had been paid to the defendants. So Mitchell looks up at him real sincere and says, 'Your honor, I've been wondering the same thing.' The shrewd bastard. Shit, I damn near exploded. What does the judge think we've been proving for the last month! I really don't understand Sirica sometimes."

"That must be some kind of press play by the judge," observed Judy Denny, one of the staff lawyers who had come in for orders.

Tony Passaretti came in. "Here's what I've got on Pappas, Jim," he said politely, handing over a yellow pad full of notes.

Jim scanned it. "I don't think I can use this, Tony."

481

Tony shrugged. "Well, here's a copy of the Pappas check," he said. "But there's no deposit slip at the bank. The account just shows a jump all of a sudden. Those guys at the Chase have been jerking us around, Jim. And old Pappas is playing games with us."

"Yeah, I see," said Jim. "But this isn't enough for tomorrow. Maybe Mitchell did borrow it to buy his damn apartment. . Just because he didn't need the money is no proof this had anything to do with Watergate."

"Maybe so," said Tony. "But there's no note, and there's no collateral for any loan. It's fishy as hell. Maybe I'll go up to New York myself and see if I can dig up the rest of the story."

"Okay," Jim replied, seeming glad to put the issue off. "Let me know what you come up with."

Later, out of curiosity, I asked Tony what became of his investigation. "Another unanswered question," he said. "I had to drop it. I got stonewalled at the bank."

Later in November 1974

"John, I really don't think this is appropriate." Henry Ruth, replacement as Special Prosecutor, was frowning. "If the press got hold of this, they'd go crazy." He threw a "JOHN DEAN" office name plate down on my desk and waited for an answer.[*]

---

[*]   By this time, on days I was not taken to Jim Neal's office at the Federal Courthouse to be available to answer his questions, I was taken to the K Street offices of the Watergate Special Prosecution Force, to work with other prosecutors. Literally, I was going to K Street one day and the Courthouse the next. The Marshal's were told each day where to take me. The Watergate prosecutors were leaving few stones unturned, and gave me assignments like reading all of Pat Gray's testimony during his confirmation hearings to see if I recognized any lies. I found many, but without the assistance–and corroboration depending on the facts–of John Mitchell, John

"Well, Hank," I sputtered. I didn't know whether to take his remark seriously. "I didn't put that on the door. One of the secretaries did it as a joke. They think I'm almost one of the guys."

"I know," he said flatly. "But we can't afford this kind of stuff. I'm already catching a lot of flak about the office you've got."

"Okay, I understand."

I knew there was some resentment that I had fared so well in the office shuffle at the Special Prosecutor's K Street headquarters. When the Watergate trial team had moved down to the courthouse, I had been assigned Neal's old office on the ninth floor—a corner location with lots of windows. Several of the lawyers consigned to the eighth floor cubbyholes had vied for it.

Soon I was in Jill Vollner's old windowless cubicle, which was decorated with poster pictures of windows. These posters sell well among Washington bureaucrats.

"John, let me ask you something personal," said Larry Iason. "Is it true that your father-in-law was a senator and got you your job at the Judiciary Committee?"

"Larry, that's one of those stories that's been reprinted so often it's taken as fact. It couldn't be further from the truth. First of all, my first wife's stepfather was a Democrat, so he wouldn't be much help to me in getting a Republican staff job. Second, I never met the man in my life, and, third he was dead when I got the job. I got it by luck, like I got all my jobs."

"You think I could be counsel to the President by the time I'm thirty-one with enough luck?" he asked.

"Okay, okay, it wasn't all luck. There turned out to be

Ehrlichman, or Bob Haldeman, it would be my word versus Gray's—and no one else was cooperating. So Gray walked.

some pretty good opportunities about that job with the Congress. Remember, the Republican Party was ripped to shreds in the 'sixty-four election just before I got to the Hill. And I was sitting with the Judiciary Committee looking at the politics. It looked to me like the Republicans had only two possible issues to make a comeback with: crime and defense. I didn't know anything about defense, so I decided to become a crime expert. That's how I wound up in the Justice Department, with the fancy title of Associate Deputy Attorney General. I was cranking out with assignments like a drill sergeant, that bullshit on Nixon's crime policy before he was elected. And it was bullshit, too. We knew it. The Nixon campaign didn't call for anything about crime problems that Ramsey Clark wasn't already doing under LBJ. We just made more noise about it."

"So you rode in on the crime issue."

"Right. In those days, only one thing was important. Getting ahead. Why?"

"I'm not sure."

December 4, 1974

"You know, Hank, I sure do wish I could make old John Ehrlichman think we have him on tape." Henry Ruth had stopped in at the courthouse for a progress report on the trial, and Neal was in an expansive mood. "That's what I did to poor old Jimmy Hoffa at the Chattanooga trial," he mused happily. "It was a hell of a sight." Jim took out his cigar, and Henry and I settled back for a yarn. "That damn Hoffa was a good liar. One of the best I've ever seen. Hell of a witness. But we did a job on him. I had an agent carry electronic equipment in and out of my office at the courthouse. Fancy stuff, with the wires hanging out all over the place. Every day for weeks. In and out. We tried to time it so he'd walk right past Hoffa in the

484

morning and again in the afternoon. He finally took the bait. One day he stopped his lawyer and got all excited. He pointed at the agent. 'Goddammit,' he yells. 'See it! See it! I told you they were bugging me!' After that he was no good as a witness. Shit, he went tighter than a drum. Lost his spark. That was nice. We outfoxed that old bastard. Kind of clandestine, you know," he drawled, making "clandestine" rhyme with "wine."

Hank Ruth, who struck me as a mild-mannered legal scholar in the mold of Sam Dash, smiled and shook his head as Jim roared with laughter.

"I think I've got things under control down here," Jim went on. "I've got all the defense lawyers figured out. Wilson's so old he makes mistakes, although I'll bet he used to be one hell of a trial lawyer. And old Bill Frates will never rescue Ehrlichman. He's really something. The reporters call him 'W. C. Fritos.' He's too much. Hundley's good, but there's so much evidence against his man that all he can do is try to subtly stick it to Haldeman and Ehrlichman. God, I'd love to sit in on some of their strategy meetings. I think Mardian's guy is the best, but I can handle him."

"How about Sirica?" Hank inquired, glancing at me as if to say, "Watch this, Jim's higher than a kite."

"Well, I was worried about him at first," Jim declared, "but now I've decided he's a hell of a good judge. Yes, sir, he's a good judge. And I don't say that because he rules whenever I want him to rule. He reads all the homework we give him, and he relies on us to help him. What I do is let most things pass now, so when I do object to something he knows it's important. He trusts us now, and he damn sure doesn't want this case reversed because of him."

Jim ran through why things were swinging to the government's favor—expressions on the jurors' faces, rulings, dramas, miscues by the defense, the overall "feel" of the courtroom.

485

Mid-December 1974

Larry Iason walked into his office, where I worked when Neal had me down at the courthouse, laid a big pile of documents on my desk, puffed out his cheeks, and blew a long, exasperated breath. "Look at all that stuff. That's what Jim just gave me to finish by tomorrow. I tell you, I feel like Neal's Higby. We've got a bunch of real egos on this trial team, and I get all the dirty work. I'm nothing but a, a, what do you call it?"

"A gopher," I said gently.

"Yeah, a gopher." He paused, and then exclaimed, "We're like the White House. You ever think about that?"

"Well, yes, but don't tell anybody. You've got power, ambitions, office shuffles, news summaries, and a tickler system. But at least your bosses temper you. That might keep you out of jail. Ours used to egg us on."

Larry smiled. "That's for sure!"

"I'm having a lot of trouble with Mardian," said Vollner wearily. "He still denies ever having seen the FBI reports, the 302s you testified he looked at in your office. Is there anything you can think of to help draw him out?"

"I don't know. Let me think." I went back over the details, and nothing helped. Then I had an idea. "How about fingerprints, Jill? Have you tried that?"

She was intrigued. "No, we haven't checked them. You think he left any?"

"He must have. Mardian's got a thumb as big as the palm of your hand. And I tell you, I can see him sitting in my office with those things, and he'd always lick his thumb before he'd turn the pages. You know how he moves when he's excited. Slap. Lick. Slap. Lick. He must have left some big wet prints on there you can almost see with the naked eye."

486

FBI agents handed me rubber gloves and a stack of the original Watergate FBI reports a foot high. I was uncomfortable, sensing that the agents must dislike me for the black eye my testimony had helped give the Bureau. My marshals sensed it, too. The agents let me choose only a few pages out of the thousands for lab tests. It was a hopeless task. Reduced to guesswork, I failed.

"Goddammit, Jill," Jim roared. "You should have checked with me before you went off on a long shot like that! If Mardian's lawyers get wind of it, they could try to use that piddly little test to make it look like he never touched the stuff."

"I thought it was worth it," she said, standing her ground.

December 16, 1974

The Special Prosecutor's office sent a letter to the supervisor at Holabird. I was finally allowed out of my room. No more guards posted at my door. No more restrictions on my conversations.

December 17-23, 1974

Chuck and I compared notes on the Watergate mysteries. We sat up late trading information, and we commented on how much better it felt to do so without worrying about protecting anyone.

"Chuck, why do you figure Liddy bugged the DNC instead of the Democratic candidates? It doesn't make much sense. I sat in Mitchell's office when Liddy gave us his show, and he only mentioned Larry O'Brien in passing as a target. I confess that Magruder once told me you were pushing for information on O'Brien because of the ITT case, and I—"

487

"Magruder's full of shit," Chuck interrupted. "That bastard tests my Christian patience to the breaking point. I have to say special prayers to temper my feelings about that asshole. I'd like to hear him say that to my face."

"Why don't we ask Jeb to come over?" I suggested. "And I'll ask him why the hell Liddy went after O'Brien. What do you think?"

"I think it's a capital idea," Chuck replied. "I've got some ideas of my own, but I'd like to hear Jeb's explanation."

I went down to Jeb's room, thinking about Chuck's remarks. I knew Chuck had been struggling with himself in an effort to be supportive of Jeb in prison. Jeb had become extremely depressed during the past few weeks. "He's got the prison shuffle," Chuck had told me, pointing out how Jeb barely lifted his head or feet as he walked the halls. "I'm worried about him, and remember, John, he's only got a month or so on us in here. We could be shuffling around like that pretty soon, so we've all got to help each other." I had no idea what Jeb would think of our probing, but he seemed to be anxious for conversation. I invited him back to Chuck's room.

"Jeb, we've been trying to put some pieces together about why we're here," I began, "and one of the questions we can't answer is why Larry O'Brien was targeted. I guess you and Mitchell agreed to that in Florida. But why O'Brien?"

Jeb froze. His pallid face flushed crimson. He tried to find words, but only stuttered. The question had more than caught him off guard. It had overwhelmed him. "Why do you want to know?" he asked haltingly.

"Just curiosity," Chuck said.

"Well, it just seemed like a good idea," Jeb said evasively.

"Well then, why was Spencer Oliver's phone bugged?" Chuck pressed. Chuck was implying that the testimony that Oliver, another official of the DNC, had been bugged by

488

accident was not true, that there had been deeper motives.

Jeb looked at me. Then at Colson. "Why? Who wants to know?" he asked as his confusion turned to suspicion and headed toward anger.

"I don't think we ought to talk about that stuff," he said sharply. Jeb turned on his heel and walked out, leaving Chuck and me staring at each other in dismay.

Chuck broke our silence. "You know, I think I know why Jeb's so damn depressed. I think he's still holding back what he knows."

"You think maybe Mitchell didn't approve O'Brien as a target?"

"No. Well, I'm not sure. Maybe indirectly, or after the fact. I'll tell you what I think happened. I don't know exactly how it worked, but I've got good reason to believe that Bob Bennett was somehow involved in the decision to go after O'Brien."

"Bennett? Why Bennett?"

"Have you read Howard Baker's minority report on Watergate?"

"No, I haven't seen it," I said, wondering where Chuck was heading.

"You should read it. It's pretty good on the CIA angle in Watergate, and that includes Bennett. You'll see for yourself the fine hand of Bob Bennett in Hunt's activities. Like the plan to have Hunt and Liddy break in on Hank Greenspun's office out in Las Vegas. Hunt was working with Bennett's help and encouragement on that. He put them in touch with the Hughes people, who wanted anything Greenspun had on Hughes."

I remembered Greenspun, a Las Vegas newspaper publisher who, like Larry O'Brien, had had business dealings with Robert Maheu, the deposed chief of Howard Hughes's Las

Vegas empire. Jeb had testified that Mitchell had raised the potential danger of Greenspun at the February 4 meeting with Liddy, but I didn't remember it. Perhaps he mentioned it when I wasn't there.

Chuck had more. "You remember when Bennett came over to the White House in January of 'seventy-two all worked up about Clifford Irving's book on Howard Hughes?"

"Sure," I answered. "He came to see me. He wanted me to have the Justice Department investigate Irving. I passed, but I remember that Haldeman wanted to find out what was in the Irving manuscript. And somebody from the White House got a copy from the publisher. Why the hell do you think there was all that frenzy over a bogus autobiography?"

"Well, I can only speculate," said Chuck. "Everyone figured Maheu might have supplied Irving with information one way or another. And Maheu had supplied the one hundred thousand of Hughes money to Nixon through Bebe Rebozo. The way I see it, Haldeman was worried about that coming out. Another messy Hughes scandal."

"If that's true, Chuck, I'll tell you Haldeman may have been just as worried it might come out through O'Brien. I had a few meetings with Bennett when the President wanted to find out about O'Brien's retainer from the Hughes people. Bennett expressed no love for O'Brien. He said O'Brien probably knew everything about Hughes that Maheu did." Chuck's eyebrows went up at this news. I went on. "You think Bennett might have suggested to Hunt that they bug O'Brien?"

"I don't know," Chuck sighed. "I'm supposed to be the White House expert on Hunt and Bennett, and I don't know. You can twist your head into a pretzel with this stuff. But I think Bennett sure would have reason to go after O'Brien—for the Hughes people, to curry favor with us, or even for the CIA. Who knows? But I'm sure he had a lot of influence over Hunt, even though they didn't seem to like each other particularly."

"Incredible. What a mess!" I laughed. "I can see why you've started your ministry."

"Well, religion is complicated, too." He smiled. "But let me give you another brain squeezer. Do you have any idea why it was Spencer Oliver's phone in the DNC that wound up getting bugged? That's why I asked Jeb."

"No, I don't know. I assumed it was a comic error."

"Maybe so. But did you know Spencer Oliver was once planning to go into business with Bennett at the Mullen Company? Or that his father worked for Bennett at the Mullen Company on the Howard Hughes account? Or that Hunt says Spencer Oliver worked for the CIA?" (Which Oliver denies vehemently.)

"No, I didn't. But what does it add up to?"

"You tell me," Chuck suggested. "Maybe one can over-complicate things. Maybe the Sino-Soviet split started because Mao Tse-Tung just got sick of Russian vodka one day. I don't know. But it looks suspicious to me. It's incredible. Millions of dollars have been spent investigating Watergate. A President has been forced out of office. Dozens of lives have been ruined. We're sitting in the can. And still nobody can explain why they bugged the place to begin with. It's unbelievable to me that Bob Bennett has waltzed through this thing. He's got the answers to a lot of unanswered questions."

We had reached a dead end. "A lot of people have gone through this mess untouched besides Bennett," I observed. "Just look at Paul O'Brien. Hell, Ken Parkinson was only in the cover-up up to his ankles. O'Brien was in up to his knees. Paul got a walk. Ken got indicted. I'm happy for Paul, but everything is backwards."

"How come Paul never got indicted?" Chuck asked.

"Because Silbert and Glanzer gave him immunity early on. Neal told me it was just another example of how they blew it.

491

He says as soon as Paul got immunized his memory went bad. They've never even used him as a witness."

"I wonder if Bennett's been immunized," Chuck said.

"I don't think so. I think I'd have heard."

"I tell you, John," Chuck went on. "I turned into something of a CIA freak on Watergate for a while, you know, and I still think there's something there. I haven't figured out how, it all adds up, but I know one thing: the people with CIA connections sure did better than the rest of us. Paul O'Brien's an old CIA man, and he walked. David Young was Kissinger's CIA liaison, and he ran off to England when he got immunity. Bennett worked for the CIA, and he ran back to Hughes. And Dick Helms skated through the whole thing somehow. Maybe those guys just knew how to play the game better than we did."

"Maybe so," I allowed. "I tell you what. I'll ask our Mafia friend Joey what he thinks of CIA people in his business."

Chuck laughed. "That's not a bad idea."

"Old Joey's been telling me he lost all faith in Nixon when he didn't destroy the tapes. He says Nixon is a weak leader and a bad criminal. He thinks the two are the same."

"Well, I agree with him in a way," Chuck replied. "I still don't know why he didn't burn those things early."

"Well, I think he loved having the tapes at first, Chuck. He thought he could use them selectively to prove his case. And by the time he found out he couldn't, he would have been impeached if he'd destroyed them. And a lot of people would have had to go to jail to let him do it. A lot of them would have been in contempt of court, because Sirica had made them responsible for procedure in handling the tapes."

"Well, maybe so," Chuck mused. "But it doesn't make sense. I think Bob Bennett must have told Nixon to hang on to them. How's that?" We laughed.

492

December 24, 1974

Holabird was astir on Christmas Eve. Our top hit man was baking cookies and bread; he had learned the skill in another prison. A multimillionaire heroin dealer from South America was in charge of preparing a turkey dinner for about two thirds of the principals. A spirited and talented Italian crew of Mafia men was busy preparing a lasagna feast for the others, who planned to eat a separate Italian Christmas dinner in the ping-pong room, which they had decorated by draping sheets over the table and the holes in the walls. I helped decorate the tree in the main dining area, picking up an extra chore when one of the Latin heroin traffickers couldn't read the instructions on how to put up the cardboard angels. When everything was ready, I went up to my room.

"You ain't going to read all night, are you, Dean?" Vinny said as he stuck his head into my room.

"What do you have in mind?"

"Grump, Tom, and me is going to work out in about an hour. It don't make no difference this is Christmas Eve, unless you're going to Mass tonight?"

"I'm not going anywhere. The old man turned down the request Chuck and I put in to go to church. What time you going to start?"

"At eleven. Remember, you got to keep your body in shape when you're in the can." We had been lifting weights together for several weeks.

"Okay. See you at eleven."

The four of us stripped down for the workout. Grump, a hit man, was small, wiry, and quiet. Tom, another hit man, was enormous. He had a "MOTHER" tattoo on his chest. Having learned to be a hairdresser in another prison, he wore his hair long, immaculate, and fluffy. Vinny and I did most of the talking, between groans and the clanking of weights.

493

"You guys in your business have a lot of trouble with your contracts, don't you, Dean?" he asked.

"Not always," I said. "Besides, that's how we lawyers make our money. Except I'm not a lawyer anymore."

"Lotsa trouble, lotsa trouble," he said. "You guys have to go to court and mess around and pussyfoot with the fucking judges all the time. We've got a better system. I just send a guy like Grump over to see a gentleman I've got a contract with, and if he don't come to terms Grump breaks his back. I tell you, it works."

"Terrific," I said with a smile.

"Not cut out for that kind of efficiency, are you? Let me ask you something, if you don't mind. You look a little wet behind the ears to be the President's lawyer. How'd you get there so young? Your old man put in the fix?"

"No. I just kissed a lot of ass, Vinny. A lot of it."

"I'll bet you did." He grinned. "So did I."

Late December 1974

"Hi, Hank, how's the Special Prosecutor?" I asked cheerily as Henry Ruth ambled into the conference room to get his brown lunch bag out of the drawer.

"Wonderful," he replied dryly. "I'm just pulling for Neal to get that trial over so we can start thinking about shutting down our operation."

"What are you going to do when you're out of here, Hank?"

"I tell you," he sighed with a wry smile, "what I'm going to do is go out and make American Express ads. That's what I'm going to do."

"What do you mean?" I laughed.

494

"You know, like the guy who does Bugs Bunny's voice or that other guy. What's his name? Miller. The one who ran for Vice-President with Goldwater. I'm going to go on TV and say, 'You may not remember me, but I'm the Watergate Special Prosecutor.' Then I'll hold up my American Express card and say, 'I used American Express all through Watergate, because nobody knew who I was. And they still don't know who I am.'" He sighed again and walked out with his lunch.

"You know, John, I really don't want to see any of those defendants go to jail. It's not going to do a damn bit of good for any of those guys," Neal said reflectively. We'd been talking about the trial; it was almost over.

"You surprise me, Jim. I thought you were itching for us all to do a stretch—as deterrent."

"Hell, no. The worst part of being a prosecutor for me is a case like this, where I don't really want the guys to go to jail. That's why I like defending guilty men. It's not right sometimes. There's nobody the government can't nail if it really goes after him. Shit, they could get me within a year if they wanted to."

January 1, 1975

Weekends seemed particularly long when Mo was in California and I had no visitor. I was spending New Year's Day reading a book, Somerset Maugham's *The Summing Up*, poring over it, escaping my loneliness. There was a knock at the door. It was Vinny.

"Hey, listen, I thought you might like a little of this," he said, lifting his sweater shirt so that I could see the pint of vodka tucked into his pants. "You know, a little cheer for the New Year."

"No, thanks. It's a little early in the day for me," I said.

The last thing in the world I needed was to break some prison rule. Even a sip to convince him I was okay was a risk I was not about to take. Vinny was really offering his friendship, which I appreciated. "Where the hell did you get that?" I asked to be friendly.

"My old lady snuck it in. If ya'd like a cocktail, come on down to the room later. My old lady thinks you're a hell of a guy. She'd get her rocks off shooting the shit with you."

"Thanks, but I've got a bunch of letters I've got to write this afternoon. So maybe I'll take a rain check." I would have enjoyed the visit, but I was afraid to get involved with the drinking.

"Sure. Just wanted you to know you were welcome, since your old lady ain't here."

He left. I went back to my book. Only a few minutes passed before there was another knock.

"It's me again," he said.

I opened the door.

"Hey, I just heard on the radio that the jury found Mitchell and those other guys guilty.[*] Their ball game is over. You think they'll put Mitchell in here? I'd love to talk to that bastard. I've got some friends he's sent up that'd like to do more than talk to him. His ass is in big trouble in the slammer. I'm not sure he'll ever come out."

"It'll be a long time before Mitchell's ever put in jail, Vinny. He's got years of appeals. Maybe Ford will pardon him. It wouldn't surprise me, particularly if he loses the election. Anyway, if Mitchell goes to jail they'll make special arrangements for him, I'm sure. The Bureau of Prisons knows Mitchell's going to be in trouble."

---

[*] [Original Footnote:] Mitchell, Ehrlichman, Haldeman, and Mardian were found guilty. Parkinson was acquitted.

496

"That's too bad. I'd like to meet the old fart."

I'd been vindicated one more time. The jury had believed me. That gave me a wave of satisfaction long enough for me to go down to Colson's room and tell him the verdict. But I didn't ride the wave long. When I returned to my room, I saw *The Summing Up* lying on my bed, open to the page I'd just read. I picked it up:

At first sight it is curious that our own offences should seem to us so much less heinous than the offences of others. I suppose the reason is that we know all the circumstances that have occasioned them and so manage to excuse in ourselves what we cannot excuse in others. We turn our attention away from our own defects, and when we are forced by untoward events to consider them find it easy to condone them. For all I know we are right to do this; they are part of us and we must accept the good and the bad in ourselves together. But when we come to judge others it is not by ourselves as we really are that we judge them, but by an image that we have formed of ourselves from which we have left out everything that offends our vanity or would discredit us in the eyes of the world. To take a trivial instance: how scornful we are when we catch someone out telling a lie; but who can say that he had never told not one, but a hundred? We are shocked when we discover that great men were weak and petty, dishonest or selfish, sexually vicious, vain or intemperate; and many people think it disgraceful to disclose to the public its heroes' failings. There is not much to choose between men. They are all a hotchpotch of greatness and littleness, of virtue and vice, of nobility and baseness. Some have more strength of character, or more opportunity, and so in one direction or another give their instincts freer play, but potentially they are the same. For my part I do not think I am any better or any worse than most people, but I know that if I set down every action in my life and every thought that has crossed my mind the world would consider me a monster of depravity.

497

January 8, 1975

"Hey, Dean, telephone!" a voice shouted up the stairs.

"Okay, be right down," I called back, and gathered up the papers I'd spread out on my small desk. I had been computing the debts I'd amassed in the twenty months I'd been without a pay check. We'd sold everything we could sell, except the house in California. Mo had told me she was ready to get a job if I thought it was necessary. I slipped the papers into the drawer hurriedly, and ran. "Okay, okay, I'm coming," I answered again. I headed down the stairs to the wall phone in the main hall. "Hello."

"You standing or sitting?" It was Charlie. I didn't like his opening question. During the last week he had been in discussions with Henry Ruth about where I was going to be sent to serve the rest of my jail term. Holabird was being closed down.

"I'm standing. Why?"

"Well, sit down!" he ordered.

I untangled the cord and sat on the bottom step. "Okay. Let's hear it. I'm sitting."

"You're about to find out what a fine goddam lawyer you've got, and I hope you appreciate it."

"We'll see," I said tartly. "What do you have?"

"I just had a call from Sirica's clerk, and the good judge has seen the wisdom of our motion to reduce sentence, and, to get right to the point, you're a free man!"

"Charlie, don't play around. Tell me what the hell the judge has done."

"I just did. He's freed you. He granted our motion and reduced your sentence to time served."

"You're shitting me?"

498

"No, sir. Now go pack your bags and I'll make sure the judge's order is out there as fast as possible."

"You're serious, aren't you?"

"You bet your ass. I told you I was a good lawyer! No, the reason you're free is that you..."

I listened but didn't hear. It was true. Charlie wasn't kidding. I was free. I'm free, was all I could think about. I didn't know whether to laugh, cry, or scream, or what to do next. When Charlie said he'd call back, all I could say was, "Thank you, I'll talk to you then."

I hung up the telephone. Jeb was coming down the hall. I wondered how he'd receive the news. Maybe Sirica had freed him too, and Herb. Or maybe he hadn't. I wanted to avoid Jeb and hurried back to my room. I stood looking out the window.

"The nightmare is over." I was talking out loud to myself. "It really is over," I repeated and listened to my own words. I couldn't stop shaking my head as I gazed out the window, nor could I stop the tears.

Everything is different now.

NEW EDITION
AFTERWORD

WHEN I FINISHED WRITING the first edition of this book, I truly believed that Watergate had resulted in changes that would affect the way government operated in Washington for the better. The presidency, as *Washington Post* reporter Bob Woodward wrote in *Shadow: Five Presidents and the Legacy of Watergate* (1999), had been changed. But that shadow has now faded.

These events certainly changed my life, and there was no question for me, at the time I wrote this book, that everything would be quite different because of this experience. After publishing and promoting *Blind Ambition*, I soon entered night school to study accounting (for five years) because it is the language of business. For the next several decades I was engaged in acquiring, merging and then selling small and middle market businesses, and with my partners we enjoyed success at what I called "private investment banking." I also was blessed with an exceptional son, who graduated Phi Beta Kappa and then graduated at the top of his class in business school, before going on to succeed in business and life, marrying a college classmate and adding a lovely daughter-in-law and three beautiful little girls to the family. Because I do not believe in retirement, I returned to writing when I turned sixty years of age, an activity I enjoy and plan to do as long as I am able to do so. I could never have predicted, however, that I would find it necessary to defend myself against the false claims of people who would seek to reinvent this history for political or financial gain, or both. This new Afterword addresses those efforts, while explaining what, in fact, actually occurred. I have divided the material into three sections: Part I – An Overview of What Really Happened at the Nixon White House During Watergate; Part II – Watergate Revisionism or

Sex, Lies and Bogus History; and Part III – A Few Persistent Questions About Watergate All These Years Later.

This Afterword is based on material I have gathered in the three-plus decades since I wrote this book; much of this information was unearthed when my wife Maureen and I filed a defamation lawsuit against the early Watergate revisionists. Although I discovered nothing in all these intervening years that would change anything I have written in the proceeding pages, I have, during that time, uncovered facts that further illuminate and clarify the earlier information I reported. Before turning to these subjects, however, it might be valuable for me to explain how this book was written.

Writing the First Edition of This Book

In 1974-75, when I was working on this book, very little information about the Nixon White House was available. I had been denied access to my White House files before I testified as well as when I worked on this book. Since then, and over the past three decades, a virtual tsunami of information has become available. The voluminous records of the Senate Watergate Committee, the House Impeachment Inquiry, and the Watergate Special Prosecution Force have been made public. Hundreds of hours of secretly-recorded conversations on Nixon White House tapes have been made public. Many of my former colleagues have written their accounts of what happened, and countless historians and journalists have written about these events.

Until 1991, I largely ignored all this material, but when I was forced to file a lawsuit to set the record straight, I read massive amounts of material that related to the activities at the Nixon White House. Nothing I learned from this material changed my mind about what I had written. To the contrary, I found solid corroboration. In addition, I learned a great deal more about Watergate and the Nixon White House.

Blind Ambition was not written to explain Watergate; rather, it is a memoir of a few years of my life. Because I am trained as an attorney, however, I had a unique problem when writing it: How should I deal with my own testimony? I knew that I could not repeat it, verbatim, in the book, for it was as flat and dull as testimony tends to be. (It also ran over 61,000 words!) At first, I tried to quote select passages and explain my feelings about the matters involved. I proceeded in this fashion because I was concerned about changing so much as a word in my testimony—which might cause me to be asked, "Which is true, Mr. Dean, Blind Ambition or your testimony?" However, my literary agent, David Obst, and then my editor at Simon & Schuster, Alice Mayhew, told me that my effort to tell the story in this fashion did not work. David had an idea, however: He would get Simon & Schuster to hire another of his writers, Taylor Branch, to help me pull it together—in less than a month we had reworked the material into the narrative you have just read.

The Assistance of Taylor Branch

Taylor is a few years younger than I. He is a wonderful writer and editor with a great eye for the story that should be told.[*] After Taylor went through what I had written, he said he

---

[*]   At the time, Taylor was a writer at the *Washingtonian Magazine*, where he had reported on Watergate, so he knew the subject. Today, he is best known for his Pulitzer Prize-winning series on the life of Dr. Martin Luther King and the Civil Rights Movement: *Parting the Water: America in the King Years, 1954-63*; *Pillar of Fire: America in the King Years, 1963-65*; and *At Canaan's Edge: America in the King Years, 1965-68*. As I write this Afterword, Taylor is completing his next project: *The Clinton Tapes: Wrestling History with the President*. (Taylor, Bill Clinton, and Hillary Clinton (then Hillary Rodham) became friends during the 1972 presidential campaign when working for the Democratic standard-bearer, Senator George McGovern. During Clinton's presidency, President Clinton had Taylor come to the White House from time to time, typically at night, so

believed that my testimony must be the core of the book. Taylor felt the fastest way to work would be for us to discuss what occurred, event by event, with him making notes. We quickly fell into a pattern of doing this in the afternoon and evening, often over cocktails and dinner. The next day, Taylor would assemble a draft section, sometimes including details that had been inappropriate for testimony. I would then go through the revised draft, where Taylor had blended material from my manuscript, my testimony, and our conversations, to make sure I was comfortable with the way he was dramatizing the narrative.

By reason of this process, I knew I had a foolproof explanation if anyone claimed a difference between my testimony and the book, for I could explain how the book was assembled. For over a decade, I maintained all our drafts and working papers in storage, only to discover the box had been placed under a leaking roof, and mildew had disintegrated the materials. (Only recently did I find a few remnants of our work that had been misfiled and thus escaped water damage.) Reconstructing how *Blind Ambition* was written would become important during our lawsuit, because just as I had feared, the Watergate revisionists claimed the book was, in fact, evidence that I had perjured myself before the Senate. This is false, and the revisionists have raised differences so insignificant they are not worth addressing other than to show the extremes to which they will go to try to discredit me. (I provide a few examples in Part II.)

Had I the chance to do it over again now, after acquiring a better understanding of the book business as a result of writing and publishing ten books, I would give Taylor a "written with" credit, but at the time it never occurred to me, Taylor never mentioned it, nor did Alice or David suggest it. Not until the

---

they could talk about events. Taylor's book is based on recordings they made of their sessions, which spanned the years of the Clinton presidency.)

revisionists made a big deal out of how the book was written was the matter even relevant.

Everything in this book came from my memory, my testimony, my journal, my first draft of the manuscript, and my agreement as to the way Taylor and I would assemble and present it all. As I understand the term, this book was not "ghosted," [*] as some have claimed, for Taylor used verbatim portions of my earlier draft (some of which were cut and pasted as we assembled the draft for the typist). In addition, there are parts of the book that Taylor had no involvement in writing whatsoever, like the 24,000 words we took from my journal to close out the story, which I tweaked to conform to the narrative style of the earlier parts of the book after Taylor departed. According to my wife's calendar, we completed the revised manuscript's ten chapters from start to finish in twenty days, with interruptions for a few social evenings. Having written a bi-weekly column for the past nine years, along with countless articles and book reviews for many different publications, and having written eight non-fiction books in the same period, I consider myself a relatively fast and experienced writer. Thus, I feel confident in saying that no one could have ghosted this book in twenty days; instead, Taylor provided invaluable assistance and editing in that time. He was indispensable in this way, and also in providing me with the editorial assistance that allowed me to flesh out some parts of my testimony while condensing others, and making it more readable and vivid.

Frankly, I wish Taylor and I had recorded our discussion sessions, for he was good at drawing me out, and it was much easier for me to talk about these events with someone who was

---

[*] According to *Safire's New Political Dictionary*, a "ghostwriter" is "one who surreptitiously prepares written and oral messages for public figures...." There was nothing surreptitious about Taylor's role, which I acknowledged in the opening, thanking him for "his talented assistance and patient tutoring," and I spoke openly about his role when this question arose while promoting the book.

genuinely curious about them, than it was for me to decide, sitting in front of a keyboard, what I should or should not address. Today, three decades after writing the book, there is no way I can recall the emotions I felt during these events, which were still quite fresh in my mind when writing this book.

Part I

An Overview of What Really Happened Inside the Nixon White House During Watergate

With the distance of time, and the availability of new information, it is now quite clear, at least to me, how the bungled burglary on June 17, 1972 at the Democratic National Committee (DNC) Watergate offices unraveled the presidency of Richard Nixon, ultimately forcing him out of office. The hallmarks of this troubling episode in American history are not only venality and criminality, but also banality and stupidity. If one looks back through the wreckage, there are a number of key events that conflated to ruin the Nixon presidency. Over the years, some of us who were involved in different aspects of these events have tried to figure out what happened and why. For example, I have discussed these matters at length over many years with Alex Butterfield, who had no involvement whatsoever in any criminal activity, and Bud Krogh, who pled guilty to his involvement in the break-in at Dan Ellsberg's psychiatrist's office. In addition, the evidence is now available to confirm what occurred. As a result, there are no major unanswered questions regarding Watergate, although Nixon apologists and Watergate revisionists like to pretend otherwise. There is certainly no mystery about why Watergate happened or about the pure stupidity of it either.

505

The Release of the "Pentagon Papers" – Nixon's Newly Exacerbated Attitude

Everything changed in the Nixon White House in mid-June 1971, following the leak by Dan Ellsberg of the so-called Pentagon Papers (the classified Defense Department study of the origins of the war in Vietnam). While Nixon had always been concerned about leaks of national security information, which made it difficult for him to govern, this massive release of classified national security information took his concern to new levels. Nixon's dark mood and growing anger are evidenced by the White House tapes of this period.[*] It was at this time that Nixon sought to enjoin the *New York Times* and other newspapers from publishing the leaked documents. It was at this time that Nixon ordered a break-in at the Brookings Institute in Washington, DC, believing that the Institute possessed government documents related to the Pentagon Papers. It was at this time that Nixon created a special unit within the White House to investigate leaks; that unit would break into Dan Ellsberg's psychiatrist's office looking for information. This was also when Jack Caulfield arrived in my office to tell me that Chuck Colson had ordered him to "fire-bomb" the Brookings Institute, and then to send burglars in to retrieve government papers related to what the President wanted, which prompted me to fly to San Clemente to try to put an end to the craziness. When I wrote *Blind Ambition*, I was unaware that Nixon himself had ordered the break-in. I learned that fact

---

[*]   A few tapes have been transcribed by The National Security Archive at George Washington University, and transcripts for June 13, 14, and 15, 1971 are available online. In addition, the Presidential Recordings Program of the Miller Center of Public Affairs at the University of Virginia has transcripts of a few conversations from this period (for June 14, 15, 17, 18, 22 and July 1, 5, and 24, 1971) and are online as well. Stanley L. Kutler's *Abuse of Power: The New Nixon Tapes*, provides transcripts for June 17, 23, 24, 29, 30, July 1, 2, 5, 5, 20, 27, August 9, 12, September 8, 10, 12, 13, 14, 17, 18, and 22, 1971.

only in 1997, when historian Stanley L. Kutler published *Abuse of Power: The New Nixon Tapes*.

Nixon's reactions define the period. For example, on June 17, 1971, Nixon demanded, "Goddamnit, get in [the Brookings Institute] and get those files. Blow the safe and get it." During a conversation on June 30, 1971, Nixon again issued an order: "They [the Brookings Institute] have [a] lot of material... I want Brookings, I want them just to break in and take it out. Do you understand?... You talk to [White House aide Howard] Hunt. I want the break-in. Hell, they do that. You're to break into the place, rifle the files, and bring them in." During an early-morning conversation with Haldeman and Kissinger on July 1, 1971, Nixon rhetorically and sarcastically asked, "Did they get the Brookings Institute raided last night? No. Get it done. I want it done. I want the Brookings Institute's safe cleaned out and have it cleaned out in a way that makes it somebody else...." Again, the next day, when talking with Haldeman and Colson, Nixon made himself very clear: "Also, I really meant it when—I want to go in and crack that safe. Walk in and get it." While this was bad, it would get worse.

Nixon wrote in his memoir that he "considered what Ellsberg had done to be despicable and contemptible—he had revealed government foreign policy secrets during wartime." (Nixon names no important secrets and they have never truly been found. What was found was a lot of over-classified information from newspaper clippings to politically-embarrassing analysis material that should not have been classified Top Secret.) Nixon was repulsed that Ellsberg "was lionized in much of the media." He wanted Ellsberg prosecuted and destroyed. Enter G. Gordon Liddy, whom Bud Krogh placed on the staff of the Plumber's Unit.

For years, Gordon Liddy refused to testify or say anything about his activities at the Nixon White House. Not until he was under investigation by the Internal Revenue Service (IRS) for the unaccounted-for money he received for his intelligence-

507

gathering activities at the Nixon re-election campaign, and forced to either explain what he had done with all the money, or pay taxes on it, did he start talking. At the time, he was unemployed and needed to earn a living. (In 1977 the IRS filed a notice of a six-figure deficiency for his 1972 taxes. To prove to the Tax Court that he had not personally received any of the money he had been given for his intelligence gathering activities, Liddy had to reconstruct, as best he could, what he had done with the money. While he recalled spending $2,270 on prostitutes, and other details, in the end he could not explain $45,630 for which he remained liable.) It appears to me that since he was being forced to talk to the IRS, he decided to sell his autobiography *Will* (1980)—and he has never stopped talking. Liddy's account, however, was written long after the events, eight to nine years later, and it is not likely that Liddy thought much about these matters during his four-plus years in prison, where he says he was primarily thinking about surviving.[*] Nonetheless, it appears that Liddy tried to reconstruct events as best he could recall them in *Will*. Not surprisingly,

---

[*] I am not sure Liddy actually knows the truth; rather he may have convinced himself that the facts are those he has reconstructed long after the events, and those beliefs have become his truth. I have serious doubts about him for good reason. The difference in Liddy before and after he went to prison is striking. Clearly, he has always exhibited aberrant behavior, and he seems to relish sharing his dysfunctional personality with the world in *Will*. Having known this strange fellow before he went to prison, having seen him in the prosecutor's office while he was in prison, and observing him since his release, it seems prison was something of a finishing school for his criminal disposition. But it also illuminates his nature. At one point in our lawsuit, I thought it appropriate to do research on sociopathic personalities because Liddy's behavior appeared to fit so many of the traits. Needless to say absent clinical evaluation by a trained professional it is not possible to know if Liddy is, in fact, a sociopath but his behavior certainly strikes me as a good imitation: superficial charm, egotistical (if not narcissistic), easily untruthful, no sense of remorse, shame or guilt, scapegoats others, need for stimulation, remorselessly vindictive when thwarted or exposed, and total lack of self-understanding – to name a few.

just as he was unable to explain what he did with all the money, Liddy gets many dates and facts mixed up, but by writing *Will* he has at least enabled others to better understand his lunacy. With a fellow like Liddy working for Nixon, the fact that Nixon's presidency fell apart should not be a surprise. No one describes Liddy better than Liddy, who boasts that it was he who:

- organized the Plumbers Unit, dubbing it ODESSA— the acronym for "Der Emerlingen Schutz Staffel Angehorigen," the post-World War II network of former Nazis that smuggled former high-level Nazi officials, including many of the worst war criminals, to safety in places like South America.

- reported to his superiors in writing on August 2, 1971, not long after the unit was created, that the FBI was not aggressively investigating Ellsberg, and that the FBI was no longer conducting "clandestine operations," and then cautioned that "any further discussions" of these activities "should be oral."

- arranged for a special screening at the National Arc-hives of Leni Riefenstahl's infamous Nazi propa-ganda film, *Triumph of the Will*, inviting select guests from the White House staff to the event. (I was not invited.)

- suggested that the Department of Justice wiretap the *New York Times* to learn more about how they re-ceived the Pentagon Papers from Ellsberg.

- encouraged his superiors to request that the CIA prepare a psychological profile of Ellsberg (notwith-standing the fact that the CIA is prohibited from en-gaging in such domestic activities), and when

509

unhappy with the profile that had been prepared (which was based on information Liddy had assembled from the FBI investigation of Ellsberg), requested a second profile. (Liddy believed that Ellsberg had leaked the material to the Soviet Union, although there has never been any credible evidence whatsoever to support that claim. To the contrary, although a Soviet double agent said that the Russian Embassy had received a copy—before reading it in the *New York Times*—there is no evidence whatsoever that Ellsberg was connected to the Russians' receipt of a copy, although this fact did not stop the Nixon White House from smearing him with the charge.)

• recommended (actually, he sold to his superiors) a scheme to burglarize Ellsberg's psychiatrist's office in Beverly Hills, California. Liddy assured his superiors that such a covert action could be undertaken and could not be traced to the White House. However, he later acknowledged that although he was "forbidden to participate directly in the mission," he broke his agreement with Krogh, and served as the lookout man for his team of burglars when they broke into the building to retrieve Ellsberg's medical files. If the police had shown up, Liddy said his plan was to distract them by "fleeing ostentatiously to draw them off, confident I could elude them." And if that did not work and "there were no other recourse," he had his "knife, but use it I would, if I'd had to; I had given my word that I would protect [my men]." (The ludicrousness of this action is patent. Liddy's belief that he could outrun policemen, their cars, and their dogs, and that all of them would follow him, rather than assume he was merely a lookout, defies common sense. Had the police come by, there would have been no Watergate. Rather, it would have been The Fielding Affair that might have brought down Nixon. And had Liddy killed a police officer, he would still be doing time. Most remarkably, the burglary was a fishing expedition, all risk and no possible reward, because, in fact, there were no Ellsberg files in Dr. Fielding's office.)

- concocted a plan to drug Ellsberg with "a fast-acting psychedelic such as LSD-25," when Ellsberg was scheduled to speak at a dinner at a Washington hotel, to "befuddle him, make him appear a near burnt-out drug case."

- was ready to assassinate newspaper columnist Jack Anderson.

- hired thugs to physically attack anti-war demonstrators on Capitol Hill, during an Ellsberg speech.

This was the sorry state to which the Nixon White House fell after the leak of the Pentagon Papers. Nixon pounding on his desk, demanding a break-in at the Brookings Institute; Chuck Colson (or was it Jack Caulfield?) calling for a firebombing at the Brookings Institute; and placing a man on the White House staff with the mentality of Gordon Liddy. Bud Krogh later apologized to me for suggesting Liddy as the general counsel of Nixon's reelection committee when I was trying to find someone to fill that post. Krogh told me the reason he had done so was that he and Ehrlichman had wanted to get Liddy out of the White House. They realized he was a disaster. Mistakenly, they thought that Liddy could cause no problems working at the reelection committee.

Bug Krogh wrote in his book (co-authored with his son, Matthew Krogh) *Integrity: Good People, Bad Choices and Life Lessons from the White House* (2007) that "[t]he break-in and burglary of Dr. Fielding's office was the seminal event in the chain of events that led to Nixon's resignation on August 8, 1974." Bud explained what too many do not understand:

...the burglary [at Ellsberg's psychiatrist's office] set a precedent that two members of the Plumbers [referring to Liddy and Hunt] could rely on when planning and executing the Watergate break-in of 1972. They knew that under certain circumstances the White House staff would tolerate an illegal act to obtain information. Later, during the intensive Watergate investigations, a major reason for the cover-up by President Nixon and former members of his staff was to prevent investigators from discovering information about the 1971 crime. Extreme illegal acts were undertaken to prevent this discovery, including perjury, obstruction of justice, and the payment of hush money to the perpetrators of the 1971 crime to keep them from revealing it during the Watergate investigation. Several members of Nixon's top staff [here, Krogh is referring to Haldeman and Ehrlichman] feared that discovery of the 1971 events would imperil them and the president himself. Former attorney general John Mitchell, when apprised in 1972 what had happened in 1971, accurately described the 1971 events as the White House "horrors."

The Reason for the Break-ins at the Democratic National Committee

Notwithstanding overwhelming evidence, there remains confusion (for far too many) about why the Democratic National Committee (DNC) was the target of Liddy's intelligence-gathering operation after he joined the Nixon reelection campaign committee. Many wonder why anyone would undertake ventures as high-risk as two break-ins and bugging the DNC given the low potential gains, since the DNC had little, if any, information that might help Nixon win reelection in 1972. The answer is as simple as it is unsatisfying: It was folly (if not stupidity) and hubris.

What in fact occurred is traceable to the dark side of Richard Nixon, who became angry and upset when the Democrats rained on his parade following his historic trip to China, cutting short the political benefits emanating from his visit. They did this by claiming that the Nixon Administration had settled an antitrust case in exchange for a large campaign contribution. This negative news cut short the positive politics of Nixon's China initiative. In fact, Nixon, who played hardball politics, set in motion the activities that culminated with the arrests of people working for his reelection committee at the DNC. This is not to say that the president ordered the break-in and bugging of the DNC, for he did not. Nor is it to say that he had advance knowledge of these actions, for he did not. And it is not to say that anyone at the White House was directly involved in these actions. It is to say, however, that it was the quest to get the very information that Nixon had wanted, and repeatedly requested, that resulted in bungled bugging and burglaries at the DNC. Set forth below is the clear evidence that leads me to this conclusion, most of it not available until long after I had written and published *Blind Ambition*.

Looking for Financial Dirt on the Democrats

As I reported (on pages 51-67), in early March 1972, the so-called ITT (International Telephone and Telegraph) scandal erupted when syndicated columnist Jack Anderson published a memorandum written by Dita Bread, an ITT employee and lobbyist, claiming that ITT's $400,000 contribution to the Nixon campaign for its convention in San Diego had influenced Nixon's Justice Department in settling a major antitrust lawsuit against ITT. Anderson's story was published the day after Nixon had returned from his triumphant visit to China. In fact, there had been no quid pro quo as the Anderson story suggested, but the Democrats—particularly DNC Chairman Larry O'Brien—were making great political gains with the charge and were successfully taking much of the luster off of Nixon's China trip, supplanting it with a seedy front-page political corruption story. Few people were higher on Nixon's enemies list than O'Brien, whom he believed was a puppet for one of his top enemies, Senator Edward Kennedy.

Jeb Magruder, in his autobiography, *An American Life: One Man's Road To Watergate* (1974), explained what occurred that piqued White House interest in locating negative information as a means of countering the Democrats' ITT attacks. Jeb reported that in early March, 1972, Nixon's campaign "had a tip from Kevin Phillips, the conservative columnist, that the Democratic Party might be involved in a kickback scheme in connection with their convention. The report was that the Democrats would lease space to individual exhibitors and kick back part of the fee to the Democrats." It is very likely that Kevin Phillips, who had once worked for John Mitchell (during the 1968 campaign, as well as after Mitchell became Attorney General), had spoken directly with Mitchell. Mitchell had great respect for Phillips and would not have lightly dismissed such a tip from him—nor would Haldeman or the President. While the evidence of Nixon's reaction may be incomplete, I have found clear signposts, which show his direct orders to go after the Democrats, including:

March 5, 1972: The President, returning to the White House from Key Biscayne on Air Force One, met with Haldeman, who made the following note: "Do some [checking] on where the Democratic money for Miami is coming from—re ITT Sheratons what contracts they have made." (The Democrats were going to hold their convention in Miami.)

514

March 7, 1972: Haldeman dictated an Action Memo, which was sent to Larry Higby, who added a handwritten inquiry to Haldeman: "Put Dean, Colson & Magruder to work on this? Dean in charge?" Haldeman responded with a handwritten answer: "OK - not by memo." Haldeman further instructed Higby to get a response by March 10th.

March 7 or 8, 1972: When Higby passed this assignment on to me (as I later testified), he did not place me in charge of anything. Rather, he informed me that Magruder and Colson were investigating to determine if the Democrats were running a "kickback scheme" of some sort in Miami, and Higby said that he had told Magruder to check with me to be certain there was, in fact, solid evidence of a kickback scheme before anyone leaked anything to the media.

March 8, 1972: The President asked Haldeman if there was "anything on the Miami investigation?" As the recorded conversation reveals, the President rhetorically inquired: "Why can't we find some dirt on Democrats? We should be able to counter attack, put them on [the] defensive." Because this conversation had not previously been transcribed, I listened to it in order to prepare a partial transcript. Nixon was very unhappy with the media flak he and his former Attorney General were getting over the ITT matter, which he believed to be totally unjustified. The following exchange occurs during the conversation:

NIXON: One thing I was going to tell you to do, and I assume our boys are smart enough to do, they may be smart enough but they aren't doing it—has anybody thought to check to see what Miami Beach hotels have underwritten the [Democratic] Miami convention, and second, this is what they have to check. There probably is more than one or two over

	there that doesn't have gangster money, have they thought of that?
HALDEMAN:	We're, we'll get...the Miami story on, on, the, their support thing...
NIXON:	I advised Mitchell and his gang, and Ehrlichman all along, and they have not followed through when I ordered this two years ago, go after the bastards, you know, we've got to have dirt to throw at them, correct? I'll tell you, I don't know what they've done. I don't know where it is? Anything, throw it up there.

March 8, 1972: Following this session, Haldeman issued another Action Memo. After suggesting options to deal with the news media, Haldeman added: "In any event, we need a counterattack. We must not let them get away with the only attack on this. We've got to build up the Miami story and anything else we can... We've got to find a way to turn around the PR on this. We're getting taken unfairly and we should be taking some initiative ourselves." Haldeman added in a handwritten note to Colson: "We need an attack on the Democrats for the contributions for individuals and to the party. There should be a careful investigation of the financial support of their convention and that should be put together as material for an attack." Haldeman wanted a fast follow-up on all this.

According to the records of the Watergate Special Prosecutor's office, at this time Jack Caulfield dispatched Tony Ulasewicz to Miami. Ulasewicz met with two men from the IRS (Caulfield had extensive contacts in the Treasury Department and the IRS). Ulasewicz told the IRS men that "he was investigating rumors concerning who was paying for the Democratic Convention and that there might be some mob connections."

March 13, 1972: The President dictated a lengthy memorandum to Haldeman in which he explained why he was so troubled by the adverse publicity from the charges regarding ITT:

This brings me to the point. It is very much in our interest, of course, to keep the China story alive in terms of the enormous public impact that it has had... As a matter of fact, the IT&T case I think was deliberately surfaced at this time for the purpose of knocking down public interest and coverage of the China visit. In that connection, it was a brilliant success although not a total success due to the fact that we had a few announcements to make after the IT&T story broke. But make no mistake about it. This is exactly why Kennedy et al. broke that story at this point. They have had it for a long time and they saved it up for right now so that they could torpedo the China visit. I am sure that Henry [Kissinger] and others concerned would not understand that this is what the deal was all about, but I could see it the moment that I saw the stories begin to surface on Friday after we had returned from China on Monday.

March 14, 1972: Again, in a recorded conversation, the President pushed Haldeman for negative information about the Democrats: "Do we have anything new on the investigation into the Miami Beach, ah, convention?" the President asked. Haldeman replied that there was nothing yet. That afternoon, the frustrated President pressed further: "Can't we find some dirt on the Democrats?" Haldeman started to reply, "Yep. We sure—," when he was interrupted by the President, who was clearly giving an order, although that is not clear on the tape, except when he curtly added: "You better." Haldeman wrote in his diary that Nixon wanted to start counter-attacking the Democrats, "instead of just reacting" to them.

517

March 15-16, 1972: At about this time, Caulfield provided me with newspaper clippings that Ulasewicz had gathered during his investigation in Florida, none of which indicated any improper funding by the Democrats of their convention. In addition, Magruder hand-carried a copy of a March 15, 1972 memorandum that Gordon Liddy had written to John Mitchell, reporting on the investigation that Magruder had instructed Liddy to undertake into the Democrats' convention funding and the alleged kickback operation. Liddy's memorandum contained a sweeping conclusion, based on information purportedly given to Howard Hunt by "an experienced political correspondent for major news media in the Miami area," that the DNC would be "receiving a 25 percent kickback from the funds raised through the exposition to be held at the Fontainebleau Hotel and Convention Hall" during the July 1972 Democratic National Convention. Magruder delivered this memorandum to me because of Higby's earlier instruction, not to mention the fact that John Mitchell, who had resigned as Attorney General effective March 1, 1972, was extremely busy helping his successor, Dick Kleindienst, win Senate confirmation, which had been stalled by the ITT flap. Magruder wanted my opinion as to whether he should leak Liddy's information to the press, charging the Democrats with operating a kickback scheme. After reading Liddy's memorandum, I concluded that the information was ambiguous at best, and advised Magruder to do nothing without better information. Because Liddy's conclusion was attributed to an unnamed newsman, I suggested to Magruder that he get more information about that newsman so he could assess it. I jotted a note—"need more info"—on the memorandum to make a record of why I had killed any idea of leaking the information, and filed it. (Later, I turned it over to the Senate Watergate Committee.)

Liddy's plans for illegal intelligence-gathering were not approved by Mitchell until the end of March, when Magruder met with Mitchell, who was vacationing in Florida, as the political attacks by Larry O'Brien and the Democrats regarding ITT continued. Magruder testified before the Senate Watergate Committee that when Mitchell approved Liddy's plans on March 30, 1972, those plans called for "initial entry into the Democratic National Committee headquarters in Washington, and that at a further date, if the funds were available, we would consider entry into the Presidential contenders' headquarters, and also potentially at the Fontainebleau Hotel in Miami."[*] A year later, during an interview with the Watergate Special Prosecutor, Magruder explained (according to the prosecutor's notes) what it was that Liddy was to look for at the DNC, and why the Fontainebleau Hotel:

> Liddy understood that photographs were to be taken of any documents in the DNC that would be valuable in terms of the intelligence that Liddy was supposed to be providing at that time, which included, in particular, anything that would demonstrate that the Democrats had agreed to the kick-back scheme at the Fountainblue [sic] that Kevin [sic] Phillips had previously reported.

I must pause for just a moment to note the extraordinary nature of the activity that was transpiring in March 1972. Because the president wanted dirt on the Democrats, and wanted to counter the negative charges regarding ITT, Haldeman had Colson (and his staff) working on it; he had Caulfield send Ulasewicz to Florida to dig up information; he instructed

---

[*]   Earlier, when recounting events, I mentioned that only once did I ask Mitchell if, in fact, he had approved Liddy's plans at a meeting with Magruder on March 30, 1972. Mitchell told me he had done so. See page 275. Years later, when Haldeman published his diaries, I found that on that same day, March 28, 1973, ironically almost exactly a year after the fact, Mitchell told Haldeman the same thing, which Haldeman entered in his diary: "Mitchell and Magruder both told [Dean] that they had both signed off on the project [referring to Liddy's illegal plans], which Mitchell told me, also."

Magruder to turn Liddy loose to dig up what he could find; and I had been instructed to evaluate the information before anything was leaked. In addition, Kleindienst's confirmation hearings were ongoing. In fact, witnesses appeared before the Senate Judiciary Committee on March 2, 3, 6-10, 14-16, 26, 29 and April 10, 11, 13, 14, 17-20, and 27, 1972, which provided the grist for daily headlines and nightly television network news. The Nixon Administration was taking a political beating. It is long forgotten now, but by the time Kleindienst was confirmed by the Senate on June 8, 1972, the Nixon Administration had been hammered, day in and day out, for months, and been badly stung by the Democrats' charges.

It was a presidential election year, and Liddy's intelligence-gathering activities were approved at the height of the ITT controversy, at a time that Haldeman (acting for the President) was still pressing hard for negative financial information concerning the Democrats and their convention. Magruder has testified repeatedly and consistently to these facts. When cooperating privately with the prosecutors (as noted above), he told them the same facts, explaining that they were looking for information to run down the alleged kickback scheme.

The Burglars Were Looking for Financial Information

The events that followed the approval of Liddy's plans are best recalled by those who were directly involved in the two break-ins at the DNC. Because Liddy was running this operation, I have started with his memory of the events. Liddy wrote in *Will* that his team broke into the DNC's Watergate office, the first time, on May 28, 1972, and that, when doing so, he was acting at the request of Jeb Magruder, who had asked him a very direct question, "near the end of April," when ITT was still making headlines: "Gordon, do you think you could get into the Watergate?" Liddy answered that he could. Magruder then asked: "How about putting a bug in O'Brien's office?"

After discussing the fact that O'Brien was in Miami preparing for the Democratic National Convention, Magruder—according to Liddy—said he wanted "to know whatever's said in his office." In addition, Magruder said to Liddy, "And while you're in there, photograph whatever you can find." In short, there was no specific information sought. Rather, Magruder was merely seeking whatever a bug planted in O'Brien's office might produce, and whatever the documents they found and photographed might reveal. It was another fishing expedition, but because this operation was screwed up beyond belief—bungled every step of the way—many overlook the lack of specificity as to what it was that they were fishing for, thinking that there must have been more going on than has been revealed. In fact, the operation was even more badly botched than has been reported.

There were five people who entered the DNC on May 28, 1972: four Cuban-Americans and Jim McCord, a former FBI agent and retired CIA electronics specialist. Virgilio Gonzales, the locksmith, and Frank Sturgis, were to be lookouts once they got inside. Bernard Barker was to locate documents, and Eugenio Rolando Martinez was to photograph them. Those involved in the first entry at the DNC were told by Hunt to look for financial documents—anything with "numbers on them." To make it appear to be a national security operation, Hunt told the Cuban-Americans (who knew Hunt as a CIA operative who had been involved in the Bay of Pigs invasion) to look for foreign contributions, particularly from Fidel Castro. Hunt understood that this deception would produce financial information. Hunt and Martinez, the most knowledgeable, have repeatedly testified to these facts.

Howard Hunt, notwithstanding his admission that he initially lied, has testified consistently as to what he told the Cuban-Americans whom he recruited for the Watergate break-ins. Hunt, who first agreed to testify truthfully during the *United*

521

States v. Mitchell trial, succinctly explained what they were looking for in the DNC:

[Testimony regarding the first break-in at the DNC]

Q: Now, can you tell us what instructions were given to the men under your command, to Mr. Barker and his men?

A: That they were to make the entry and photograph anything with a figure on it.

Q: When you say a figure, you are referring to financial type material?

A: Yes, sir.

Q: This is in the office of the Democratic National Committee Headquarters?

A: Yes, sir.

Q: What about Mr. McCord? Did you know what Mr. McCord was supposed to be doing in there?

A: I knew that Mr. McCord would either be bugging or wiretapping.

[The questioning here moved to cover the second break-in at the DNC]

Q: What instructions were the men who were to photograph documents given?

A: They were to photograph everything that was available with particular reference to any papers with financial figures and computations on them, anything that looked like contributors. In fact, a second camera had been procured for that purpose, together with a large quantity of film.

Q: Did you know what Mr. McCord was supposed to be doing on the second entry?

A: He was supposed to be either replacing or repairing an electronic device that for some reason was not functioning properly.

Martinez, who also testified in a deposition in my wife's and my own defamation lawsuit, has consistently said that they were looking for financial information regarding contributions from Fidel Castro. Martinez added that, at that time, it seemed a credible story. Asked to be more specific, Martinez explained, "I want to say the document that might represent that there [was] money coming in or money going out, some accounting thing, anything related with money coming from Cuba...anything that we could find out about that, that is what we were told."

Alfred Baldwin was the man assigned to listen to the conversations at the bugged DNC offices. He was hired at the time of the first break-in by Liddy's "wireman," James McCord. Al Baldwin moved into the Howard Johnson Hotel, and took a room facing Virginia Avenue, thus facing those of the Watergate offices of the DNC that were directly across the street and also faced Virginia Avenue. Baldwin, also a former FBI agent, cooperated with the prosecutors after the arrests of Liddy's men during the second entry, and was never prosecuted. Baldwin testified against Liddy and McCord at their trial, and fleetingly during the Senate Watergate hearings, but he was never closely questioned about what exactly happened, until a deposition in our lawsuit.

When we questioned Baldwin he confirmed (under oath) Liddy's men never entered O'Brien's office during the first break-in. Baldwin described Liddy's operation as a joke, comic, a "Katzenjammer Kids" operation—it was "just totally unorganized." During the first entry into the DNC, the burglars never got anywhere near O'Brien's office, for good reason—they did not have a clue where it was located. As a result, no bug was ever placed in O'Brien's office, and no photographs

523

were taken in or near his office. O'Brien's office was located in a separate suite of offices within the DNC complex and behind a locked glass door that was never opened during the first break-in. It was McCord's job to place the bug in O'Brien's office, but Baldwin testified during his deposition that it was not until shortly before the second entry, on June 12, 1972, that McCord instructed him to visit the DNC to find the location of O'Brien's office. Baldwin did this by pretending to be the nephew of a former DNC chairman (a person Baldwin actually knew). Knowing that O'Brien was out of town, he asked O'Brien's secretary to show him the chairman's office, which was located in the back of the building, where the listening post at the Howard Johnson Hotel would not have been able to pick up the signal from a bug. Baldwin drew a crude floor plan so that McCord would know where to go when they entered the second time.

As late as 1980, when he was writing *Will*, Liddy believed his men had entered O'Brien's office during their first entry because one of the burglars (Bernard Barker) had reported, as Liddy wrote, that "Barker had two rolls of 36-exposure 35-mm film he'd expended on material from O'Brien's desk, along with Polaroid shots of the desk and office before anything was touched so that it could all be returned to proper order before leaving." In fact, these pictures could not have been of materials on O'Brien's desk. Liddy added, when recounting these events in *Will* that the next morning he "reported to Magruder the successful entry into the Democratic National Committee headquarters in the Watergate. For proof, I showed him Polaroid photographs of the interior of Larry O'Brien's office." In fact, the suite of offices that McCord bugged (and the office Barker had no doubt photographed) belonged to the Chairman of the Democratic State Governors, and included the office of the Director of the Office for the State Chairman, R. Spencer Oliver, and the office of his secretary, Ida M. Wells. McCord placed a bug in the telephone system of this suite of offices, which faced the Howard Johnson Hotel across the street, and said that he planted a room bug, as well, that never worked. Since the Democratic State Governors office was frequently empty, and Spencer Oliver was often traveling, the conversations that Baldwin overheard using the bug were largely of the secretaries who made use of this phone system in these empty offices. (They liked this phone system because it did not go through the DNC's switchboard operator.) Baldwin estimated that he may have heard as few as "60" and possibly as many as "100" or more different people use the phone that McCord had bugged, and none of them was Larry O'Brien or any member of his personal staff.

While Liddy apparently did not know his team had never made it to O'Brien's office, he did know that the bug McCord had installed was not picking up anything regarding O'Brien. He wrote in *Will* that by June 9, 1972, Magruder had looked at the summaries of the conversations that Baldwin was overhearing—no electronic recordings were made because McCord could not figure out how to connect his taping machine to the radio receiver intercepting the calls, so Baldwin made notes and Liddy had his secretary retyped them—Magruder found the material "hardly worth the effort, risk, and expense."

After further conversations with Magruder, Liddy set up a second entry into the DNC to repair the defective bug and to take more photographs of financial material in the DNC files. It would be done the same night that they planned to break into and bug Democratic presidential candidate George McGovern's headquarters on Capitol Hill. In discussing the second DNC break-in, Liddy wrote, "Magruder didn't tell me what he either expected, or was afraid, we'd find in O'Brien's files," only that he wanted his men "to photograph everything in his desk and in those files." (While Liddy did not recall what Magruder wanted when writing *Will*, as noted earlier, Hunt recalled clearly, and Hunt had received this information from Liddy to impart to the Cuban-Americans. This, however, is typical of Liddy's selective or poor memory in reconstructing these events so long after they occurred.)

False Protests of Ignorance, With Occasional Slips, At the White House

Protests of ignorance about why anyone would break into the DNC offices were rampant after Liddy's men were arrested. Neither Nixon nor Haldeman wanted to recall the actions they had earlier demanded be taken to look for financial dirt on the Democrats, nor did they want to recall putting pressure on everyone to find such intelligence. Notwithstanding these protests of ignorance, however, both Nixon and Haldeman slipped from time to time and revealed their knowledge when discussing what, in fact, had happened. Unfortunately, there is no single collection of all the transcribed Nixon taped conversations, and most of the conversations have not been transcribed. One day, it will be possible to do a digital search, which will help locate the hidden nuggets. Still, proceeding the old-fashioned way—by reading—I have found conversations that show that Nixon and Haldeman, in fact, knew exactly what had occurred at the DNC and why it had happened. Below are a few examples, and I do not doubt that, one day, more will be found:

On June 20, 1972, just three days after the arrests at the Watergate, and on his first day back in his office, Nixon had the following exchange with Haldeman. (The emphases are mine):

NIXON: My God, the [Democratic National] committee isn't worth bugging in my opinion. *That's my public line.*

HALDEMAN: *Except for this financial thing.* They thought they had something going on that.

526

NIXON: Yes, I suppose.

Nixon and Haldeman discussed the fact that they were looking for financial information in the DNC during a conversation on January 3, 1973 (again, emphases are my own):

NIXON: I can see Mitchell, but I can't see Colson getting into the Democratic office.

HALDEMAN: The stupidity.

NIXON: What the Christ was he looking for?

HALDEMAN: They were looking for stuff on two things. One, *on financial.*

NIXON: Yes.

HALDEMAN: And *the other on stuff that they thought they had on what they were going to do at Miami to screw us up, because apparently—a Democratic plot.* And they thought they had it uncovered. Colson was salivating with glee at the thought of what he might be able to do with it. And they were very reluctant, the investigator types were reluctant, to go in there. They were put under tremendous pressure that they had to get that stuff. None of this— I don't know any of this firsthand. I can't prove any of it, and I don't want to know it. As I pointed out, if I ever get called in I'll be ignorant, which I am.

Among the references that I have found (so far) regarding the President's interest in the financial activities of the Democrats, is a conversation I had with him on February 28, 1973. In the middle of this conversation, and literally out of nowhere, Nixon asked me a question: "What in the name of God ever

527

became of our investigation of their [referring to the Democrats] financial activities? Jesus Christ, they borrowed—they cancelled debts, they borrowed money. What the hell is that?" At the time, I was not certain what the President was taking about, because I had been only incidentally involved in the earlier full-court press to dig up financial dirt on the Democrats, so I stammered and mentioned the fact that his opponent Senator George McGovern's finances were in "bad shape," and then proceeded to another topic. Reading the transcript of this conversation years later, I realized that Nixon was testing me to see how much I did or did not know about these earlier efforts, and when he realized I did not know anything, he, too, moved on. The subject would come up again.

On March 13, 1973, in a conversation with me, the following exchange occurred (again, emphases are my own):

DEAN: A lot of people around here had knowledge that something was going on over there. They didn't have any knowledge of the details of the specifics of, of the whole thing.

NIXON: You know, that must, must be an indication, though, of the fact that, that they had God damn poor pickings. Because naturally anybody, either Chuck or Bob, uh, was always reporting to me about what was going on. If they ever got any information they would certainly have told me that we got some information, but they never had a God damn [laughs] thing to report. What was the matter? Did they never get anything out of the damn thing?

DEAN: No. I don't think they ever got anything.

NIXON: It was a dry hole, huh?

DEAN: That's right.

NIXON: Jesus Christ.

DEAN: Well, they were just really getting started.

NIXON: Yeah. Yeah. But, uh, Bob one time said some-
           thing about the fact we got some information
           about this or that or the other, but, I, *I think it
           was about the Convention, what they were plan-
           ning*, I said [unintelligible].

Today, I have no doubt that Nixon understood that his request for dirt about the financial activities of the Democrats
was the catalyst that resulted in Mitchell's approving Liddy's
operation that resulted in his men getting arrested in the
Democratic headquarters. This was not information that Nixon
was about to admit to anyone, other than through his oblique
admissions to Haldeman. This, of course, raised the following
question: If Nixon's involvement in the ruinous Watergate
operation was so tangential, and if no one at the White House
was involved directly in the conspiracy to burglarize and bug
the DNC, then why did the cover-up occur, when the cover-up
appears to have made it so much worse for everyone?

Reasons for the Watergate Cover-up: More Stupidity, Including My Own

Bud Krogh's explanation as to why the cover-up occurred—that the Ellsberg-related burglary was at the core of
the cover-up—is correct, at least as far as the White House was
concerned. This fact was well understood by all who were
involved in the cover-up, although it has been left to only Bud
and myself to acknowledge it, since Haldeman, Ehrlichman,
and Mitchell went to their graves either pretending they did not
understand why the cover-up occurred or denied that anything
untoward had, in fact, happened.

Initially, and during the first few days after learning of the
arrest of Liddy's team at the DNC, there was considerable

confusion at the White House about what, in fact, had truly occurred. Certainly, no meeting was held where everyone sat down and planned a cover-up. No information was more incomprehensible and difficult to understand than the fact that not only had Liddy used James McCord—head of security at the Committee to Reelect the President, who was then in jail—but Liddy had also used the same men he had employed to burglarize Daniel Ellsberg's psychiatrist's office. As for Liddy's contingency plans in the event that his men got caught and were arrested, he had absolutely none, so he laid it off on the reelection committee and the White House to take care of such problems as providing support money and attorneys' fees for those who had been arrested—a sure and short route to obstruction of justice. In fact, a panicked Liddy had tracked down Attorney General Kleindienst at his golf club, confessed that his men had been arrested at the DNC, and requested that Kleindienst get them out of jail—as if he could, in fact, actually do that without obstructing justice, not to mention the attorney general of the United States had no jurisdiction over the District of Columbia jails.

Liddy was confident that no investigator could trace him to the events at the DNC, or to Hunt. Yet it was quickly discovered that Liddy—as general counsel at the reelection committee—had laundered campaign money for the committee through the bank of Barnard Barker, who, after his arrest at the DNC, was in the District of Columbia jail. The address book of another of the men arrested at the DNC and put in jail included Howard Hunt's White House phone number. As Nixon said at the time, if we did not know better, it would have all looked to us like it had been intentionally botched. When the FBI entered the case, its investigation quickly revealed that Liddy had left a trail all over the country when he had traveled and tried to recruit former CIA and FBI men to join his team, making it clear that he was planning illicit operations.

Personally, I felt that I had no criminal exposure from Liddy's failed operations. While I had little knowledge of the criminal law, I knew just enough to convince myself that I had withdrawn from the conspiracy to burglarize and bug the DNC. I had thrown cold water on Liddy's proposal during the second meeting in Mitchell's office, and told Haldeman I wanted nothing to do with Liddy's crazy schemes, to which Haldeman had concurred. And I'd had no further dealings with Liddy's illegal activities, and was not aware that they had been approved.

In truth, I was deeply ignorant about the criminal law, and it had never occurred to me that the Counsel to the President needed to be (or have access to) a criminal lawyer. If I had been aware, I would have hired one for my staff. At the Nixon White House, the White House Counsel's Office needed a highly-trained criminal lawyer. I had never heard of the crime of obstruction of justice until well into the cover-up, when I pulled out a copy of the federal criminal code to determine what, if any, laws we might be breaking. Had I better understood the criminal law, my antennae would have been fully extended. Instead, I learned about obstruction of justice the hard way and paid dearly for my stupidity. (Remarkably, over a dozen attorneys ended up on the wrong side of the law in the course of Watergate, a fact that I attribute to lack of knowledge of the criminal law and to the instinctive loyalty widely felt toward the office of the president, regardless of the occupant.)

There is no doubt in my mind that if Liddy, and Hunt, had not undertaken earlier illegal activities for the White House, then Haldeman and Ehrlichman would have urged the President to cut all ties with his friend, former law partner, and campaign manager John Mitchell. Mitchell might have agreed, and indeed urged that very action, had he not learned about Liddy's activities at the White House, which he later described as "the White House horrors." (At one point after the cover-up had collapsed, Mitchell made an offer to the Watergate Special

Prosecutor that he would plead guilty if they would back off the investigation of Nixon, but by then, it was far too late.)

Mitchell learned about Liddy's and Hunt's activities at the Plumber's Unit in great detail from Bob Mardian, who had become Mitchell's aide at the reelection committee. Mardian and Fred LaRue debriefed Liddy shortly after the arrest of his men at the DNC, and Liddy shared all the ugly details. As a result, Mitchell was concerned that the Ellsberg break-in was potentially even more serious politically for Nixon than the bungled break-in at the DNC offices, for no one was sure if Nixon had been directly involved in the Ellsberg break-in. If Mitchell ever asked the President about the Ellsberg break-in, which there is no indication that he did, he would have learned that Nixon had not authorized it.

Liddy's and Hunt's activities at the Plumber's Unit were called "national security" work (and at one point, Nixon forbade me to discuss these activities with prosecutors for this reason). But no one knew what that meant and whether it justified illegal conduct, not to mention covering up that conduct. These questions were never discussed. Rather they just loomed in the background, based upon indirect references. If, in fact, Nixon did not know about the Ellsberg break-in until I told him about it on March 17, 1973, which he claimed to be the case, then Ehrlichman and Haldeman were keeping information from Nixon that he needed in order to understand what was taking place. While I have not listened to enough of the Nixon tapes to know, I would be stunned to find that Nixon was not aware of this fundamental problem long before I told him about it.

As to whether it was a legitimate national security matter, two courts have examined the issue. When Ehrlichman, Liddy, Barker, and Martinez were on trial for the Ellsberg burglary, this issue arose. Ehrlichman claimed that Nixon had authorized the Ellsberg action; in particular, he said they had discussed it while walking on the beach in San Clemente. But

Ehrlichman had no solid proof of this fact (because there was none) and Nixon was too ill at the time to testify (which helped Ehrlichman). Ehrlichman's fallback argument was that regardless of whether or not the President specifically authorized the break-in itself, such authority had been delegated by the President to the Plumber's Unit. The trial judge ruled that even if the President had the authority to authorize such an act, he could not have delegated that authority to any of the defendants since they were not law enforcement officers and their claims for delegated authority were based on "vague, informal, inexact terms." Accordingly, all were convicted following a jury trial. When their convictions were appealed, however, the U.S. Court of Appeals for the District of Columbia was all over the lot. In affirming Ehrlichman's conviction, the court held that there could be no "national security" exception without specific authorization by the "President or Attorney General."

Nonetheless, this area of law is anything but easy, even for judges. In this split and internally-inconsistent decision, the Court of Appeals also reversed the convictions of burglars Barker and Martinez, because Hunt had described the operation at Ellsberg's psychiatrist's office as a national security matter, when he asked Barker if he would become operational and help conduct a surreptitious entry to obtain national security information on "a traitor to this country who was passing...classified information to the Soviet Embassy." At trial, the jury was instructed by the judge that "an individual cannot escape the criminal law simply because he sincerely but incorrectly believes that his acts are justified in the name of patriotism, or national security...or that his superiors had the authority without a warrant to suspend the Constitutional protections of the Fourth Amendment" (which requires a warrant). But the Court of Appeals found this to be a faulty instruction. They held that Barker and Martinez should have been given an opportunity to show that they believed Hunt, who was then working at the White House, and that they acted on his authority as a government official. After their convictions were set aside, the Watergate Special Prosecutor's Office declined to pursue Barker and Martinez further.

Frankly, since the day Nixon told me I was the first to inform him about the Ellsberg break-in, I have not believed that it could have been a national security undertaking. I understood then, as I do today, that such actions require direct Presidential approval and if Nixon had not heard of it, he surely could not have authorized it. But I did not raise the Ellsberg break-in here in order to resolve this issue. Rather, I do so because I believe that, just as Bud Krogh observed, the efforts to cover up the Watergate break-ins cannot be understood without understanding its relationship to the Ellsberg break-in. This fact exacerbated the tension between those most at risk for authorizing Liddy's illegal activities, John Ehrlichman (the break-in at Ellsberg's psychiatrist office) and John Mitchell (the DNC break-in), who had been at odds long before the arrests at the DNC.

It had been fascinating to watch, as I did from my White House perch, as Ehrlichman slowly but steadily undercut Mitchell's authority and standing with the President. Initially, no one had President Nixon's ear and attention more than his attorney general, John Mitchell, who had not wanted the job and had accepted the post only as a favor to Nixon, who had pushed him hard. Neither Mitchell nor Ehrlichman were familiar with the ways of Washington. Mitchell had been a bond lawyer in New York; Ehrlichman, a real estate lawyer in Seattle. But Ehrlichman was a faster student than Mitchell, and he had closer proximity to Nixon, for he saw him daily, while Mitchell was running the Justice Department. Every time Mitchell made a mistake, and there were many (like his flawed Supreme Court nominees), Ehrlichman made sure the President understood it. By the time I arrived in the White House from Mitchell's Justice Department, eighteen months into Nixon's first term, Ehrlichman's Domestic Council was increasingly making domestic policy decisions as to what the Department of

534

Justice should or should not be doing. Observing Ehrlichman and Mitchell together at White House meetings, I noticed that there was always an edge, and both men seemed to force civility. Ehrlichman blamed Mitchell for the ITT scandal disaster, which had blunted the political pluses from the China trip, the centerpiece of Nixon's reelection bid. After Mitchell departed the Justice Department in March 1972, and Dick Kleindienst took control, Ehrlichman was telling the new attorney general how to run his department. The cover-up cannot be fully understood without appreciating the personalities involved, principally those of Ehrlichman and Mitchell. At the time, they were two of the most powerful men in Washington.

As White House Counsel, I was a second-level staffer in the Nixon White House who reported to Haldeman, the chief of staff. I had no access to the President, other than through Haldeman, or if the President called me. The reason I quickly found myself in an increasingly significant role in dealing with the dire problems that instantly arose after the arrests of Liddy's team at the DNC headquarters was because of the strained, if not toxic, relationship between Ehrlichman and Mitchell. While Mitchell could talk with Haldeman, for whom he had great respect, he found Ehrlichman arrogant and insufferable, so he had nothing to say to the man unless absolutely necessary. In meetings, rather than address each other directly, they would talk to anyone else attending in order to make their point or communicate information that the President needed. Having worked for Mitchell, I knew he trusted me. By June 1972, when Liddy's disaster arrived at the backdoor of the White House, I had been there long enough to have earned Ehrlichman's trust. So the two communicated with each other, regarding the subject of dealing with the problems Liddy had created, through me. I could feel the leverage each was placing on the other.

Again, Ehrlichman blamed Mitchell for approving Liddy's harebrained scheme, which had resulted in the arrests at the DNC, notwithstanding the fact that Ehrlichman himself had failed to warn anyone about Liddy's foolish behavior at the White House before going to the reelection committee. Mitchell blamed Ehrlichman for Liddy's "White House horrors." Ehrlichman, with Haldeman's concurrence, was directing the White House response to Liddy's disaster; Mitchell was directing the reelection committee's response (even after he quickly resigned from his post as Nixon's campaign manager). Because both Ehrlichman and Mitchell had potential criminal liability for authorizing Liddy's illegal actions, they seemed to convince themselves that by protecting themselves, they were protecting the President. As the cover-up progressed and as Liddy's men were demanding more money, not to mention Hunt and, soon, McCord demanding a promise of clemency, Ehrlichman instinctively sought to keep the White House out of it all, while Mitchell needed the assistance of the White House not only in raising money, but also because only the President could grant clemency. It fell to me to communicate between these two camps, and I effectively became the desk officer for the cover-up or, as I said earlier, the linchpin in the conspiracy to obstruct justice (an investigation that might uncover the Ellsberg related break-in).

The fact that Ehrlichman and Mitchell had each other over a barrel in the end hurt Nixon. Neither man was interested in accounting for his behavior, by owning up to approving the disasters Liddy had delivered. This, in turn, created a situation where there was no intelligent discussion and analysis of the problem, for I do not doubt that both men sincerely believed (and went to their Maker believing) that they had undertaken the illegal action only because they were doing what Nixon had wanted. In the end, no one benefited from the disdain with which each of these important Nixon aides viewed the other.

So what can we see at this distance, so many years later, about the Watergate break-ins and cover-up? Most clearly, for anyone who looks, is the fact that the atmosphere that Nixon created in his White House was bound to result in trouble, given the attitude that anything the President did was considered legal and the fact that the President was willing to do anything, more or less. It was almost inevitable that something like the amateurish Ellsberg and Watergate break-ins would have occurred with someone as lacking in judgment as Gordon Liddy in charge. Although the orders for Liddy's illegal activities did not come from Nixon, both operations sought to obtain information Nixon wanted (in both instances, information to discredit his perceived enemies). Moreover, Nixon never considered anything other than an effort to cover up the illegal activities, and it was as amateurish as the illegal activities that were being hidden. In hindsight, it appears that Nixon had only one real option after the arrests at the Watergate, which was to come clean immediately and completely. Had he done so, he might have had a few weeks of ugly publicity, although probably not much worse than the kind he suffered from the ITT scandal, which was baseless. Since America was not about to elect Senator George McGovern, the American people would likely have appreciated Nixon's candor had he exercised it. Sadly, however, neither Nixon's character nor his politics were capable of such sorely needed public truthfulness.

The greatest, and maybe only lasting, lesson of Watergate is that when presidents screw up and make a mistake, they must admit it and not try to hide it. For example, most recently President Bill Clinton learned this lesson the hard way by failing to admit to his illicit affair with Monica Lewinsky. President George W. Bush did not learn the lesson either, and his presidency is going to be haunted as history digs out the horrific mistakes he made by authorizing torture and jeopardizing the civil liberties of Americans in his "war on terror."

One morning while working at the National Archives at College Park, Maryland on the book that would become *The Rehnquist Choice* (2001), a distinguished-looking gentleman with a British accent approached me. He too was doing research and he said that he recognized me, introduced himself, said he was an historian, and asked if I might join him at lunch later in the cafeteria. I had no plans, so I told him I would be pleased to do so. At lunch, an American woman who was his research assistant joined us. He said he wanted me to know this was all off-the-record, should we stumble into anything interesting. We talked about the value of documents and the unique record that Nixon had created of his Presidency, which is probably the best-documented Presidency that will ever exist since no sane President will, again, tape his conversations. My new historian friend lamented that notwithstanding the remarkable record of what occurred during the Nixon years, he had recently read a book about Watergate that he had picked up in a used bookstore: *Secret Agenda: Watergate, Deep Throat and the CIA* (1984) by Jim Hougan, that distorted that record. He said the book had caught his attention because he was visiting the National Archives to do some work with World War II papers. He had been retained by a London law firm, a team of lawyers who were deeply involved in a case dealing with Holocaust deniers, who claim that Hitler might have been hard on the Jews, but the Holocaust was a myth. He said he had been stunned to find signs of a similar and incipient revisionism regarding Watergate in the Hougan book. He mentioned that he hoped that it was not a sign of a "Watergate denial" movement, akin to what had been developing more slowly with the Holocaust. When I told him about Watergate revisionism—and the nine years of litigation I had only recently ended—he was horrified. "Don't let the bastards get away with it," he pleaded. I assured him I would fight them until my last breath.

I understand that there will always be those who will argue that the earth is flat; that the Bible is the literal truth; that

538

evolution is wrong; that there was no Holocaust in Germany; that Franklin Roosevelt was the cause and not the solution to the Great Depression; that mobsters or Castro or Lyndon Johnson, not lone gunman Lee Harvey Oswald, assassinated President John Kennedy; that James Earl Ray did not shoot Dr. Martin Luther King; and that Nixon was an innocent victim of Watergate—to mention a few areas where conspiracy theorists delve. The deliberate distortion of history may sell books, settle scores, and satisfy ideology, but it does little to help us understand ourselves and the real world.

Part II

Watergate Revisionism, or Sex, Lies, and Bogus History

One reason I have explained here, in some detail, how and why the break-ins and cover-up occurred, is because of the effort to falsely rewrite these events for political and financial gain, or both. There is a small group of revisionists, all of whom seem to know one another and work together in their efforts to reject the "received wisdom" about Watergate. The word "cabal" is too pejorative, although they meet the definition; I might call them a "conspiracy," but because they include so many conspiracy buffs, it could be confusing. I think they can best be described as a "clique" because of their working relationships. Some in this clique are merely out to make money, while others are ideologically-driven, and have adopted a "we got it right and everyone else is wrong" attitude, even as they deeply distort the historical record. Because I do plan to fight these people as long as I am able, and after discussing it with counsel, I am only addressing two of the revisionists' works. They have forced me to become litigious, and I am actively considering taking legal action against several of them. Nor will I list them, for they love such publicity, and would only play on it if I did. But a discussion of the two principal

539

works will give you the gist of their work and explain, to some extent, how they develop their new (and bogus) accounts.

Secret Agenda: Watergate, Deep Throat and the CIA

Watergate revisionism efforts began with *Secret Agenda: Watergate, Deep Throat and the CIA* (1984) by Jim Hougan. The fly-leaf on the book jacket of his sensational work summarizes its contents:

> The generally accepted belief about the affair has always been that White House spies bugged the Democrats in their headquarters at the Watergate complex—apparently to gain political intelligence. *Secret Agenda*, however, reveals that accounts of the break-in have been deliberately falsified by a CIA cover story. The readers also learn that;
>
> - The Democrats' Watergate headquarters was never bugged;
>
> - The President was spied upon by his own intelligence agents;
>
> - The CIA tried to manipulate the press to conceal the agency's involvement in forbidden domestic operations;
>
> - False evidence was planted for the FBI to find in Democratic National Committee headquarters;
>
> - Sexual espionage—and not election politics—was at the heart of it all.

Doing what all revisionists and conspiracy theorists do, Hougan, a freelance journalist, went digging into the minutiae of Watergate. This first effort at revisionism did not seek to question the broad outlines of the events, which were still well-known a decade after they occurred, when Hougan was writing. Rather, Hougan sought to raise questions, leaving it for those who might follow him to add to his account (and many

540

have obliged). Hougan claims that the CIA (always a good target for conspiracy theories) was deeply involved in Watergate from start to finish. He accuses former CIA employees Hunt and McCord of having still been connected to the agency when working for Nixon, and he claims that McCord sabotaged his own work to make sure everyone was caught. In addition, Hougan states that the CIA was operating a call-girl ring near the Watergate complex that became involved in all of it.

Reviewing Hougan's work for the *New York Times Book Review*, Watergate author and journalist Anthony Lukas credits Hougan with having been enterprising in his digging, but is forced to question the findings because Hougan "piled premise upon premise" until Lukas found himself "tottering on a tower of unproven assumptions." This is a nice way to describe it. As for my take, I feel Hougan's work can be dismissed because it falls squarely within the analysis of Princeton philosopher Harry G. Frankfurt's classic work *On Bullshit* (Princeton University Press, 2005). Hougan's evidence is pathetic. Take, for example, his claim that McCord botched the break-in and bugging in order to protect his former employer, the CIA. Here, Hougan mistakes McCord's conspicuous ineptitude for skill. Yet McCord had never been a spy or covert operative at the CIA, a position that would have been way above his pay-grade. Rather, he was something of an electronics janitor who swept CIA facilities to be certain they were not bugged. Hougan appears to misunderstand the fact that the CIA's relationship to Watergate began as a red-herring argument to defend Nixon—an argument that had been cooked up by Chuck Colson, working with Senator Howard Baker. The Watergate Special Prosecution Force investigated the CIA's role in Watergate and found the CIA to be a lot smarter than the efforts of Nixon, Mitchell, Haldeman, and Ehrlichman to involve the CIA in Watergate.

The New York Times, which received a copy of Hougan's book shortly before publication, tried to generate news from it.

On November 6, 1984, the *Times* used the inside-page headline "'72 Data Show FBI Questioned If Burglars Bugged The Watergate." The headline refers to an FBI memorandum Hougan obtained through the Freedom of Information Act that reported that the FBI laboratory "doubted that telephone taps found at the Watergate complex in Washington were compatible with eavesdropping receivers used by" Liddy's team. Earl Silbert, the Assistant U.S. Attorney who had prosecuted McCord and Liddy (Hunt and the Cuban-Americans had all pled guilty), was quoted in the FBI materials as having "strenuously challenged the FBI's conclusions" at the time, as he did when the *Times* contacted him. Silbert then believed, as he does today, that the FBI lab screwed up. Baldwin testified at the McCord and Liddy trial that he had listened to as many as hundreds of conversations (and, as noted earlier, these involved 50 to 100 or more different people) from a bug in the DNC, just as he did again during our lawsuit. Hougan handles this conflicting information by simply expressing his confidence that the FBI lab was correct, and that there was no bug in the DNC. However, Hougan's explanation is absurd. He claims that Baldwin was not overhearing conversations in the DNC, but rather was listening to conversations at a nearby call-girl ring located at the Columbia Plaza—a covert operation run by the CIA, according to Hougan. Baldwin's testimony completely undermines this claim. That the *Times* would think this nonsense was news, however, is not surprising.

The Washington Post, which understands Watergate, largely ignored Hougan's book. *The New York Times*, on the other hand, which was scooped by the *Post* on the biggest story of the last quarter of the Twentieth Century and has never recovered from its weak Watergate reporting, prominently reviewed Hougan's work and declared it one of the best nonfiction books of 1984. (Fiction, maybe, but nonfiction?) The *Times* has consistently promoted Watergate revisionism, for it seems that its institutional memory is so jealous of the drubbing the *Post* handed the paper during Watergate that the *Times* keeps looking for information that might somehow show that the *Post* got it wrong. Thus, they are overly willing to promote any other version of this history.[*]

In fact, the *Times* should have looked into the history enough to know that virtually every sensational claim in Hougan's book was wrong. For example, Hougan's candidate for Deep Throat, *Washington Post* reporter Bob Woodward's notorious unidentified Watergate source, was about as off-the-wall and inaccurate as the rest of the book. Hougan deduces that because Deep Throat never told Woodward about Al Baldwin, the "FBI's top echelon and many of its agents" must be eliminated as candidates for consideration—thus eliminating Assistant FBI Director Mark Felt, who we now know was, in fact, Deep Throat. Hougan felt it was "ultimately fruitless to speculate about Throat's identity," but still suggested that Throat "could be part of the Old Boys' network, in which case Admiral Bobby Ray Inman must be a leading candidate."

---

[*]   Most recently, while working on this Afterword, I arose on Super Bowl Sunday (February 1, 2009) to discover the following front-page headline in the *New York Times*: "John Dean's Role at Issue in Nixon Tapes Feud." The accompanying article addressed a bogus contention by the Watergate revisionists that Professor Stanley Kutler had somehow doctored his transcripts of the Nixon tapes to absolve or lessen my guilt in Watergate because we were friends. In fact, we did not become friends until after he published *Abuse of Power: The New Nixon Tapes* (1997) with the transcripts in question. The story was based on an article submitted to—not yet published by—an academic journal by an ardent Watergate revisionist. (The article had been published earlier online and was riddled with errors, typical of Watergate revisionism, and ultimately rejected by the journal.) The *Times* reporter on the story called me, but never told me the gist of her story. Until I read it, I did not have a clue what, in fact, she was writing about. I merely expressed my amazement that the *Times* even found news in the baloney the revisionists were pushing. The last reporter to pull such a ploy on me was from the *National Enquirer*. The fact that the *Times* editors considered this front-page news was a sad commentary of their understanding of this history. I published my response at Tina Brown's *The Daily Beast* at http://www.thedailybeast.com/blogs-and-stories/2009-02-04/the-times-has-lost-the-watergate-plot/.

Admiral Inman surely must have gotten a few laughs from Hougan's nomination.

Despite the deep flaws of *Secret Agenda*, it remains the starting point for most Watergate revisionists, who, in turn, consider Hougan no less than the Godfather of their splinter history. In truth, Hougan's work is a sorry example of history. It is not untypical, nonetheless, of Watergate revisionism's selective use of evidence, conspicuous deficiencies in critical thinking, remarkable disregard for common sense, and its deliberate manipulation of the evidence to reach predetermined and sensational conclusions. In reality, historical consensus is seldom fundamentally wrong, and there can be wisdom in crowds. Sadly, dubious (or worse) scholarship has dominated Watergate revisionism, and no more so than with those who have picked up where Jim Hougan's work left off, and pushed the boundaries even further.

Silent Coup: The Removal of a President

In 1991, St. Martin's Press published *Silent Coup: The Removal of a President* by Len Colodny and Robert Gettlin. The book is divided into three sections. The first rehashes the infamous Moore-Radford incident at the Nixon White House, when it was discovered that the Joint Chiefs of Staff (Moore) assigned a Navy yeoman (Radford) to the National Security Council with the task of spying on Nixon and Kissinger. It seems that the Joint Chiefs were worried because the Nixon White House was so secretive that they did not know how to effectively provide military assistance to their Commander-in-Chief. The authors used this story to provide a nasty, highly-distorted portrait of a young Bob Woodward, which was designed to call into question the honesty of his reporting. (The authors failed to mention, however, that they both had bones to pick with Woodward. Colodny, once a liquor sales-man and would-be Maryland political figure, was infuriated that Woodward revealed him as the source of stories published by the *Washington Post* when Woodward was the Metropolitan Editor. The stories concerned a liquor scandal in suburban Maryland based on Colodny's illegally-recorded telephone conversations. Gettlin, a would-be journalist, had been turned down by Woodward for a job at the *Post*.)

The next section of the book, its centerpiece, invented a totally new account of Watergate, to which I will return shortly. The third and last section claimed that Nixon's post-Haldeman Chief of Staff, Alexander Haig, had forced Nixon to resign in order to protect himself from his involvement in the Moore-Radford incident, claiming that Haig had orchestrated "a silent coup," so to speak. It also argued that Haig was Deep Throat. While Haig could be devious and duplicitous, he did not force Nixon to resign. Rather, by the time Nixon left, most everyone in the White House wanted him to leave because they were terrified they were going to go to jail like their predecessors if they continued defending the indefensible Nixon. There was nothing silent about the rumblings and the "CYA" memos written during those final days. Nor was there a coup, under any definition of that word.

The core of *Silent Coup* is found in its twelve chapters (over 180 pages and almost half the book) relating to Watergate. It is a complex and convoluted account that claims, in short, that the Senate Watergate Committee, the House Impeachment Inquiry, the FBI, the Watergate Special Prosecution Force, along with countless journalists and historians, all got Watergate wrong. As I understand, the gist of *Silent Coup* is that I was, in fact, responsible for the Watergate break-ins and cover-up. I purportedly ran a rogue operation, and after the arrest of Liddy's men, I tricked my superiors into covering it up. Indeed, I manipulated the President of the United States as if he was a puppet. For this account to fly, of course, it means that virtually everything I testified about, or have written about in this book, is a bald-faced lie.

545

According to *Silent Coup*, I became aware of a call-girl ring, located in the Columbia Plaza Apartments (near the Watergate complex), which operated in association with the Democratic National Committee. I had learned about this operation from my fiancé and later wife, Maureen. The call-girl ring was allegedly managed and advised by a Washington, DC attorney, Phillip Mackin Bailley, who was arrested and indicted by the U.S. Attorney for the District of Columbia on prostitution charges shortly before the second Watergate break-in. Just before Bailley's arrest, the story goes, I summoned the Assistant U.S. Attorneys handling the case to my office at the White House and instructed them to bring Bailley's address book, where I discovered the name of my fiancé—Maureen Biner. For reasons not fully explained in *Silent Coup*, I ordered the second Watergate break-in because I was looking for something inside the DNC. It was Colodny's collaborator—another St. Martin's author—Gordon Liddy who filled in the blanks when he openly joined Colodny and Gettlin to promote *Silent Coup*.

Liddy's Collaboration in, and Promotion of, *Silent Coup*

Liddy's account is quite convoluted as well, but he repeated it time and again during radio interviews throughout the United States when promoting *Silent Coup*, and in a new Postscript to *Will* that incorporated as much as St. Martin's would allow of this new account. Liddy developed a bizarre monologue describing what occurred, in which he explains away his own bungled Watergate activities, while inventing a new story out of whole cloth in order to place the blame for everything that went amiss on me. Liddy has also sullied the names of two innocent women in his quest to accomplish his dirty work—the woman who was a victim of his earlier criminal activity, Ida Wells, and my wife, whom he attacks in order to hurt me.

Below, I have condensed Liddy's monologue by removing the stuttering, the "ahs" and "hmms," as well as a few extraneous comments, in order to focus on the relevant parts of his fantasy. I have added, in brackets, a few points to clarify Liddy's material, and broken it into paragraphs to make it more readable:

[Dean] was in business for himself...I was the cutout in the classic parlance of the intelligence community. And the real "ops officer" was E. Howard Hunt, who was nominally my subordinate. And so [Dean] would tell Jeb Stuart Magruder orders [for] me. Magruder would then relay them to me. And about the only thing in this world that I agree with Jeb Stuart Magruder on is what my orders were. And my orders, which came from Dean through Magruder, were to go into the Watergate office building where the Democratic National Committee then had its headquarters on the sixth floor and to install wiretaps on the telephone of Larry O'Brien, who was then the Chairman of the DNC, and also put in a room monitoring device and go into his desk drawer to find out whatever dirt he might have on the Republicans so we could [deal with] it.

Well, the men went in and instead of putting, they didn't go anywhere near Larry O'Brien's office. The lookout wasn't set up to see Larry O'Brien's office, it was to see into three offices which were [across the street], one was that of R. Spencer Oliver, the other was his secretary Ida Maxie Wells, and the last was a very infrequently used office of the Chairman of the State Democratic Governors. And that makes no sense at all. I didn't realize, of course, at the time, they told me they'd gone in they'd put it into Larry O'Brien's, and I'm getting this feed back [from the wiretap], of nonsense, hairdressing appointments and things of that sort, which were incidentally not recorded. All I got was what they said they were listening to.

What has been found out is, and this is in *Silent Coup*, in the Columbia Plaza apartments, which was not very far from [the Watergate complex], there was a call-girl ring operating.

A very, high-priced, high-class call-girl ring by all accounts. And the DNC decided to just sort of tap into that for the entertainment for visiting firemen [referring to visiting officials]. And according to *Silent Coup*, the madam was a woman whose real name was Heidi Rikan, whose alias was...Cathy Dieter. And the counsel, the lawyer for Cathy Dieter was one Steven [sic] Mackin Bailley. Well, apparently, what was going on was my men were monitoring the telephone calls of people who were calling over to make appointments with the call girls, photographing them, tele-photo lenses, cause they could see right across the street to what they were doing.

So I, learning of this call-girl ring, and we'll get to how he [Dean] learned in a minute, learning of the call-girl ring he [Bailley] directs, you know, [and] this surveillance through Hunt. [Liddy says in other monologues that I directed this surveillance of the call-girl operation through Hunt.] Well then there was sort of an accident. Now if you read both *Silent Coup* and you read my book, which is a commentary on *Silent Coup*, it doesn't go into this, but there is a standard that the authors of *Silent Coup* held themselves to—they wanted to have two sources for everything. [St. Martin's Press would not let Liddy include this material in his addendum to *Will*.]

Well unfortunately for this piece of information one of the sources is dead. Heidi Rikan is now dead. So [Colodny] went to Phillip Mackin Bailley and because they only had one source they didn't put this in, so because this is my life we're talking about, I subsequently went to Phillip Mackin Bailley and I talked to him. And I found him very credible. He said look, I was the lawyer for Heidi Rikan or Cathy Dieter, I was not a pimp, even though he was arrested and, and charged with the white slave traffic act.

And to make a long story short [according to Phillip Bailley] what happened was there was an envelope, a manila envelope that had an assortment of photographs of women in see-through nighties, plus one group photograph, which was given to the DNC as a sort of a catalogue. And it was kept in a particular desk, which could be observed directly by the people who were working for John Dean, ostensively for me. And that [catalogue] was, you know, what you see is what you get. You go in there and you look. And there came a time when the roommate of the madam, one Maureen Biner, established a relationship with the Counsel to the President of the United States, John Dean.

And according to Phillip Mackin Bailley she was one of the girls, but her photograph was not in that thing [referring to the envelope]. In any event, after she established this relationship, some of the other girls in the ring became offended because, according to them, again, according to Bailley, she started putting on airs and acting as if she was better than the rest of them. So one of the girls who was down, according to Bailley, from the Xaviera Hollander ring up in New York, one Marion Taylor I think it is, who was the woman principally offended by Maureen Biner, whose code name by the way was Clout, given to her by the other girls because of this relationship. She [Marion Taylor] stuck two photographs of Maureen Biner in the envelope and said let's see how Clout likes getting this exposure.

Well, in the meanwhile, Phillip Mackin Bailley was arrested and his notebooks were seized by the police and they had the names of the girls and their code names, such as Clout, listed. Along with the names of his other clients and other people that he knew. And John Dean called the—this is in *Silent Coup*—John Dean called the prosecutor, whose name was [John] Rudy, Assistant United States Attorney, demanded that he come up with the photographs and come up with the notebooks. And to [Dean's] horror, in the [Bailley] notebook, is the name of Maureen Biner, code-name Clout. And not too long after that it is speculated by Bailley, someone must have called Maureen.

But at any rate, [after Dean talked to the prosecutor] then I received instructions to go back into [the Watergate building], this is the second entry into the DNC. First one was successful. And I was told that the wiretaps were not working properly, put in new ones, photograph everything and so on. And I passed this information which I received from Jeb Stuart Magruder on to Hunt. And I assumed that was what Hunt was doing. What actually happened was Hunt gave to one of the Cuban cohorts Eugenio Rolando Martinez ...unbeknownst to me, a map of the interior of the DNC. On that map marked with an X was a particular desk, which of course was the desk in question where these photographs were. They [Dean and Hunt] gave him a key and when he was arrested, he had the map and the key and he tried to get rid of it. His instructions according to him, which is reported in *Silent Coup*, were to...retrieve the contents of the desk, give them to Hunt, who presumably I guess would give them to John Dean. Because he certainly wasn't going to give them to me, because I had no idea that any of this was going on. [In other monologues, Liddy would discuss the desk that belonged to Ida Maxie Wells, and then repeat Phillip Bailley's false charge that she was booking dates for men visiting the DNC with prostitutes at the Columbia Plaza.]

Taking Legal Action

I first learned about the publication of *Silent Coup,* and its incredible account, shortly before its publication, when Mike Wallace of *60 Minutes* called to quiz me about it, and to request I go on camera to respond. They were going to do a story on it, and Mike told me that *Time* magazine was going to run an excerpt, for both considered it a major news story. To make a long story short, after a bit of digging, both *60 Minutes* and *Time* cancelled their stories, although both were all but ready to go, with *Time* pulling its story after it had already gone to press. As soon as I learned about the book, I asked Wallace to send me a copy. He said he could not, for St. Martin's had required *60 Minutes* to sign a confidentiality agreement. A similar arrangement had been made with *Time*, which was prohibited from showing the book to Hays Gorey, who had covered Watergate for them, and to Carl Bernstein, Woodward's partner in covering Watergate for the *Washington*

Post, who was then working at *Time*. St. Martin's refused to discuss this with me, so I placed them on notice, informing them that the book was bogus, and advised them that if they published it, the Deans would file a defamation action.

To say I was shocked by this account is a gross understatement. To say that my wife was stunned and deeply hurt is also a major underestimation. She is not a political person, other than to be an informed citizen who cares about her country. One reason that Watergate was such a difficult time for her was because I had told her nothing about what was happening at the Nixon White House, and she did not think, when marrying the Counsel to the President, that her husband would someday be headed to prison. By 1991, when *Silent Coup* was released, our lives had returned to normal. We had become relatively private people, and placed the past behind us. All that changed, however, with the promotion of *Silent Coup*, and Liddy—who I believe was largely motivated by nothing more than revenge against me for attempting to stop him and then testifying truthfully about it all—traveled the country telling every radio and television station that would have him that my wife was a call girl, and that this was the reason I had cut him out of the real action with the burglary and bugging of the DNC.

Liddy had never met Maureen, and all who know her understand that she is not someone who could ever engage in prostitution. It was tragic what Liddy and Colodny did to her. By nature a happy, highly self-confident person, who loved to be with other people, she fell into a deep depression, even needing medical attention. That depression would last for years, which is one of the reasons I have not previously spoken about this publicly. Even to this day, she remains withdrawn, shy, and concerned that other people may have heard about *Silent Coup* and Liddy's charges, and may believe that these false statements are true. Until you, or someone you love, have been so brutally and falsely attacked, it is difficult to understand the impact, but it is devastating.

People like Liddy and Colodny do not seem to understand how deeply untrue words can hurt. To the contrary, they have relished praise from right-wing ideologues (like the crowd at Fox News in Washington). Their mentality is foreign to me: How could these men attack innocent women merely to politically attack me or make money? I was so troubled by their false claims that I wrote a book about such personalities to better understand them.[*] They are, in short, people who simply have no conscience. They have no real feeling or empathy for others, only for themselves and those with whom they are close. If I had thought as Liddy did, the solution would have been simple: I would have done to Colodny and Liddy's wives, or some other family members of theirs, what they had done to mine, as revenge for the pain and suffering they caused Maureen. But I do not think like this, and there are rules in our civilization, even if others do not play by them. In truth, a lawsuit is a legally-authorized brawl, and win, lose, or draw, the suit itself can cause no end of grief for those who sue and are being sued. In this case, however, I believed we could win, and I also knew that the lawsuit would enable us to figure out how this bogus history had been assembled, so that we could show it for what it truly was. But we proceeded carefully, for I was aware that the only litigation nastier than a defamation lawsuit is one in the area of domestic relations. When Maureen said she was up to the undertaking, regardless of how unpleasant it would be—because it was as strong a statement as

---

[*]   See John W. Dean, *Conservatives Without Conscience* (Viking 2006). Liddy, whom I only mentioned in passing in this book, is, in fact, a prototypical authoritarian conservative. Colodny appears motivated not by ideology but money; he does not appear to fall within these conservative personality types but he showed he too was without conscience in attacking my wife, dragging her into Watergate when, in fact, she had no involvement whatsoever.

we could possibly make that the charges against us were false—we proceeded.

The law of defamation is stacked against public officials (which I had been) and public figures (which we assumed Maureen might be considered, very unfairly, because the revisionists had tried to drag her falsely into Watergate or simply because she had been a public official's wife). In fact, Nixon and I had an Oval Office conversation about *New York Times v. Sullivan*, the seminal Supreme Court defamation case. We had discussed how difficult the U.S. Supreme Court has made it for the public-person plaintiff to find redress through the American courts. As a private New York lawyer, Nixon had argued a case before the Supreme Court under the impossible standards of *Sullivan* and lost. *Sullivan*, and its progeny, hold that a public official (and later any public-figure) plaintiff must prove that the defamatory statement at issue was published with "actual malice"—a misleading standard because it does not really involve malice in the traditional sense of ill-will or hatred. Rather, the "actual malice" standard requires that the person publishing the defamation either knew that the statement was false when publishing it, or acted, when publishing it, in reckless disregard as to whether it was true or false. This standard is daunting because no defendant is about to admit that he or she thought the statement they published was false or reckless regarding whether it was false. To the contrary, every defendant will claim that he, she, or the company believed that the published statement was true, so it takes a lot of digging to show the defendant knew the statement to be false or acted with reckless disregard to its truth or falsity. The Supreme Court demands clear and convincing evidence on this score. (Indeed, making things even more difficult for plaintiffs, in this area of law appellate courts will take the almost unheard-of measure of nullifying jury findings if they do not think the evidence was truly sufficient for the jury to reach the conclusion it has reached.)

The rationale of *Sullivan* and related cases is well-meaning: It is the belief that freedom of speech and of the press, under the First Amendment, need breathing room, and that defamation lawsuits at times chill even valuable speech. For these reasons, the High Court has made it particularly difficult for public people to prevail in such lawsuits, because they can defend themselves in the marketplace of ideas instead. Public people, the thinking goes, have access to the media to deny false and damaging charges. While that might be true, in practice it is also correct (as the old saying goes) that the truth cannot get its boots on before the lie has traveled the world. In addition, this body of law has become a refuge for people like Liddy, who use it for personal reasons to strike out at others, knowing that it is difficult (not to mention monumentally expensive) for the object of their defamation to prevail in court. In our case, St. Martin's was well-insured against such a lawsuit, so the Liddy actually encouraged us to sue. He may have hoped that the lawsuit would draw attention to *Silent Coup*, and sell more copies, because if a public person enters the public debate, it draws more attention to the false charge.

The defamations in *Silent Coup*, and Liddy's follow-up actions, were so egregious that I had no doubt that we could prove actual malice and win the lawsuit. Although we issued a denial, we made no public appearances, knowing it would only draw more attention to the book. Indeed, we wanted to wait until the book had run its course before filing our lawsuit, to avoid giving it publicity. In the interim, we undertook a search for the right lawyers, an effort that proved worth the time. We wanted to find a firm that would take the case on a contingency-fee basis, because not only would this hold down our expenses, but it would also mean the firm believed it could win the case.[*] We interviewed high-profile and low-profile

---

[*] A typical contingency agreement shares a third of the winnings with the lawyers, but requires the client to pay all out of pocket expenses of

attorneys, preferring the latter. A friend suggested the attorney whose law firm that had taken the *National Enquire* to task for publishing false information about Elizabeth Taylor, Neil Papiano of Iverson, Yokum, Papiano & Hatch in Los Angeles. It proved a great choice. Neil assigned the case to two partners: Arnold "Doug" Larson and John Garrick (who have since opened their own firm). We would talk or visit with our attorneys almost every day for the next nine years. At one point, the defendants had no less than seventeen lawyers representing them. Yet Doug and John—and occasionally Neil or one of the firm's associates—kept the defendants' attorneys dancing full-time in what became a massive lawsuit.

Our lawsuit named as defendants Colodny, Gettlin, Liddy, St. Martin's Press and its top officers, and a number of people who had republished the material at issue. Because St. Martin's had the largest insurance policy, the company took the lead. We filed in a California court. St. Martin's got the suit removed to federal court, which we had fully anticipated, and Liddy's attorney—using dubious claims that all the witnesses and documents were back in Washington—got the case transferred back to the District of Columbia. This meant that we had to hire a Washington lawyer as well. A couple of years into the case, we hired David Dorsen as Washington counsel. David not only had extensive defamation law experience and was willing to work on a contingency fee, but he had also been Sam Dash's deputy chief counsel of the Senate Watergate Committee, and thus knew Watergate well.

I closed down my business and devoted myself full-time to assisting our attorneys. St. Martin's and all the other defendants moved to dismiss, contending that even if the facts we pled in our complaint were true, we still had no legal claim. But all those motions failed. Soon after, the defendants offered

---

the lawsuit, like mail, copying, travel, court costs, and court reporters for depositions, which can easily run six-figures a year in protracted litigation.

us a settlement if we would allow them to continue publishing *Silent Coup*. In effect, they wanted a license to defame us. We said no. While the lawsuit continued, we had the power of a subpoena, and until we learned how this bogus history had been written—which would enable us to discredit it—we had no interest in settling. Fortunately, we did learn exactly that.

One day I will deconstruct all the Watergate revisionism (but should I fail to get around to it, for there is little joy in wading in false history, the material in my files will enable others to do so). For now, I will merely show how Colodny and Liddy invented their false stories about my wife and me by using a few of the many examples, rather than by attempting to refute all their false charges, which would itself require a hefty book.

Inventing Bogus History: How Revisionists Revise

Colodny had untrue information about me or my wife on almost every page in his account of Watergate, consistently calling me a liar whenever my account differed from anyone else's. To charge a person with lying is easy, and as I will show, it can be done in a few sentences. To refute such a false charge, by contrast, typically requires many pages. Accordingly, I have selected a few typical examples of the types of charges that run throughout *Silent Coup* to show how the revisionists in general, and Colodny in particular, operate.* But also I want to show that unpacking a false charge (even in

---

* These examples, and other material relating to *Silent Coup*, are drawn from our court filings, which Colodny has partially published on his website (see: http://www.nixonera.com/library/dean.asp), where he posts material produced by other Watergate revisionists (rants based on bad information). Apparently Colodny wants to create a home base for Watergate revisionists. In addition, he continues to attack Bob Woodward and, of course, me.

summary form) is far more complex that making the charge —
and the revisionists have an endless supply of false charges.

More specifically, *Silent Coup* makes much of the "brashness of the lie" I purportedly told (at pages 100 and 102) when
I returned to the United States from the Philippines, where I
was giving a speech as Liddy's men were getting arrested
during their second entry into the DNC. Upon my return to the
office, I noted that I had had two Mondays that week because I
had started the week on the other side of the International Date
Line (the imaginary line that separates consecutive calendar
days, with the Eastern hemisphere always one day ahead of the
Western hemisphere). *Silent Coup* found it offensive that I
written that I'd had "two Mondays in a week, something no
one should have to endure." According to *Silent Coup*, "Dean
didn't have two Mondays, he had two Sundays." It then
proceeds to ask:

> Why would Dean lie about when he had left Manila? Why
> fabricate the business about two Mondays? What difference
> did it make when Dean learned of the break-in? It made all
> the difference in the world, because Dean desperately
> wanted to convince everyone that he had had nothing to do
> with the beginning of the cover-up, which started in
> Magruder's phone call to him in Manila on the night of the
> seventeenth. If he started admitting that Magruder had
> called him quite so early in the game, all sorts of inquiries
> would be stirred alive, and he would not be able to keep the
> questioners from probing his story closely, and coming upon
> such people as Perry Rivkind and his assistant Bob Stutman,
> whose testimony could have impugned Dean.

In fact, I did have two Mondays when crossing the International Date Line. Colodny located my White House travel
records at the National Archives, where he found my "travel
voucher" with my flight times from Washington to Tokyo to

557

Manila and back by the same route, and he even contacted the Bureau of Immigration in Manila to find when precisely I had departed. The voucher shows the following:

(Sunday) June 18	Leave Manila	9:00 AM
(Sunday) June 18	Arrive Tokyo	1:15 PM
(Sunday) June 18	Leave Tokyo	4:00 PM
(Sunday) June 18	Arrive San Francisco	9:00 AM
(Sunday) June 18	Leave San Francisco	12:05 PM
(Sunday) June 18	Arrive Washington	8:57 PM

At first blush, it looks like Colodny was correct, and that when I walked in my office at the White House on Monday morning, June 19[th,] and that I had had two Sundays, not two Mondays. In fact, I had had two Sundays, but I was also starting my second Monday as well. What Colodny failed to calculate before calling me a liar was the time it requires to fly between these cities. The fact that I had experienced two Mondays was (and remains) stuck in my mind for a unique reason, which I would have explained had he asked. Traveling to Manila, we had stopped in Tokyo, and shopped at the duty-free store in the U.S. Embassy, where I purchased a Seiko watch that had the day and date. Flying to Manila, I had read the instructions to figure out how to set the day and date, which was a bit tricky.

When I was flying home, after our plane was many hours out of Tokyo, the pilot came on the public address system to announce that we had just crossed the International Date Line, and he gave us an estimated arrival time for San Francisco. Earlier, I had looked at my watch and it was Monday, June 19th so I had dated several postcards I had picked up in Manila to send to my family, and on which I had written the header,

558

"Manila, June 19th," with a message that I was heading home. (I mailed them from San Francisco.) Chapter Four had originally started with a note from one of those post cards, in which I explained that although I had starting writing the card on Monday, June 19th, it had become Sunday, June 18th after crossing the International Date Line, and I was trying to figure how to reset my new watch, but to do so I had to dig out the instruction manual before I got it correct.

After *Silent Coup* claimed I had lied, I discussed my travel with a pilot who flew regularly to Tokyo, who said it would be impossible to prove—all these years later—precisely when my Northwest Airlines flight had crossed the International Date Line because it would have depended upon the weather and wind, and the flight plan that evening. However, he said that my day/date watch and the pilot's announcement struck him as being accurate—and that I had, indeed, had two Mondays. (He also offered to find an expert witness who could corroborate this, if necessary.) In calling me a lair on this bit of minutiae, Colodny simply ignored the time that it took for me to travel from Manila to cross the date line, which is thousands of miles from Tokyo. I had traveled all day Sunday, and sometime after midnight, when over the Pacific Ocean, I had my first Monday, but when we crossed the date line, I was back to Sunday.

Silent Coup claims I lied because I did not want anyone to come upon "such people as Perry Rivkind and his assistant Bob Stutman, whose testimony could have impugned Dean." This assertion, too, was false and baseless. The information with which Rivkind or Stutman might have "impugned" me was never reported, because, in fact, it did not exist. Stutman, as Colodny learned when he spoke with him, corroborated the fact that I first learned of the Watergate break-in upon landing in San Francisco on June 18, 1972. As Colodny's secretly-taped telephone conversations show, Stutman's memory of the event was clear, and neither Colodny nor Gettlin could get him to change his story, despite repeated efforts. Stutman remem-

559

bered that I told him "some assholes got caught breaking into the DNC and my office thinks I should come back to Washington." Because of what occurred later, he never forgot the poetry of my first reaction. Rather than face the facts, however, *Silent Coup* contrived an alternative, fictional universe, declaring that yours truly, "the consummate actor," had fooled Stutman (an experienced law enforcement officer) by withholding my knowledge of the break-in from him for all those hours while flying from Manila to Tokyo and then to San Francisco, but then suddenly coming up with this explanation after calling my office from San Francisco. Colodny's effort to make the facts go away by merely declaring that I was "the consummate actor" was a fiction and, because he knew this was an invented explanation, it was evidence of actual malice.

One Colodny tactic was to not allow a person with a hazy memory of events from years earlier to correct his or her memory after thinking further about the matter. This is how Colodny dealt with Perry Rivkind, who tried to recall his visit to Manila with me for Colodny many years earlier. Unaware he was being secretly recorded, Rivkind tried to recall what had occurred by thinking aloud, and thought it possible I had learned of the Watergate break-ins while in the Philippines. However, Rivkind told Colodny, "I honestly can't remember whether that's when he learned it." When Colodny pressed him on his first mistaken memory, Rivkind repeated, "I'm honestly drawing a blank."

Even though Rivkind made it clear to Colodny that he "could have it wrong" and "you better ask Stutman" and "I honestly can't remember," Colodny was determined to use the mistaken recollection whether Rivkind really believed it or not. As Colodny explained in a later conversation with Bud Krogh:

Krogh: And will Rivkind, ah, be, stand up under pressure if he is asked by others about this.

Colodny: Oh, I don't care what he does at this point [laughs].

560

If Colodny secretly got someone on tape to indifferently support his preconceived story, even if that person told Colodny that he was not sure or requested that Colodny confirm the fact with someone else, then Colodny "relied" on that person as a source. This was how Colodny has reinvented history. This was also further evidence of Colodny's actual malice.

In trying to make me a liar about hearing from Jeb Magruder while I was still in Manila, Colodny showed how he could manipulate information as he did with Magruder, literally planting information to manipulate him into recalling a telephone call, years after the event, which never occurred. Magruder never called me in Manila, and, if he had, he would have recalled that fact long before Colodny planted the thought in his mind. Colodny's conversations with Magruder are illustrative of his use of highly deceptive techniques (here, secretly recording a person when giving them false and misleading information). During a deposition in this lawsuit, Magruder was read a portion of one of his recorded conversations where Colodny repeatedly gave Magruder false information, including, most importantly, telling Magruder incorrectly that there was a record of a telephone call from California to Manila (via the White House Signal Corps switchboard, or Secret Service) on June 17, 1972. Neither the Signal Corps nor the Secret Service maintained such records, a fact formally acknowledged by both agencies to our attorneys. But Colodny's false statement convinced Magruder that he must have made the call.

Magruder explained what had occurred during his deposition in our lawsuit:

Q.   Reverend Magruder, if you could turn specifically to the bottom of page three [of the transcript of your conversation with Colodny], and I'd just like you to bear in mind where Mr. Colodny states in the second to last paragraph there: "Do you have any

561

recollection because it looks like the phone call went through California to Manila—California to the White House to Manila at 11:30 Manila time on the 17th." And then I also want to direct your attention to the middle of page six and specifically where Mr. Colodny states: "Whoever made the call, okay, rather than say you did it or somebody else did it, it went through the White House signal board." And then it drops down and he says: "There's a record of the phone call coming through at about 8:30—about 8:30 your time, 11:30 Washington time, 11:30 Washington time a call is placed to the White House signal board to Manila." Now, when Mr. Colodny gave you the information that I have just read, did you assume that it was accurate?

A.   Yes.

Q.   Did you believe, based on what he told you, that he had a record of a call from California to the White House signal board to Manila that was made at 8:30 California time on June 17, 1972?

A.   That's what he said, he had a record.

Q.   And did you rely upon Mr. Colodny's representation of having this record in responding to his questions to you about an alleged call you made to John Dean?

A.   I assumed he was correct about a call.

Q.   And subsequently, and just you can correct me if your memory is different, but I think you state to Mr. Colodny later on in one of these transcripts that it's possible that you did make that call; correct?

A.   The way the conversations went, it was narrowed down to the point where I was the only person who could have made that call, if there was a call.

Q.   And was that surmise or conclusion, however you want to characterize it, on your part, based upon Mr. Colodny's representation of having a record of that phone call?

562

A.   Based on that and based on a number of other documents that other people said that it was me who made the phone call.

When Colodny was under oath, after a good bit of misdirection (which became the norm in his deposition), he admitted he had given false information to Magruder to induce a false response:

Q.   When you talked to Mr. Magruder prior to *Silent Coup's* publication, when you first asked him about that phone call from Dean to Mr. Magruder on June 17, 1972, did Mr. Magruder remember it?

A.   Mr. Magruder—like the conversation with Mr. Liddy, the third one—at first didn't recall, didn't recall. We kept talking about the evidence that— that mitigated against the call coming—the instruction coming from Mr. Mitchell for a lot of reasons that we've already discussed, timing, the fact that Liddy says the call came from Magruder. The order had to have been given between 8:30 and 9:00 and the time when he said he hadn't even talked to Mitchell yet.

Q.   So the answer to my questions is: He did not remember it when you first asked him about it?

A.   Right.

Q.   But you told Mr. Magruder that he had made such a call, didn't you?

A.   I did not tell him that he had made such a call. *

Q.   Did you tell him that you had a record of such a call on June 17, 1972 from Mr. Magruder's hotel in

_____

* Colodny is confused, wrong or dissembling, for his own recording of his conversations proves that Colodny told Magruder he made the call to me during *repeated* conversations.

563

California to the White House to Manila at 8:30 AM? Did you tell him that?

A.   I don't know that I used a specific time.[*] I told him that—that such a record existed and—but I didn't say that that record came from him. I didn't say it was a record from him.

Q.   Okay. And did such a record exist?

A.   I had been tracing such a record based on the evidence.[**] And after numerous discussions with Mr. Magruder, while I had every reason to believe I thought we were going to get it, we hadn't. It's a technique you don't usually use, but it is used. And it's a technique where you have a lot of evidence pointing in one way, and you indicate that there's a document or person said something and see what reaction that draws sometimes. And obviously if Mr. Magruder didn't make the phone call, whether there was a call from that hotel or not, Mr. Magruder would have said "I didn't make that phone call." That is a technique, by the way, is used not only by police and journalists—although I must tell you I thought those records still existed. As I later found out, the records were destroyed by the Signal board.[***] So while I was saying to him—and I had every belief to have it—I did not have it in hand.

Q.   Is that technique you referred to called lying? [Counsel withdrew this question as argumentative, and restated it.] You didn't really have such a record, correct?...And the answer is "no," right?

---

[*]   The recording Colodny made of that conversation proves that he is once again confused, wrong or dissembling, for in fact, he was very specific on this point.

[**]   There is no evidence that Colodny ever sought such information from any of the agencies that might have possessed such a record.

[***]   We advised the court that this was untrue. The Signal Corps did not destroy such records; it never had kept or possessed them in the first place, and its representative would have so testified if necessary.

A.   The answer is no.

This is about as clear an example of actual malice as one might find, for Colodny knew he created false information by giving Magruder false information. This was the way Colodny proceeded through much of his research, employing such tactics. Based on our analysis of literally hundreds of his secretly-recorded calls with countless persons he said he had "interviewed," we summarized for the court how Colodny conducted his interviews. His principal research tool was a telephone connected to a tape recorder, which he did not explain to those he called and with whom he talked. To get the information he wanted, he used a number of methods, such as asking leading questions to obtain negative information from persons hostile to me and, by association, my wife; relying on faded memories of events occurring over 15 years earlier; and disclosing false information in order to obtain false information. He also consistently sought to prejudice persons against us by "poisoning the well" with derogatory and false information about us; frequently planted information with a person who had no memory of a particular event, and later enticed that person to repeat back to him the planted information as if it were his or her own information; he interrupted and switched the subject or ended a conversation when the information being given was inconsistent with his desired version of events; and, of course, he failed to tell anyone that his or her interview was being treated as "on-the-record" for attribution. This pattern of dishonesty repeated itself, time after time, for Colodny secretly recorded over a thousand conversations.

Colodny called this journalism. In fact, as we believe we demonstrated with clear and convincing evidence in our court filings it was deception, if not fraud. But Colodny's deceptive research methods pale in comparison to his primary new Watergate source, the man on whom he and Liddy relied to

565

turn history upside down. For not only was their new source conspicuously unreliable, they understood, in Colodny's words, that he was "crazy," not euphemistically speaking, rather they knew he was a man who was mentally disturbed, who would tell them whatever they wanted to hear, and they shamelessly exploited him.[*]

Colodny's and Liddy's New Watergate Source: Phillip Mackin Bailley

I had never heard of Phillip Mackin Bailley before his name was published in the newspaper on June 9, 1972 and his case was brought to my attention by government attorneys who sought me out to inform the White House that one of Bailley's victims was a women working in the Executive Office of the President. I did not call the prosecutors; rather, they arranged to come to the White House because the Department of Justice wanted the White House informed of the situation: A young women working there had been extorted into prostitution by Bailley, who was being indicted, and the government might need to call her as a witness in a rather seamy case, if it went to trial.

Bailley, then a seemingly attractive and fun-loving young attorney, would troll the bars in Georgetown at night, where he would seek to meet young ladies whose relationships with their boyfriends had turned bad. Soon, Bailley would be wining and dining them, and luring them back to his apartment, where he

---

[*]   In addition to the court filings in our lawsuit published on Colodny's website, I have relied on a filing not published by Colodny but found at the U.S. District Court for the District of Columbia. It is *Plaintiff's Motion (1) For Partial Summary Judgment Re: Defendant's Affirmative Defense That Actionable Statements Cannot Be Proven False and (2) For Summary Adjudication That The Falsity of Defendant's Actionable Statements Is Undisputed*, and accompanying documents, which were filed on April 20, 2000. See also Liddy's *Memorandum in Opposition to the Dean's Motion for Partial Summary Judgment and Summary Adjudication*, which was filed on May 16, 2000.

would get them high on wine and marijuana. Once they were stoned, he would get them to pose for highly compromising nude photographs. Next, Bailley would use the photos to extort the young women, telling them if they did not have sex with whomever he instructed, then he would reveal the photos to the women's parents. A coed from the University of Maryland went to the police and reported what Bailley was doing, and because taking women across state lines for immoral purposes is a federal crime, the U.S. Attorney's Office in the District of Columbia had jurisdiction. It was an awful story the Assistant U.S. attorneys reported, but the young lady they thought worked at the White House in fact worked at the Office of Emergency Preparedness (FEMA's predecessor) instead. Thus, after informing her superior of the situation, I had nothing further to do with the matter. The prosecutors did not show me an address book or notebook with Maureen's name in it, or that of anyone else for that matter. Until *Silent Coup* was published, I never again heard Bailley's name, nor did I know what had become of him.

It was Jim Hougan who first told the world Bailley's story, which Bailley had begun peddling in the mid-1970s after his release from federal prison. At that time, Bailley began telling anyone who would listen that he knew the real story of Watergate, because he had been an attorney who represented prostitutes before he got busted, and he had learned about a call-girl ring operating out of the Columbia Plaza Apartment building. When *Silent Coup* was published in 1991, I tracked down J. Anthony Lukas, who had written one of the first Watergate books, *Nightmare: The Underside of the Nixon Years* (1976), because he had reported: "So spicy were some of the conversations on this phone that they have given rise to unconfirmed reports that the telephone was being used for some sort of call-girl service catering to congressmen and other prominent Washingtonians." When I talked with Lukas, he said that when he had reviewed Jim Hougan's book for the *New York Times* and had read about Phillip Bailley in the book, he had paused

567

to wonder if this was the person he had been told in 1975-76, when he was doing research, was chatting up the call-girl rumor in Washington. He could not be certain, but felt it entirely possible. He said that when he had talked to the prosecutors and a few people from the DNC, however, he had called it what it was, a "rumor," and one he felt was not worth pursuing.

With each telling, Bailley's story got better, and soon he had every attractive woman directly or indirectly associated with the Nixon White House as part of the call-girl operation. (In addition to my wife, he falsely claimed the call-girl ring included Diane Sawyer, who had worked in the White House Press Office and later for ABC News; an assistant who had worked for John and Martha Mitchell; Debbie Sloan, the wife of the reelection committee treasurer, Hugh Sloan, who was briefly portrayed in the movie "All the President's Men"; as well as many others.) When Colodny tracked down Bailley and started talking to him, Colodny believed he had struck it rich. Bailley agreed with everything Colodny would tell him, and added even more. Colodny was so excited that he went to St. Martin's and told them that he was going to totally re-work his Watergate material. While I would remain his villain, he had discovered totally new information that he felt changed everything.

There was one problem, however, with using Bailley as a source: He had been in and out of mental institutions and mental care for his entire adult life. After his arrest for extorting women, and before his guilty plea, he had been sent to St. Elizabeth's in Washington, DC, so that the prosecutors could evaluate whether he was even mentally fit to stand trial. After his release from prison, where he claims he talked with Hunt and Liddy, he falsely confessed to being the Green River Serial Killer when living in the Seattle area and after being arrested

568

naked in the middle of a highway.[*] Bailley was thrilled that Colodny was taking him seriously and giving his (concocted) story the credit he believed it deserved. With Colodny, Bailley thought he had struck it rich, as Colodny coached him to fill the gaps and holes in his story. Colodny made it easy for Bailley because he explained that he was not interested in any of the other supposed call girls, only Maureen Dean.

Colodny shamelessly manipulated Bailley into elaborating his fantasies, letting his imagination run wild. Did Colodny know what he was doing? He knew exactly what he was doing, and recorded himself doing it. Colodny understood that Bailley was mentally unbalanced, if not insane. In fact, Colodny told just about anyone to whom he spoke (except Bailley, of course) that Bailley was crazy. For example, when discussing Bailley with the man who had prosecuted Bailley for extortion, John Rudy, Colodny said, "Bailley's the last guy I want to talk to at this point. I want to know what's going on before I ever approach Bailley. Because everybody's gonna say he's crazy." To which Rudy replied, "And they may not be very far from the truth." Later, after Colodny had been dealing with Bailley, Colodny was asked by a former Mitchell aide, Steven King, "How do you perceive Bailley?" Colodny answered, "Bailley's crazy, there's no question about it." Colodny obtained Bailley's criminal case file, a public document, from which he learned that government lawyers believed that Bailley was not only crazy, but also a liar. For example, prosecutor John Rudy had stated the following to Federal Judge Charles Richey, who had jurisdiction of Bailley's case:

> During the investigation—and I will not go into the grand jury testimony, but it pretty well followed the rest of the investigation—many, many witnesses—and there are

---

[*]   The true Green River Serial Killer, Gary Leon Ridgway, was not found until November 2001, when he was linked by DNA to the murders of four women. In 2003, Ridgway pled guilty, pursuant to a plea bargain that spared him the death penalty.

very few exceptions—or the people that I talked to in my office concerning the allegations against Mr. Bailley expressed to me that they thought Mr. Bailley ranged from being weird in his actions to outright paranoia.

Now, of course, these were not expert witnesses. These were male and female persons who were associated with Mr. Bailley going back to 1969. But they found in their association with him that his conduct was bizarre at times and that he would say one thing and turn around the next moment and deny that he had ever said any such thing.

Colodny also found in Bailley's federal case file letters from two psychiatrists, retained by Bailley, who said that he was a sexual deviant who found gratification in "humiliating" or "degrading" women. One doctor noted that Bailley had alcoholic blackouts that occurred during the very time period for which Colodny relied on Bailley's memory. Colodny told John Ehrlichman, who was cooperating fully on his project, "I mean you cannot believe how sick this guy is, he has this thing about women, he hates women." No less a witness than Bailley's own sister confirmed this fact:

Colodny: Because, Sheila, everyone who knows him says he hates women.

Sheila: I, I think, I'd say that's true, the way he's been treating all of us, I, I, that's real evident to me.

It's no surprise, then, that Colodny had little trouble getting Bailley to make false statements about my wife. Colodny spent more time talking to Bailley about *Silent Coup* than he did talking to anyone else about the book, except perhaps for John Ehrlichman and John Mitchell. Mitchell had died before Colodny got to the Watergate material, but when Colodny mentioned Hougan's call-girl story to Mitchell, Mitchell correctly thought it a hoax. It was, however, material that had

570

been given to Mitchell by Hougan about the alleged call-girl operation—material that was sent to Colodny after Mitchell's death—that triggered Colodny's interest again. In addition to conducting many conversations with Bailley, Colodny asked for and received a number of tape recordings from Bailley, which were rambling, semi-coherent monologues and which constituted powerful evidence that Bailley was a very sick man.

Notwithstanding the fact that Bailley might have been the worst source in the annals of history, Colodny and Liddy still relied on him as their principal (and in many instances, *only*) source for their preconceived story about my wife and me.[*] Colodny relied on Bailley, it appears, because his behind-the-scenes collaborator, Liddy—who was helping Colodny make all the pieces of his story worked—kept pushing him to include the charges against Maureen. Less than six months before *Silent Coup* was published, Liddy and Colodny had the following exchange:

> Liddy: But why are we backing off on [Maureen] being a hooker?

---

[*]   Phillip Bailley was a defendant in our lawsuit, and as an attorney by training, he represented himself (with assistance from Liddy's attorneys). Shortly after introducing himself to our attorneys, John Garrick and Doug Larson, he informed them that, in fact, he was a space captain from Alpha Centauri, who had been abandoned on earth. Before he was deposed, he requested that his then-current psychiatrist Cyril Hardy, M.D., be deposed. Dr. Hardy explained that Bailley was incapable of distinguishing fact from fiction. As Dr. Hardy explained, Bailley had "hallucinations" and "difficulty differentiating between reality and fantasy." Dr. Hardy testified, based on his expertise, that Bailley probably had suffered from these conditions since he was around 30 years of age (in other words, since the mid-1970's) and would suffer from them the rest of his life. When Bailley was deposed, he took the Fifth Amendment (among a number of privileges he invented) and refused to testify. Bailley is truly a remarkable source on which to rewrite history, as Colodny and Liddy have attempted to do.

571

Colodny: Well, we're not, the, it isn't a question of backing off per se. It's a question of not being able
to flat out state it cause we don't have the evidence.   In fact, the girl in Houston [attorney
Candace Cowan who knew Maureen during the
relevant time period] hurt me more than helped
me.   I thought she was talking about Mother
Theresa when she got through telling me about
[Maureen].

About a month later, Liddy again asked Colodny: "You still
don't have Maureen doing tricks yet?"   Colodny answered:
"No." At his deposition in our lawsuit, Liddy was asked why it
was important that Maureen be involved with a purported
prostitution ring with a connection to the DNC, the point he
kept pushing:

Q: Mr. Liddy, prior to the publication of *Silent Coup*
and Postscript to your book, do you recall telling Mr.
Colodny on more than one occasion that you wanted
him to be sure to get the information relating to
Maureen Dean being a prostitute into his book?

A: Yes.

Q: Why did you tell him that?

A: Because the significance of Maureen Dean being a
prostitute is that it provides the motivation for doing
what [John Dean] did.

When *Silent Coup* was published, it did not claim any direct connection between Maureen and any call-girl operation,
but it was written with heavily vetted innuendo to give the
reader the impression that Maureen had ties to just such an
operation.   Liddy determined that if St. Martin's would not risk
it, he would.   Accordingly, he met personally with Phillip

572

Bailley, declared him sane and a reliable source, and began repeating Bailley's story (as he did in the monologue I inserted earlier). Liddy's promotion of *Silent Coup* pushed it onto the *New York* Times bestseller list, and his attacks on me and my wife earned him his own talk-radio show, plus he sold a few more copies of the reissued paperback edition of *Will*. For Liddy, trashing my wife and me proved a positive career move, and he is not a man likely to have second thoughts about destroying the lives of innocent people in the process. Not only did he severely damage my wife, he also turned on Ida Maxie Wells—whose life he had already disrupted by bugging her telephone when she worked at the DNC in 1972. He had gone to jail for that activity, and seemed to hold against her the fact that she had testified against him. Liddy likes his revenge however he can get it.

The Settlement and Ida "Maxie" Wells's Lawsuit

In February 1972, the then 23-year-old Ida "Maxie" Wells joined the staff of the DNC as a secretary to Spencer Oliver. Having her telephone bugged, however, had not been a pleasant experience. She left the DNC in July 1972 to take a vacation to get away from it all. In September, however, she was called back to testify before a grand jury in Washington—for she had been the victim of Liddy's criminal behavior. After the 1972 Presidential campaign, Maxie moved to Atlanta, and in 1976, she joined the Presidential campaign of Jimmy Carter, becoming his personal secretary and the traveling companion to Mrs. Carter. When President Carter was elected, Maxie served as his personal secretary during the transition and then, following a full-field FBI security check (which surely would have revealed whether she had done anything like what Liddy and Bailley claimed), she joined the White House staff, where she served the President and First Lady in a host of capacities during Carter's term in office. In 1986, after working at the Carter Center in Atlanta, Wells decided to return to college to seek a Ph.D. in Twentieth Century American Literature. She was a graduate student at Louisiana State University when we deposed her in our lawsuit.

During her deposition, under oath, she denied any knowledge of a call-girl ring or prostitution activities at the DNC; she also testified that she did not know Phillip Bailley, notwithstanding his claims to the contrary; and she stated that she had never had pictures of Maureen in her desk at the DNC, as Bailley claimed, nor had she arranged dates for men at the DNC with prostitutes, as Liddy claimed Bailley had informed him she had done. After the deposition, our attorney John Garrick visited with Maxie. (John appreciates and knows good literature, including Southern literature, which was Maxie's interest.) He asked her why she had done nothing about Liddy's false charges, and she explained that she had wanted to avoid anything that might distract her from completing her doctorate and dissertation, so she had worked to ignore Liddy—although that had been difficult because his claims that she procured women for men visiting the DNC and that she was affiliated somehow with a prostitution operation troubled her deeply. At our request, John Garrick told her that if she decided to take action, we would be pleased to assist her in any way we might.

By spring 1997, Maxie felt she had to do something. She hired an experienced defamation attorney based in Washington, DC, David Branson, who contacted me (through David Dorsen) to ask if our offer of assistance was still open. It was, indeed, so I arranged to meet Branson while he was in California for another case, so that I could assist him in gathering basic information and documents about the case. (We encouraged David Dorsen to assist Branson in any way he could, and it worked out nicely for all, for soon Dorsen joined Branson's law firm.) When we visited and chatted, Branson indicated that Maxie had had her fill of Liddy. Maxie's mother had heard Liddy on the radio talking about her daughter arranging for dates with prostitutes while she worked at the DNC, and claiming that she had pictures of prostitutes for men to look at in an envelope in her desk. It upset her mother. And it disturbed Maxie's friends as well. She was going to file her defamation suit, and she did so, in Maryland, where Liddy had a home, on April 1, 1997. (Because there is a one-year statute of limitations on filing such lawsuits, much of what Liddy had said could not be sued upon. Dorsen and Branson, however, had located a few examples of Liddy trashing Maxie just as he had Maureen, including a lecture Liddy delivered that Dorsen himself attended and recorded.)

By the time Maxie filed her lawsuit, the senior-status judge who had been assigned our case, Harold H. Greene, had become impatient with the massive filings by the defendants. Colodny had filed one motion that actually required a dolly to move it, at 4,200 pages. St. Martin's, as well, had filed enormous motions. It was all part of their scorched-earth effort, which was backfiring.[*] Rather than burying us, we were making the lawsuit painfully expensive for the insurance carriers pay the bills of the defendants. Within a few months of filing our lawsuit, we became a well-tuned machine, able not only to respond instantly to the endless motions and actions filed by the defendants, but also to keep the initiative in the lawsuit. We never departed from our game plan of slowly tightening the noose on St. Martin's top management, while gathering information about how this bogus account had been assembled. Colodny had taped everyone, and the tapes made quite clear that all the key players knew this was faux history, because they knew that Bailley was not believable.

---

[*] My index alone for the *Silent Coup*-related materials connected only with the litigation runs 60 pages, with the dated entries single-spaced, and in 10-point type. There are roughly 2,400 separate entries, each representing a matter that itself might range from as few as five pages to Colodny's 4,200 page monster. Today, this material fills about two hundred filing boxes.

Meanwhile, Liddy had filed a lawsuit against me. His complaint read like something he and his son (an attorney) had drafted on the kitchen table after too many beers. Based on the (false) charges in *Silent Coup*, Liddy claimed that if he had known that I had allegedly ordered the break-in on June 17, 1972, then he would not have participated, nor would he have remained silent. Because I had allegedly concealed my activities for the past (then) twenty years, he contended that I had defrauded and injured him. The lawsuit was absurd. Unfortunately, when Judge Greene dismissed the suit for, among other reasons, Liddy's "unclean hands," he did not publish his memorandum dismissing the case. I suspect Liddy's frivolous action cost St. Martin's insurance company, which was covering Liddy's legal fees, quite a bit.

Colodny, and his then-attorney, pursued one of the most noxious and specious of all the defendants counter measures: They took the unheard-of step of suing our attorney, John Garrick. When Colodny and St. Martin's had filed various motions to block us from obtaining Colodny's illicitly-recorded conversations, Colodny's attorney began attaching news articles from a columnist/reporter for *The Tampa Tribune*, Ray Locker. The articles were meant to bolster the motions, which was pure bootstrapping, because Colodny was feeding information to Locker that he repeated like a parrot. For this reason, John Garrick sent a strong letter to Locker—not for publication, but rather to call him on what he was doing. Locker, however, had the letter printed in the "commentary section" of the newspaper. In the letter, Garrick took issue with Locker's statements (in several columns) that Colodny's unlawful tape recordings "provide[d] the heart of Colodny's defense," and that Garrick (and his law partners) were trying to suppress these tapes. Of course, that claim—which Garrick called "absolute hogwash"—got what was occurring precisely backward. As Garrick stated, "To the contrary, we are confident that full disclosure of all the tape recordings made by Colodny will expose Colodny's book *Silent Coup* as a fraud." Based on this statement, Colodny sued Garrick and his law firm for defamation. The case ended up in the U.S. District Court for the Middle District of Florida, Tampa Division, before Judge Elizabeth Kovachevich, who eventually granted Garrick and the firm summary judgment, ruling that Colodny was a public figure in connection with *Silent Coup*, and that, as a matter of law, there was no evidence that Garrick acted with actual malice. The judge also pointed out that a jury might well agree with Garrick that the book was a fraud, and noted that Garrick was expressing "pure opinion," which would not support a claim of defamation. This frivolous litigation no doubt cost Colodny's insurance carriers quite a bit, too.

St. Martin's scorched-earth strategy was making a lot of lawyers wealthy, costing the insurance carrier dearly, and not advancing the defendants' situation in any way whatsoever. Thus, it is no wonder that St. Martin's wanted to talk settlement. By then, in 1998, we understood exactly how Colodny had invented his new history, based on Phillip Bailley's sick fantasies, and we were therefore ready to discuss settlement. Because we reached a confidential settlement, unfortunately, we are precluded from discussing it, except to say we were satisfied by the terms of the agreement that was reached.

Like St. Martin's, Gettlin was ready to settle, but Colodny and Liddy wanted to fight on. Colodny's insurance company was not prepared to risk more, however, so they simply paid Colodny (he claims he was paid $400,000) to allow them to settle with us, ending our action against him. Accordingly, we agreed to dismiss St. Martin's, Colodny, Gettlin, and Bailley "with prejudice," meaning the litigation was over for them, and began to prepare for our trial with Liddy.

Liddy had no reason to settle, since he was in a fight with Maxie Wells, and he had gotten lucky; *Wells v. Liddy* was assigned to U.S. District Court Judge J. Frederick Motz, who had been appointed to the bench in 1985 by President Ronald Reagan. Judge Motz consistently ruled for Liddy. First, he granted Liddy's motion for summary judgment, declaring that Wells was an "involuntary public figure"—the rarest of rarities in the defamation law, so rare that only about two of them have been found since the beginning of time. According to Motz, the very fact that Maxie's telephone had been bugged by Liddy's wireman, McCord, made her an object of interest, and that fact—together with the one that Bailley had spent years spreading false stories about her—combined to make her a public figure. As a public figure, Maxie had to prove Liddy had acted with actual malice. Judge Motz then ruled that, as a matter of law, she could not prove actual malice, and he therefore dismissed her lawsuit against Liddy, just over a year after it had been filed.

Fortunately, there is nothing that David Dorsen loves more than an argument before an appellate court. By this time, David was deeply involved in the Wells case, so he prepared the brief appealing Judge Motz's ruling, and argued it before the U.S. Court of Appeals for the Fourth Circuit. In July 1999, the Fourth Circuit reversed Judge Motz, and sent the case back for trial. The appellate court held that Maxie was not an involuntary public figure, and that, as a private figure, all she had to do was show the jury that Liddy had acted negligently (rather than knowingly, or with reckless disregard regarding the truth or falsity of his statements). Liddy's lawyers then requested that Judge Motz send the Wells case to the District of Columbia to combine it with our lawsuit, which he did. But the situation had changed. On January 29, 2000, Judge Harold Greene passed away; now our case was assigned to U.S. District Court Judge Emmet Sullivan. Judge Sullivan saw the ploy of Liddy's counsel to combine the cases for what they were, and on February 24, 2000, he sent the Wells case back to Judge Motz. We also took some delight in the fact that Liddy no longer had St. Martin's insurance company paying his attorneys' fees. Now, he was facing two trials where each could easily cost $1 million in attorneys' fees.

In addition, we had developed a strategy that would limit our trial and give us a ruling that Liddy's statements regarding myself and Maureen were false: We filed a motion seeking partial summary judgment that would gut Liddy's case. It is unusual for plaintiffs to seek summary judgment, particularly in defamation lawsuits, but the situation was unusual. Liddy asserted only two defenses as we headed to trial: that the statements he made were true and that he had not made those statements with actual malice (that is, knowing they were false or with reckless disregard as to whether they were true or false). Our motion sought to remove one of Liddy's defenses by showing the court, before trial, that Liddy had no admissible evidence to demonstrate that the statements Liddy had made regarding Maureen were true. After nine years of discovery, and millions of dollars of investigations and depositions by the defendants, the undisputed evidence showed that Maureen had never been associated with prostitution, not withstanding Liddy's false claims to the contrary.

After years of digging, Liddy had but one source for his claims that my wife had been involved in prostitution: Phillip Mackin Bailley. For good reason, Liddy had not listed Bailley in his pre-trial statement setting forth the witnesses he would call. Liddy could not rely on Bailley, whose psychiatrist had explained did not know how to separate truth from fantasy regarding the false information he had provided. Thus, Liddy had no evidence to prove what Maureen denied, and her denial was corroborated by many witnesses who knew her at the time Liddy claimed she had been involved in these activities. Liddy had no admissible evidence that her photograph—or for that matter any photographs—had been in Maxie Wells' desk and Maxie herself had denied ever seeing or possessing such photos. Liddy did not have even a scintilla of evidence that Maureen had ever told me about a call-girl operation at the DNC, because it had never happened. Nor did Liddy have any admissible evidence that a woman Maureen had once known, Erika Rikan, had used the alias Cathy Dieter, as the madam of

579

a call-girl ring. To the contrary, Colodny had discovered before publishing *Silent Coup* that Rikan was not Dieter, but since Rikan was dead, Colodny had proceeded to make the claim anyway. In short, Liddy had no probative evidence whatsoever to prove the truth of his claims, while we had solid proof to show the statements were false.

In addition, just as Liddy's lies about Maureen were unsupported by viable evidence, he similarly lacked evidence for his claim that I had ordered the Watergate break-ins and committed perjury. Liddy had claimed that he himself had not known that Jeb Magruder and Howard Hunt had been acting at my direction. In fact, neither had Magruder or Hunt known this and both denied it under oath. Indeed, Hunt, according to Liddy the key player on my behalf, had actually told Colodny that the target of the break-ins had *not* been the offices and telephone of Spencer Oliver and Maxie Wells; Hunt said that that had been "McCord's mistake...nobody was interested in Oliver, for God's sake." Liddy had absolutely no evidence to support his claim that Hunt was the "only person" aware of my role and my setting the real target, a fact both Hunt and I denied under oath. Magruder also denied under oath that I provided him false orders, for he testified that he never discussed the break-ins with me. Finally, not only is there no evidence that either my wife or I had any knowledge of a call-girl operation at the DNC, there is clear evidence that everyone who made this claim relied on Phillip Bailey. Not a single person who worked at the DNC was aware of such an operation.

As for Liddy's claim that I committed perjury that sent an innocent John Mitchell and John Ehrlichman to prison, again, Liddy had no evidence to support his charge. First, Liddy had no evidence that Mitchell and Ehrlichman were innocent. In fact, both had been found guilty beyond a reasonable doubt of conspiracy to obstruct justice, obstruction of justice, and perjury. When reviewing their convictions, the U.S. Court of

Appeals for the District of Columbia found the evidence "overwhelming" to support the jury's verdict, noting that Mitchell had been convicted not merely on my testimony, but also on that of Magruder, Fred LaRue, and Herb Kalmbach, not to mention on the basis of White House tapes that contained statements by Nixon, Ehrlichman, and Haldeman that "implicated Mitchell in the crimes of which he was convicted." Similarly, Ehrlichman was convicted of perjury based on his statements before the grand jury and the Senate, and openly admitted his perjury during the deposition in our lawsuit, which undercut Liddy's claim.

Liddy's response to this motion was technical, claiming these were facts that should be tried before a jury. But the rules of procedure give the judge the power to narrow the issues for trial to keep the trial focused. After Judge Sullivan received the weak response from Liddy's attorneys, he called all counsel to his chambers in Washington. He advised Liddy's attorneys to settle the case because, he suggested, he was inclined to grant our motion for partial summary judgment, which would effectively gut Liddy's defense. The only issue at trial would be whether he had made the defamatory statements with actual malice, and we were confident that any jury would agree that relying on Phillip Bailey—when one was aware of his mental condition, as Liddy had been—was proof of actual malice. We were later told that Liddy's lawyer, John Williams, in essence, explained to Judge Sullivan that Liddy would never settle, but also that Williams recognized the problems they faced. After more jockeying, Judge Sullivan said he was going to dismiss the case "without prejudice," which means the matters had not been resolved. Informally, too, Judge Sullivan advised our lawyers that if we felt it necessary to proceed in the future, he would reopen the case right where it had ended, with our pending motion for partial summary judgment. This ended the matter for us, but not for Liddy, who was still dealing with Maxie's lawsuit.

After the Fourth Circuit Court of Appeals sent the case back to Judge Motz, Liddy was forced to go to trial. David Dorsen tried the case for Maxie, and Williams handled the case for Liddy, in a jury trial that began on January 16, 2001. Shortly before trial, Motz made evidentiary rulings that indicated he was going to allow Liddy to go wherever he wished, while keeping a tight rein on the evidence Maxie could present. David was deeply frustrated by Judge Motz's handling of the case, but there was nothing he could do. When the jury got the case for deliberation, however, they could not reach a decision. At that point, Judge Motz issued another remarkable ruling for Liddy, claiming that "no reasonable jury" could have found in favor of Maxie on the issue of whether Liddy had been negligent in making the remarks at issue despite the fact the Fourth Circuit has said precisely the opposite. Again, Dorsen returned to the Fourth Circuit Court of Appeals, and again they reversed Judge Motz, calling for another trial. This time, Judge Motz had a scheduling conflict so he passed the case to another judge. Again, we were delighted because this was either cost Liddy money, or his law firm was losing money if they were doing it for free. For Dorsen, who had once been deputy chief counsel to the Senate Watergate Committee, it had become a matter of not allowing Liddy to distort history, and he was willing to fight as long as necessary.

Aside from the good news, as I saw it, that it was getting expensive for Liddy (or his attorneys), the bad news was that even though Judge Motz was gone, he had already created the law of the case; his evidentiary rulings from the prior trial would govern the second one as well. David knew this was a problem. The case went to the jury on July 3, 2001. Ready to go home for the Fourth of July holiday, the jury deliberated about 45 minutes, and returned with a ridiculous verdict, notwithstanding the show Liddy was able to put on: Liddy statements that Maxie had sued on were not "of and concerning" her, another requirement of libel law. Liddy had talked, at the event Dorsen had recorded, about photographs of prostitutes in the desk of Maxie Wells, yet the jury decided that did not mean Liddy accused her (in the statements at issue) of being involved in prostitution.

While Liddy escaped liability, he won nothing. He certainly did not establish the truth of his claim that there was a call-girl operation, nor did the jury reach a decision about whether he made the statements with actual malice. Maxie, understandably, was exhausted and wanted to get on with her life, which she would do by teaching literature to college students.

In short, the litigation ended with a whimper. This was fine by us, because we now had all the evidence that will ever be needed for any sane and honest historian to see the Colodny and Liddy Watergate revisionism for what it really is: a total distortion of the historical record. Sadly what these revisionists have done is typical of what those who have followed them have done as well. I welcome honest revisions in history. However, I will fight dishonest revisionism, for we learn nothing when history is distorted.

Part III

A Few Persistent Questions that Remain about Watergate, Even All these Years Later

Hopefully, in the preceding pages of this Afterword I have answered most all of the significant questions that remain about Watergate. I have been guided by questions that I have been asked over the years. However, there have been a few other persistent questions that I have not addressed in Parts I and II, which I have set forth below, in no particular order, along with my answers. As well, I have a closing question of my own. After the rather heavy material in the preceding pages, I thought it might be appropriate to end with some straightforward answers to the questions that I am frequently

583

asked by persons interested in these events, and about which I feel uniquely qualified to answer without merely speculating:

Q: Did *The Washington Post* crack the Watergate case and force Nixon from office?

A: No. This is not to say that the *Post* did not play a vital role, for it did. When no one else was covering the Watergate story, the *Post* was making it front-page news. While the *Post* did not crack the case, so to speak, they made it an important story inside the Beltway, which made it important to members of Congress, prosecutors and judges—who did crack the case. Had the *Post* not given the story the attention it did, the matter would have ended long before Nixon's reelection in November 1972. Bob Woodward and Carl Bernstein did a great job reporting the story, and great credit goes to Ben Bradley, the editor in chief who had the guts to keep pushing on and Katharine Graham, the owner and publisher, who supported Bradley all the way.

Q: What about Woodward's notorious source, Deep Throat, who turned out to be Mark Felt, the Assistant Director of the FBI, and the number-two man?

A: It was well-known that Felt was a leaker, but it was not known that he was leaking to Woodward. In October 1972, Assistant Attorney General Henry Petersen, who headed the Criminal Division of the Department of Justice, told me that an attorney for *The Washington Post* (presumably Edward Bennett Williams, an experienced criminal defense lawyer) had expressed concern to Petersen that Felt was leaking to the *Post*. (Peterson said Felt was known in the Justice Department as "the white rat," for his prematurely white head of hair and his squealing

584

whenever he thought it might help Mark Felt.) In turn, I reported this to Haldeman, who advised the President of Felt's reputation. At one point in their conversation, Nixon said to Haldeman, "You know what I would do with Felt, an ambassadorship." This was how Nixon placated former CIA Director Richard Helms, who went quietly on to become the U.S. Ambassador to Iran. So clearly, Nixon was worried about Felt. Frankly, I was hoping that Deep Throat was someone with more noble motives than Felt possessed; Felt was trying to undercut Acting FBI Director Pat Gray, so he could become Director himself.

Q: Would Watergate and the Nixon presidency have turned out differently if the Republicans had controlled Congress instead of the Democrats?

A: Absolutely. Had Republicans been in control, there would have been no Watergate investigations and no pressure to prosecute anyone. While those caught breaking into the DNC and trying to bug Larry O'Brien would have been prosecuted, and the FBI would have found out that Liddy and Hunt were in charge, the investigation would likely have ended with Hunt and Liddy. Nixon might have openly pardoned them all, explaining that they had also engaged in national security operations for the White House, which he would have refused to discuss. Democrats would have been outraged, but unable to do anything about it. One need merely look at how Republicans responded when the Bush/Cheney Administration flagrantly violated the most fundamental American laws (to engage in massive electronic surveillance of Americans, the arrest and detention without charge of perceived enemies including American citizens, and the use of torture to extract information) to see what a Republican Congress would likely have done had Republicans been in power during Watergate.

Q: What was the most difficult moment, or moments, you experienced when going through the account you related in *Blind Ambition*?

A: There was no single difficult moment; rather it all was a rather unpleasant experience. Re-reading this book after all these years was not what I call a pleasant experience either. Nonetheless, Watergate was a very maturing experience for me. I see now that I lacked experience in the criminal law, which I sorely needed. But otherwise, I feel that the Office of the White House Counsel performed very well during my tenure in the post, except with respect to Watergate. In the years since serving, I have had occasion to look at records from the office, and we did top-quality work. We also did a lot of business. The files from my office at the National Archives constitute one of the larger collections. But I did not write about what we did right in *Blind Ambition*; rather, I focused on what I did wrong. It was not pleasant having to turn on Nixon and those who had once been friends and colleagues. But when they refused to do the right thing and end the criminal activity, and then tried to blame me for what had gone wrong, they had selected the wrong person to scapegoat. Just as Liddy was the wrong person to hire to do illegal acts, because he was incompetent, I was the wrong person to seek to use to perpetuate an indefinite cover-up, because I refused to live on the wrong side of the law and to lie.

Q: Why did you not return to the practice of law?

A: While still working at the White House, I had
      planned to leave the practice of law and go into in-
      vestment banking, which I did after Watergate (and
      after returning to night school for five years to study
      accounting). While I was disbarred for my actions
      during Watergate, I have actually had invitations to
      get readmitted to the practice of law by bar counsel
      and others who wanted to sponsor my readmission.
      But because I do not want to practice, I have not
      considered it necessary. I treasure my legal educa-
      tion, and there is not a day I do not rely on it. I
      have kept abreast of legal developments in the areas
      of law that interest me, I write about legal matters,
      but I have never had the urge to practice. During
      our lawsuit, I prepared the first drafts of countless
      pleadings and motions and became well-versed in
      the federal rules of civil procedure, so I got a good
      taste of the law for some nine years, and it did not
      entice me to practice either.

Q: Did you ever talk with Richard Nixon, or the others
      at the Nixon White House, after Watergate?

A: I never talked to Nixon, but I did talk with almost
      everyone else. Talking to me was not the sort of
      situation that Nixon could have handled. He be-
      lieved that I should have fallen on my sword for
      him. Loyalty, to me, is a two-way proposition, and
      as the tapes show, Nixon did everything in his pow-
      er to undercut me and to make me not only his sca-
      pegoat, but Haldeman's and Ehrlichman's as well. I
      realize now that Nixon was simply not capable of
      doing the right thing; it was not in his character. I
      ran into Bob Haldeman coming out of an elevator in
      Westwood, California, where he was working. We
      had a very friendly exchange, he gave me his card,
      and he encouraged me to call and arrange a lunch. I

regret that I did not do so, for he passed away not long afterward. John Ehrlichman wanted revenge, and teamed up with Leonard Colodny to do whatever he could to cause me damage.

Unlike Haldeman's taped conversations with Colodny, Ehrlichman's conversations were pathetic. Ehrlichman had once aspired to high office, starting with the U.S. Senate. Listening to his taped conversations with Colodny, I felt very good that I had cut short his political career, for this was not a man of character. The only time I talked to Ehrlichman was during his deposition in our lawsuit, as we were riding down to lunch in the elevator. Colodny had so embittered Ehrlichman that he literally foamed at the mouth with saliva during the deposition, exuding hate, plainly feeling very put-upon by being forced to testify (although St. Martin's, not we, had called for his deposition), and being as nasty as he could. He looked awful, and was quite overweight, and soon I realized he had lost his once-sardonic wit and personality as well. During the elevator ride, he refused to look at me, so I said to him as we arrived at the first floor, "Well, John, after listening to your testimony, I guess I won't be getting a Christmas card this year?" Expecting the old John to have a quick comeback, I was stunned when he became nearly catatonic from thinking he had somehow been sending me Christmas cards in earlier years, which I assured him had not been the case. John Garrick, who was the attorney conducting the deposition—and whom Ehrlichman had compared to former assistant Watergate Special Prosecutor Richard Ben Veniste trying to intimidate a non-intimidateable Garrick, who took it as a compliment—looked at me after we got out of the elevator and asked, "Was he always so out of it?"

588

Q: Do you regret joining the Nixon White House?

A: Not at all. It was a great experience. There were more good days than bad, and relatively speaking, Watergate activities were not where I spent most of my time. It was a phenomenal education, for from the White House Counsel's Office, you can truly see how the government operates.

Q: Other than Watergate, what kind of President was Richard Nixon, and will he ever be judged other than through the lens of Watergate?

A: As President, Nixon was remarkably progressive, and for this reason, conservatives have never liked him. He will forever be credited for his China initiative, which also was a highly progressive move, as was his creation of the Environmental Protection Agency. But Nixon will always be viewed through the lens of Watergate and his abuses of power. Still, the perspective on those abuses will likely change because of the Bush/Cheney Presidency, which in my view (and I believe history's as well) will be judged, to borrow a title from one of my books, to have been worse than Watergate.

Q: If you had it to do all over again, what would you do differently?

A: I should have resigned when I told Haldeman, in September 1971, that I wanted to leave. By then I could smell the rot, and wanted to get away from it. Haldeman more or less threatened me if I left, but enticed as well by commenting that I would get better offers after Nixon was reelected. Had I left, I could have been a spectator, rather than a participant.

Q: (This is my question regarding the comment I made that there was nothing I would change in *Blind Ambition*.) Is there anything that I should have included but failed to do so in the original narrative?

A: Yes. When writing *Blind Ambition*, I tried to avoid being self-serving, and I have not changed my thinking about that. But I probably should have included an important fact about why I was ready to do what had to be done, and if it sounds self-serving, I apologize, but it is the way I thought back then and still think today. I talked about this on one occasion, and I probably should have included it in *Blind Ambition.*[*]

When you are working for the executive branch of the federal government, you take an oath to "support and defend" the Constitution, not the President of the United States. While the President's staff serves at his pleasure, the Counsel to the President's first job is to protect the office of the Presidency, not the man who occupies that office. When I broke rank, I understood that my doing so would be characterized by some as the action of a snitch, a rat, a tattletale, an informant, a stool pigeon, or a whistleblower. Or, as Richard Nixon would have it, a traitor. Ugly labels, for sure. None of them, however, troubled me then or now, because I know what actually happened and why. How others perceive it (so long as they are honest) is not very important, as I shall explain.

---

[*]   I have discussed this point on one previous occasion, when I prepared an article for the *Hastings Law Journal* for their symposium marking the passage of twenty-five years after Watergate. I have drawn from that article to answer this question. See John W. Dean, "Watergate: What Was It?" *Hastings Law Journal* (April, 2000).

Ironically, what I felt I had to do had actually arisen, albeit indirectly, in a conversation with the President on February 28, 1973, when talking about leaks and informants. At that time, the President made a comment about a person with inside information who went public, observing that "everybody would treat him like a pariah. He's in a very dangerous situation. These guys you know—the informers, look what it did to Chambers. Chambers informed because he didn't give a Goddamn." I knew exactly what it had done to Whittaker Chambers, the President's favorite informant, since he had received the information from Chambers—and it launched Nixon's political career.

Whittaker Chambers, of course, had testified that he had once been an active organizer for the Communist Party, working the corridors of government power in Washington. But when Chambers learned of the true nature of communism, and of his former friends who still embraced it, he broke rank and became a witness against these people and their thinking. Years earlier, I had read Chambers's book about being a witness—appropriately titled *Witness*. While I found no similarities between Whittaker Chambers's life and my own, I had discovered an eloquent writer, and I had not forgotten the message of one passage in particular, which I later discovered I had underlined:

I had begun to understand that to be a witness, in the sense in which I am using the term, means, ultimately, just one thing. It means that a man is prepared to destroy himself, if necessary, to make his witness. A man does not wish to destroy himself. To the full degree in which he is strongest, that is to say, to the full degree of force that makes it possible

591

for him to bear witness at all, he desires not to destroy himself. To the degree that he is most human, that is to say, most weak, he shrinks from destroying himself. But to the degree that what he truly is and what he stands for are one, he must at some point tacitly consent in his own mind to destroy himself if that is necessary.

Nixon had it wrong with Chambers: Chambers did give a damn, and that was why he had taken the actions he did in testifying against Alger Hiss and others. Within a few weeks of that February 28, 1973 conversation, I knew exactly what Whittaker Chambers was talking about.

During the last ten days of March 1973, a confluence of events forced my decision. I had told Haldeman, Ehrlichman, and the President that I had no solution to the problems of Watergate, but that I believed that the President had to end the Watergate cover-up. Then on March 23, 1973, U.S. District Court Judge John Sirica, who had been presiding over the Watergate criminal cases, revealed in open court the letter from James McCord charging that he and others involved in the Watergate break-in were under political pressure to plead guilty and remain silent, that perjury had been committed during his criminal trial, and that higher-ups were involved in the break-in. It had long been anticipated that McCord would do something like this. It was no surprise. We knew that he was correct, but we also knew he had no hard evidence to support his charges. He was relying on hearsay from Gordon Liddy, who would likely kill McCord before he would corroborate his allegations.

When McCord blew the whistle, it was time for my decision. Could the cover-up go on? Absolutely. Could it succeed? Almost for certain, particularly if the cover-up were justified for "national security" reasons, and if, when called to testify, I had supported the earlier testimony by Mitchell and Magruder (which was false) about the meetings with Liddy in the Attorney General's office—by lying. In short, my options were clear: either I could go forward and live the lie or I could do exactly what Whittaker Chambers accurately described—consent to the inevitable self-destruction that would be necessary to tell the truth. While I thought about it carefully during a long visit to Camp David, I knew before I started where I would come out. I really had no choice. I was disgusted with my own behavior, I was deeply troubled by the pervasive criminality within the Nixon White House, and I believed Americans deserved better from those in the White House. I made the decision that, regardless of the consequences, I was going to tell the truth, and, as they say: The rest is history.

Because of the great number of persons who have political, economic, and emotional ties to any President, when you tarnish that President, his followers feel that you tarnish them as well; when you harm that President, you harm them as well; and when that President strikes out to defend himself against you, his followers will do likewise. When you do the kind of damage I found necessary to do, the attacks against you never end, because Presidents, and those who have hooked on to a President's star, are not only concerned with protecting his incumbency but his legacy as well. I have little doubt that those who want to refurbish Nixon's deeply tarnished image will never stop attacking me. It is the price I must pay for having told the truth and for continuing to do so.

UPDATED EDITION
ACKNOWLEDGEMENTS

While Polimedia Publishing is a new publisher, I have been working with the organization's principles – Charles Lago and Chris Johnson – for many years, for they have assisted with book promotion tours, principally in California, with my last four books, arranging events and selling books. They know the book business well and because they frequently were asked if *Blind Ambition* was available for sale, they helped convince me that it should not remain out of print. Charles and Chris have handled the technical matters of reproducing this book like old hands, for which I am appreciative. Family friend David Cason, whose design talents have long been invaluable to the Deans, assisted with the new cover.

Special thanks to wife Maureen, who made the initial read of the new Afterword. In addition, I requested my FindLaw editor Julie Hilden to run her sharp eyes over this new material, and as always, she had helpful suggestions. Ms. Samantha Greenhill did a nice job of copyediting and updating the index to include the Afterword. Finally, David Dorsen, whose name you will recognize from the narrative of the Afterword, offered several helpful suggestions for the Afterword, as did Thomas Long, with whom I am working on a book about the Watergate cover-up trial for the University of Kansas Press. As always, however, all errors are mine, not those who helped me assemble the book.

ABOUT
THE AUTHOR

Before becoming Counsel to the President of the United States in July 1970 at age thirty-one, John Dean was Chief Minority Counsel to the Judiciary Committee of the United States House of Representatives, the Associate Director of the National Commission on Reform of the Federal Criminal Laws, and Associate Deputy Attorney General of the United States. He served as Richard Nixon's White House lawyer for a thousand days.

Dean did his undergraduate studies at Colgate University and the College of Wooster, with majors in English Literature and Political Science. He received a graduate fellowship from American University to study government and the presidency, before entering Georgetown University Law Center, where he received his JD in 1965. After having retired at age sixty from a successful career as a private investment banker (acquiring, merging and later selling middle-market companies), he returned full-time to writing and lecturing.

John, who regularly appears on MSNBC's "Countdown with Keith Olbermann," has been described as one of the most knowledgeable and candid commentators about the ways of Washington and the workings of our government. He writes as a guest columnist for a number of publications (The Huffington Post, Truthdig, The Daily Beast – to mention a few) and has written a regular a bi-weekly column for FindLaw.com for the past nine years. He is currently working on his next book. He lives in Beverly Hills, California with his wife Maureen.

INDEX

This Index includes both the material from the narrative of *Blind Ambition* and the new Afterword. To distinguish the material, pages relating to the Afterword have been marked in italics.

601

605

Magruder, Jeb Stuart, (*Cont.*)
152, 200-201, 228, 251, 307
protected by cover-up, 154, 155-156, 218
scapegoat candidate, 235, 305-306
accused of prior knowledge of break-in, 267, 268-269, 284-285
his grand-jury testimony, 270, 274, 322, 377
implicates Mitchell, 310-311
sentencing of, 445, 448-449
testifies at cover-up trial, 449, 456, 490
in jail, 456-459, 461, 466, 488-490, 499
and burning of CRP documents, 479-480
reason for break-in and bugging, *515-516, 518-521, 525-526, 547, 550*
on being mislead by Colodny, *557, 561-563, 565, 581*
Maheu, Robert, 73-75, 85, 490-491
Manila, 100, 208, 294, *557-562, 564*
Mansfield, Mike, 240
March Air Force Base, 205
Mardian, Robert C., 40, 45
and ITT case, 54, 60
in Watergate cover-up, 121-123, 135-138, 153-154, 294, 295, 307
and FBI Watergate data, 143, 486-487
indicted, 435 fn.
trial and conviction, 473, 480, 486-487, 497 fn.
Marshal's Service, 457
Martinez, Eugenio R., 155 fn., *521-523, 533-534, 550*; *see also* Cubans
Maugham, Somerset, 496
"Mayday" demonstration, 39-42, 76
Mayflower Hotel, Washington, 405-407, 429
Mazo, Earl, 14
McCandless, Robert, 267-268, 335, 348, 355-367
and Ervin hearings, 364, 376, 380, 381-382, 383, 393, 401, 404

McCandless, Robert, (*Cont.*)
general representation, 348
McCord, James W., Jr., 101-103, 111, 121-122, 139, 144, *522, 522-526, 530, 536, 541-542, 578, 581, 593*
Caulfield and, 103, 248
White House strategy on, 141-142, 168-169
indicted, 155-156 fn.
threatens to talk, 212-213, 216-217
implicates higher-ups, 259-260, 262, 284
McCrone, Walter, 59, 61
McGovern, George, 99, 114, 148-149, 348, 358, 367, *503 fn., 526, 529, 537*
McKinney, Marshal, 454-455, 462
McLaren, Richard, 51
McNamee, Wally, 359
McPherson, Bud, 447, 453-455, 462
Melbourne, Fla., 410ff.
Metropolitan Club, New York, 189, 476
Metropolitan Police, 40, 105, 108, 125
Mexico, 31
Miami, 52 fn., 91, 93, 408, *515-519, 521, 528*
Miller, William E., 496
Millhouse: A White Comedy, 37
Mills, Wilbur, 49
Minnick, Walter, 183-184, 187
Mitchell, John N., 6, 7, 29, 69 70
advice to Dean, 2, 3
and Nixon, 8-9, 13, 122
and Huston memo, 32, 33
kills Huston Plan, 34-35
Ehrlichman moves in on, 47-52, 183-184, *534-535*
resigns as Attorney General, 52, *519*
and Kleindienst-ITT hearings, 62, 265
and early campaign-intelligence plans, 78, 80-83
Liddy plan presented to, 88-97, 103, 115, 127, 184-185, 226-227, 487-490
hostile to Colson, 89, 128-129,

610

Petersen, Henry E., (*Cont.*)
Dean is grilled about, 387-388
takes over Watergate inquiry, 429-430
Playboy, 189
Plumbers' Unit, 20, 46, 58, 143, 203, *508, 509, 510, 532, 533*
Poff, Richard, 49, 433
Powell, Lewis F., Jr., 49, 50
Public Health Service, 132

Ratenoff, Teddy, 38-39
Rebozo, Charles G. "Bebe," 70, 72, 491
Redman, Albert, 376, 415-416
Re-election Committee, *see* Committee to Re-elect the President
Rehnquist, William H., 50
Republican Party, 52, 156, 484
Richardson, Elliot L., 371 fn., 427
Richey, Charles, 160, 172, 569
Rient, Peter, 432
Roosevelt Room, 68, 155, 174, 175, 215
Rothblatt, Henry, 218
Ruby, Operation, 91-92
Ruckelshaus, William D., 427
Rumsfeld, Donald, 81
Ruth, Henry, 483-486, 495-496, 499

St. Clair, James D., 434, 441-442
Sanchez, Manolo, 225
San Clemente, Calif., Western White House at, 2-13 *passim*, 16-17, 45, 149, 281, 284, 287, 507
San Diego, Calif., 52, 65, 90, 514
Sandwedge Operation, 80-82, 85-86, 92
Sapphire, Operation, 93-94
Saturday Night Massacre, 427, 431
Scanlan's Monthly, 27-32, 35, 69
Schorr, Daniel, 355, 356-357, 407
Scott, Hugh, 60, 61
Seale, Bobby, 457
Secret Service, 21, 23, 30, 40, 124, 189, 191, 367, 561
Securities and Exchange Commission, 367

Sedan Chair, 91
Segretti, Donald H., 79, 165, 170-171, 177, 185, 282, 437 fn.
Select Committee on Presidential Campaign Activities, *see* Senate Watergate Committee
Senate:
votes Watergate probe, 220-221, 222 fn., 239-240,
see also
Senate Watergate Committee
confirms Krogh appointment, 239
see also
Senate Commerce Committee
and executive privilege, 265
immunity powers of, 364
Senate Commerce Committee, Krogh confirmation hearings, 203, 215, 241, 250
Senate Foreign Relations Committee, 36
Senate Judiciary Committee:
Kleindienst-ITT hearings, 52, 53-54, 58-67, 265, 399-400
Gray hearings, 221, 236, 239-240, 258-259, 292-293
Senate Watergate Committee (Ervin Committee), 221, 222 fn., 240-241
Nixon strategy toward, 222, 223-224, 229, 379-380, 381, 398, 401-403
Dean considers going to, 335-337, 352, 359, 363-366
immunity question, 354, 362, 365, 390
leaks from, 362, 378-380
Dean prepares to testify before, 373, 375-381
hearings, 365-366, 373, 383-409, 410, 419, 442 fn.
Sequoia, 304
Shaffer, Charles N., 271-272, 276-281
early dealings with prosecutors, 284-291, 294-296, 298, 311-313, 315
advises Dean on Mitchell, 298-299, 302-303, 305-307

613

614